Jesus and Early Christianity in the Gospels

A New Dialogue

by

Daniel Jalal Grolin

George Ronald
Oxford

George Ronald, *Publisher*
46 High Street, Kidlington, Oxford OX5 2DN

To my parents and my two brothers

A catalogue record for this book is available from the British Library

ISBN 0–85398–462–X

Typeset by Stonehaven Press, Knoxville, Tennessee
Printed and bound in Great Britain by Biddles Ltd,
www.biddles.co.uk

Contents

Introduction

Just over a century ago Charles A. Briggs started his volume *General Introduction to the Study of Holy Scripture* with the words, 'Biblical Study is the most *important* of all studies, for it is the study of the Word of God, which contains a divine revelation of redemption to the world.' Such a perspective is, of course, that of a religious person and there can be no doubt that were it not for the belief that the Bible is the Word of God it is unlikely that there would be faculties of biblical studies at universities all over the world, let alone colleges set aside for that field only. It is indeed with this belief that the vast majority of pupils enter the study of biblical scholarship, although some enter with little more than curiosity. For those who are only curious, their interest needs no explanation other than curiosity itself.

For a religious individual, the value of such studies may also seem obvious at first sight. Yet precisely the religious value of such study becomes more and more difficult to perceive as one becomes more and more familiar with the methods involved in such studies. The basis of these methods is that we can study the Bible without accepting the statement of faith that the Bible is the Word of God. That it can be studied thus does not, of course, mean that someone doing biblical studies cannot believe in the Bible's sacredness.

The author of this book is a follower of the Bahá'í Faith which has a long-standing tradition of showing reverence to prophets by referring to them and to God with capitalized pronouns. While this book is written using methods that by their very nature are agnostic, the author is not agnostic and will therefore, as a reminder of this fact to the reader, follow the above-mentioned convention. This is because while all methods are designed to assist one to be as objective as possible, the selection of method and material (the subject of our first chapter) is still in the hands of a subjective individual.

A student of scripture or literature in general must be alert to the fact that any act of interpretation is a double-edged sword. Interpretation is a translation of symbols. When an author, any author, decides to write, he or she does so by means of words which are themselves symbols for that hidden image to which they refer. That hidden image is to be found only in the mind of the author and at his or her death the only 'real' image is irretrievably lost. The only means by which we can reconstruct an approximation of the lost image is to search out what was formative to the image at the time the author wrote. What sustains any attempt to reconstruct such formation is that any system of symbols exists in order to communicate. As such, a system of symbols must, in order to function as a means of communication, be common to those who seek to communicate.

The act of interpretation, therefore, is to attempt to understand the meaning of those symbols, to find the hidden image. In the case of biblical literature, the problem is that the system of symbols that was common to Jesus or to the evangelists is distant from the system of symbols of our time. The experiences that were formative for the system of symbols with which the Bible was written have been lost with the passing of time. Thus any interpretation requires a translation from one system of symbols to another and therein lies the peril of interpretation, for it is a translation of something foreign to something familiar. In that process it is almost inevitable that something is lost in the translation, just as it is inevitable that the message will take on attributes that are inherent, not to the original system of symbols, but to the new one.

Rudolf Bultmann was one of the leaders of the development of the biblical criticism known as 'form criticism'. In the recurrent surges of interest in historical reconstructions of Jesus (referred to as 'Quests for the Historical Jesus'), he is credited with putting an end to the second of such surges. In his only book devoted specifically to the historical Jesus, *Jesus and the Word*, he commented on this interaction between subject and object:

> Man, if he rightly understands himself, differentiates himself from nature. When he observes nature, he perceives there something objective which is not himself. When he turns his attention to history, however, he must admit himself to be a part of history; he is considering a living complex of events in which he is essentially involved. He cannot observe this complex objectively as he can observe natural phenomena; for in every word which he says about history he is saying at the same time something about himself. Hence there cannot be impersonal observation of history in the same sense that there can be impersonal observation of nature. Therefore, if this book is to be anything more than information on interesting occurrences in the past, more than a walk through a museum of antiquities, if it is really to lead to our seeing Jesus as a part of the history in which we have our being, or in which by critical conflict we achieve being, then this book must be in the nature of a continuous dialogue with history.
>
> Further, it should be understood that the dialogue does not come as a conclusion, as a kind of evaluation of history after one has first learned the objective facts. On the

> contrary, the actual encounter with history takes place only in the dialogue. We do not stand outside historical forces as neutral observers; we are ourselves moved by them; and only when we are ready to listen to the demand which history makes on us do we understand at all what history is about.[1]

All of this may seem quite theoretical, so let us consider two concrete examples. The first example pertains to the English language. If we look at the adjective 'radical' such as it was understood by Dr Samuel Johnson in 1756, when he published the first dictionary of the English language, we find that it was defined as 'Primitive, original *Bacon* Implanted by nature. *Ibid.* Serving to origination.' Yet today if something is 'radical' it is understood to be extreme, straying far from the average. So if the evangelists had described Jesus' religion in 18th century English as a 'radical' movement, it would be misunderstood by today's reader as meaning that Jesus had started an extreme movement; many would associate the word 'radical' with politics. Yet as we see from Dr Johnson's dictionary, this would be to misunderstand what the evangelist was writing. The intent would be that Jesus had originated a simple religion or perhaps a movement that sought the original form of religion. In other words, the symbol (the word 'radical') had a meaning that was in its true and precise sense understood only by the writer but was shared generally with his or her audience. Yet today we would not have immediate access to the meaning of the symbol. The change in the meaning of the word is caused through its changed use. As it is applied to objects, concrete 'radical' movements, for example, the original hidden image is universally changed to contain the universally perceived one. The radical movement becomes the defining image for the symbol 'radical'.

Now this was a fairly simple example. Sometimes the symbol involves more complex events or structures to explain a common frame of reference. Many are probably familiar with the highly syndicated situation comedy *The Nanny* with Fran Drescher. For those unfamiliar with the sub-culture of the Jews of New York, much of the humour is lost. That Fran's parents wish to move to Florida and live in a condominium is a cliché that the scriptwriters presume is known and understood by the audience, understood because it belongs to a common experience of the Jewish sub-culture of New York.

What then is the difference between the exegete and the theologian? The exegete attempts to recover the lost hidden image behind the symbol; the theologian seeks to create a new coherent image, coherent not only unto itself but coherent with the experience of his or her present. Thus it would seem that the exegete and the theologian have no common ground, though they read the same scripture. Yet the exegete cannot ignore scripture's meaning and its purpose in life, nor the theologian help but wonder what those words meant to those who first heard them.

Exegesis is one of the primary interests of this book – to recover the world in which the gospels were written and the world in which their traditions were transmitted before they came into the hands of the evangelists. Another question this book will deal with is that of historicity. This is a question that is by far more controversial than the need for exegesis. Is it necessary to question whether or not an event described in the Bible actually happened?

The problems here are manifold. Besides the problems already discussed, the question of historicity seems to draw out more controversy than anything else. Above we looked at the duality of the theologian and the exegete, now we will look at the duality of myth and history.

From the outset there is a difficulty understanding the meaning of the words 'myth' and 'history'. One might say that their popular usage is not sufficient to explain in detail the problems and their solutions. First the word 'myth'. By 'myth' often is understood 'something commonly held but not true all the same'. This is not, however, the meaning with which it is intended in this book. What is meant is a bit more complex. A myth is a story or narrative which is told about the past or the future in order to explain the present. The present experience is perceived as disconnected with the sacred and the narrative explains the path back to the sacred. The myth takes on many forms. This definition is one that serves our purpose well in this book because it describes the material of the gospels so well. A myth may recount events that either happened or did not. That is not an issue *per se*. The point is not whether or not an event happened but whether the story performs the mythic function, to lead the reader from the mundane to the sacred. On the other hand, the word 'history' is often understood as meaning 'what really happened'. The problem with this sort of definition is that it is in fact useless because once the event has occurred it is lost, just like the 'hidden image'. What remains are the consequences and the recollections of those who witnessed the events. However, in looking at the event it is impossible not to look for meaning, impossible not to select the details of the event to be restrained by the perspective that the situation makes available to the observer. What 'really happened' is neither available nor is it interesting. History is only interesting inasmuch as it has the power to explain the present; it is the answers we seek that makes us ask the questions to which we look to the past for those answers. History does not connect with the sacred; rather it asks questions that deal not in meaning but in event and consequences.

The object of history is not and cannot be to disprove myth. History can observe the presence of myth and can attempt to determine whether or not a historical event lies behind it but ultimately it cannot determine the truth value of the myth. Conversely, myth is not being deceptive when it recounts a story which has no historical background. So just as the theologian and the exegete operate in two different spheres, so also do myth and history. However, myth and history, too, can have an area of intersection.

In the case of Christianity this intersection has been, from the very beginning, the belief in the significance of a historical event, the life of Jesus of Nazareth, believed to be Messiah, the Saviour of mankind and Logos incarnate. Because of this intersection between history and myth we may acquire history through the mythic narrative of the gospels and may gather mythic value from the enquiries of history. Because of this intersection the historian can draw out history from the religious narratives of the gospels and the theologian can extract religious meaning from the conclusions of history.

And this, one might say, is one way of understanding the subtitle of this book, *A New Dialogue*. The dialogue is the ongoing process between the events of the past and how they impact on the present. The dialogue is always new whenever a new person takes up the task of uniting the two worlds, the sacred past with the profane present, translating the symbolic world of the past to the symbolic system of the present. This book, however, seeks to be historical and exegetical rather than mythic and theological.

Finally, it is proper to define the extent of the book in terms of contents and intended use. This book deals only with the gospels, not because the remainder of the New Testament is not interesting or relevant but merely because it is too extensive to be included here. This is a study guide, which means that it is intended to be used in a study of the actual text. It is not sufficient to read this book (or any other) without having delved into the text in question. This is not intended as a commentary, for its purpose is not merely to comment on specific verses but rather to demonstrate a type of methodology.

The approach used in this book is to take different traditions of the gospels and ask of each: 1) Where does it come from and how was it understood? 2) The evangelist has taken it and used it; has he changed its meaning, and if he has, how? 3) How was the tradition, as we find it in the gospels, used later by Christians? This basic structure should be fairly visible. The present author has attempted to do this in each section where it was possible. It is, of course, lacking where it is not applicable, either because it was the evangelist's construction (1 is missing) or it held no major significance for later Christians (3 is missing).

The first chapter will deal with these methods and introduce the basics of the different critical sciences that will be used throughout this book. The second chapter provides an introduction to 1st-century Palestine, its peoples and its literature. With these two chapters as foundation stones, the third chapter embarks on the first piece of the gospels, the beginning of a new dispensation, what happened in the period before the ministry of Jesus. Here the question of who Jesus was becomes a central theme and has been dealt with extensively. In the fourth chapter the baptism of Jesus is discussed, as well as John the Baptist and the institution of baptism. The fifth chapter deals with Jesus' speeches and how they are critically evaluated. The sixth chapter attempts to deal with the miracles of Jesus and how they are to be placed in proper historical perspective. In the seventh chapter we resume the chronology at Jerusalem and Jesus' entry into that city. Much attention is here devoted to the history of Jerusalem from the earliest times until the monumental entry of Jesus into its walls. It also discusses Jesus' relationship to the temple. The eighth chapter discusses the prophecies of Jesus, the Olive Discourse as well as the problematic Farewell Discourse. The ninth chapter deals with the Last Supper and the institution of the Eucharist. The tenth deals with the arrest, trial and execution of Jesus. Here there is also some discussion of the theology that developed after the event and how it was understood in different early and later branches of Christianity. The eleventh chapter deals with the resurrection and ascension and its import in the early church and today.

Foreword

It is my privilege to provide *Jesus and Early Christianity in the Gospels* by Daniel J. Grolin with a Foreword. A privilege, since this book not only offers a sound introduction to the gospels – which in itself is a purpose fulfilled – but it also invites you to participate in a dialogue on the person of Jesus Christ, whatever religion or faith you may belong to.

This book clearly belongs to the research which has been carried out within the framework of the so-called 'Third Quest for the Historical Jesus'. This quest has now been pursued for some decades and is a renewed interest in establishing the historical facts behind the life and teaching of Jesus the man from Nazareth; an objective that for many years had been renounced as the sources for such an endeavour were considered too scarce and too biased.

Interestingly enough, the original quest for the so-called Historical Jesus in the age of the Enlightenment had the purpose of setting free the teaching of Jesus from the bonds of the Church. In the case of this author's use of the Historical Jesus research, the intention is quite the opposite: to find a neutral platform for the discussion of the figure of Jesus Christ, he uses the methods and the insights of the Historical Jesus research. From here on he invites everybody to enter into a fruitful inter-religious dialogue on the impact of Jesus on his or her religion.

As a Christian I must at the outset acknowledge the fact that the person of Jesus Christ plays a role in other religions and faiths such as Judaism, Islam and Bahá'í but also in

Hinduism, for instance in the figure of Mahatma Gandhi, who in his non-violence campaign took inspiration from the teachings of Jesus, or most recently in Buddhism, say in the reading of the gospels by the Dalai Lama. In socialism the revolutionary teaching of Jesus has always played a role. In other words: as Christians we have to give up the notion of the exclusiveness of the figure of Jesus to Christianity. We may discuss the interpretation of the life and sayings of Jesus but we must accept the role of Jesus in other religions. Not only should we accept this fact but be inspired by it and maybe even see herein an opportunity for a new basis for inter-religious debate and understanding.

The book is well-written and unbiased as it does not get caught up in the strong emotions and differences of opinion evolved from the interpretation of the sayings and doings of Jesus Christ but rather assumes as granted that the story about Him can be told in a straightforward manner. Having discussed the methods of modern biblical scholarship and in particular the methods of the Historical Jesus research and its evaluation of sources and especially the criteria for genuine and non-genuine Jesus-words, the author carries on along this path. After a very instructive chapter on the Jewish context of the gospels, the book describes the contents of the gospels starting with 'The Birth of a New Dispensation'. Then follows chapters on the baptism of Jesus, His preaching and His mighty works, His entrance into Jerusalem and His prophecy, the last supper with His disciples, His crucifixion and resurrection. Thus the main points in the life and death and views of Jesus Christ are presented and discussed. Not only the canonical gospels and texts are used for this purpose: the author reveals a comprehensive knowledge of non-biblical literature of the era, first and foremost of the Gospel of St Thomas. As already stated, it is a sound introduction to the world of the gospels and in its own right an account of the life and death of Jesus Christ and the foundational ideas of the era He instigated.

In Appendix 1 the author undertakes a survey of the impact of the gospels on Bahá'í writings and shows how essential events in the gospels are interpreted into the general Bahá'í context and in Appendix 2 he offers an outline for a New Inter-religious Dialogue.

I can only welcome this endeavour and recommend this book as a highly competent introduction to the intriguing and disquieting world of the gospels.

Jens Buchwald Andersen
University Chaplain of the
University of Southern Denmark,
Odense

Acknowledgements

I would like to thank the following people for their contribution to the publication of this book: Kaiser Barnes and Patrick Barker, who both encouraged me to approach a publisher when the work was still in its infancy stage; Ian Semple, who read and commented on early chapters, and Hooper Dunbar, who was continually encouraging youth to study religion in the context of history; Science of Religion Professor Christopher Buck, who helped reshape the structure of the book; the former University Chaplain Erik Strid in Odense, who read, commented and engaged me in thought-provoking conversation; the current University Chaplain Jens Buchwald Andersen, who has seen this manuscript on its way to publication and whose thoughts and encouragement were an enormous assistance; and Science of Religion Professor Knud Rendtorff, who read the manuscript and whose comments assisted me in subsequent revisions. Other great sources of assistance and inspiration were three academic e-mailing lists to which I have been subscribed: X-Talk, dedicated to the discussion of the Historical Jesus; Synopt-L, which is dedicated to the discussion of the Synoptic Problem; and Corpus-Paul, dedicated to Paul and Pauline literature.

1
The Critical Sciences

The last two centuries have seen a remarkable development within the field of biblical scholarship, much of which has been kept in scholarly circles. This is partly because scholarship itself has been divided over the legitimacy of these new sciences but also because of the vast tradition of the exclusiveness of scholarly knowledge. Some of the pioneers of these sciences were ostracized, persecuted or even excommunicated from their churches or synagogues and sometimes charges of heresy were laid against them. The fact that secularization promoted these sciences made the delineation even more distinct. Today the warring factions have made their arena public and the media is used more relentlessly, so the existence of these sciences is generally known but their significance is still generally poorly grasped.

Methods

An attempt to uncover the origins of Christianity, its history and its beliefs, must necessarily involve methods and materials. Below we will start with a discussion of the methods with which we will analyse the gospels.

Source Criticism is the science that attempts to identify dependence and independence of sources. This is the science used when one attempts to determine the relationship between the gospels. Almost since Augustine, the dominant model has been that Matthew first composed his gospel and that Mark took the former and edited away much material and thus produced his own, adding very little himself. Luke had both gospels and from those composed his own, adding some of his own material. Lastly John composed his, omitting much that came before but putting in much that was new. This hypothesis is still favoured by some but generally now the assumption is that Mark came first, which solves some problems but also creates new ones. First, it explains why so much relevant material was edited away in Mark (it wasn't, Mark never saw Matthew). It also explains why the chronological order given by Mark is never opposed; that is, that there is no instance where both Matthew and Luke change the order of things in a similar way: Mark is always supported by one or the other. An intercalation is a structure in which there is a compound of two different stories, one occurring within the framework of the other. Intercalations occur only in Mark. None of the other gospels has this construction independently of Mark. This suggests that the other authors found the structure awkward but were willing to copy it from Mark. Also, there are instances where Matthew makes changes in the Markan source but does not change other parts, thus making the text internally inconsistent. This also strongly suggests dependence. In addition, it seems more logical to assume that Matthew and Luke improved Mark's grammar than that Mark lowered the standard.

This raises the problem of the vast amount of material in common between Luke and Matthew, sometimes with word for word agreements. This has generally, but not unanimously, been solved by supposing a common source shared by Matthew and Luke called (for the sake of having a common reference) 'Q', from the German word *quelle* meaning 'source'. The reconstruction of Q shows that it is largely but not solely a sayings source with only a few narrative sections. While reconstruction is tentative, most studies today, like this one, presume the existence of this source. Theological studies have been made of the community in which Q came into being. A theory of stratification of Q has also received much attention and recognition. By stratification is meant that the collection of sayings came into being in strata: certain themes became interesting to the community and were added to the text in its next revision.

Still problems remain. There are the so-called minor agreements, text agreements between Matthew and Luke, not always word for word, which cannot be explained adequately by Q. Sometimes we find that Matthew and Luke agree to omit certain words of Mark. As a solution to these problems it has been proposed that Mark existed in a more primitive version and that Matthew and Luke used that version and that the version we have today is a revision made subsequently. This primitive version is referred to as either Ur-Markus or proto-Mark. There is no agreement regarding John. Yet there is increasing support for Markan dependence. This book, however, does not presuppose this thesis.

The test of these solutions is in their application in the sciences described below. If these are true hypotheses then they will assist us in the reconstruction of our texts; if not, they will lead us astray but it is not possible to avoid making these decisions.

Redaction Criticism is the effort to determine how the writer of the gospel used his literary sources and thus establish general patterns that are specific for the authors in question. For example, if it can be established that an author always inserted a particular interpretation into his source, we will know, even when we do not have the source, that this is characteristic of this author. An example of this is that Matthew always changes 'kingdom of God' into 'kingdom of heaven'. This demonstrates a redactional policy on Matthew's part: not to offend Jewish sensibilities. This, plus countless other similar changes, tells us how Matthew operates and how we can expect him to use other literary sources that we do not have available to us. Here we test our source hypothesis, seeing whether a coherent redaction pattern emerges and whether the end result can be explained by looking at the sources and the editorial practice of the author.

Form Criticism is interested in investigating smaller units within the gospel text. These units then make up the component parts of the gospel. Amongst these are collections of sayings of Jesus, collections of parables, a small apocalypse, a passion story and a collection of miracle stories. An additional source that has been proposed is a collection of proof-texts.[2]

Collections of sayings are found in the hypothetical source Q[3] as well as in the Gospel of Thomas (discussed below). A collection of parables is found in chapter 4 of Mark, though the sayings sources seem to include parables as well, which seem to have been united prior to Mark's use of them. These collections will be discussed at length in chapter 5. Collections of miracle stories are believed to have circulated as well. The marks of a collection are especially strong in the Gospel of John, as has been posited by Rudolf Bultmann.[4] Other sources include confessional statements and early church liturgy.[5] Certain units are longer. The small apocalypse in Mark 13 is a collection of sayings[6] which probably came into being well before the composition of Mark (see chapter 8). The passion narrative, whose purpose it was to explain the death of the Messiah, also circulated in various forms prior to its inclusion in Mark. The Gospel of Peter (discussed below) represents a late version of the genre in question. All of these different sources provide the material that the evangelist edited and placed into a continuous narrative form.

Historical Criticism attempts to reconstruct the historical situation, or lack of it, behind the account given. It draws from general circumstances known from other sources regarding the place and time and evaluates what is the most likely historically. Questions such as the historicity of the infanticide of Herod, the census, the naming of Simon Peter, John the Baptist's acceptance of Jesus, John the Baptist's execution and a host of other events qualify for this line of enquiry. Knowledge of 1st century history of Palestine is, of course, a prerequisite but the sciences described above also form the necessary background for such evaluations.

Textual Criticism attempts to reconstruct the gospel text as faithfully as possible to that of the author. It deals with a multitude of documents, Greek or otherwise, to establish the text that is to be used for our studies. The Greek text generally used today is mainly Alexandrian. The Alexandrian text is a group of documents, some amongst the oldest available, belonging to a family of manuscripts that is linked to Alexandria through its use by Alexandrian Church Fathers. The Western text group is very ancient but often also very unreliable, so that it has been termed a sort of unrevised text. The Caesarean text is very rare but appears to have been brought by Origen (the Church Father) to

Caesarea from Egypt, so it must have been in use in Egypt at the beginning of the 3rd century. Lastly there is the Byzantine text group, which on the whole represents a mixture of older text families. This group is by far the best represented text and was the basis of the Greek text from which the King James Version (KJV) was translated.

In this connection it should be noted that some of the current debate between those who favour the King James Version and those who favour a modern translation, such as the New International Version (NIV), completely ignores the fact that the variation between them is as much a question of translation as one of which Greek text is employed.

Patriology is not strictly speaking a biblical science. It deals with the Church Fathers, the early Christian writers who helped shape the Christian community. The body of literature that belongs to this category is immense but cannot wholly be ignored when trying to understand how today's church came into being. Furthermore, some of the Church Fathers recorded early traditions that are not found in the New Testament literature.

The sociological perspective is a newcomer to biblical study. The purpose is to understand not only the historical circumstances, the active force in a community, but also the sociological, which constitute the reactive force in a community. In order to understand the texts belonging to a community one has to understand what sort of a community it is.

Each of these disciplines deserves a book by itself and the short introductions given here can only be considered a bare minimum.

The word *canon* denotes ecclesiastical approval. In this book we will refer to canon in terms of which books were considered 'authoritative' in the church or synagogue. In the wake of the Jewish wars, in the seventies, the Jewish canon was selected and became a model for the building of the New Testament.[7] One should not assume, however, that the existence of the Old Testament canon can be understood as the motivating force behind the New Testament canon. In fact, during the authoring of the New Testament the 'scripture' refers to Old Testament literature. The impetus for creating a New Testament canon came from the conflict with Marcion, who believed the Old Testament to have been spurious rather than holy. He replaced the Old Testament with his own canon consisting of a modified Gospel of Luke as well as some letters of Paul.[8] The Catholic Church rejected Marcion but created in response a counter canon, a broader canon. The canon does not just canonize 'the unity of Christianity, but also . . . canonizes the diversity of Christianity'.[9]

Materials

In this section we will discuss the texts that this book will refer to in order to contextualize the gospels and the Christian tradition of the 1st and 2nd centuries.

The Gospel of Thomas is undoubtedly the most significant discovery in recent times for New Testament studies. Thomas is a collection of sayings attributed to Jesus: 'aphorisms, proverbs, wisdom sayings, parables, prophetic sayings about the "Kingdom of the Father", and community rules.'[10] As a sayings collection it provided the first positive evidence of the existence of a literary genre which matched that of the hypothetical Q source. Like Q, Steven Davies argues, the Gospel of Thomas can be dated to the mid-1st century when this genre was used. It fell out of use with the advent of the gospel genre.[11] Koester comes to a similar conclusion. He argues an early date for Thomas as Davies does (though not as early) on the basis that Thomas is independent of the canonical gospels, reasoning that if Thomas had been written after the canonical gospels, it would have used their material.[12] That independence has only recently become the consensus. Hitherto is has been held that the Gospel of Thomas was a Gnostic work that drew its material from the canonical gospels. But the Gnostic origin of Thomas is now also equally doubted[13] and is today recognized as belonging to the Jewish wisdom tradition, such as the Wisdom of Solomon.[14] There has been some discussion regarding the ordering of the sayings of Thomas. Comparing the Gospel of Thomas with reconstructions of Q, it becomes immediately clear that unlike Q, which has definite thematic units and sequences, Thomas has nothing of the kind. It is generally agreed that certain words link certain sayings with those that follow. Koester finds such connections to be products of almost casual compilation.[15] Crossan, on the other hand, feels that randomness rather than being 'a sign of literary incompetence' should be considered 'indicative of a particular theological vision'.[16] In testing the hypothesis of a Gnostic theological view in the Gospel of Thomas, it is important to note the absence of Gnostic mythology. It does not seem, therefore, that any reasonable definition of Gnosticism can make it an appropriate label. Even 'proto-Gnostic' seems an unwarranted tendentious designation. There are certainly instances where Thomas is not just more original (or primitive) than either Matthew or Luke but is even more original than Q. The reverse, however, also appears to be true. The two written sources probably share both oral and written sources, each redacted in accordance with its perspective.

The Gospel of Peter is a narrative of the passion and resurrection of Jesus purported to be reported by Peter. Immediately upon being discovered it was pronounced dependent on the canonical gospels.[17] A fragment of the gospel dating to about 200 CE puts the latest date at that time but *terminus ad quem*[18] can be placed further back by a reference to it in the work in Serapion.[19] There are, however, certain features in the Gospel of Peter that seem to come from an early tradition, for example, the lack of direct quotations with introductory formulas and independent usage of Old Testament material. Koester and Crossan both believe that the Gospel is a witness to an early tradition. Crossan proposes a 'Cross Gospel', which is an early textual passion narrative used by the canonical evangelists. In his hypothesis, the Gospel of Peter is an important witness to the Cross Gospel.[20] In Crossan's Cross Gospel 1) Jesus was buried by his enemies, 2) the disciples are absent and 3) all heavenly beings leave the tomb. In the canonical stage there is a reversal: 1) Jesus is buried by friends, 2) the apostles are present and 3) there is one heavenly being in the tomb. In order to have this happen a redactional stage is inserted which includes: 1) Joseph of Arimathæa appears to aid the takeover of Jesus' body, 2) the apostles hide but mourn and 3) a heavenly figure descends to wait in the tomb. Koester notes three problems with Crossan's hypothesis. First, the most extensive text is late and may have been influenced by canonical texts through subsequent scribal transmission. Second, the hypothesis suggests that the oral process stopped influencing written records at a very early stage. Finally, the proposition that John is dependent on Mark remains a minority view.[21] Current source-critical studies of John hold that the passion narrative of John was part of the Sign

Source.[22] It is particularly problematic, as Koester notes, that Crossan assigns the last epiphany on the lake to the intra-canonical stage, since its equivalent (John 21:1–14) is considered to be a latecomer to the canonical gospel.

The Infancy Gospels centre around the youth of Jesus and the life of His parents. There are two 2nd century Infancy Gospels, the Infancy Gospel of Thomas (miracles of the infant Jesus) and the Gospel of James (the life of Jesus' parents), each representing a further development in the legendary portrayal of Jesus. A third book of interest is the Arabic Gospel of Infancy, which belongs to the 6th century.

The Gospel of the Hebrews is no longer available to us except through quotations in the Church Fathers' literature. Furthermore, it is believed that there was not one but three different gospels called thus by the Church Fathers. Each quotation has been assigned to either the Gospel of the Hebrews, the Gospel of the Nazaraeans or the Gospel of the Ebionites. Each of these gospels belonged to a Jewish-Christian community, that is to say a community in which the Christians were Jewish converts. Ebionites were more radically Jewish than were the Nazaraeans, the former rejecting the virgin birth and the later accepting 'Son of God' as the title of Jesus. Both observed the Law and required circumcision and the keeping of the Sabbath.

The Secret Gospel of Mark is believed to be preserved only in a few quotations by Clement of Alexandria, a late 2nd century Church Father. The letter of Clement, which preserves two quotations from the gospel, was only recently discovered in a manuscript that can be dated to the 18th century. Owing to various problems finding the manuscript for further analysis, at the time of writing there is only a photograph of the text available. The text has a Markan style to it but fragments have a more mystic content. The value of the Secret Gospel of Mark has generally not been recognized but the work has two very significant advocates in Koester and Crossan, who both believe it to be Ur-Markus (see above).[23]

The Gospel of Mary has not received much attention; its inclusion here is therefore due only to the present author's own interest in this work. The composition has been dated to the end of the 2nd century on the basis of an extant manuscript.[24] The work is a story of Mary Magdalene consoling the disciples after the crucifixion and ascension. It includes two Gnostic dialogues in which esoteric questions are asked and answered. There also appears some synoptic material that is of questionable dependence.[25] In the view of the present author, the narrative section belongs to a feminine oral tradition from a somewhat 'orthodox' community.

The Didache (the teaching) is a catechism which prescribes a certain way of living one's personal life and communal religious life and conducting community administration. As a document it has long been regarded as one of the most significant contributions to our knowledge of early Christianity. It is composed of four distinct sections: The Way of Life and the Way of Death take up the first six chapters. In it is described the way one's personal life should be conducted (the Way of Life) and how it should not be conducted (the Way of Death). The second part (chapters 7–10) describes the sacraments: baptism, fasting, prayer and the Eucharist. The third part discusses the ecclesiastical structure (chapters 11–15) and it ends with a short eschatological discourse (chapter 16).

Determining the origin of the Didache has proved a complicated affair. The history of research can, according to Clayton N. Jefford, conveniently be divided into three schools.[26] The French school tends to date the Didache to the middle of the 1st century and places it in Palestine or Syria.[27] The German school proposes dependence not only on the synoptic gospels but often on Apostolic Fathers such as the Epistle of Barnabas and the Shepard of Hermas. Dates ranged from the beginning to the middle of the 2nd century and the suggested location is most often Egypt.[28] The third school, which comprises British and American scholars, has not found as much unanimity as the two other schools. In general, this school has not endorsed the early dates proposed by the French school but has supported a Syrian location over an Egyptian.[29] This book will assume the position that the Didache is not dependent on the gospels, though it does not presume an anti-Paul background.

Summary and Conclusion

What methodologies can supply us with is ultimately 'plausibility': a plausible history of the gospel tradition, plausible editorial practices and plausible social and historical contexts. A historian is at all times dependent on colleagues to share, to some degree, his or her sense of 'plausibility'. The problem here is that even what seems coherent and plausible to a majority of scholars, at any given time, may be the outcome of a common experience of reality that is entirely different from the one that was experienced by the author of the text that is being scrutinized. What seemed coherent and logical to Matthew may not seem so to a reader today. This is not merely a question of being familiar with context but also with mind set.

Evaluation of the materials can only take place through the use of methodology. Dating and determining interdependence of other sources, context and intent of a work are crucial to assessing the inherent value of the source. Is there not then a danger of circularity? Is it not possible that the lack of access to the mind set will contaminate the process from the very outset? Whether one ascribes to such a methodological pessimism or not will very much depend on how one evaluates one person's ability to make a bridge from one mind set to another. The premise behind this chapter and its presentation of methods and sources is that there is an essential common experience among all people, that despite the unique individual experiences that diversify human perception, there are certain features of human existence that make at least a partial bridge possible. It is with this cautious note in mind that we set out to explore the gospels.

2
The Jewish Context

This chapter deals in particular with the different types of Jewish communities of the 1st century. In this connection we shall also look at some of the most important Judaic writings. This will form a basis for understanding the historical setting of Jesus and His ministry.

Contemporary Judaism

Judaism today is generally homogenous in its beliefs; there are few disputes on the matter of what is canonical and what is not. Divisions occur mostly on the extent to which one follows these laws. However, this chapter is not about contemporary Judaism but about that which was contemporary with Jesus and His disciples and to some extent the first community and the evangelists. As Sarah J. Tanzer in her article 'Judaisms of the First Century' writes: 'It has become clear that in the first century CE Judaism was not monolithic but highly variegated throughout the Greco-Roman world, and diverse and complex even within the borders of Roman Palestine.'[30]

Bruce Chilton succinctly explains how we can understand this diversity: 'religions find definition to begin with not in doctrine let alone in a book or rite but in social entities, e.g. communities of faithful.'[31] In other words, the formation of sects or groups is a function not of a random set of people agreeing on the same system of beliefs but of social conditions which make certain sets of beliefs more tenable. We should not therefore be surprised when we find that the sects that we are going to look at have diverse social parameters. Bruce J. Malina suggests that a group starts when someone is displeased with the present state of affairs, perceives the possibility of changing this and then shares it with others who evaluate and join if they agree with the assessment.[32] If one considers this a reasonable model then it follows that groups are formed with individuals who are able to communicate and agree on the common goal of such a group.

We shall now undertake a survey of some of the most significant sects of 1st century Judaism.

The Pharisees

The most prominent sect of Jews in the time of Jesus was the Pharisee. The word 'Pharisee' derives from the Hebrew word *perusim* (פרוים) meaning 'separate ones', which in the Greek New Testament is transliterated as *pharisaioi* (φαρισαῖοι). Thus from the name itself questions arise: from whom are they separate and is this name given or taken by them? Irving Zeitlin suggests that from the Mishnah's[33] lack of use of the term, the term was applied to them rather than adopted by them.[34] He feels that the term 'party' or 'sect' is an improper term for such a popular group and regards them rather as a 'socio-religious movement'.[35] But by any of the social-scientific models currently used in New Testament (NT) studies, this is not true. A socio-religious movement or a 'faction' is generally expected to fade quickly, either realizing its goal, failing and dissolving or becoming institutionalized and developing means of permanence, which in turn means developing sectarian qualities.[36] Malina finds that it is better described as a 'countermovement organization' because they 'focus on stability and permanence'.[37] An analysis of the Mishnah will indeed show that it is 'their [Pharisees of the Mishnah] halakhah [normative law] not *the* halakhah'.[38] Zeitlin also states that their self-perception was that they were 'brothers of the Covenant', that they did regard themselves as 'the true community of Israel' and finally that they probably kept apart from those who 'fell short of the Pharisaic standards of purity'.[39] According to Horsley and Hanson, the Pharisees had been a 'religiopolitical party' during the period in which they had Hasmonean support[40] but when they lost power they became a brotherhood in the Law.

The main historical sources of the history and theology of 1st century Judaism remain Josephus[41] (a Pharisee himself) and Philo of Alexandria.[42] Furthermore, Paul the apostle was a Pharisee before converting to Christianity. The Pharisees believed in the resurrection, free will, predestination and the immortality of the soul, which was a major shift from ancient Judaism in which the only afterlife was through one's children, procreational afterlife.[43] This concept will be discussed further in the section about the Sadducees, who held these ancient beliefs. The Pharisees were strict observers of the Torah, which they held to be of two kinds: written and oral. The Oral Torah comprised the traditions carried from generation to generation, much the same way as the Catholic Church has its tradition. Observance of the written Torah included keeping the Sabbath and certain Levitical hygienic regulations, while observance of the Oral Torah required keeping the fast and strict observance of tithe donation and purity rules. They are recognized by these features throughout the gospels, and being the major opponents of Jesus, one may indeed say, to some degree, that Jesus' teachings were defined against the Pharisaic tradition, or perhaps more accurately, Pharisaic practice, particular when His teaching travelled to urban areas where Pharisees were more common. One should not forget, however, that Matthew encouraged following the prescripts of the Pharisees and only condemned the spirit in which they were customarily carried out in his time: 'Saying, The Scribes and the Pharisees sit in Moses' seat: All therefore whatsoever they bid you observe, [that] observe and do; but do not ye after their works: for they say, and do not' (Matthew 23:2–3 KJV).

In some sense Matthew probably considered himself a converted Scribe who, unlike Paul, still considered Judaic law to be valid.[44] Luke portrays an occasion when Jesus was invited to the home of a Pharisee. The story is recounted differently by two other independent sources, in Mark and John, and probably circulated in an oral form. While the words may be the construction of the evangelist,[45] the story probably represents an ancient witness both of things that Jesus might have done as well as things Pharisees might have done. This shows that, though opposed to Him, not all the Pharisees considered Jesus unclean. An example of this is when Jesus went to the home of the Pharisee named Simon and a woman who was known to be a sinner came to adore Jesus by washing His feet with her tears, wiping them with her hair and kissing and anointing them. Luke says that the Pharisee thought that this was a sign that Jesus did not have the prophetic vision which would have allowed Him to know that the woman was a sinner and that she should therefore be avoided (Luke 7:36–9).

If something like this truly happened, then it says

something significant about the Pharisees. Claims by some that their influence was diminished by strict rules of cleanliness, which did not allow them to mingle with commoners, should be considered critically. It should be noted that this sect had very few adherents. Josephus writes regarding the end of the 1st century BCE:

> . . . for there was a certain sect of men that were Jews, who valued themselves highly upon the exact skill they had in the law of their fathers . . .These are those that are called the sect of the Pharisees, who were in a capacity of greatly opposing kings. A cunning sect they were, and soon elevated to a pitch of open fighting and doing mischief . . . these very men [as opposed to all other Jews] did not swear [support to Caesar], being above six thousand . . .[46]

From this two important facts emerge. First, there were only about six thousand Pharisees at the beginning of the 1st century and, second, although they made no open revolt, they did not hide their contempt for the Roman overlords. So while few wanted to follow the laws as rigidly as the Pharisees did, many probably regarded them as ideals both in their attitude towards law and in their outspokenness about government. Their theological opinions are explained by Josephus:

> Now, for the Pharisees, they live meanly, and despise delicacies in diet; and they follow the conduct of reason; and what that prescribes to them as good for them, they do; and they ought earnestly to strive to observe reason's dictates for practice. They also pay a respect to such as are in years; nor are they so bold as to contradict them in anything which they have introduced; and, when they determine that all things are done by fate, they do not take

> away freedom from men of acting as they think fit; since their notion is, that it hath pleased God to make temperament, whereby what he wills is done, but so that the will of men can act virtuously or viciously. They also believe that souls have an immortal vigour in them, and that under the earth there will be rewards or punishments, according as they have lived virtuously or viciously in this life; and the latter are to be detained in an everlasting prison, but the former shall have power to revive and live again; on account of which doctrines, they are able greatly to persuade the body of the people; and whatsoever they do about divine worship, prayers, and sacrifices, they perform them according to their direction; insomuch that the cities gave great attestations to them on account of their entire virtuous conduct, both in the actions of their lives and their discourses also.[47]

There can be no doubt that Josephus is quite partial to the Pharisees and he is probably exaggerating when he claims that the vast majority of the Jewish people supported them. The reason for their popularity given above is that their doctrines were appealing but Josephus gives us another reason as well. Here he speaks of Hyrcanus the high priest who banished Ptolemy, first favouring the Pharisees and wanting to join them. Being slandered required that the felon be punished: the Sadducees required one's death but the Pharisees only 'stripes and bonds': 'and, indeed the Pharisees, even upon other occasions, are not apt to be severe in punishments.'[48]

It is possible that the Pharisees were indeed more lenient in their pronouncements on the Law than their counterparts the Sadducees, for they would, for example, understand 'an eye for an eye' not as a retribution but would allow the offender to compensate with a monetary sum.[49]

But an important and salient question remains about the extent to which the Pharisees influenced the general opinion of the people. Was there an active attempt to draw people who were not of that sect to follow them? That Paul was a Diaspora Jew[50] and a Pharisee prior to his conversion suggests that Pharisees were at least geographically spread and probably present in most metropolitan areas. Paul's early missionary activity, which was also in the Diaspora, was first directed towards Jews who attended synagogues. Were these, like Paul, more or less affiliated with the Pharisees?

In the Mishnah, which we shall discuss further below, we find support for the contention that the Pharisees did indeed attempt to be influential amongst all people.

> Hillel said: Be of the disciples of Aaron who loved peace and pursue it; so you should love all men and attract them to the study of the Law. He used to say: Whoever magnifies his own name destroys it; whoever does not increase his knowledge of the Law shall be cut off: whoever gives himself the crown of the Law shall be consumed. He also said: if I do not do good works, then who will do them for me? And if I think only of myself, then what am I? And if not now, when? Shammai used to say: Let your study of the Law be fixed; say little and do much and receive all men with cheerfulness.[51]

From this there can be no doubt that the Pharisees felt obliged to receive all and encourage them to observe the (Pharisaic) law and that they were told the terrible consequences for people who were not reached. Richard Horsley, however, points out that the Rabbis do not appear to have enjoyed the company of uneducated peasants. As evidence he cites a tradition on the authority of Dosa b. Harkinas:

'Morning sleep and midday wine and children's talk and sitting in the assemblies of the peasants put a man out of the world.'[52] This probably represents the predominant view, while Hillel and Shammai seem more like an ideal. This will be explored further below when we look at the specifically Galilean situation.

The theological proximity of the Pharisaic sect and nascent Christianity probably contributed to the continued conflict between these two factions, even in the century immediately after the crucifixion of Jesus. The problem emerged as an internal conflict, as the Pharisaic practices were imposed on the newly-converted Gentiles. These advocates of the full application of the law were later named 'Judizers' (Gk. *Ioudaizo*) and contributed to some of the inner turmoil in the newly-emerged church. Although we shall learn more about this conflict in the chapters to follow, let it suffice for now to mention that this problem caused some division between Paul, who openly advocated the complete annulment of these Pharisaic traditions, and the church in Jerusalem, which still followed these laws.

The Sadducees

The Sadducees are known to us only through the eyes of their opponents, for they have left no writings of their own.

Although the Sadducees appear in a similar context in the gospels (i.e. as opponents of Jesus), their theology differed greatly from that of the Pharisees, particularly in their rejection of the authority of Pharisaic traditions and the existence of spirits, angels,[53] the soul and of the resurrection.

The Sadducees distinguished themselves in another way. They were a small but powerful elite, some of whom descended from Zadok (hence the name Zadokite, which was transliterated from Hebrew *zaduqim*, צדקים), who was the high priest under King David. They exercised great influence in the temple of Jerusalem but had to struggle against the Pharisees at the royal court. Their loyalty to the Roman emperor may well be understood as a logical consequence of their theology, inasmuch as they rejected the concept of an afterlife and believed in punishment and rewards being granted by God in this life. Thus that they were occupied by Rome could only be viewed as the Will of God. Their theology indicated to them that as long as they followed their temple cult, a just God would protect them. This also explains why they stopped existing as a group after the destruction of the temple in 70 CE, as this destroyed the Sadducees' centre of authority and clearly showed that dedication to the temple cult was not sufficient to maintain God's covenant.[54]

This may in part justify Josephus' claim that the Sadducees were not popular amongst the underprivileged, for they held that the way things were was God's justice, while the Pharisees held that this justice was reserved for the afterlife. Such doctrines could only be held by those who were satisfied with their condition in life, which must have been a minority group. Josephus says of this group that 'the Sadducees are able to persuade none but the rich, and have not the populace obsequious to them'.[55]

The groups that conceivably could have belonged to this party include priests, aristocrats and the wealthy. The wealthy were a newly-emerged class of people who had, through commercialization, gained a position in life. Another group that might have belonged to this sect was the military, which had been employed by the Sadducees during one of their campaigns.

On a couple of occasions the Sadducees appear in the gospels to ask questions that could not have been asked by the Pharisees. One was the question about the doctrine of the resurrection:

> The same day came to him the Sadducees, which say that there is no resurrection, and asked him, saying, Master, Moses said, If a man die, having no children, his brother shall marry his wife, and raise up seed unto his brother. Now there were with us seven brethren: and the first, when he had married a wife, deceased, and, having no issue, left his wife unto his brother: Likewise the second also, and the third, unto the seventh. And last of all the woman died also. Therefore in the resurrection whose wife shall she be of the seven, for they all had her (Matthew 22:23–8 KJV).

The question here is based on the law of Deuteronomy (25:5) which states that when a man dies and has not brought forth one to be the seed of his house, it is the obligation of the brother to marry the widow so that the house (i.e. the family) may live on. The law hints at the Sadducean belief that the only afterlife is through the seed.[56] It thus can be said to reflect an older thought pattern which is totally devoid of Hellenism. This concept is also exemplified by the curse put upon the idol-worshippers: 'Thou shalt not bow down thyself to them, nor serve them: for I the LORD thy God [am] a jealous God, visiting the iniquity of the fathers upon the children unto the third and fourth [generation] of them that hate me . . .' (Exodus 20:5 KJV).

The answer of Jesus, however, rejects the concepts of both procreational afterlife and an earthly resurrection (i.e. as conceived by the Pharisees). It seems to be a compound of two answers: 'Jesus answered and said unto them, Ye do err, not knowing the scriptures, nor the power of God. For in the resurrection they neither marry, nor are given in marriage, but are as the angels of God in heaven' (Matthew 22:29–30 KJV).

The first reply seemingly answers the question on the assumption that the resurrection deals with afterlife, especially with reference to the 'angels of God in heaven', which indeed would seem to be a provocation to the Sadducees who did not believe in their existence. 'But as touching the resurrection of the dead, have ye not read that which was spoken unto you by God, saying, I am the God of Abraham, and the God of Isaac, and the God of Jacob? God is not the God of the dead, but of the living' (Matthew 22:31–2 KJV).

The first part of the answer is a quotation from Exodus 3:6, in which God presents Himself to Moses as the God of His forefathers. The second statement, 'God is not the God of the dead, but of the living', is Jesus' own. First He shows that God is the God of the forefathers of the Jews, who are physically dead but who are, according to the logic of this verse, 'of the living'. Viewed in connection with the first statement, which made all the resurrected 'the angels of God in heaven', the resurrection had somehow come to pass. This had come in the past through the advent of these illustrious forefathers and hence they are still accounted as living.[57] Thus Jesus clearly refuted the Sadducees' view of the resurrection (and perhaps also that of the Pharisees). This shall be discussed in detail in later chapters.

Though we have no positive way of knowing this, it is quite conceivable that the Sadducees had their own tradition. Certainly they differed in their understanding of the questions of ritual purity and Sabbath observance.[58] But perhaps far more interesting is the theory that they rejected all of the canon with the exception of the Pentateuch,[59] like the Samaritans. It was the prophets who introduced such concepts as resurrection, so the rejection of these concepts may in fact indicate a rejection of the authority of the prophets. The problem of this theory is that it leaves the justification for the existence of the temple and its cult in an tenable situation. Most likely such rejection was held privately, for it is not mentioned by opponents. If this was the case, perhaps it is indicated by the Mishnah when it says: 'The daughters of the Sadducees, if they follow after the ways of their fathers, are deemed like to the women of the Samaritans; but if they have separated themselves and follow after the ways of the Israelites, they are deemed like to the women of the Israelites.'[60]

In a New Testamental context the Sadducees are also interesting for their prominent role in the crucifixion of Jesus.

The Essenes

The Essenes were members of a sect of Judaism who lived in seclusive communities. They strictly observed the Law and had rigid ascetic practices. The Qumran community, to which the Dead Sea scrolls belonged, is believed to have been part of this sect. Although the word 'essene' does not occur in the Dead Sea scrolls, most of the practices reflected in those documents seem to match those of the Essenes. We should also remember that the 'Pharisees' too are rarely mentioned in the Mishnah, so their absence is hardly decisive.[61]

Pliny in his massive work *Natural History* sets forth a host of knowledge. In a description of Palestine we find:

> On the west side of the Dead Sea, but out of range of the noxious exhalations of the coast, is the solitary tribe of the Essenes, which is remarkable beyond all the other tribes in the whole world, as it has no women and has renounced all sexual desire, has no money, and has only palm-trees for company. Day by day the throng of refugees is recruited to an equal number by numerous accessions of persons tired of life and driven thither by the waves of fortune to adopt their manners. Thus through thousands of ages (incredible to relate) a race in which no one is born lives on for ever: so prolific for their advantage is other men's weariness of life![62]

Josephus in his book *The Jewish Wars* describes the Essenes at length.[63] The present author will quote selectively from this and will attempt to sum up pertinent points. The Essenes were generally monastic but received children into their midst for education, presumably by adoption. The absence of women claimed by Josephus is supported by the total absence of reference to them in the community writings found at Qumran.[64] Josephus also mentions another group of Essenes who allowed marriage for the purpose of procreation, these having a trial marriage of three years to see if they were able to produce children.[65] There is a discrepancy between the description given by Josephus and that of the sect of Qumran, which is the community's isolation. Josephus writes: 'They have no certain city, but many of them dwell in every city.' It is difficult to reconcile the life style described by Josephus with a community living in a metropolitan area. Urbanization intrudes on the life of asceticism, where women are not allowed and where all goods of the community are shared freely. Most likely the group lived in communities like the Qumran sect, in colonies not too far away from cities so that candidates and adoptive children could come easily while being remote enough so they were unlikely to be invaded by the commercialism of the urban environment. It also appears that all work was carried out in the community by the community itself. Josephus says: 'After this every one is sent away by their curators, to exercise some of those arts wherein they are skilled, in which they labour with great diligence till the fifth hour.' As to their scripture, we are told that they 'take great pains in studying the writings of the ancients, and choose out of them what is most for the advantage of their soul and body'. Whether this means a selective canon or not is difficult to determine but the evidence from Qumran shows that the Prophets were used a great deal but there was a somewhat relaxed attitude towards the Other Writings.[66] They also composed their own religious scripture, the status of which within the community is difficult to determine. This overlay of tradition and interpretation did not soften the application of the Law; in fact, it made it quite a bit more strict.

Josephus says that each member was under oath that he would not 'conceal anything from those of his own sect, nor discover any of their doctrines to others, no, not though any one should compel him so to do at the hazard of his life'. How Josephus then came to learn of their doctrines he does not reveal and we are bound to be somewhat sceptical about this secrecy. However, if the Qumran are, as the present author believes, an Essene community, then Josephus either did not know all of their doctrines or did not wish to publish them. Josephus in his autobiographical account *Life of Flavius Josephus* states that during three years, from the age of 16 to 19, he acquainted himself with the three main sects (the Pharisees, the Sadducees and the Essene), as well as following an ascetic named Banus.[67] His choice, as noted above, finally fell on the Pharisees. It seems doubtful that Josephus in those three years could gain entrance into a community like Qumran. He could possibly have visited a community and there may have been common lore circulating about them but he probably never gained a membership that would give him access to knowledge beyond what was generally known. At most we can entertain, as Hadas-Lebel suggests, that Josephus followed the sect for a year but 'drew back' at the end of the year because of the oath necessary to go on to the two following years that were required before attaining membership.[68]

The doctrine of the Essene, Josephus writes, was

> That bodies are corruptible, and that the matter they are made of is not permanent; but that the souls are immortal, and continue for ever; and that they come out of the most subtle air, and are united to their bodies as in prisons, into which they are drawn by a certain natural enticement; but that when they are set free from the bonds of the flesh, they then, as released from a long bondage, rejoice and mount upward.

We also find references to angels within the Qumran scripture[69] but rather than a similarity with Hellenism, which Josephus appeals to, these are to be compared with Zoroastrianism. No single sect of Jews exhibits such a clear theological relation to Zoroastrianism as does the Qumran. Here dualism is ever present and apocalyptic works also draw several parallels.

Lastly, there is an aspect that is purposely completely

ignored by Josephus, namely the apocalyptic expectation of the group, which was so central to the whole community. The community did not only read what was beneficial to the soul, neither did it carry weapons merely 'for fear of thieves'. Their literature shows that their expectation of two Messiahs also had great military repercussions but, unlike the Zealots, this was not directed towards the Romans as much as against the present rulers of the temple. These are depicted as the 'sons of error' who are led by the 'wicked priest' and 'the spouter of lies'.

Regarding the controversy of whether the Qumran community was Essene or not, the following should be kept in mind: The Qumran literary body is by no means monolithic and reading through does not give an altogether consistent picture. This is generally accounted for by the fact that the community was a living and changeable one. Another point was that Josephus was not an insider and there is a difference between 1) what people outside see, 2) what insiders write about themselves and 3) what the reality of the community is. Furthermore, the Qumran literary corpus may indeed not be the product of a single community but the collection of like-minded communities with some historical or theological relationship.

The impact these and like communities had on the general population was probably not great. Their secrecy around doctrine and their seclusiveness made them insignificant when it came to popular beliefs. They were probably highly regarded for their observance of the Law, for otherwise we cannot explain people willingly entering or children willingly being given to be raised. The strictness of their application of the Law, however, was probably considered unattainable by most of the populace and so probably the Pharisee interpretation remained the most feasible and popular.

Samaritans

In addition to these three major sects of Judaism, there were other groups, including the Samaritans, who were a separate people by virtue of their rejection of the temple of Jerusalem. The Samaritans, the inhabitants of Samaria, were a people alienated from the rest of Judaism and widely held to be untouchables, as is well reflected in the New Testament: 'There cometh a woman of Samaria to draw water: Jesus saith unto her, Give me to drink. (For his disciples were gone away unto the city to buy meat.) Then saith the woman of Samaria unto him, How is it that thou, being a Jew, askest drink of me, which am a woman of Samaria? for the Jews have no dealings with the Samaritans' (John 4:7–9 KJV).

From this story we also note that Samaritans had messianic expectations (verse 29). It is conceivable that the expression 'Saviour of the world' (ὁ σωτὴρ τοῦ κόσμου; verse 42[70]) which occurs nowhere else in John, has a distinct Samaritan origin. The title 'Saviour' for Christ was particularly common amongst Gnostics and as the first known Gnostic, Simon Magus, came from Samaria, a connection is plausible. Irenaeus writes that Simon Magus was believed to have come to confer 'salvation upon men'.[71] It is also peculiar that the reason why Jesus was believed was because He knew things about the woman; later, others believe in Him because of 'his word' (τὸν λόγον αὐτοῦ) this too is consonant with Gnosticism.

Van Groningen notes the following about Simon Magus and his beliefs: They were informed about the Jewish faith or the Samaritan Pentateuch,[72] Samaritanism was generally well-disposed to Jesus' message because of the attitude He took to some of the later developments in Judaism[73] and, finally, that 'Samaritanism was in fact one of the main environments and soils from which Gnosticism arose'.[74]

The Samaritans, as already mentioned, had the same Pentateuch the Jews had but they rejected the other scripture (the Prophets being predominantly Jerusalem-centred) and instead placed their centre of worship on Mount Gerizim.

> When the Lord your God brings you into the land of Canaan which you are entering to take possession of, you shall set up there stones and plaster them with plaster, and you shall write upon them all the words of the Law. And when you have gone over Jordan, you shall set up these stones, concerning which I command you this day, on Mount Gerizim. And you shall build an altar to the Lord your God.[75]

The Samaritan Pentateuch is often dated to the break with the Judaic Jews in the 5th century but recent studies have placed the final breach in the post-Hasmonean period at the beginning of the 1st century BCE.[76] According to Deuteronomy (27:8–13), Simeon, Levi, Judah, Issachar, Joseph and Benjamin were directed to stand on Mount Gerizim to bless the people as they moved across the river Jordan.

The Samaritans were considered unclean, for while the Jews had been in exile in Babylon the Samaritans had remained behind and intermarried with heathen settlers.[77] When the Jews returned from exile the Samaritans wished to help reconstruct the temple but were not accepted as Jews anymore and thus could not partake in the privilege.[78] It is at this point that their shrine was set up on Mount Gerizim. Though there were wars between Jews and Samaritans after this, they enjoyed some peace during the reign of the Romans but still remained a despised and unclean people. So despised were they that they were almost proverbial and became the perfect object of that famous didactic story in Luke 10:30–5.

Herodians

The Herodians were a political party rather than a religious sect and appear in the gospels as the supporters of Herod. According to the gospels, they supported the Pharisees in their contentions against Jesus and tried to frame Him (Mark 3:6). The fact that these two factions disagreed on the Herodians' most important *raison d'être*, namely the legitimacy of the current reign, makes their alliance appear all the more desperate. These are probably the people who assisted Herod in gaining the crown instead of the Maccabean Antigonus in 70 BCE. According to Epiphanius, the Herodians were a group that believed that Herod had fulfilled messianic expectation, having fulfilled Genesis 49:10.[79] Little else is known about them, as they were a relatively short-lived political party whose main interest was to maintain the *status quo*.

The Fourth Philosophy and the Sicarii

For a long time scholarly surveys of 1st century Judaism have compounded several different movements into a single entity called the 'Zealots'. As a consequence of Horsley and Hanson's ground-breaking study of popular movements at the time of Jesus, such a construction is no longer tenable. The 'Zealots' proper were a popular movement and will be discussed below. A group usually categorized under 'Zealots' is the Fourth Philosophy. This group was called by Josephus 'the fourth sect of Jewish philosophy' and was authored by 'Judas the Galilean', who is mentioned by Luke in Acts 5:37. Luke purposely tells this story to show that Christians knew that they were comparable to this sect but also that they were aware that they were different in that Christianity had a divine origin.

Josephus tells us that 'these men agree in all other things with the Pharisaic notions; but they have an inviolable attachment to liberty; and they say that God is to be their only Ruler and Lord'.[80] He goes on to describe their fearlessness but says nothing more about their doctrines. Horsley and Hanson conclude that the movement resisted payment of tax because of its religious convictions, considering them to be a compromise of the covenental principle of serving no one but God.[81] They were a peaceful resistance group that was willing to suffer the punishment of torture for what they believed.

This 'philosophy' also spawned the sect known as Sicarii, which assassinated those who collaborated with the Romans.[82] Horsley and Hanson speculate that the change of strategy was necessitated by a change in social conditions that left no options open other than terrorism.[83] Later they played a lesser role in the revolt of the mid-sixties, in which they finally committed mass suicide on Masada.[84]

Popular Movements

The movements discussed so far have been upper class, scribal or ethnic movements. When we use the term 'popular' below it refers to movements that operated by orality rather than scribalism. These movements usually supported lower-class ethics and lacked the intellectual sophistication to argue from scripture in the way Scribes did.

The Zealots

The Zealots were, to Josephus, ultimately responsible for the destruction of the temple of Jerusalem. The movement began when the approaching Vespian army in the mid-sixties started conquering northern Judea and systematically killing every member of the lower class in the area. Fleeing peasants gathered in Jerusalem, forming the resistance movement which, although it consisted of a relatively small number, played a vital role inasmuch as it prevented the ruling class of Jerusalem from negotiating the surrender of the city.[85] Horsley and Hanson conclude that the movement was democratically oriented and elected an uneducated Zaducite to the office of high priest in accordance with tradition.[86]

Bandit Movements

Bandit movements were drawn from the impoverished people of the countryside. These movements may in their Palestinian form best be termed 'social banditry', since they represented the sense of justice of the common people. Horsley and Hanson explain: 'Social bandits also generally share the fundamental values and religion of the peasant society of which they remain at least a marginal part. They may be defenders of the faith as well as of what is right.'[87] Freyne states that there is a 'religious aspect of social banditry, representing as it does the divine justice that is actively engaged in bringing about the new order that is hoped for.'[88] There are instances where peasants sheltered brigands or asked for help when the authorities were to slow to dispense justice.[89]

Josephus regularly reports the formation of large groups of brigands who, with their stronghold in caves, managed to become a serious military threat. These were found in Galilee,[90] in Syria[91] and in Idumea on the border of Arabia.[92] On the road to Beth-horon some brigands led by Eleazar managed to rob Stephen, a servant of Caesar.[93] The same Eleazar made raids in northern Judea and Samaria[94] and was only captured and sent to Rome for trial and execution after a 20–year long career.[95] According to the gospels, Jesus was crucified together with thieves (see chapter 10).

Messianic Movements

The word 'messiah' (= Christ) is almost unknown in Jewish literature in the sense we find it in the New Testament. The concept itself, however, is found in both popular and official versions. Messiahs were royal pretenders, individuals who were to replace the current illegitimate royal rulers and usher in the true rule of God. Followers of popular messianic movements were usually armed and ready to assist the royal pretender in his conquest of dominions. By nature such figures followed popular tradition, whereby royalty was elected by the people as their military leader, as were Saul and David (2 Samuel 2:4, of Judah; 5:3, of Israel).

A case of particular interest is that of Simon bar Giora, who started off as a leader of outlaws. He captured Hebron,[96] where David had been anointed king over both Judah and Israel. After he had conquered all of Idumea he was welcomed into Jerusalem by its inhabitants in order to fight the Zealots who had taken the temple in Jerusalem. When the Romans captured Jerusalem they found Simon adorned in royal clothes, a white frock and a purple cloak. He was taken to Rome and paraded and publicly executed in celebration of the Roman victory.[97] This indicates that both Simon and the Romans understood him to be the king of Israel.

According to Josephus, Judas son of Ezekias stormed the royal armoury at Sepphoris in his pursuit of a royal rank.[98]

Prophetic Movements

Prophetic movements were similar to the messianic in that they were headed by a single figure whose followers considered him the inaugurator of the rule of God. Unlike messianic movements, the followers of prophets were unarmed inasmuch as they believed that God Himself would intercede and assure the salvation of His people. These prophets would therefore follow certain patterns which were popularly known to have been followed by Moses or Elijah-Elisha, such as going into the wilderness and performing miracles, parting seas and so forth. These sorts of prophets may be termed 'action prophets', in contrast with 'oracle prophets'.

Oracle prophets are foretellers of bad fortune, in line with such prophets as Jeremiah and Amos. These often proclaimed the displeasure of God and His approaching judgement. Such pronouncements could also include explicit mention of the deeds that had made God discontent, so that the prophet often also acted as a critic of current authorities.

Four years before the war with the Romans a peasant, Jesus son of Hananiah, appeared in Jerusalem proclaiming: 'A voice from the east, a voice from the west, a voice from the four winds, a voice against Jerusalem and the holy house, a voice against the bridegrooms and the brides, and a voice against this whole people!'[99] He was publicly whipped and ridiculed but continued unperturbed to proclaim his woes on Jerusalem for seven years until the day he was killed by a catapulted boulder as he was proclaiming, 'Woe, woe to myself also!'

Just before this story Josephus mentions in passing an anonymous (false) prophet who had claimed 'that God commanded them to get up upon the temple, and that there they should receive miraculous signs of their deliverance'.[100]

These are both cases of popular oracle and action prophets. But prophets and prophecy were also present in scribal communities such as the Essenes.[101] The Pharisees did not have prophets as such but had a strong reputation for foreknowledge.[102] Indeed, when Josephus himself was captured by Vespian, he made a prophecy about his coming success.[103]

There are examples of action prophets amongst both the Samaritans and Galileans. The Samaritans had a prophet during the time of Pilate who gathered people on Mount Gerizim with the promise that he would show them sacred vessels placed there by Moses. The people, however, were stopped by Pilate who slaughtered a great many of them.[104]

Amongst the Galileans arose Theudas the son of Judas the Galilean (mentioned above) who led his followers across the river Jordan, which he promised that he himself would divide, presumably in remembrance of Moses (Exodus 14:21) or Elijah and Elisha (2 King 2:8, 14). Fadus, however, sent in troops, executed Theudas and paraded his head in Jerusalem.[105]

An Egyptian Jew arrived in Jerusalem and called on people to gather on the Mount of Olives. From there, he promised, he would command the walls of Jerusalem to fall and would then give them free entrance into the city.[106] This was probably a form of re-enactment of Joshua's capture of Jericho (Joshua 6:20).

Apparently a prophet appeared in connection with the Sicarii who led people into the 'wilderness' with a promise of deliverance.[107]

Judaism in the Diaspora

Judaism had prior to the 1st century spread to virtually every part of the Roman Empire. As such it had come into, indeed had been immersed in, a sea of Hellenistic social and philosophical influences. In the words of Aune, Judaism in the Diaspora had been in an 'uneven process of Hellenization since the late fourth century BC'.[108] Almost a century ago Friedländer wrote his seminal article on the diversity of Judaism in the Diaspora.[109] In it he proposes that many of the antinomian[110] tendencies in early Christianity were a consequence of various groupings with such tendencies already existing in Diaspora Judaism. Antinomianism invariably stemmed from an allegorical interpretation of the Law. Rodney Stark explains Jewish antinomianism in the Diaspora as a response to the social pressures of Greek society in which Jewish Law made social interaction with Gentiles highly problematic.[111] Friedländer argues that some of these diverse groupings later formed Gnostic groups.[112]

It was in the Diaspora that the synagogue developed the features that Palestine later gradually adopted. E.P. Sanders lists some of the most important rights that Jews had acquired in the Roman Empire: 1) the right to assemble or have a place of assembly, 2) the right to keep the Sabbath, 3) the right to have their 'ancestral' food,

4) the right to decide their own affairs and 5) the right to contribute money.[113] Sanders proceeds to summarize evidence for the Jewish activities in the Diaspora, such as keeping the Sabbath, refraining from eating pork, circumcision and their abhorrence of idols. The synagogue, however, was the centre of the Jewish community in the Diaspora. It was here that the Law was learned and worship took place.[114] While the temple existed, Jews from the Diaspora made yearly pilgrimage and paid their dues to the temple fund. After it was destroyed, however, Sanders notes that the Diaspora synagogues 'began to take some of the characteristics of the temple earlier than did the synagogues in Palestine'.[115]

Religion in Galilee

It is important to distinguish between the religious environment of Galilee and that of Judea. So far our discussion has largely centred around the religious environment of the latter. No one has done more to emphasize this point than Burton L. Mack and Richard Horsley. In his book *The Lost Gospel* Mack devotes all of chapter 4 to make clear this distinction. Below we shall consider the proposition offered by Mack as well as how these fit Horsley's conclusions in his book *Archaeology, History and Society in Galilee*.

First, Mack notes that while the kingdoms of Israel (which includes Galilee) and Judea were united under David and Solomon, this was so only for about a century after which they divided and Israel established its capital at Shechem. After this it was annexed to Assyria, then neo-Babylon and finally came under Persian rule. Mack insists that Galilee 'had never been fully incorporated into the cultural entity that Christians imagine as "Israel"'.[116] This cannot be accepted without some qualification. Galilee was never fully integrated into the kingdom of Israel, the temple state established by David and Solomon. Galileans were, however, part of the tribes of Israel, tribes that were united by the Mosaic covenant, a common myth of Exodus/Passover and an alliance of military cooperation. Horsley demonstrates that the Israelite community was not substantially invaded by foreign peoples as Mack posits.[117] Galileans were resistant to foreign dominion whether it was Greek, Roman or a Judean monarch, though the latter was certainly preferable.

Mack also recounts the events surrounding the Samaritans, concluding: 'And as for Galilee, it was known among Jews as "the land of the gentiles".'[118]

This designation, which Mack cites as common lore,[119] comes from Isaiah 9:1 (MT[120] 8:23). The expression 'הגוים גליל' might simply be translated more literally as 'Galilee of the nations/peoples'. The former translation is supported by the Vulgate reading *Galileae gentium* and to a certain extent by the LXX which reads γαλιλαία τῶν ἐθνῶν[121] but which, however, includes the insertion of the words τὰ μέρη τῆς Ιουδαίας (part of Judea).[122] This shows that at least in the Diaspora (certainly in Alexandria), Galilee was considered part of Judea, or more likely the ideal Israel, as early as the second century BCE.

1 Maccabees (5:15) describes the uprising against Maccabeans by Ptolomais, Tyre, Sidon and 'all Galilee of the Gentile' (RAPC). Seán Freyne sees this as a borrowing from Isaiah 8:23, and not 'an ethnographic description of the province as a whole'.[123] But the expression πᾶσαν Γαλιλαίαν ἀλλοφύλων is perhaps better understood as meaning the 'whole of gentile Galilee' (NJB). In other words, rather than the whole of Galilee being Gentile, there was

a part of it that was. It was not all of Galilee that arose, it was Gentile Galilee, the Greek city states, that rose up against Judas Maccabeus. Right after the report of the uprising was received Judas told his brother Simon to go and help his brethren in Galilee. This underscores the need to distinguish between the two groups present in Galilee: one was rebellious (Gentile) and one was the brethren (Jewish). It would be a mistake, however, to accept the narrative of 1 Maccabees at face value. The Galileans certainly were not conquered in the same sense as the Idumeans, since combat had been against the Itureans; however, neither were they Judeans and the new Judean overlords required that 'the laws of the Judean' be enforced.[124]

Mack goes on to point out that in the regions around Galilee, cities built on the Greek model started to emerge. All of the signs of Hellenism were well represented in these cities and yet 'they did not generate a revolution like that of the Maccabees in Judea'. This is true. But does this mean that the general population felt any less Jewish than that in Judea? This is a very worthwhile question to pose. John D. Crossan sets out to answer this question in his book *The Birth of Christianity* and concludes, through the study of anthropology, that the lack of such revolution lies in the inability of peasantry to organize such efforts.[125] All power was concentrated in those cities which were built after the Greek model and the Jewish peasants were severely exploited under these conditions.[126] So the lack of Galilean revolution does not demonstrate disloyalty to Jerusalem or acceptance of Roman rule; it merely shows that there was a lack of retainers. A lack of retainers supportive of peasant concerns produced 'social banditry', in which the cause of the poor was championed by Robinhood movements (see discussion above).

The Maccabees gained independence for Jerusalem in 140 BCE but did not recapture Galilee completely until 100 BCE when the sway of Roman power took the crown from the Hasmoneans and gave it to the Herodians. Mack discusses the rich resource of Galilee and asserts, but does not present, conclusive evidence of a non-Jewish presence in the rural areas. To restate the Galilean situation: There was a basic dichotomy between the city states based on the Hellenistic model and the countryside whose population comprised mainly Jewish (former) landowners and craftsmen. In the northern territories this resulted in open animosity when Jews or Gentiles took power.[127]

Next Mack discusses the synagogue (the building) of which no traces are found in Galilee until the 3rd century.[128] Mack reasonably concludes that 'before the Roman period it seems highly unlikely that Jews moving to Galilee would have considered themselves living in the Diaspora or have formed congregations on its model'.[129] He further states that villages, not only in Judea but also in Galilee, had a model independent of that of the Diaspora. In the Judean-Galilean model, 'the *ma'amadoth*, or priestly-scribal "stations" in the village square'[130] functioned as the local administrator and religious leader.

Then Mack comes to the questionable conclusion that although 'the Samaritans had certainly kept alive the old traditions of "northern" Israel focused on Shechem/Samaria . . . they were not for that reason Jews'.[131] Though he qualifies this conclusion with 'at least the fact of Jewish presence in Galilee allows the myth of common Jewish culture to continue', the question still begs: How does Mack define a Jew? Is a Jew not one who believes in Moses and the God of Moses and strives to follow the Laws that He enjoins? In the Mishnah we find the statement, 'The daughters of the Sadducees, if they follow the ways of their fathers, are deemed like the women of the Samaritans [that is, unclean]' (Niddah 4:2). There is absolutely no statement of this character in the Mishnah about Galileans. Why then should we consider them apart from Judean Judaism? Why should we consider them to be non-Jews? To accept that Judaism was diverse is to accept that each group had a claim to being Jewish. Mack in *A Myth of Innocence* charges that the term 'Jewish' has 'been defined frequently in self-serving, theological terms, not by means of inquisitive historical description'.[132] To define Judaism in terms of temple cult and loyalty to the temple, as Mack does, is nonetheless extremely problematic. Horsley and Hanson's reconstruction of Jewish origins places the centre of faith not in the temple or kingship, which were late-comers, but in the rural independent farmers' worship of Yahweh, with whom they had a covenant.[133] Notwithstanding this, Theissen notes two instances when Galileans acted positively towards the temple. The first was during the Caligula crisis when a statue of the emperor was about to be erected in the temple and the Galileans made massive protests in Tiberias (see chapter 8). The second was in the late sixties when Josephus was successful in collecting tithes.[134] As for the former, Horsley points out that one cannot take Josephus' interpretation of Galilean motives at face value. He suggests that rather than protecting the temple, the Galileans were reacting to an affront to the Mosaic covenant.[135]

Next Mack touches on the question of the presence of the Pharisees, stating, 'Even conservative Christian scholars have begrudgingly had to admit that there is only the spottiest evidence for the presence of Pharisees in Galilee before the Roman-Jewish war, and nothing to suggest that they had any position of power there.' He further states, 'It is extremely important to know that the Pharisees were not officials in charge of Jewish synagogues.'[136] Neusner explains the difference between the Scribes and Pharisees as follows: 1) Pharisees believed that 'ordinary people' should follow the laws of sanctification so as to 'pretend to be of the priestly caste'[137] and 2) while scribalism proclaimed universal teaching and following of the Law, its social vision did not include 'everyone' becoming 'qualified to join their profession'.[138] These two features, the present author would venture, were the prime factors in the Pharisees' lack of success in gaining members amongst Galilean rural Jews.

One must, however, ask how it is that the Pharisees came to appear in the Q material which belongs to the early fifties through seventies in Galilee. First of all it must be conceded that Q is a text that belonged to a literate people, a people who lived in those cities that were big enough to have a class of retainers but which at the same time could attract travelling Christians.[139] At this stage, these sorts of cities would probably have had some Pharisees living in them. But why were the Pharisees the target of this criticism and how far back was it directed at this sect? Q 11:40–6 presents the traditions that most explicitly deal with the Pharisees. The criticism is a charge of 1) hypocrisy and 2) striving for (undue) recognition. These are not charges one levels at those who are superior to one in power but at one's equal. The Pharisees did not lead the synagogue; they strove for the higher seats in the synagogue. If they were in power they could take those seats with authority. But this was not the case, for they had to resort to hypocrisy (acting) to gain them. The picture that emerges is that of two competing

Jewish sects, one local, the other Judean. Both tithed but one did so in hypocrisy; both used the synagogue but one only to get illicit recognition. The woes of verses 40–6 are not supported by the Gospel of Thomas as referring to Pharisees in particular. But Q 11:52 has a parallel with Thomas 39:1–2 and 102. 'Jesus said, "The Pharisees and the scribes have taken the keys of Knowledge and hidden them. They themselves have not entered, nor have they allowed to enter those who wish to"' (Thomas 39).

This suggests that there is a tradition (the Common Saying Source) that goes further back than Q which also saw the Pharisees as the competition. It is therefore not inconceivable that some Pharisees worked in the lesser urban areas, not as a religious authority but as a sect competing for ascendancy.[140] Saldarni also presumes that the Pharisees were not in power but he argues that they could travel up to Galilee and were supported by local landowners as a social stabilizing factor.[141]

From here Mack embarks on the reign of Herod and notes that 'after Herod's death in 4 BCE, Judas the Galilean, son of the slain Hezekiah, stormed the military installation at Sepphoris to get at the armoury. The Roman legate from Antioch responded by burning Sepphoris to the ground and, according to Josephus, sold the people into slavery.'[142] One cannot but wonder how Mack can, in a discussion of the religious climate of Galilee, pass over this event with such brevity. Possibly this is because 'Richard Horsley has shown that the very notion of Zealots as a typical phenomenon rests upon a mistaken reading of Josephus'.[143] All the same, Horsley clarifies in his introduction that 'most of the ideas believed to be distinctive to the Zealots, almost all of them widely attested in our limited sources, were probably common Palestinian Jewish ideas'.[144] The event is significant because it is an example of a popular messiah movement in Galilee (see above). It should be noted that this attempt at gaining kingship employed none of the religious Judean motifs that we saw in Simon bar Giora; rather it presented a pragmatic attempt at establishing a king who at least supported common Galilean concerns.

No mention is made of another Galilean Judas who founded a scribal movement, the Fourth Philosophy (see above). Speaking of this, Josephus notes that Judas was assisted by a Pharisee named Saddok and that they appealed to the religious sentiments of people to further their design. In the text of Whiston we read that the nation 'was infected with this doctrine to an incredible degree'.[145] The reach of this sect is noted in other places and is lamented by Josephus who, writing to a Roman audience, cannot justify this sect's existence amongst the Jews. It is in Josephus' best interests to play down both the spread of this sect and its religious nature, for it reflects ill both on his people and on his religion, and yet he can deny neither. The thesis advanced by Heinrich Graetz is that the Zealots (i.e. the Fourth Philosophy) in fact received support for their doctrines amongst some Pharisees, namely the followers of Shammai.[146]

Another popular movement with its origins in Galilee that often goes unmentioned is the prophetic movement of Theudas (see above).

So what can we know about the Galilean halakhah? Theissen and Merz are cautious because the Galilean halakhah has been 'concealed by the later transformation of Galilean piety by the rabbis on the one hand and Christianity on the other'.[147] However, they outline two features that seem to have been specific to the Galilean halakhah: 1) stronger anti-pagan tendencies and 2) fewer rules of cleanliness.[148] Vermes notes that Judeans in general found Galileans incompetent in their dealings with temple regulations and that their rabbis engaged unaccompanied women in conversation on open streets.[149] On the other hand, the Mishnah notes that the Galileans suspended work the entire day of Passover (Pesahim 4:5). This strongly suggests that Galilee had its own observance of Passover independently of Judean tradition.

This short survey of Judaism of the 1st century CE should suffice for an understanding of the role of the main protagonists and antagonists of the New Testament. But to understand the sources, format and style of the New Testament, we will now look at the scripture current amongst the Jews at the time of Jesus.

The Mishnah and the Talmud

The Mishnah (*hnvm*, Hebrew for repetition [of Law]) is a compilation of the oral law dealing with the different aspects of the written law applied to everyday life. It was compiled in the later part of the 2nd century by the Rabbi Judah Ha-Nasi. The Mishnah is divided into six major topics rather than sources.[150] The first of these is the topic of agriculture, farming in accordance with rules of the Torah and maintaining the seeds and grains of the different crops. The second section deals with holy days and the rules associated with them. The third is on women and their functions in the home, the relationship between man and woman and the transition of the woman from the domain of her father (or caretaker) to the domain of her husband. The fourth section deals with politics, government and economics. The fifth deals with the sacred (i.e. the temple), the rites of worship, especially those of sacrifice. Lastly, in the sixth section, the laws and ordinances of purity and cleanliness, both at home and in the temple, are dealt with.

The Mishnah contained the so-called Oral Torah and the various traditions which were regarded as coming from Moses Himself. The Mishnah itself claims this:

> Moses received the Torah from Mount Sinai and committed it to Joshua, and Joshua to the elders, and the elders to the Prophets; and the Prophets committed it to the men of the Great Synagogue . . . Shemaiah and Abtalion received [the Law] from them . . . Hillel and Shammai received [the Law] from them . . . Rabban Johanan b. Zakkai received [the Law] from Hillel and Shammai . . .[151]

The whole tradition is more mythical[152] than historical. Even the last link between Hillel and Shammai and Rabban Johanan ben Zakkai must be considered questionable. Johanan became prominent when he founded the Tannaim[153] in Javneh after the destruction of Jerusalem in 70 CE. Most of Rabban Johanan ben Zakkai's contemporaries had received their education through someone who had been a student of either Hillel or Shammai.[154] Acts 22:3 presents Paul, who certainly was Rabban Johanan ben Zakkai's junior, as a disciple of Gamaliel, the grandson of Hillel.

Hillel and Shammai were the founders of two Pharisaic schools, the former generally milder and more popular while the latter was stricter. Often these two are cited each after the other as to their pronouncement on a particular subject.

Within a generation of the composition of the Tannaim, the Sanhedrin, which had ruled Jewry so far back that its origin was shrouded in legend, was re-established. Once the Mishnah had been compiled there emerged about a century later a tradition of interpretation, which eventually became the Talmud. The Talmuds were produced in Israel in the 4th century and in Babylon in the 5th or 6th century. While the former was immediately considered authoritative, the latter grew in authority slowly but soon left the former in disuse. It is worth noting that the Mishnah, although compiled at the end of the 2nd century, was not committed to writing until the Talmud was completed in the 6th century.[155] Still, it can be considered a somewhat reliable source of 1st century Pharisaic thought and theology. Indeed, a few sayings found in the gospels, which are attributed to Jesus, find their parallel in the Talmud.

The Targums

The Targums are Aramaic (which, as mentioned before, is the language that Jesus used) paraphrased translations[156] of the Old Testament books. These were the translations that Jesus and His apostles probably used in their ministry and after them the evangelists may conceivably have been influenced by them. They started as oral translations no earlier than the 2nd century BCE, and although they are conserved mainly in medieval transcriptions, there were also fragments found in the Qumran caves (in particular, of a Job Targum) and a Palestinian Targum of the Pentateuch. Although scholars dispute just how great the influence of the Targum was on the New Testament (depending often on the dating of the Palestinian Targum), there is reasonable evidence that some texts were available to people in the vernacular language. First of all, when one compares the quotations in the New Testament with the Old Testament, out of the 278 citations, 53 agree with both the Septuagint[157] and the Masoretic[158] text, 10 agree with the Masoretic text alone, 37 with the Septuagint alone and 175 agree with neither (the three remaining cannot be identified with the Old Testament at all). This suggests that there was a text available to the evangelists that is different from the Septuagint translation and the Masoretic text.[159] Furthermore, certain interpretations correspond with the Targum interpretation, such as the exposition of Psalm 68:18 in Ephesians 4:8 or when in Mark 4:12 forgiveness is linked with healing as in the interpretation used in the Targum for Isaiah 6:10.[160]

The Mishnah sets clear guidelines for the translation[161] and use of the scripture in the synagogues. It also specifically bans written Targums, presumably so that the sacredness of the original text would not be compromised. One must therefore wonder at this event recorded in the Gospel of Luke:

> And there was delivered unto him the book of the prophet Esaias. And when he had opened the book, he found the place where it was written, The Spirit of the Lord [is] upon me, because he hath anointed me to preach the gospel to the poor; he hath sent me to heal the brokenhearted, to preach deliverance to the captives, and recovering of sight to the blind, to set at liberty them that are bruised, to preach the acceptable year of the Lord. And he closed the book, and he gave [it] again to the minister, and sat down. And the eyes of all them that were in the synagogue were fastened on him (Luke 4:17–20 KJV).

The first verse should be clarified: the book (*biblion*, βιβλίον) was a scroll, as rendered in all the newer translations, since codices[162] were not really available in Palestine until the 2nd century. The word translated 'opened' (*anaptuzas*, ἀναπτύξας) must be understood as 'unrolled'. This is strange in view of the fact that there was a ban on written Targums. Either we must assume that the ban on Targums was not generally accepted or that Jesus both spoke and read Hebrew, an uncommon skill for a son of a carpenter.[163] Special Sabbath readings were available for services in the synagogue,[164] which were called Haphtarot. Although there was apparently not a fixed selection in the 1st century, in the 2nd century the Mishnah did provide one.

LXX – The Septuagint

This translation of the Jewish scripture into Greek was made in Alexandria starting some time in the 3rd century BCE until its completion about a century later. According to legend, 72 scholars came together and each produced a complete translation of the scripture. When they had finished, each translation was checked against the other and was found to be in complete agreement. This legend clearly illustrates the great acknowledgement the translation received from Jews in the Diaspora everywhere. When the Christians started using it, this soon changed and the glory of the LXX was quickly overturned. That the LXX at times was inaccurate or merely freely translated must be granted. However, some of the writings from Qumran have proved that some of these apparent discrepancies were not caused by the carelessness of the translator but occur because another Hebrew text was used.[165]

This has restarted the discussion of whether one should give more credence to the LXX than has hitherto been given. The oldest Old Testament manuscripts we possess are of the LXX, yet the Hebrew has always been considered the norm. The former come from the a, B and A manuscripts of the 4th and 5th centuries while the latter comes from the Leningrad manuscript of the 10th century. The Hebrew has long had precedence over the LXX because the LXX no longer held any authority in the debate with the Jews. So in the 3rd century Origen had already set out to produce the Hexapla. This momentous work had six columns of scripture: the Jewish scripture, first in Hebrew, then in Hebrew transliterated into Greek, and then four different Greek translations. When Jerome prepared the new official Bible of the Roman Church, the Vulgate, he did so from the Hebrew.

This LXX is the Bible used by the evangelists, often with word for word accuracy. However, certain liberties are taken by the evangelists in their editorial work on the text used to prove Jesus' messiahship.

Summary and Conclusion

This chapter has attempted to describe Jewish movements and literature of the first couple of centuries. We found that as well as the groups of movements that had specific names and known theological positions there were also movements that were popular and led by single charismatic leaders. The prominence of the first category in the gospels is clear; the second is less obvious but perhaps even more germane to our understanding of early Christianity.

In the following chapters we shall see that early Christianity in many ways was characterized by its popular origin. Most significantly, we have seen that popular movements often compensated for their lack of ability to proclaim through writing or through scholarly knowledge with acts of emulation (or promise of emulation) of former prophetic or messianic figures. Through emulation they spoke eloquently to their peers about their prophetic or messianic claims. For obvious reasons this line of proclamation was generally unconvincing to people of a scribal tradition. Scribal movements, on the other hand, drew their authority from their ability to read and interpret the Law.

In the following chapters we shall see how the gospels represent an adoption of popular traditions into a scribal representation. This adoption, we shall see, in some instances transforms the tradition in order to make it more acceptable to its scribal audience.

3

The Birth of a New Dispensation

This chapter deals with what happened before the baptism of Jesus, which is referred to in the following passages:

Matthew 1:1 to 3:12
Mark 1:1–8
Luke 1:1 to 3:20; 3:23–38
John 1:1–35

This chapter establishes the foundation of most of the doctrines about the nature of Jesus, the pre-existence of the Word, its role in the birth of the world of creation, Jesus' descent from the house of David and the miracle of His virgin birth.

The Word: John 1:1–14

The Logos, or the Word, is first described in the Christological[166] hymn of the first chapter of the Gospel of John. This small section of the New Testament contains some of the most influential theological statements found in the gospels. It utilizes concepts first brought into the Bible by Hellenism.[167] The introduction of these new elements[168] has over the years been a source of criticism because they have been regarded as an intrusion into the 'pure Christian way of thinking'. Such comments, however, ignore the great trends in Jewish thought that adopted these concepts.[169] Philo had developed an exegesis where 'the "breath of God" was the Holy Spirit and Wisdom who fill all men with wisdom'[170] and Moses is 'the Sage in whom the Spirit of God resides with permanence'.[171]

Zeitlin traces the divine Messiah back to Jewish apocalyptism,[172] which in itself seems quite plausible.[173] While there are no traces of apocalyptism in the Gospel of John, there is, nonetheless, a great affinity with wisdom. The Gospel of Thomas shares this affinity, which stems not from Philo but from a long tradition of Jewish Wisdom literature.[174] Robinson draws a parallel between Proverbs 1:23–33, which we find cited in 1 Clements (57:3ff) letter to Corinth, and Thomas 38:[175] 'Jesus said, "Often you have desired to hear these sayings that I am speaking to you, and you have no one else from whom to hear them. There will be days when you will not find me" '(SV).

The latter part of the saying has a parallel with John 7:34: 'Ye shall seek me, and shall not find me: and where I am, ye cannot come' (ASV). There is, of course, a difference in 'Gatung' or genre between the Gospel of Thomas and that of John and in this John remains a rather unique synthesis.

Excursus: Trinitarianism and Christology

At the end of the 3rd century a doctrinal conflict issued from the rising of Arius,[176] who claimed that the Son (Jesus Christ) was not of the same substance as the Father, that is, *anomoios*.[177] Throughout the history of the church different movements have countered orthodox ideas about the nature of Christ and each time they have moved orthodoxy closer to the present-day doctrine of the Trinity. Below is the final version of the Nicene Creed (325 CE), which won general consensus after the death of the last Arian emperor in 378 CE.[178]

> We believe in one God the Father almighty, maker of heaven and earth, and of all things visible and invisible; and in one Lord Jesus Christ, the only-begotten Son of God, begotten of the Father before all ages, (God from God); Light from Light; true God from true God; begotten not made, [who is] of one substance with the Father, [and] through whom all things were made; who for us men, and for our salvation, came down from heaven, and was incarnate by the Holy Spirit of Virgin Mary, and was made man; and was crucified also for us under Pontius Pilate; he suffered and was buried; and the third day he rose again in accordance with the Scriptures, and ascended into heaven, and is seated at the right hand of the Father; and he shall come again, with glory, to judge both the living and dead; [and] his kingdom shall have no end; and [we believe] in the Holy Spirit, the Lord, the Life-giver, who proceeds from the Father [[and the Son]],[179] who with the Father and the Son together is worshipped and glorified, who spoke through the Prophets; and [we believe] in one holy and catholic and apostolic Church; we acknowledge one baptism for remission of sins; and we look for the resurrection of the dead, and the life of the Age to Come. Amen.[180]

It is worth noting how various creeds throughout history were formulated as a response to minority opposition. Thus Christianity was formulated and shaped through the resolution of these internal conflicts. Before looking at more contemporary material, it is necessary to review the Chalcedonian Creed to get a feeling for the doctrinal shift over 70 years which precipitated the emergence of a new conflict. This time the question no longer involved the divinity of the Son but rather His two natures – the human and the divine. The Chalcedonian Creed, though not specifically against Modalism, clearly denies it. This is perhaps a response to the charges levelled against Alexander of Sabellism (a form of Modalism) by Arius or perhaps as a response to Marcellus'[181] teachings.

> Following, then, the holy fathers, we unite in teaching all men to confess the one and only Son, our Lord Jesus Christ. This selfsame one is perfect both in deity and in humanness; this selfsame one is also actually God and actually man, with a rational soul and a body. He is of the same reality as God as far as his deity is concerned and of the same reality as we ourselves as far as his humanness is concerned; thus like us in all respects, sin only excepted. Before time began he was begotten of the Father, in respect of his deity, and now in these 'last days', for us and behalf of our salvation, this selfsame one was born of Mary the virgin, who is God-bearer in respect of his humanness. We also teach that we apprehend this one and only Christ-Son, Lord, only-begotten – in two natures; and we do this without confusing the two natures, without transmuting one nature into the other, without dividing them into two separate categories, without contrasting them according to area or function. The distinctiveness of each nature is not nullified by the union. Instead, the'properties' of each nature are conserved and both natures concur in one 'person' and in one reality. They are not divided or cut into two persons, but are together the one and only and only-begotten Word of God, the Lord Jesus Christ. Thus have the prophets of old testified; thus the Lord Jesus Christ himself taught us; thus the Symbol of Fathers 'the Nicene Creed' was handed down to us.[182]

The conflict was rooted in the rise of Nestorianism,[183] which held that Christ had two separate 'natures' (i.e. divine and human). Nestorius argued that the essence or substance (*ousia*) of things is not changeable and thus in the incarnation it is not that God becomes human but that God changes His appearance (*schêma*) or outward property. Nestorius made the analogy of the water being in essence the same although it changes appearance when it freezes.[184] What Nestorius actually meant by *prosôpon* is difficult to determine and is a disputed matter. We may understand it to mean the inner property, which is the reflection of the essence (*ousia*) but which allows multiplicity of appearances (*schêma*). The inner property of water (i.e. molecules) determines the outward appearance.

Further conflicts were to arise later but the concepts of the Trinity and the nature of Christ have been largely unchanged since the Definition of Chalcedon. Generally, both Catholics and Protestants agree on these creeds. This is easily observed when comparing this with a strictly Protestant confession such as the Westminster Confession:[185]

> 2. The Son of God, the second Person in the Trinity, being very and eternal God, of one substance, and equal with the Father, did, when the fullness of time was come, take upon him man's nature, with all the essential properties and common infirmities thereof; yet without sin: being conceived by the power of the Holy Ghost, in the womb of the Virgin Mary, of her substance. So that two whole, perfect, and distinct natures, the Godhead and the manhood, were inseparably joined together in one person, without conversion, composition, or confusion. Which person is very God and very man, yet one Christ, the only Mediator between God and man.[186]

This is a very close echo of the Chalcedonian Creed. Thus these Trinitarian and Christological doctrines were preserved and have remained largely unchallenged to this day (except by a few minor groups such as the Unitarians and the Jehovah Witnesses, who have upheld the 'heresy').

* * *

To return to the main theme, the Word, further analysis of the verses in question is needed to understand their implicit statements. In the analysis below the present author proposes that the entire prologue is best understood as operating strictly within a Philonic cosmology.[187]

Almost all English translations of the gospels start more or less as the KJV does in the first two clauses of John 1:1. 'In the beginning was the Word, and the Word was with God.' This clearly states that the Word existed before Creation and, as stated below, Jesus is identified with the Word. One should remember, however, that there is a distinction between being pre-existent (i.e. having existed before birth) and existing before creation. The second part of John 1:1 is usually translated 'and the Word was God' (KJV). However, *The New World Translation of the Holy Scripture* (NWTHS), a translation made by Jehovah Witnesses, translates it 'and the Word was a god'. In a footnote this is justified by the fact that the word used for God is simply *Theos* (θεὸς) and not *ton Theon* (τὸν θεόν), which has the definite article. The absence of the definite article does not, however, justify the indefinite article used in this translation. The nature of Koine Greek (common tongue) makes the distinction rather difficult. The five words that are involved are: *kai* (καὶ, and), *Theos* (θεὸς, God), *en* (ἦν, was), *ho* (ὁ, the) and Logos (λόγος, Word). In Koine Greek, the function of the words is not dependent on their position in the sentence but rather on their endings. The *os* ending implies that the word is a subject and an *on* ending implies that the word is an object (e.g. *theon*). Hence in the third clause the first word in the English translation (the subject) is not found by the suffix, since both are in a 'nominal inflected form' (i.e. end with *os*) but by which has the definite article. By placing *theos* first in the clause, emphasis is added to *theos*, which disallows 'a god' as a justifiable translation. The absence of the definite article, however, makes *theos* descriptive rather than identificational. One may therefore wish to opt for the New English Bible's translation: 'What God was the Word was.' Another explanation of the word order is the suggestion that the liturgy is set according to the old rules of Hebrew parallelism in such a manner that Logos appearing last in 1:1a is connected with Logos, the third word in 1:1b, which in turn connects *theon* at the end of 1:1b with *theos*, the second word in 1:1c and so on. Irenaeus, who was a disciple of John and an early Church Father, wrote in his book *Against Heresies*: 'But God being all Mind and all Logos, both speaks exactly what He speaks. For His thought is Logos, and Logos is Mind, and Mind comprehending all things is the Father himself' (2:28:5). Another suggestion is made in James Moffatt's translation, which reads 'the Logos was divine'.

In his commentary on the Gospel of John, David J. Ellis writes:

> The fullness of the Godhead and the Word are identified. The active Word immanent in the world is no less God than the transcendent God beyond all time and space. The absence of the definite article in front of 'God', taken by some to mean that the Word possessed something less than full deity, implies, however, that other persons exist outside the second Person of the Trinity.[188]

This, as we shall see, ignores the Judaic nature of the Johannine Prologue.

The Vulgate, the Catholic authoritative Latin text, keeps the order of the Greek text and therefore reads '*et Deus erat Verbum*' (Vul) which translates 'and God was the Word'.[189] The theological implications of the reversal of the two subjects is not very different from the New English Bible (NEB) text.[190]

Briefly, the Trinity, as defined by most Christians, is commonly referred to as the threefold personality of God: God the Father, God the Son and God the Holy Ghost. These separate Persons equally share in will and power and have no conflict between them. All three Persons are God but they are not the same, i.e. the Son is not the Father, the Father is not the Holy Ghost, etc. but each of them is considered God.

If, however, we suppose that the Philonic cosmology forms the background for this statement, we gain new insight. Ronald Williamson in his *Jews in the Hellenistic World: Philo* gives the following exposition of Philo's thought about the Logos:

> The precise relationship of the Logos to God is not easy to define. The use of the expression the 'first'-God (*Leg. All.* III.207), implies the existence of 'the second God' (*Quaest. in Gn.* II.62) and the propriety of applying the term *theos* to the Logos. There is a sense in which the Logos is *theos*, more than *theios* (divine), without being 'God', for the Logos is God's Logos, not God. The Logos does not exhaust the being of God. However, as Philo puts it in *Conf. Ling.* 95–7, those who 'serve the Existent', led by Moses ('the nature beloved of God'), 'shall behold the place which in fact is the Word, where stands God, the never changing, never swerving' and also 'the world of our senses' . . .

> Inevitably, since the Logos is the expression of the Thought of God, is in fact God's Expressed Thought, there is for Philo a very close link between the Logos and the world of Ideas or Forms which he adopted – and adapted – from Plato.[191]

Williamson emphasizes elsewhere that the reader of the initial Johannine statement would not be surprised to find that Philo

> . . . without intending to infringe his Jewish monotheism, and without in fact doing so . . . calls the Logos 'the second God', in whose image man has been made (*Quaest. in Gn.* II.62) . . . In *Som.* I.229–30, as we saw in the previous chapter, only when the word *theos* denotes God himself is the article used. The title, *theos*, without the article, is, however, given to 'his chief Word'. In other words, though the Logos is neither God nor a god, it is the primary, secondary layer (as it were) of the effulgence or emanation of the divine light, the Thought of God – and therefore appropriately called either 'the second God' or allowed the title *theos* – expressed, for example in the rational order of the universe intelligible to the human mind. It is doubtful if we should do justice to Philo's view of the Logos if we described it as an intermediary. To regard the Logos as an intermediary in the proper and fullest sense would perhaps involve a departure from the Jewish view of God as a living God, himself active in the world and history – a step not taken by Philo. It cannot be emphasized enough that the Logos for Philo is God's Logos, the incorporeal Word or Thought of God, not a distinct and separate being having its own divine ontological status, subordinate to God.[192]

In the third verse, most translations agree: 'Through him

all things were made; without him nothing was made that has been made' (John 1:3 NIV). The Logos would seem to be the agency through which God created the world. This too is consistent with the image portrayed in the Wisdom literature about the pre-existent Wisdom. Philo would, in no uncertain terms, agree with this too. Williamson states:

> Philo uses the idea of the creation of the world by God using his Logos as his instrument (*organon*) to express his belief that the universe – except for the physical body and the irrational element in man – is a reflection of the ideal pattern in God's mind.[193]

Erwin R. Goodenough explains that the Logos was the emanation of God which subsequently 'streamed' into the Creative Logos and the Ruling Logos (to which we shall return later). The emanation of the Logos is a part of the process by which creation comes into being. Philo presents two distinct theories with various details. Common to them both, however, is the fact that 'creation is not something done by a remote force or mind, but that the divine is left permanently in the world to be its guide, to fill it with providential care'.[194] Williamson further states:

> If Moses was an incarnation, the process of occupation of a human life by the divine Logos went so far as to result in an almost total exclusion of the human flesh of Moses. However, though the 'bodily region' was placed in a position of subjection within Moses' life, it was by 'that Word by which also the whole universe was formed'.[195]

Next is the statement of John: 'In him was life; and the life was the light of men. And the light shineth in darkness; and the darkness comprehendeth it not' (1:4–5 KJV).[196]

Those who refute the power of Light, that is to say Jesus, remain in darkness and do not comprehend it. For John it is important to point out that it is not merely Jesus, the envoy of God, that these people have refused but rather the incarnation of Truth (or Light or Life, all of which are equivalent expressions). Here again imagery is borrowed from Philo, who, seeing the Logos as he does, would find that 'Not surprisingly, therefore, just as God is Light and the archetypal source of every other light, so is the Logos'.[197]

Now from the void of timelessness, John brings us to the time of John the Baptist. John is presented as a witness of the Light.[198] As the herald of the Dispensation of Christ, his station is less than the Light. 'He came unto his own, and his own received him not' (John 1:11 KJV). 'His own' must in this context be the Jewish people whom the Word had in the past made His own, through prophets and covenants with the Patriarchs. 'Yet to all who received him, to those who believed in his name, he gave the right to become children of God' (John 1:12 NIV). Here 'the children of God' are those who enter the new covenant and 'believed in his name' may mean to believe in the name Jesus the Christ, i.e. He is the fulfilment of the prophecies about the Messiah. Alternatively, John may equate the name with the essence of His being, the Logos.[199] 'Which were born, not of blood, nor of the will of the flesh, nor of the will of man, but of God' (John 1:13 KJV). To be 'born' in this passage refers to the birth of faith in the heart of man. The gift of faith can only be given by God. As with the Nicodemus pericope (John 3:1–21), birth is here seen as a metaphor for a spiritual event. 'And the Word was made flesh, and dwelt among us, (and we beheld his glory, the glory as of the only begotten of the Father,) full of grace and truth' (John 1:14 KJV). This is often referred to as the incarnation (literally meaning 'in flesh'). It is, as we have seen above, more likely to be a restatement of Philo's wisdom that receives permanence in a historical individual, a new Moses. The Weymouth translation is, therefore, theologically more logical, for while 'made' is a more literal translation of *egeneto* (εγένετο) it does not seem like John suggests that spirit is a substance that becomes physical.[200] 'And the Word came in the flesh, and lived for a time in our midst, so that we saw His glory – the glory as of the Father's only Son, sent from His presence. He was full of grace and truth' (John 1:14 WEY) This 'incarnation' is mirrored in Philo's idea of who Moses was. Goodenough states: 'This extremely complex idea was expressed legally by describing the ideal man [Moses] as νόμος ἔμψυχυς, *lex animata*, the incarnate representation of the supreme universal Law. In him that Law, itself unformulated, could, become vocal, λογικός.'[201] Even more to the point are Williamson's comments:

> The question that has been raised of the possibility of an incarnation of the Logos within the human life-history of Moses raises also the question of whether or not the Logos of Philo was personal. Philo certainly speaks of the Logos in personal terms, as, for example, the Son of God (*Conf. Ling.* 146). The same implication seems to lie behind such titles as a 'high-priest' in *Som.* I.215, but it is doubtful if personification proceeds to the point of personalization. The Logos of Philo is never, as it was later in Christian theology, a 'person' within the one Godhead . . . Philo did perhaps think in terms of the deification of Moses, but not of an incarnation within Moses' life of the divine Logos. Because of the diametrically opposed qualities of flesh and spirit, the deification process involved the gradual and finally total eradication of flesh from the life of Moses.[202]

This is by some regarded as a central theme of the Gospel of John, that the divine took on human form and lived amongst men. But perhaps the emphasis is more on the second sentence, that men or the Christians or perhaps the community of John saw this and were affected by it.

If we look at verse 17 there is, it seems, a conscious use of the Philonic ontology: 'For the law was given through Moses; grace and truth came through Jesus Christ' (ASV). We should note that while the law was given (ἐδόθη) through (διὰ) Moses, grace and truth came (ἐγένετο) through (διὰ) Jesus. Although the acts are described by two different verbs, the same preposition ('through') is applied. We recall Goodenough's model of the emanation of the Logos which divides into two streams which manifest themselves as the Law-Making Power (Δύναμις Νομοθετική) and the Power of Mercy (Δύναμις Ἵλεώς).[203] Thus the two emanations of Logos each came through two different figures, first the Law-giver and then the Mercy-bringer.

Finally we should consider the title applied to the bearer of the declaration of the unseen Father (verse 18), namely the 'Only-begotten' (μονογενὴς). Vine states: 'The expression also suggests the thought of the deepest affection, as in the case of the O[ld]T[estament] word *yachid*, variously rendered, "only one" Gen. 22:2, 12 . . .'[204] Following the idea that this is an allusion to Isaac, whom Abraham was to sacrifice to God, we come to see this title as independent of the Philonic ontology discussed so far. The suspicion that this is indeed what John was thinking of is enforced by the statement placed on the lips of John the Baptist: 'Behold, the Lamb of God, that taketh away the sin of the world! This is he of whom I said, After me cometh a man who is become before me: for he was before me' (John 1:29–30 ASV).[205] The title, therefore, is not so much about Jesus' relationship with the Father as about what He did for the world, namely that He came and was sacrificed for it. Grappe also cites some antecedents for the title in designating prophetic figures.[206] Afterwards, however, he goes on to discuss the possibility of the Isaac allusion, which he concludes fits 'perfectly'.[207]

The Genealogy: Matthew 1:1–17, Luke 3:23–38

Genealogies fill a special role in the Bible and come from long-standing Jewish traditions. However, they have an additional function in the New Testament. Beyond merely asserting the legal right of Jesus to the Davidic throne, they are also, in Matthew, structured in such wise as to show how all through history certain events mark (at intervals of 14 generations) a major Jewish event. Some biblical scholars have used the conflicting genealogies as an argument for the Bible to be treated as a fallible historical text, since a divinely-inspired and infallible text could obviously not contain such clear contradictions. Over the years, however, as a countermove, many valiant efforts have been made to 'harmonize' such apparent contradictions and we shall presently view examples of these.

Two problems become obvious even at a superficial first glance: 1) The number of generations between David and Jesus in the two genealogies differ and 2) the names do not correspond in the genealogies, with the exception of Shealtiel and Zerabbabel.

In response to the first problem we must keep in mind the Jewish context in which the gospels were written. To account for every generation was an unnecessary task. One could easily call the grandson of somebody the son. All Jews proclaimed themselves to be the 'sons of Abraham'. Jesus, whose father was from Bethlehem, was a 'son of David' and

Elizabeth whose husband was a priest was a 'daughter of Aaron'.[208] In the same manner one should not interpret 'begot' as meaning literally 'son of'. In view of this fact, the genealogy of Matthew, which has obvious omissions when compared with historical accounts,[209] may be taken as an arbitrary arrangement to fulfil the 3 by 14 dispensational model.[210]

To solve the second problem, several suggestions may be taken into consideration. The first suggestion theorizes that Matthew gives the genealogy of Joseph's actual father Jacob, whereas Luke traces it through his legal father Heli. This would occur through leviratic marriage, meaning that Joseph's actual father, Jacob, died and, as he did not have any offspring nor any brothers, his wife was forced to marry into another family (with a different heritage) that was descended from Solomon. Hence Joseph would inherit the Davidian throne through his legal father (Heli) and so would Jesus.

The second suggestion postulates the opposite: namely, that Matthew gives the legal descent and Luke the physical. The reason for this reversal lies in the failure of Solomon's line. Jechoniah was the heir to the Davidic throne but by his deeds he brought a curse on himself which also resulted in the Babylonian exile (see Jeremiah 22:30 and Matthew 1:11–12). It suggests that because of the failure of the line of Solomon, the rights to the Davidic throne were transferred to Nathan. Both the first and the second suggestion fail to provide any evidence for a leviratic marriage. Indeed, the second suggestion fails to provide a legal basis for such a transfer.

A third solution would be that Luke in fact does not give the genealogy of Joseph but that of Mary. The reason for the appearance of Joseph's name instead of Mary's is founded in the theory that Heli, Mary's father, died without sons and that Mary then became heiress to Heli's house, which in turn is given to Joseph through marriage. Thus Davidic descent would be traced through both Joseph and Mary. Unfortunately, there is nothing to support the theory of Heli being sonless.

A fourth theory also purports the same as the third (i.e. that Luke's genealogy belongs to Mary) but for other reasons. Here Heli is considered to be the father of Mary and hence the father of Jesus. Joseph's inclusion in the genealogy is only parenthetical: Luke 3:23 'When he began, Jesus was about thirty years old, being (the son, as was thought, of Joseph) son of Heli' (NJB, parenthesis mine).

The placement of the parenthesis is justified by the fact that Joseph's name appears without the word *tou*.[211] This breaks the basic pattern of the genealogy and shows that Joseph is not to be seen as part of the genealogy. Also, Luke's interest in Jesus' humanity (presumably why he traces it back all the way to Adam) would have him trace his actual parentage (i.e. not legal). One may also notice that Luke does something untraditional by reversing the genealogy (moving from Jesus to Adam instead of Adam to Jesus). This disregard of tradition may also account for Luke using the genealogy of a woman (Mary). Matthew, on the other hand, would then trace the legal line, which runs through Solomon and gives Jesus the legal right to the throne while at the same time avoiding the curse put on Jechoniah (since Joseph is not the actual father of Jesus). Furthermore, Matthew makes sure, at the end of his genealogy, not to imply that Jesus was born of Joseph, by breaking the pattern and mentioning that Joseph was the 'husband of Mary, of whom was born Jesus' (Matthew 1:16 KJV) . The Greek makes clear that 'whom' (ἧς, hes), being feminine, refers to Mary, as is reflected in the NJB: 'of her was born Jesus'.

There seems to be little point in arguing the authenticity of the genealogy.[212] However, it is interesting to investigate the function of the genealogy in Christian theology. First, it would seem obvious that one purpose is to confirm Jesus' right to the Davidic throne. David was the first great monarch of Israel. He was chosen by God and anointed to kinghood through the prophet Samuel. This point (of being anointed) is of utmost importance because it was a custom in Old Testament times to anoint prophets and it was a necessary rite before assuming kingship. The king was considered to have entered into a special covenant with God in which, through his anointment, he would become adopted and thus be 'the Son of God'.[213] It is for this reason that it is important for the evangelist to confirm this right to the Davidic throne, for this would have some weight with the Jews, who would understand the meaning of being anointed and sonship.

The Jews had an interest in proving a different genesis for Jesus. Gustaf H. Dalman suggests in his book *Jesus Christ in the Talmud, Midrash, Zohar and the Liturgy of the Synagogue* that Jesus was of Roman origin. The 4th century Jewish scholar Ulla is quoted as saying that 'Jesus was related to the authorities', that is to say, Pontius Pilate.[214] Dalman also notes that 'the Targum Sheni on the Book of Esther (iii. 1) names Pilate also with Jesus among the ancestors of Haman'.[215] Dalman further notes that all public genealogies were destroyed by Herod to hide his own less than honourable background. Genealogies, therefore, only survived through private records.

There is only one reputed mention of Jesus in the Mishnah, which records that Simeon ben Azzai had found a genealogical record in Jerusalem which stated that 'so and so' (generally believed to be the cover name for Jesus) was 'a bastard son of a married woman' (Yebamoth 4:13). The interpretation in the Babylonian Talmud, however, does not present this interpretation (Yebamoth 49 b).

It is most likely that Mark did not believe Jesus to be a descendant of David, as he records Jesus' defence that the Messiah need not be a descendant (Mark 12:35). The question asked of Jesus presumes two things: 1) that Jesus had claimed to be Messiah and 2) that Jesus did not trace His genealogy back to David. Against this reading of this controversy narrative Funk writes:

> Yet it is unlikely that Jesus' own lineage through David would have been introduced into the genealogies of Matthew and Luke so readily if he had himself carried on a polemic against the idea. It is more likely, in the view of most scholars, that it comes from a segment of the Jesus movement in which there was some tension between the Messiah as the son of Adam (a heavenly figure) and the Messiah as the son of David (a political, royal figure). Admittedly, there is very little evidence for such tension, but there is even less evidence for such a debate in Jesus' own time.[216]

The present author disagrees with this assessment. The controversy narrative first appears in Mark, which does not have the genealogy of Jesus. That both Matthew and Luke ignore the original intention of the story can hardly be surprising.[217] A biblical scholar, however, cannot do this. First let us consider that the intention is to argue against the idea that the Messiah is the son of David. Next let us consider how the counterargument is made: by citing scripture. This is a scribal portrayal of Jesus, just like the original concern (the origin of the Messiah) is of a scribal nature. This is therefore a debate that takes place within a single social stratum and not between those who hold the Son of man/Adam (Galilean) concept and those who hold the Davidian (Jerusalem).

The earliest community probably knew that Jesus was not a descendant of David and, more significantly, so did some scribal opponents.[218] Soon, however, the polemic stopped and the community started to use the story differently. As Funk notes, the psalm became a favourite of the early church. Another indication is John 7:40–2, which relates a discussion that arose between those who believed that Jesus was Christ and those who did not. Those who believed He was not presented two arguments: 1) He was from Galilee and 2) He was not a descendant of David. John presents no argument or refutation of the allegations, which suggests that he accepted them. Bruce J. Malina explains the production of the genealogies:

> Mediterraneans were anti-introspective. Instead of judging people individually and psychologically, Mediterranean elites and non-elites utilized stereotypical descriptions and explanations.
>
> For example, genealogy can be deduced from one's subsequent behaviour and character (and behaviour/character offer solid indication of one's genealogy). Social standing necessarily determines one's abilities or lack of them (and ability or inability is clear proof of one's social standing). A person who does something for all mankind is of divine birth (and divine birth points to benefits for all mankind).[219]

Although these genealogies filled some needs in Christian self-definition, they seem to have been the cause of some debate in later years. The epistle's warning is a witness to the ongoing nature of the debate: 'Neither give heed to fables and endless genealogies, which minister questions, rather than godly edifying which is in faith: [so do]' (1 Timothy 1:4 KJV). And 'But avoid foolish questions, and genealogies, and contentions, and strivings about the law; for they are unprofitable and vain' (Titus 3:9 KJV).

The Birth of Jesus: Matthew 1:18–25, Luke 2:1–20

It is a well-known fact that the Virgin Mary plays a much more prominent role in Catholicism than in Protestantism. Thus she is called by the Catholics the 'Mother of God' (Greek, *theotókos*) and is regarded as having a special role in God's plan of salvation. She is considered to be sinless and exempt from original sin through the divine grace of God. In 1483, by papal decree, she was considered to be herself born immaculate.[220] In 1854 Pope Pius IX issued a statement with the papal definition of this doctrine in the document known as '*Ineffabilius Deus*'.

There is, in fact, no scriptural backing for this doctrine. Yet such was the regard for Mary that she was considered perpetually virgin. Notice, however, that verse 1:25 of Matthew implies something other than perpetual virginity. 'And knew her not *till* she had brought forth her firstborn son: and he called his name JESUS' (KJV, italics mine). The Catholic translation, the New Jerusalem Bible, reads: 'he had not had intercourse with her when she gave birth to a son; and he named him Jesus' (NJB).

The implication of the words *heos hou* (ἕως οὗ) seems to be the termination of an action (refraining) on the fulfilment of a condition (the birth of Jesus).[221] It would thus follow that James, Joses, Judas (not Iscariot) and Simon (not

Peter) are full brothers of Jesus and not half-brothers (sons of Joseph from another marriage) or cousins.

But to return to the matter at hand: Here are two verses from the gospels that imply the virgin birth of Jesus: 'Behold, a virgin shall be with child, and shall bring forth a son, and they shall call his name Emmanuel, which being interpreted is, God with us' (Matthew 1:23 KJV). 'And the angel answered and said unto her, The Holy Ghost shall come upon thee, and the power of the Highest shall overshadow thee: therefore also that holy thing which shall be born of thee shall be called the Son of God' (Luke 1:35 KJV).

In Matthew the virgin birth is viewed as the fulfilment of the prophecy of Isaiah (7:14) which says, 'A virgin shall conceive, and bear a son', whereas in Luke it is merely stating it in the context of the storyline. The interpretation given by Matthew, of the verse from Isaiah, is rather anachronistic for in its original context it refers to a span of time ('from time of conception to he knew to refuse evil', verse 16) and is part of the prophecy to Ahaz about the imminent fall of his enemies. The Hebrew word translated as 'virgin' (העלמה) merely means a maiden or someone of marriageable age. In Matthew's defence it should be said that he is true to his source, the LXX, and that the Greek word used there, *parthenos* (παρθένος), does carry the modern sense of the word 'virgin'.

Crossan sees the (independent) agreement of Matthew and Luke on both the virgin birth and the birthplace as a consequence of a tradition of exegesis of two Old Testament texts, Isaiah 7:14 and Micah 5:2.[222] While this is certainly true, as is evident from textual comparison, there is, the present author feels, a distinction between the usage of the two passages. Generally, as we shall see in the last chapters of this book, proof-texts that support narrative are there to prove that Jesus was the Messiah in accordance with scripture. But while there is certainly good reason for Jesus being born in Bethlehem, as the Messiah should be a descendant of David, there seems to be nothing, however, to suggest that the Messiah should be born of a virgin. Searching scripture, there seems to be no prophecies that remotely suggest that the Messiah should be born thus and while there certainly is biblical precedence for miraculous births, there is none that would suggest this. Indeed, one might say that there is a tension between the virgin birth and the common expectation of the Messiah being born of the family of David. Though Jesus qualifies through a technicality (kingship through adoption), it is doubtful that such a combination could come out of the same exegetical needs (i.e. that Jesus is Christ).

In other words, while exegesis of scripture created the story about Jesus' birth in Bethlehem (Jesus is Messiah → exegesis of Micah → Jesus born in Bethlehem), it was doctrine that necessitated exegesis in the case of the virgin birth (doctrine of virgin birth → exegesis of Isaiah → story of Jesus' virgin birth). What occasioned the doctrine of the virgin birth must remain speculation.

The controversy surrounding the virginity of Mary is deeply rooted in the Jewish tradition too. The Toldoth claims that: 'At the close of a certain Sabbath, Joseph Pandera, attractive and like a warrior in appearance, having gazed lustfully upon Miriam, knocked upon the door of her room and betrayed her by pretending that he was her betrothed husband, Yohanan. Even so, she was amazed at this improper conduct and submitted only against her will.'[223] Tertullian, writing some time towards the end of the 2nd or the beginning of the 3rd century, has Jews making the accusation of Jesus being 'a harlot's son' in the late 2nd century.[224] Celsus, a pagan philosopher of the 2nd century, was familiar with some traditions, among them the above, that later appeared in the Toldoth.[225]

The Three Wise Men: Matthew 2:1–23

Three different places have been suggested as the origin of the wise men, the *mágoi*,[226] who came 'from the East': Persia, owing to the extensive study of stars which was made in that region at the time; Arabia because of the gifts – gold, frankincense and myrrh – which originated in that area; and lastly Babylon, owing to its large community of Jews. As early as the 2nd century the wise men were thought of as kings and were even given the names Balthasar, Melchior and Gaspar, which have remained in Western traditions.

It is interesting to note that according to the Arabic Gospel of the Infancy,[227] these Magi were 'Magicians that had arrived from the east in Jerusalem, as Zoroaster had predicted'. Early tradition linked the Magi with Zoroaster, so much so that when the Persians invaded in 614 CE, one of the friezes of the wise men at the entrance of the Justinian Church of the Nativity looked so Persian that the church was spared from destruction. The tradition has been carried over into many different accounts. Ugo Monneret de Villard in his book *Le Leggende sui Magi Evangelici* (*The Legends about the Magi of the Gospel*) made a thorough survey of the legends concerning the Magi but space will allow only a few references to his findings.

He holds a book called *Libro della Caverna dei Tesori* (*The Book of the Treasure Cave*) to be of some importance. It tells of the Magi in Persia and Chaldee who saw the star, in which was to be seen a maid with a child with a crown on its head. Consulting the 'Oracles of Nimrod', they found that the meaning of this star was that the King of the Jews was born. They then went to Mount Nud[228] where they got the gifts for the new-born king. These gifts had been left there, in what is called 'the Treasure Cave', by Adam and Eve after they had been banished from the garden of Eden. From there the Magi proceeded to Herod and Bethlehem.

A parallel is to be found in rabbinic narratives of Abraham in which Nimrod is warned of the birth of one who shall conquer the world. The astrologers and councillors propose that a great infanticide take place. This advice is followed but Abraham is hidden and survives. Consulting other traditions about the Oracles of Nimrod, Monneret de Villard reaches the conclusion that Nimrod 'who is called "the great leader of the Magi" and which the Book of the Treasure Cave describes, as we have already seen, as the founder of the religion of fire, is no one if not Zoroaster'.[229] He likewise concludes that evidence equally suggests that Balaam, whom Eusebius and Gregory of Nyssa designate as the forefather of the Magi, is also to be identified with Zoroaster.

Prophecies about Jesus were attributed to Zoroaster and circulated with great accuracy.[230] In them Zoroaster talks of a virgin birth at 'the end of time and the final dissolution' and of one who would be persecuted and finally crucified with the appearance of great signs. This individual's descent and ascension are also mentioned and he is called the Word which establishes nature. Zoroaster is asked who is greater, He or the one to come, and Zoroaster answers that He will be one of Zoroaster's descendants and that 'I am he, and he is I; he is in me and I am in him'.[231]

The account of the wise men in Matthew demonstrates the supranational nature of the mission of Jesus, these three men from abroad being the first to recognize the 'King of the Jews'. Whether there is a historical core in the Magi myth or not, it plays an important role in the Gospel of Matthew. Nepper-Christensen suggests that Matthew is contrasting heathen worship with Jewish rejection and persecution.[232]

According to the gospels, Herod was still king when Jesus was born. Herod the King,[233] however, was already dead in the year 4 BCE. This inconsistency may be due to a traditional failure to fix the year of Jesus' birth.[234] There is, furthermore, a problem with Jesus' stay in Egypt. Matthew 2:13–15 fixes a time limit for the stay of 40 days, after He goes to Jerusalem, as recorded by Luke 2:22–4, as required by the Law.[235] The other problem is that in Matthew, after the family had been in Egypt, they wanted to return to Judea (presumably Bethlehem), indicating that it was their home. Indeed, Matthew does not mention that they were travelling to reach Bethlehem but merely mentions that Jesus was born there. Luke, on the other hand, tells of the travel and records that they 'returned into Galilee, to their own city Nazareth'. In view of these discrepancies it seems necessary to either chose to believe one or other account or to reject both. Both are legends but we may still approach a conclusion about the date of Jesus' birth. There is a conflict between Luke's accurate pinpointing of the start of Jesus' ministry and the fact that Herod was king of Judea at His birth (1:5) and died 34 years and not 30 years earlier. This may be resolved if the Herod referred to is Archelaus, who was not king but tetrarch over Judea (and Idumea and Samaria). Though Luke appears to be careful not to call Herod Antipas 'king', his source for the birth narrative (or its historical date) may not have been as discerning. That Herod was 'king of Judea' rather than Israel may be an indication that the tetrarch was thought of rather than King Herod the Great. Implicit to this, of course, is a complete rejection of the time frame presumed by Matthew. On the other hand, Luke explicitly mentions that the census (one which we have no mention of, except as occurring in the mid-seventies) was made during the Syrian governorship of Quirinius. Quirinius, however, did not become governor before 6 CE. The Lukan assertion that Jesus was about 30 when He began His ministry may be taken as an ideal age established by David (2 Samuel 5:3) and Joseph (Genesis 41:46).[236]

There is general scepticism about the massacre of the infants of Bethlehem, which seems an outrageous act to commit on the basis of the sayings of a few foreign astrologers: 'Then Herod, when he saw that he was mocked of the wise men, was exceeding wroth, and sent forth, and slew all the children that were in Bethlehem, and in all the coasts thereof, from two years old and under, according to the time which he had diligently inquired of the wise men' (Matthew 2:16 KJV). In defence of this unlikely account (and ignoring the problem of how such speedy access to King Herod was given to the Magi and the fact that no other records are provided by other historians of that time), it may be said that King Herod was indeed by reason of his family life poisoned with suspicion and was by character rash and ill-tempered. Wracked by disease, old age and the constant intrigue of his wives[237] to make their sons the heir to the throne, Herod executed no less than three of his own sons, all three designated as heir to his kingdom in one of his six wills. His first two sons, Alexander and Aristobulus, were named his successors in his first will but after alleged plots against him, followed by reconciliation and then renewed hostilities, they were executed by strangulation. The sole heir to the throne, designated in Herod's fourth will, was Antipater, his third son. Five days before his death, Herod ordered the execution of Antipater and wrote the sixth will in which he designated Archelaus as king and his brother Antipas and half-brother Philip as tetrarches.

Josephus recounts an uprising during this period when certain Jews provoked Herod by cutting down the golden eagle[238] at the gate of the temple:

> He then returned back and came to Jericho, in such a melancholy state of body as almost threatened him with present death, when he proceeded to attempt a horrid wickedness; for he got together the most illustrious men of the whole Jewish nation, out of every village, into a place called the Hippodrome, and there shut them in. He then called for his sister Salome, and her husband Alexas, and made his speech to them:– 'I know well enough that the Jews will keep a festival upon my death; however, it is in my power to be mourned for on other accounts, and to have a splendid funeral, if you will be subservient to my commands. Do you but take care to send soldiers to encompass these men that are now in custody, and slay them immediately upon my death, and then all Judea, and every family of them, will weep at it whether they will or no.' [239]

Shortly after, Herod fell sick and one day, fearing natural death, he attempted suicide with a knife but was prevented by his cousin, Achiabus. On hearing this, Antipater, who had already been incarcerated, greatly rejoiced and was emboldened enough to attempt to bribe the guards to release him. Herod, however, became informed of his plan and commanded his immediate execution. From this it becomes clear that King Herod had no regard for his own family or for innocent subjects. Indeed, could not the suggestion of a new King of the Jews, not of his own line, be sufficient reason for this crazed king to kill the innocent infants of Bethlehem? Certainly Matthew would not find it hard to convince the reader, who was familiar with Herod, that this was the case. However, the absence of such a story in Josephus' histories seems to strongly support sceptics of its historicity, as it seems unlikely that he would let pass such a splendid opportunity to vilify the Herodian king.

Matthew is explicit that Herod the Great attempted to kill Jesus when He was under two years of age and he specifically notes the change in reign from Herod the Great to Archelaus (which occurred in 4 BCE): 'But when he heard that Archelaus did reign in Judea in the room of his father Herod, he was afraid to go thither: notwithstanding, being warned of God in a dream, he turned aside into the parts of Galilee' (Matthew 2:22 KJV).

Crossan points out the striking features between popular accounts of the birth of Moses and Matthew's version of the birth of Jesus. Below is Josephus' story in *Antiquities* 2:9:2–3:

> While the affairs of the Hebrews were in this condition, there was this occasion offered itself to the Egyptians, which made them more solicitous for the extinction of our nation. One of those sacred scribes, who are very sagacious in foretelling future events truly, told the king, that about this time there would a child be born to the Israelites, who, if he were reared, would bring the Egyptian dominion low, and would raise the Israelites; that he would excel all men in virtue, and obtain a glory that would be remembered through all ages. Which thing was so feared by the king, that, according to this man's opinion, he commanded that they should cast every male child, which was born to the

> Israelites, into the river, and destroy it; that besides this, the Egyptian midwives should watch the labours of the Hebrew women, and observe what is born, for those were the women who were enjoined to do the office of midwives to them; and by reason of their relation to the king, would not transgress his commands . . . Accordingly God had mercy on him [Amram], and was moved by his supplication. He stood by him in his sleep, and exhorted him not to despair of his future favours. He said further, that he did not forget their piety towards him, and would always reward them for it, as he had formerly granted his favour to their forefathers, and made them increase from a few to so great a multitude . . . Know therefore that I shall provide for you all in common what is for your good, and particularly for thyself what shall make thee famous; for that child, out of dread of whose nativity the Egyptians have doomed the Israelite children to destruction, shall be this child of thine, and shall be concealed from those who watch to destroy him: and when he is brought up in a surprising way, he shall deliver the Hebrew nation from the distress they are under from the Egyptians. His memory shall be famous while the world lasts; and this not only among the Hebrews, but foreigners also: – all which shall be the effect of my favour to thee, and to thy posterity.

Here we should note that these elaborations on the canonical narrative of the first two chapters of Exodus are parallelled by Matthew's narrative of Jesus' birth. First of all, the triggering event in Josephus' narrative is the prophetic warning of a sacred scribe, whilst in the canonical narrative it is the growing populace of the people of Israel. This parallels the Magis' prophetic warning to Herod. Second, God's prophetic dream given to Amram, which has no parallel in the Exodus, parallels the dream of Joseph.

Summary and Conclusion

In a certain sense, this chapter began the chronology by revealing the conclusion. As in a mystery novel, we have started out with the murder and will in the following chapters uncover what really happened. With John's representation of Jesus as the embodiment of the Logos of God, we stand at the end of the transmission of the Jesus tradition, such as it unfolds in the New Testament. Where does it begin and in what sense can we speak of an evolution?

The most straightforward answer, of course, is that Jesus represents the beginning of the evolution which culminated in the perspective of John. The problem here, as suggested by the second question, lies in the word 'evolution'. The term implies necessary steps between two levels. So it is often said that there was an evolution from a low Christology to a high Christology and one imagines that Christians became bolder and bolder in their claims on behalf of Jesus. The problem here is the assumption that the development of high Christology is the inevitable outcome of a uniform process in the same sense that we imagine that species evolve to 'higher' life forms. However, there is no natural imperative that necessitates evolution towards a higher life form. Evolution is not a process that impels a species to become better but rather a process that impels it to adapt to circumstances. We know that once our planet was dominated by dinosaurs but that a radical change in environment caused them to die out. Only species that could adapt to the new circumstances could survive. Likewise, the evolution of the tradition about Jesus did not progress towards something higher; rather it adjusted to a new environment. So once it is asserted that John's perspective of Jesus evolved from an earlier perspective, it must immediately be asserted that such an evolution was adaptive in nature. When the tradition about Jesus came into a society that was familiar with the writings of Philo, nothing short of making the claims he made for Moses would be acceptable to it.

We have also in this chapter seen examples of evolution in the Synoptic Gospels. In Mark, Jesus was the Messiah but not born of David, in accordance with popular tradition. In Matthew and Luke this changes as the Jesus tradition takes on the scribal prerequisites for messiahship and Jesus is provided with a genealogy connecting Him with the family of David.

Another development that seems to have taken place between Mark and Matthew and Luke is the emergence of the doctrine of Jesus' virgin birth. Here the origin is more obscure. Certainly Jesus' very existence is elevated to the miraculous. The miraculous purpose that God has for Jesus is reflected in the miracle by which Jesus is brought into the world. Other motifs such as the similarity between Moses' birth and that of Jesus equally provide clues as to how Matthew understood Jesus.

When Mark uses the title 'Son of God', it appears as if this is a title he connects with Jesus being the Christ. The term appears in the Markan narrative (3:11 = Luke 4:41 and 5:7 = Matthew 8:29 = Luke 8:28), where it is spoken by a demon. This is part of the literary work of Mark.[240] In other words, it is not an integral part of the miracle tradition but is part of Mark's literary framework. In the interrogation Mark (14:61) uses the term 'son of the Blessed' (εὐλογητοῦ), which Matthew interprets as Son of God (26:63). Clearly in Mark's context this is connected with whether Jesus is Christ. Luke here shows his dislike of the term as he removes it here and in the following.

Finally it is spoken by the centurion in the passion narrative (15:39 = Matthew 27:54. Luke has the same scene but changes the term). Again, this is doubtful as a received tradition. It appears as a literary construct by Mark. Mark and the Markan community clearly used the term Son of God about Jesus but it does not appear to have been derived from the tradition used in his gospel.

In the chapters to come we shall consider further views of Jesus that are less evolved than the ones we outlined in this chapter, views that were adopted by people who lived in the same social and intellectual environment as Jesus.

4
Baptism

In this chapter we shall deal with the rise of John the Baptist and the baptism of Jesus and also see how the custom of baptism developed after the martyrdom of Jesus.

The Advent of John the Baptist: Matthew 3:1–17, 11:11–15, 17:10–13; Mark 1:1–8, 9:11–13; Luke 3:1–20; John 1:19–28

Shortly before the appearance of an angel to Mary, according to Luke, one also appeared to Zechariah, the husband of her kinswoman, Elizabeth, to promise him the child he wanted. This child was John the Baptist.

As far back as the Christian tradition can be traced, John the Baptist was considered the forerunner of Jesus and the return of Elijah[241] promised by Malachi (4:5): 'Behold, I will send you Elijah the prophet before the coming of the great and dreadful day of the LORD' (KJV). He described his own work with the prophetic words (Matthew 3:2–3): 'And saying, Repent ye: for the kingdom of heaven is at hand. For this is he that was spoken of by the prophet Esaias, saying, The voice of one crying in the wilderness, Prepare ye the way of the Lord, make his paths straight.' We shall discuss later the subject of return. For now, let us look at the historical John the Baptist.

Baptism was commonly practised when converting Gentiles to Judaism. In a Jewish conversion the proselyte would first be circumcised, then have a ritual bath[242] and finally (before its destruction), make an offering in the temple. He would also take a Jewish name and stop using his pagan name.[243] But when John the Baptist baptized people, it was not to a new faith (i.e. that of John the Baptist) that he converted them but to something more akin to a renewal movement within Judaism, similar to other sects or movements of the time.[244]

The main theme of John's ministry was baptism for the remission of sins and proclaiming the advent of the Kingdom of God, that is, 'making the path straight' and being the one who 'crieth in the wilderness'. Catchpole, however, points out that the version given in Mark 1:2b seems to be a combination of Exodus 23:20 and Malachi 3:1, which is the same combination we find in Q 7:27. The awkwardness of the Malachian verse is suggested by the common removal of it in both Matthew and Luke[245] and its appearance in Q suggests that Mark was dependent on Q in some form or another.[246]

John the Baptist must have remained a central figure of the early community and it may be conjectured that there continued to be a good or at least amiable relationship, as well as conflict, between those who followed John and those who followed Jesus. It is possible that the former were almost entirely absorbed into the latter after the demise of John. An indication of this may be found in the saying attributed to John in the Gospel of John (3:30): 'He must increase, but I must decrease.' This saying perhaps forms the core of a speech placed in the mouth of John the Baptist and expounded by the evangelist. If some of the members of the Baptist movement later joined the Johannine church, this remark would render their presence in the community intelligible to the community itself.

Baptism was a central teaching of John the Baptist, and although it has remained a part of the Christian ceremony of initiation (in contrast to the Qumrans, with whom it was a daily ritual),[247] it does not have the same importance as it had during his ministry. For John, his own baptism was not one of conversion as such, rather the baptism was a preparation for the coming of the Kingdom of God. According to Christian sources, his call to repentance[248] was not moralistic but an eschatological call.[249] It was the last chance for Israel to ready itself for the final day of God. In recounting the Jewish reaction to Herod (Antipas) being defeated by Aretas, King of Arabia, Josephus has the following to say about John the Baptist:

> Now, some of the Jews thought that the destruction of Herod's army came from God, and that very justly, as a punishment of what he did against John, that was called the Baptist; for Herod slew him, who was a good man, and commanded the Jews to exercise virtue, both as to righteousness towards one another, and piety towards God, and so to come to baptism; for that the washing [with water] would be acceptable to him, if they made use of it, not in order to the putting away, [or the remission] of some sins [only,] but for the purification of the body: supposing still that the soul was thoroughly purified beforehand by righteousness. Now when [many] others came to crowd about him, for they were greatly moved [or pleased] by hearing his words, Herod, who feared lest the great influence John had over the people might put it into his power and inclination to raise a rebellion, (for they seemed ready to do anything he should advise,) thought it best, by putting him to death, to prevent any mischief he might cause, and bring him-

> self into difficulties, by sparing a man who might make him repent of it when it should be too late. Accordingly he was sent a prisoner, out of Herod's suspicious temper, to Macherus, the castle I before mentioned, and was put to death. Now the Jews had an opinion that the destruction of this army was sent as a punishment upon Herod, and a mark of God's displeasure against him.[250]

There are some interesting discrepancies in the two portrayals of John the Baptist. For Josephus it is important to emphasize John's righteousness and virtue. These are, to Josephus, central and the baptism is merely a bodily seal for the cleanliness that the soul has already attained. Josephus mentions nothing of John's eschatological teachings. This, the present author believes, is an omission on Josephus' part rather than an invention of the evangelists, for there were plenty of people who preached righteousness, so this alone cannot explain the crowd that John attracted.[251] Indeed, Josephus is careful not to portray him as an eccentric who was 'clothed with camel's hair, and had a leathern girdle about his loins, and did eat locusts and wild honey' (Mark 1:6 ASV). Risto Uro makes a thorough analysis of the material available in Q and Mark in order to judge the message of John the Baptist and its implications.[252] He concludes that Mark is the more original and that John's apocalyptic message may be a later invention of the Q community but he is by no means certain.[253] It is certain that righteousness played a central role in the Baptist movement but it differentiated itself from other movements such as the Pharisees in calling for a single rite of salvation.[254] This act was highly anti-establishmentarian in two ways: First, it took authority away from the Jerusalem cult, which performed this function, and second, it presumed that this act was somehow different from an ongoing manifestation of righteousness, as was the rite performed by the Pharisees.[255] This of and by itself was not an uncommon element in popular Palestinian movements. However, the present author thinks an even more radical criticism was implied by the rite.

In Q 3:7–8 John warns that 'fruits worthy of repentance' should be brought forth, for 'begin not to say within yourselves, We have Abraham to *our* father: for I say unto you, That God is able of these stones to raise up children unto Abraham.' This, the present author would argue, is central to John the Baptist. Baptism was, as already mentioned, used as a daily ritual amongst the Qumran sectarians but was also part of the conversion ritual of Gentiles. First the Gentile would be circumcised, then he would have a ritual bath and finally he would offer at the temple. He would also stop using his pagan name. Now to a Jewish audience all except the baptism would be natural (circumcision, offerings at temple and Jewish name) and so by requiring baptism John is making everyone a Gentile. This is not, however, a positive statement about the Gentiles but a negative one about the Jewish assumption of being protected by the Abrahamic covenant. This may have had an impact on the later expansion of Christianity outside Jewish communities.

With this in mind, John the Baptist as an apocalyptic preacher becomes all the more likely. Furthermore, his execution on the grounds that he might cause sedition (*stasei*) also suggests that he may have aroused messianic expectations. John's criticism of Herod also suits the prophetic role as well. Q calls John the Baptist a prophet who predicts the advent of the 'Coming One'. Neither of these points are corroborated by Josephus but appear unlikely to have been Christian constructs. Beyond calling him a prophet, John is portrayed as a prophet: he lives an ascetic life style at the periphery of society and calls people to prepare for judgement. John the Baptist mentions the 'Coming One', an expression that is only found on the lips of John and his disciples but which Q otherwise never uses about Jesus and which Jesus Himself is extremely vague about accepting.[256] This also appears to be historical.

The quote from Isaiah in Mark makes John the precursor to Yahweh; in the Q tradition, however, John is the precursor to the Coming One. Q (Matthew 11:10 = Luke 7:27) uses the prophecy in Malachi 3:1[257] with the same sense of relationship between John the Baptist and Yahweh. It is conceivable that John used the quote in Mark and Q and interpreted it in terms of the Coming One. However, it is more likely that both prophecies represent a scribalization of John's message.

Theissen points out that Mark 1:4 states that John baptized in the wilderness (ἐρήμῳ), which might appear odd, for where can one baptize in a desert? Later it is mentioned that people are baptized in the Jordan river and Luke this adjusts by saying that John received his call in the desert but baptized in the Jordan river. Matthew solves it by saying that John preached in the wilderness. However, Mark is not wrong because there are indeed places where the desert comes very close to the river. Furthermore, Q also associates John the Baptist with the wilderness.[258] Kloppenborg includes in Q an introduction in which the circumstances of John's ministry take place (i.e. in the beginning of Q and not in Q 7:24) but Neirynck doubts this.[259]

Josephus does not mention that John had launched accusations against Herod that it was unlawful for him to marry Herodias, the wife of his brother Philip (Mark

6:18).[260] Theissen concludes that Mark's story is derived from a popular tradition rather than a scribal, since they are not informed about the details of the legal problem. It is not unlawful to marry your brother's wife, unless he is still alive.[261]

Both the evangelists and Josephus agree that righteousness was a prerequisite. Q (Matthew 3:8, Luke 3:8) writes, 'Bring forth therefore fruits worthy of repentance.'[262] Josephus omits mentioning the criticism that John launched against the religious authorities, stigmatizing them specifically, according to Matthew, with the name 'generation of vipers'.[263] While both Matthew and Josephus each have a vested interest – Matthew in accusing the Pharisees and the Sadducees and Josephus in maintaining that Jews in general and Pharisees specifically were righteous and beyond reproach – only one of the two reflect the truth of the matter. It appears likely that Matthew is right but perhaps Josephus was not aware of the criticism directed against the Pharisees, for most likely no one would openly admit to having been the target of the criticism. We have the story reported in Mark 11:27–33 in which Jesus is questioned about the source of His authority and to which He reportedly posed a counter question of where the authority of John the Baptist came from. The answer was not forthcoming because, as Mark explains their reasoning: 'If we shall say, From heaven; he will say, Why then did ye not believe him? But should we say, From men – they feared the people: for all verily held John to be a prophet' (Mark 11: 31–2). Q levels another accusation at 'this generation' and its rejection of John the Baptist (and Jesus) by saying: 'For John came neither eating nor drinking, and they say, He hath a devil' (Matthew 11:18, Luke 7:33).[264] So when Josephus says that all supported John, this may merely reflect the fact that no one dared publicly denounce him. Josephus' attitude towards John the Baptist is particularly curious in view of the generally negative attitude towards popular movements. Rather than discrediting John as he does other popular leaders, he, or more likely his source, recasts John into a role acceptable to a non-popular audience.

This brings us to another question, namely John's imprisonment. For Josephus there was no interim period, for John was apprehended and immediately sent to Macherus, a castle on the border between the dominion of Herod and Arabia. The reason given makes no sense. Why should he be sent there to be executed away from 'Herod's suspicious temper'? According to Josephus, Herodias was residing in Macherus, which allows for the scene portrayed in Mark to take place there. Josephus' portrayal of Herod as a despotic and irate ruler is not sufficient reason for the suggestion that Herod did not immediately execute John because he feared popular reaction. There is no way of confirming the story of the Baptist's execution but there seems to be no good reason why Mark should transfer some of the guilt to Herodias,[265] who by the time Mark wrote had been banished and made destitute with her husband. That John was held imprisoned over a longer period of time, as suggested by Mark, is supported by Q (Luke 7:19 = Matthew 11:2), which speaks of John having sent some disciples and Jesus sending them back with an answer. For this scene to have taken place we would have to assume that time had passed between John's imprisonment and the time Jesus started preaching independently, time for the rumour to have reached John and for him to have sent disciples.

Q's eulogy in Luke 7:24 (= Matthew 11:7) harks back

to a common sayings source to which Thomas had access:

> Thomas 78:1–2: Jesus said, 'Why have you come out to the countryside? To see a reed shaken by the wind? And to see a person dressed in soft clothes, [like your] rulers and your powerful ones?'

> Luke 7:26: Come on, what did you go out to see? A prophet? Yes, That's what you went out to see, yet more than a prophet (Malachi 3:1).

> Thomas 46:1–2: Jesus said, 'From Adam to John the Baptist, among those born of women, no one is so much greater than John the Baptist that his eyes should not be averted. But I have said that whoever among you becomes a child will recognize the Father's imperial rule and will become greater than John (SV).

Theissen suggests that both a literal and metaphorical reading of the reference to the reed suggests that Herod Antipas is its subject. In its literal sense the reed was the emblem used by the tetrarch[266] and in the metaphorical sense it was fitting, for as a political survivor he seemed able to bend when it was necessary.[267]

Luke has a special source that tells us about the ethical teachings of Jesus:

> And he answered and said unto them, He that hath two coats, let him impart to him that hath none; and he that hath food, let him do likewise. And there came also publicans to be baptized, and they said unto him, Teacher, what must we do? And he said unto them, Extort no more than that which is appointed you. And soldiers also asked him, saying, And we, what must we do? And he said unto them, Extort from no man by violence, neither accuse any

> one wrongfully; and be content with your wages (Luke 3:11–14 ASV).

These are not radical teachings but exhortations to justice: share wealth out of abundance, take no more than is lawful. What is significant here is that, unlike the addresses to the scribal class, these words seem to address people who were inclined to accept John's message: the poor but self-sufficient, the unpopular tax-collectors and the soldiers.[268] The exhortations themselves, however, benefit the group that probably made up the majority of John's followers, the destitute and the powerless. It was they who would find themselves without a shirt or food, overtaxed by the tax-collectors and threatened and assaulted by soldiers.

The continued importance of John the Baptist is seen by the inclusion of an infancy narrative in Luke, where he is presented as Jesus' cousin and receives angelic exaltation comparable to that which was received by Jesus.[269]

Christ's Baptism : Matthew 3:13–17, Mark 1:9–11, Luke 3:21–2, John 1:29–34

The setting for this event is described in two short verses in the Gospel of Mark:

> And it came to pass in those days, that Jesus came from Nazareth to Galilee, and was baptized by John in Jordan. And immediately coming up out of the water, he saw the heavens opened, and the Spirit like a dove descending upon him: And there came a voice from heaven, saying, Thou art my beloved Son, in whom I am well pleased (Mark 1:9–11 RW).

In Matthew's account, John the Baptist recognizes the

station of Jesus and pleads with Him, that he should be baptized by Jesus. Jesus, however, refuses and is Himself baptized. This is unique to Matthew and shows an issue that apparently was alive in the Judeo-Christian church.[270] Evans suggests that Luke also shows his 'embarrassment' by rewriting it into a single sentence in which 'astonishingly, the man Jesus is introduced onto the scene for the first time by means of a subordinate participle clause (*and when Jesus also had been baptized*)'. He further points out that the baptism story is (owing to the obvious discomfort it evinced) not invented by Christians.[271]

Luke offers that the Holy Spirit descended in 'bodily form'.[272] John, on the other hand, says that John the Baptist had no knowledge of the station of Jesus prior to His baptism. It is interesting to note that in the Gospel of John the event is narrated by John to his disciples a day after the event happened, pointing out Jesus and calling Him 'the lamb of God'. Thus John the Baptist not only first recognized that Jesus was the Christ but he also viewed the Messiah as one who would suffer rather than conquer.[273]

Matthew has a problem of consistency, in terms of when and how John the Baptist recognized Jesus, for the statement before the baptism conflicts with the enquiry made by John during his imprisonment through some disciples, saying, 'Art thou he that cometh, or look we for another' (Q, Matthew 11:3, Luke 7:20)? Seeing that the first words of recognition are a Matthean addition with a theological intent, the Q story seems the more likely.[274]

The words of the Father in the Synoptics, 'Thou art my beloved Son; in thee I am well pleased', are also interesting in the connotation they seem to have had for early Christians. D, one of the major manuscripts,[275] reads, 'today I have begotten you' and thus refers to Psalm 2:7: 'I will declare the decree: the LORD hath said to me, Thou art my Son; this day have I begotten thee.' The D thus fully complies with the LXX. The same words are connected to the baptism by 2nd century Church Father Justin Martyr in his *Dialogue with Trypho* (chapter 103.1).

The baptismal formula of Matthew 28:19, the baptism 'into the name of the Father and of the Son and of the Holy Spirit' (ASV) is also found in the Didache 7:1,3. It is odd that this formula should occur in two so markedly Judeo-Christian texts. Müller judges that the Matthean baptismal formula has its background in the account of Jesus' baptism.[276] It should be noted that in Acts of the Apostles converts are baptized only in the name of Jesus Christ (Acts 2:38, 10:48 and 19:5). Wedderburn considers some of the possible significances of the expression εὶς τὸ ὄνομα (into the name) by postulating a Semitic background in which the above expression is traced back to the Hebrew *l^e sem*, which we find in a ritual ablution that frees a slave. Following the argument of Strack-Billerbeck, Wedderburn concludes that the 'phrase indicated how the baptized was bound to the one into whose name he was baptized and that this bond carried with it an obligation'.[277] If this is a reasonable interpretation, then we may well understand the expansion of the original formula, which we know from Luke and Paul, to include both the Father and the Holy Spirit, to be a sign of dissatisfaction on the part of Judeo-Christians that God, and the Holy Spirit that moved the church, were not included in the bond that was being formed in the rite of baptism.

What can the reason be for Christ to be baptized? Was He in need of it? H. L. Ellison in his commentary on Matthew writes: 'Jesus was "born under law" (Galatians 4:4); since John was God's messenger, he had to fulfil all righteousness (15) by accepting his baptism, though he did not need it.'[278] Some Christians have linked the baptism to the crucifixion, making it a preparation for 'the taking of humanity's sins upon His shoulders'. Alternatively, some believe that it was merely to show the rightful authority of John to baptize for the remission of sins. The word 'righteousness' in Greek is *dikaiosune* (δικαιοσύνη), meaning either (as Paul most commonly uses it) the gift of righteousness of God to man (through the sacrifice of Christ) or as doing what is right in the sight of God. Thus Jesus, being the perfect example of righteousness, showed His followers that in the sight of God it was righteous to be baptized. Müller points out that the expression is a favourite with Matthew (Mark does not use it and Luke uses it only once) but that it should not be understood in the sense that Paul uses it but rather should be understood in the sense of what is achieved through deeds.[279]

The question should perhaps be reformulated as: How did Jesus' contemporaries understand baptism? Baptism, of course, implied an acceptance of the premise for the need of baptism and that the proposed solution (baptism) was effective. As stated above, there is an implicit arrogation of authority in John's claim. It is John who stands with the means of salvation in the imminent judgement and therefore it seems quite likely that Jesus was perceived as a disciple of John. This is implied by Mark 1:14–15 in which Jesus returns to Galilee proclaiming John's message. John states: 'When therefore the Lord knew that the Pharisees had heard that Jesus was making and baptizing more disciples than John (although Jesus himself baptized not, but his disciples)' (John 4:1–2 ASV). This is probably an anachronism with a historical core. It is probably true that Jesus did not baptize. Mark does not mention any baptism performed by Jesus; indeed, we only see the imperative to follow Him. John's statement that the disciples converted more people than John the Baptist is probably an anachronism, which was probably true by the time John was writing his gospel. According to John, Jesus preached in Judea with the disciples baptizing, while John was baptizing in Aenon prior to his imprisonment (John 3:22–4).

Excursus: The Baptismal Sacrament

This sacrament is a beautiful symbol which uses the imagery, on the one hand, of dying to this world and rebirth as a new beginning or, on the other hand, as a cleansing of sins.[280] In John the later imagery is used:

> Jesus answered and said unto him, Verily, verily, I say unto thee, Except a man be born again, he cannot see the kingdom of God. Nicodemus saith unto him, How can a man be born when he is old? can he enter the second time into his mother's womb, and be born? Jesus answered, Verily, verily, I say unto thee, Except a man be born of water and [of] the Spirit, he cannot enter into the kingdom of God. That which is born of the flesh is flesh; and that which is born of the Spirit is spirit (John 3:3–6 KJV).

We shall now see how the practice of baptism developed through the centuries. In the Westminster Confession of Faith (6.154–6.160) we find 1) the almost magical influence of the sacrament is confirmed, 2) the ministers are given exclusive right to administer it, 3) the sprinkling of water is as valid as full immersion, 4) infant children of a believing parent are to be baptized, 5) grace and salvation may be conferred without baptism and baptism does not ensure salvation, 6) its effect is instantaneous and 7) it is a once-in-a-lifetime sacrament.

Each of these points is better viewed either from a theological or from a historical perspective: 1, 4 and 6 perpetuate the movement away from symbolical interpretation to more literal interpretation. The Protestant movement's rejection of papal authority did not abolish the power of the church and the vast number of illiterates left ministers with some authority, which is maintained by article 2. The institution of ministers, deacons and bishops is mentioned in the Pauline letters and is thus, to some degree, biblical. It is, however, questionable whether baptism was restricted to officials of the church at that time.[281] The expression 'lawfully called' probably stems from the biblical account of the apostle being called by Jesus and given 'power [against] unclean spirits, to cast them out, and to heal all manner of sickness and all manner of disease' (Matthew 10:1). The question of the validity of the baptism by someone who is somehow disqualified is an old one. As far back as the 3rd century the question of whether the converts from heretical sects should be re-baptized was one that divided the Roman from the North African church. The matter was first settled through the influence of Augustine, who insisted that it was not who did it but how it was done ('*non cogitandum quis det, sed quid det*'). Typical for movements that started in colder climates, article 3 allows sprinkling rather than full immersion, which could represent a danger to the health of the baptized. Another trait of the reformed church is, as mentioned before, emphasis on grace and salvation being possible despite sin, as in article 5. The seventh article raises another interesting point, namely that a person is to be baptized only once. This, no doubt, is to counter those 'anabaptist' (from the Greek 're-baptizers') movements which were severely denounced by the Protestant reformers. In the 4th and 5th centuries it became common to receive clinical baptism, which meant that one was baptized only when one was close to death in order to escape from sin after the once-in-a-lifetime complete cleansing. The practice, however, soon fell into disuse and in its place infant baptism became the norm.

Comparisons between Protestant and Catholic articles of faith regarding the rite of baptism show no significant diversions. Beliefs in this regard remained largely unchallenged until the 17th century. At this point a new denomination arose from English and then American Protestantism, the Baptists, which challenged many of the conventional views:

> 1. Baptism is an ordinance of the New Testament, ordained by Jesus Christ, to be to the person who is baptized – a sign of his fellowship with Christ in His death and resurrection; of his being engrafted into Christ; of remission of sins; and of that person's giving up of himself to God, through Jesus Christ, to live and walk in newness of life.
> 2. Those who actually profess repentance towards God, faith in, and obedience to, our Lord Jesus Christ, are the only proper subjects for this ordinance.
> 3. The outward element to be used in this ordinance is water, in which the person is to be baptized in the name of the Father, and of the Son, and of the Holy Spirit.
> 4. Immersion – the dipping of the person in water – is necessary for the due administration of this ordinance.[282]

The first article makes baptism 'a sign' instead of a magical union in the body of Christ. The second article, the qualification of a candidate to baptism, utterly denies the possibility of infant baptism.[283] The third article fixes the element of the baptism as water but emphatically calls it an 'outward element'. The fourth article specifies that baptism has to be done by 'immersion – the dipping of the person in water' for it to be valid.

* * *

The Temptation of Christ: Matthew 4:1–11, Mark 1:12–13, Luke 4:1–13

This is another subject which might seem perplexing for Christians who view Jesus as being sinless. The whole concept of the Son of God being tempted seems to contradict Christian theology on an intuitive level. For this reason the Devil has become such a vivid image.

To properly understand the implications of statements such as 'Being forty days tempted of the devil', we most look at the original meaning of the word 'tempted'. The words *peirazo* (πειράζω) and the more intensive form *ekpeirazo* (ἐκπειράζω) are used similarly (1Corinthians 10:9 uses both words). In their original language (Koine Greek) both are devoid of the implication of being touched by temptation or, as it might be more correctly translated, 'tested'.[284] In fact, this is how the New Jerusalem Bible renders it: 'for forty days being put to a test by the devil' (Luke 4:2 NJB). The story is found in two versions.[285] One sums up the whole event in one verse: 'And he was there in the wilderness forty days, tempted of Satan; and was with the wild beasts; and the angels ministered unto him' (Mark 1:13 KJV). The story of Elijah's stay in the desert between Beersheba and Horeb which took 40 days and in which he was tended to by an angel (1 Kings 19:4–8) seems to be a most significant parallel. It is the key to understanding how Jesus' act was interpreted.

The accounts given by Matthew and Luke are more detailed. But whereas Mark omits to mention fasting, he does mention the presence of wild beasts. Pedersen proposes that there is a new Adam typology involved in Mark's account, in which Jesus is in paradise with animals and is tempted by the snake. Thus Jesus' resistance of this temptation signals the re-establishment of paradise.[286]

Mark also appears to see Christ's stay in the wilderness as a fulfilment of Isaiah's prophecy (Isaiah 11:6–10) in which animals who are prey and predator live in peace and a child remains unmolested by animals that would otherwise be a threat to it. This prophecy also mentions the son of Jesse which the Gentiles shall seek.

Both Matthew and Luke give accounts of the particular temptations proffered by the Devil in an attempt to deter Jesus from His messianic mission. Both mention three scenes in which the Devil presents a temptation and suggests its legitimacy with a quotation from scripture or merely indicates that Jesus is the Christ and it is therefore His right to accept it. These are then refuted by Jesus with other quotations from Deuteronomy.

Matthew		*Luke*	
DEVIL'S SUGGESTION	CHRIST'S REPLY	DEVIL'S SUGGESTION	CHRIST'S REPLY
turn stone into bread (?Isaiah 49:10)	Deuteronomy 8:3	turn stone into bread (?Isaiah 49:10)	Deuteronomy 8:3
cast thyself down (Psalms 91:11)	Deuteronomy 6:16	worship me (for a worldly dominion)	Deuteronomy 6:13
worship me (for a worldly dominion)	Deuteronomy 6:13	cast thyself down (Psalms 91:11)	Deuteronomy 6:16

It is quite plausible to see this account from Q as a casting of Jesus in the role of Moses, who received manna and 'tempted' His Lord by striking the rock to receive water and who was angered by the making of the golden calf when the people should only worship the Lord.[287] It is likely that Luke retains Q's original order,[288] as he does most often, but it is difficult to see why Matthew should change the order.[289] Perhaps it is not a redaction within the domain of the evangelists but a redaction within Q which they have received.

Theissen provides an alternative interpretation which employs a historical context as an exegetical key. Theissen points to three motifs within the second Lukan temptation that indicate that Caligula, the Roman emperor, was the individual who was being portrayed as the Devil: 1) He required prostration of his subjects, 2) he had the power to confer dominion and 3) he represented an affront to Jewish monotheism.[290] This amongst other things leads Theissen to suggest that the story was composed sometime between 40 and 55, and since it belongs to the last strata of Q, it is also indicative of Q's final place and date of redaction.[291] Yet he also contends that both Nero and Domitian could fit the role as well.

The third request (with Luke) has not really been satisfactorily explained. However, the present author would like to suggest that if we allow for the composition of the temptation narrative to be placed two decades later than Theissen would, a possible explanation may emerge. This would make Nero the object of the second temptation, whom Theissen also grants as a possible candidate. The Devil suggested to Jesus that He throw (βάλε) Himself down from the pinnacle (πτερύγιον) of the temple.

This temptation story bears a striking resemblance to the 2nd century martyr narrative about James[292] preserved in Hegesippus,[293] Clement of Alexandria[294] and The

(Second) Apocalypse of James.[295] Behind these narratives we can see a traditional oral narrative which combined two independent narratives, one about James being thrown from a height of the temple and the second a story about his death. It is the first story that will primarily interest us here. Regarding the second story we have a short note on James being tried.

From Josephus we know that about the year 61 Festus, the procurator of Judea, had died, leaving the region temporarily in disarray. At this point, we are told, Ananus took advantage of the power vacuum to have James and some others brought before the Sanhedrin and sentenced to stoning.[296] What brought on the charge of breaking the Law (παρανομησάντων) Josephus does not reveal. According to the Mishnah (Sanhedrin 7:4), one of eight offences one can be stoned for is instigation to apostasy. It is conceivable that this is the specific charge brought against James. Josephus does not say that he was thrown off the temple but that he was brought before a court and condemned to stoning on false charges (or incorrect interpretation of the Law). Hegesippus too says that James died from stoning,[297] since the fall did not kill him, but in the drama it is a hammer or a club that delivers the final blow.

Turning to the temptation story in Q, we must ask if the story about James influenced it, how can we best understand the motif that it uses? In Q Jesus is not thrown from the pinnacle of the temple but James was. While the second version has Nero portrayed as Satan, here the Pharisees (or other Jewish groups) are the ones represented as Satan, who wants to have Jesus thrown down from the pinnacle of the temple. This, however, seems to give mixed messages. On the one hand we should resist the temptation of property, represented as breaking the fast by turning stones into food, which was actively done in the Christian Jerusalem share community.[298] In addition, we should resist the temptation of Caligula and Nero to submit to Roman polytheism. But on the other hand, we should not allow ourselves to be martyrs at the hands of Jews (or Pharisees). Is it possible that some Christians did not approve of James' boldness when it put the whole community in danger? In the two first temptations the temptation was shared and rejected with fellow Jews to some degree. The last, however, is the temptation to divide oneself from the Jewish community. According to Hegesippus, James was encouraged to speak from the pinnacle of the temple by the very people who threw him down. The last temptation is written by a countermovement inside the Christian community of Jerusalem. In other words, Jesus is used as an ideal who rejected the temptation that James 'failed' inasmuch as James proclaimed a message that made Christianity unacceptable to fellow Jews.

Attaching the two stories, we can comfortably infer, changed the genre of the first story from a miracle story into a component part of a passion narrative. In all three versions of the story mentioned above (Hegessipus, Clement and Apocalypse), James quite miraculously survives the great fall. This is also true in the later narrative in the romance *Recognitions*,[299] though it is likely that it has detached the story from a traditional passion rather than preserved it from its pre-passion version. When we consider this together with Q's temptation narrative, we can deduce that the original miracle story understood James' survival of the fall to be a miracle accomplished by a host of angels. This image was appropriately removed when the story became part of a passion story.

The temptation story's heterogeneous nature is also

noticeable on closer inspection. It is clear that the story is a scribal tradition from its citation of the Law and that it is plausibly placed in Jerusalem from its interest in the temple. This is reinforced by the portrayal of Jesus as one who fasts, something that appears to be absent in Galilean traditions.[300] The story's use of the title 'Son of God' is interesting in two ways, first because it ties the tradition to Judea[301] and secondly because it is ambivalent about accepting the title. The author of Mark, we shall see in chapter 8, erects a silencing scheme, whereby those who discover Jesus' messianic secret are told not to tell others. This he does in order to account for the divergence of claims made on Jesus' behalf in Judea and Galilee. This is not the concern of the author of Q's temptation story, yet silence is part of the motif. The temptation in each case is to proclaim His messiahship through a visible miracle. Certainly, the story presumes that Jesus can make that claim but it considers such an open proclamation to be an evil inclination to be rejected as a suggestion of Satan. Just as Mark has Jesus proclaim His messiahship in the passion (14:61–82), Q has Jesus refusing such a proclamation in the temptation.

Though it could be posited that Hegesippus is late and that it is his account of James that is influenced by a story about Jesus, rather than the other way around, this remains problematic. First of all, it would then be difficult to explain the third temptation story in terms of its portrayal of Jesus as Messiah, since it is in no way related to any messianic motifs.[302] While there is little to suggest that Jesus was in Jerusalem for more than a brief period, James was the leader of the Jerusalem church for about three decades. As a figure who continued to lead the community, he must have engendered more storytelling than the long-dead founder, Jesus of Nazareth. As we shall see, hagiography is more apt to explain present events by modelling past history after it than it is to model the present to suit the past. The past is only valuable insofar as it is *made* to explain the present. Finally, for Hegesippus' story to make sense we would have to assume that its author consciously, knowing the temptation story, had James fail the test. Such a negative outlook of James, however, is not reflected in the story of Hegesippus.

Annemarie de Waal Malefijt recounts a story from the Philippines in which an *ingkantos*, a spirit that can take human form, comes to tempt a young man with a gold wristwatch. He refuses and though he becomes ill from the encounter, he becomes better with the assistance of the local healer. According to de Waal Malefijt, such stories support 'the social equilibrium by dramatizing and reinforcing the danger of coveting wealth and power unattainable within the community . . . The belief stresses the danger of foreign influences in Sibulan [of the southern Bisayan islands] and reflected the actual experiences of those members of the community who have gone to Manila or other cities to find work.'[303] Just as the people of Sibulan defended their society by telling a story about the danger of accepting the wealth of Westerners, some Jerusalem Christians told stories about the danger of proclaiming Jesus openly.

Though the first temptation is satisfactorily understood in the context of the Jerusalem share community, since such a general concern is consonant and parallel with the second temptation, yet another option is equally plausible. In the Gospel according to the Hebrews there is a tradition in which James the Just, who is the brother of Jesus, takes an oath not to eat bread until he sees the Lord risen from the dead.[304] Though it is almost certainly a myth, it may suggest that a certain type of fast was attached to certain hope. In the Mishnah certain provisions are made for a prayer for rain. If this not answered then the people start fasting. After a while allowances are made, so that people can eat 'only while day' but are forbidden to 'work, to wash themselves, to anoint themselves, to put on sandals or to have marital intercourse; and the bath-houses are shut up'[305] and Hegesippus describes James as one who 'drank no wine or strong drink, nor did he eat flesh; no razor went upon his head; he did not anoint himself with oil, and he did not go to the baths'.[306] It is possible that this same party that disapproved of James' open confession of Christ approved of his open display of righteousness arising from his Nazirite vow.[307] According to Josephus,[308] like Hegesippus, James was executed by stoning, not by a mob, but on the orders of Ananus the high priest. Perhaps Hegesippus is anachronistically placing the Scribes and Pharisees as the antagonists instead of the more logical high priest and Sadduceans. Indeed, if Hegesippus' description of James is correct, James may have been seen as challenging the legitimacy of the high priest.[309] We will see that in early Christianity in Jerusalem the temple issue was inextricably connected with Jesus' message.

There are, in the present author's opinion, common elements that belong to a pre-Q/pre-Markan oral tradition. In short, these two share the fact that Jesus went into the desert and was tempted by the Devil. All other elements, in both traditions, are secondary and belong to a scribal social world. The common traditions, however, are sufficiently archetypal in nature to have been understood as such in a popular prophetic movement. In terms of acts, this spoke loudly about Jesus' claims of prophethood.

What tradition, one may ask, does the author of the

temptation narrative follow when he uses the Devil the way he does? Elaine Pagels writes, 'In the Hebrew Bible . . . Satan never appears as Western Christendom has come to know him, as the leader of an "evil empire", an army of hostile spirits opposed to God.'[310] She goes on to give a summary of the Old Testament usage of Satan. In general, Satan means adversary and is often used in the sense of 'adversary of Israel' or of its representatives. Even in its supernatural version, Satan is not the adversary of God in any conventional sense but is rather an angel of God in the same sense as the angel of death. The supernatural agent has its origin in the conventional adversary (e.g. parties within Israel), whom some prophets described symbolically by means of Canaanite myths. Elsewhere, Satan, the angel of God, could oppose a wrong deed and speak on behalf of God.[311] Even in Job he is God's 'authorized' agent, who tests Job.[312] In view of this tradition, it is quite logical that Satan is the figure evoked by the author of the temptation narrative to test Jesus. Abraham was likewise tested by God with the sacrifice of Isaac: 'And it came to pass after these things, that God did tempt Abraham, and said unto him, Abraham: and he said, Behold, [here] I [am]' (Genesis 22:1 KJV).

The Hebrew word used here is *nasah* and was translated 'tempt' by the KJV translators as was natural with the definition of the word in the 17th century. Most of the later translators,[313] however, avoided the implication that God might have been a 'Tempter'.

Both the baptism vision and the temptation are experiences that were Jesus' alone and would not have been available to early Christians unless Jesus Himself told them. Bornkamm notes in his discussion of Jesus as a prophetic figure that a 'prophet has to produce his credentials, somewhat as did the prophets of the old covenant in telling the story of their calling and in accompanying their message with the sacred prophetic saying'.[314] Bornkamm wrongly concludes, the present author suggests, that Jesus did not speak of His calling. These two experiences, particularly the baptismal vision, were in all likelihood told by Jesus to establish His prophethood.

Summary and Conclusion

The narrative of Mark, John and Q really start, not with Jesus, but with John the Baptist. Clearly, early Christians felt that one could not understand Jesus without understanding John. Yet John the Baptist's importance quickly faded in the centuries after his execution. We see this process already underway in the gospels. Both Matthew and Luke show a concern about the discipleship of Jesus in the Baptist movement which is not present in Mark or Q. Notwithstanding this, it seems plausible to assume that there was some sort of continuity between the teachings of John and those of Jesus. Whether this holds true will be explored in chapters 5 and 8.

The teachings of John the Baptist should be understood in the context of the belief in the imminent arrival of the end. In view of these special circumstances, normal access to purging of sin through an accepted institution was no longer sufficient. The urgency of the situation not only removed authority from institutions such as the temple, something that the Pharisees and Essenes had already done,[315] but removed it from the class of people that derived its confidence from its ability to read the Law and interpret it. Extraordinary circumstances placed all under equal requirements: an immediate repentance before the intervention of God in history. Reliance on such things as the Abrahamic covenant was insufficient.

The intervention in history was in the Markan tradition referred to by citing Isaiah in which John the Baptist comes to make way for God Himself. The Isaianic text was probably understood in the sense Q alludes to by its reference to the Coming One. The function of this figure is vague at best. We may assume that standard messianic expectations were awakened by John's proclamation.

Consonant with this picture of John the Baptist's doctrine is the emulation of Elijah, following the traditional form of popular prophetic proclamation. It is no wonder that there was some confusion as to whether or not John the Baptist was the return of Elijah. When asked, John the Baptist was reported to have denied this (John 1:21) but Mark and Matthew affirm it in its Jesus tradition. As we shall see in subsequent chapters, Jesus Himself was asked the same question and He too emulated Elijah. The insistence that John the Baptist was Elijah by the evangelists was put as a response to assertions by Scribes that Elijah would come (Mark 9:11ff and para. in Matthew and Matthew 11:14) before the day of Yahweh. This issue was, as suggested by Mark himself, a scribal one which Jesus is unlikely to have addressed.

In our attempt to uncover the nature of the message of John the Baptist we have had to use several different sources, none of which actually belong to John or his disciples. All are sources that are essentially friendly towards John the Baptist but are also quite biased in their portrayal.

In the Christian tradition, John plays another role in relationship to Jesus. We have seen that when John baptizes Jesus, the latter experiences a vision in which He sees the Holy Spirit and hears the voice of God. In the Christian tradition, John not only proclaims the coming of Jesus but also anoints Him as a prophet, an adopted Son of God. This tradition is connected with the tradition that Jesus fled into the desert where He was tempted by Satan.

The temptation tradition, such as we find it in Mark and Q, is a scribal reproduction of a popular tradition. The popular tradition was a recollection of Jesus' proclamatory act. The core of the story comes to us from two independent sources, Mark and Q. In other words, it is not the invention of evangelists or even of a single community. In addition, the story meets the criteria of historical probability although the fact that Satan appears in the story may raise objections about its historical probability from a modern perspective. The question, however, is not whether there is such a thing as Satan but why such a story was told. As a story told in a popular environment, it marked Jesus as a new Elijah.

Just like the story of Jesus' calling to be God's Son at His baptism, the temptation story is a story that could only be told by Jesus Himself. Both stories recount Jesus engaging the divine. Thus we conclude this chapter by seeing that Jesus began His mission by proclaiming His Elijah-hood through narratives about Himself.

5

The Proclamation of Christ

After Jesus returned to civilization, He appointed His apostles and started to proclaim His mission. He continued where John the Baptist had left off, proclaiming the advent of 'the kingdom of heaven'. However, a change in the message suddenly appeared which was wholly unexplained in the gospels: the imminent kingdom had come.

Parables and liturgically expressed doctrines were common preaching methods and were widely used in the days of Jesus. Indeed, the gospels bear witness to the fact that the content and the authority of Jesus' words, not the form in which they were delivered, were astonishing to His contemporaries: 'And they were astonished at his teaching: For he taught them as having authority, and not as the scribes' (Mark 1:22 ASV).

Often, in recent studies, the parables of Jesus have been regarded as distinguished from traditional rabbinical parables by the use of hyperbole, exaggeration, that emphasized the point. We shall look closely at some of these in this chapter.

In recent years many historians have attempted to reconstruct the teachings of the Historical Jesus, the person who uttered words that were heard and retold again and again until someone decided to record them. Later these were placed into larger narrative frames that combined the two and the gospels came into existence, were edited, reedited and used by others to make greater and more complete stories. So to reconstruct these teachings it is necessary to learn how to eliminate first what was the creation of the evangelist and after that to undertake the more challenging task of eliminating the creations of the community in which Jesus' sayings circulated. Below we will look at how part of this operation was undertaken.

There are, of course, a host of problems and not a few controversies over how to locate the words of Jesus. Some words may stem from contemporary Judaism, others from the early church and still others that seem to come from neither. Those belonging to the last group form the core of what we know about the Historical Jesus, and with that knowledge we may sort through the other material and see what is consonant with our primary data. One cannot ignore the fact that Jesus was part of Jewish society nor that He was the initiator of the early church and that He may have said common Jewish things and that He may have said things that appear to be the church's own creation. This principle, the principle of discontinuity,[316] is not the only criterion for evaluating the historicity of words attributed to the Historical Jesus. Social context is, for example, increasingly influential in Historical Jesus studies. Ultimately every attempt to make such a reconstruction is fallible and based on what appears most sound to the scholar undertaking the endeavour.

Origins of Sayings Traditions

One important factor in analysing the sayings attributed to Jesus is to understand how His words could come from His lips to the pages of the gospels. Obviously only one group of people can be expected to have committed to memory the sayings of Jesus and that is His disciples. But who were they? Where did they come from? And how did they live?

The first answer seems implicit from the gospel tradition: they belonged to the lower classes. The lowest was the class of the destitute, of the beggars. These probably constituted the majority of Jesus' followers. The reason for this, as we shall see, is to be found in the socio-economic situation of Palestine in general and Galilee in particular. The other group was the poor working class. These separated themselves from the former in that they were able to survive on what they earned. To this class belonged craftsmen, farmers (day-workers) and fishermen.[317] This latter class became disciples by leaving their property and joining the lowest class, leaving their nets (Mark 1:18), their harvest (John 4:35), their tax-collection (Matthew 9:9). Experience showed that people of greater wealth were unwilling to leave it (Mark 10:17ff). Reading the parables attributed to Jesus also reveals His great affinity with this class of people.[318]

To understand the overwhelming presence of the lower class it is necessary to look at the economic situation of Galilee. Throughout the reign of Antipas a grand-scale economic reform took place. As Freyne points out,[319] this was quite successful but brought a massive aggregation of wealth into the hands of a few. Peasants in particular suffered in the process. They found their small plots of land were repossessed and they were forced to become day-labourers, whose pay, Crossan shows, was more or less the same as it cost to maintain an urban slave.[320]

From this it becomes obvious that the disciples of Jesus were mainly Galilean and mainly from the rural areas of Galilee. It is noteworthy that neither Sepphoris nor Tiberias, Antipas' two most important cities, are mentioned anywhere in the gospels.[321] This probably signals early Christians' antipathy for the urbanization that these cities represented. If we accept that these classes of people constituted the disciples of Jesus, it is difficult to understand the existence of written records among people who were almost all illiterate. The reason will become apparent below. The genre of wisdom was generally reserved for the educated and Jesus' use of wisdom sayings was a transgression of social boundaries in itself.[322] Stephen J. Patterson has pointed out that the sayings tradition shared by Thomas and Q, compared with other wisdom traditions in the Near East,

> . . . betrays a markedly different orientation . . .Wisdom in the ancient Near East was, for the most part, a school tradition carried on by scribes and scholars working under official sponsorship. As such, it tends to be rather conservative in its approach to the ultimate questions it raises. Its values are those of the status quo: moderation, order, hierarchy, wealth as a sign of diligence and reward, and so on. The ancient sages were not especially interested in rocking the boat or agitating for social reform.[323]

As we shall see, the wisdom of Jesus was opposed to the status quo and was intent on social reform.

Below is a list of rules kept by these disciples when they travelled, which was pretty much all the time – thus they are commonly called itinerants:

1) Go two and two (Mark 6:7)
2) Salute no one (Luke 10:4)
3) Go only to Jews (Matthew 10:5–6)
4) Bring on the journey:
   a staff (Mark 6:8), no staff (Matthew 10:10, Luke 9:3)

no bread (Mark 6:8, Luke 9:3)
no wallet (Mark 6:8, Matthew 10:10, Luke 9:3, 10:4)
no money in their purse; (Mark 6:8, Matthew 10:9, Luke 9:3, 10:4; 1 Corinthians 9:14, Didache 11:6,12)
sandals (Mark 6:9), no shoes (Matthew 10:10, Luke 10:4)
one coat (Mark 6:9, Matthew 10:10, Luke 9:3)

5) When you come to a house:
if rejected shake the dust off (Mark 6:11, Matthew 10:14, Luke 9:5)
seek out the worthy (Matthew 10:11)
preach the gospel (Mark 6:12, Luke 10:9, Matthew 10:7, Didache 11:8)
greet with 'Peace' (Luke 10:5, Matthew 10:12)
heal the sick (Mark 6:13, Matthew 10:8, Thomas 14)
exorcize unclean spirits (Mark 6:9, 6:13, Matthew 10:8)
eat what is placed in front of you (1 Corinthians 10:27, Matthew 10:10, Luke 10:7, Thomas 14)
abide in the same place till you leave (Mark 6:10, Matthew 10:11, Luke 10:7)
stay no more than two days (Didache 11:5)
eat not at a common meal you order (Didache 11:9)

From this the life style of the itinerant becomes clear. Even if he is able to acquire wealth he is not to do so, for he is sworn to a life of destitution. Why? Because through his demeanour the itinerant challenges the mercy of the householder who, if he passes the test, becomes 'worthy'. This is, of course, a somewhat internal evaluation of the situation. Declaring someone 'worthy' was a reflection after the fact. One accepted the kingdom of God, therefore God must have found him worthy.

There is a performance involved in the behaviour of the itinerants, a behaviour that by design is intended to reject social scripts and prescripts, in order to invent new ones.[324] Below we shall look at how parables aided this change of vision.

To return to the recording of the sayings of Jesus: Amongst these householders, some of whom became Christians, a few retainers recorded what they were taught by the itinerants. Both Q and the Gospel of Thomas contain sayings of these itinerants.[325] The reason for the production of these texts, however, needs further consideration. It is sometimes proposed that the writing of the gospels was occasioned by the decline in the number of people who could recite the oral tradition so that it would not be lost. Such a thesis, which could equally well be applied to Q or Thomas, would place the first forms of textualization in the latter part of the 1st century, when these appear to have started to disappear. Textualization, however, was not caused by the lack of oral reciters but by the need to control those who carried the tradition. Werner H. Kelber has advanced the following about the Markan textualization as a counter-response to the prophetic orality:

> The experience of disconfirmation undermined the credibility of prophetic authorities and faith in their oral, prophetic effectiveness. At this point, orality was ill-equipped to deal with the dilemma, for the prophetic, oral use of living words was itself a major part of the problem. Linguistically, Mark responded by disestablishing words from oral life and transposing them into a new key.[326]

This very situation must have also faced the Markan predecessors. How could one ensure that the tradition that was accepted by the community was not modified by its reciters for their own benefit and to the detriment of the community? As Kelber points out, an oral solution was impossible. Only freezing the tradition in the written media could ensure that there was no alteration. In addition to this, the textualization made the tradition independent of its reciters. One need not rely on any particular reciter for the tradition and thus the monopoly was broken. Thus the first recordings of oral tradition in text came into being not as a means of retaining a disappearing tradition but to control a living and potentially disruptive one.

The Didache refers to the itinerants who spread the oral tradition as 'prophets' (11:4, 7–12; 13), yet prophecy does not seem to have been their primary purpose. The title, therefore, is better understood as an inheritance from Jesus, whose disciples they were. These 'prophets', as we have seen, lived the life style of Jesus and spoke His words and in both ways proclaimed the arrival of the kingdom.[327] Below we will look at a saying in which Jesus designates Himself as a prophet rejected in His own home. This experience was not only Jesus' but was the experience of all the itinerants who had lost their homes and families.

Reflecting on the Old-testamental use of the word 'prophet' (נביא), one finds it to have a very broad usage. In general, by 'prophet' is meant a spokesperson. Aaron was made a prophet for Moses so that Moses could be God's spokesman to Aaron and Aaron could be Moses' spokesman to the people (Exodus 7:1). The followers of prophets are sometimes called prophets themselves, although their only task is to praise God and to turn the people towards Him.

In 2 Kings 4 a story is recounted of the wife of a deceased member of a prophetic brotherhood under Elisha who appealed to him to save her from the creditors.[328] In 1 Kings 20:35 a 'son of the prophets' commands another to smite him but the other does not and his imminent death by a lion is prophesied for his disobedience to Yahweh.

1 Kings 22 offers an interesting insight into the use of 'prophets'. As the king of Israel readied himself for war, he consulted with four hundred prophets[329] who all foresaw him successfully conquering 'Ramoth Gilead'. He purposely did not invite Micaiah because Micaiah did 'not prophesy good concerning' him, thus clearly demonstrating that the office of prophecy was granted only to those who would agree with the will of the king.

In 1 Samuel 19:20 a messenger of Saul encounters a 'company of the prophets prophesying, and Samuel standing as head over them, the Spirit of God came upon the messengers of Saul, and they also prophesied' (ASV). These could thus be considered the prophets of Samuel.

Understanding this relationship of the 'master' prophet and 'servant' prophets, we can understand the Didache's use of the term 'prophet' as it applies it to the radical itinerant preachers. These disciples of Jesus should therefore be considered not only 'prophets' in a generic sense but as 'prophets of Jesus'. This term should be chosen above more descriptive titles (such as radical or itinerant) because the Didache uses it and because it properly explains their life of emulating their master, Jesus the prophet. They, according to Didache 11:8, 'have the behaviour of the Lord' and he teaches 'others to do as he does himself . . . for so also did the prophets of old' (11:11).[330] In Q (or perhaps an independent oral tradition in Matthew and Luke) the prophetic master/servant relationship is expressed in terms of: 'He that receiveth you receiveth me, and he that receiveth me receiveth him that sent me' (Matthew 10:40). Or in the Lukan reversal: 'He that heareth you heareth me; and he that rejecteth you rejecteth me; and he that rejecteth me rejecteth him that sent me' (Luke 10:16). To which Matthew adds 'He that receiveth a prophet in the name of a prophet shall receive a prophet's reward: and he that receiveth a righteous man in the name of a righteous man shall receive a righteous man's reward' (10:41 ASV). In 1 Thessalonians 1:6 Paul writes to his followers 'And ye became imitators of us, and of the Lord, having received the word in much affliction, with joy of the Holy Spirit' (ASV).

That Jesus may have been thought of as an Elijah figure is also attested by a Markan source which repeats popular rumours (6:15, 8:28) and which necessitated the differentiation between Jesus and two past prophets, Elijah and Moses, in the transfiguration (9:28) and which finally led the crowds in the crucifixion scene to believe that Jesus was calling for Elijah (15:35). In a Lukan tradition, Jesus refers to a comparison between His own behaviour and that of Elijah and Elisha (4:25–7).

The life style of these prophets of Jesus has been compared to that of the Cynics.[331] Cynicism was a popular Greek philosophy, or rather a popular religious movement, whose members were also wanderers who lived a life of abstinence.[332] However, there is no evidence whatsoever to suggest that Jesus had any contact with Cynicism and there is no sign in Q of any affinity with Hellenism. Kloppenborg states: 'This [the similarities between Q and Cynics] is not to suggest that the Q group imitated the Cynics or borrowed and adapted their ideology. The Jesus of Q is not a paradigm of Cynic παρρησία [outspokenness] or, still less, of ἀναίδεια [shamelessness], as an expression of the freedom and self-sufficiency of the sage.'[333]

There is also a significant difference in the social origin of the two movements. The Jesus movement had its origin in the rural areas as a consequence of urban oppression. The Cynic movement came from the urban environment but rejected its ensnaring materialism.[334] The Cynics were educated philosophers who were obliged, even after abandoning their families, to ensure that their children had the means to get an education for themselves.[335] Crossan notes that the Cynics' attire was a sign of their independence from material things, while for the prophetic itinerants it was a sign of communal dependence.[336] As such, Crossan finds the idea of a Cynic Jesus, as a replacement for a Jewish Jesus, to be a 'little short of absurd'.[337] Even Mack does not see these people (whom he terms 'Jesus people') as undifferentiated groupings:

> The difference between the Jesus people and the Cynics was the seriousness with which the Jesus people took the new social vision of the kingdom of God. This reflects the influence of Jewish concern for a real working society as the necessary context for any individual well-being. It was this interest in exploring an alternative social vision that set the Jesus movement apart from a merely Cynic-like call for an authentic lifestyle only in the interest of individual virtue or integrity.[338]

Nevertheless it must be granted that the Cynic parallels to the Q itinerants are striking and not of a superficial nature, as some have charged.[339] The correlation lies in the particular use of behaviour that by its nature commands respect and illustrates the criticism that is vocalized.

Jonathan Z. Smith, one of Burton Mack's conversation partners, has criticized the tendency in comparative studies to dismiss similarities between early Christianity and other religions of late antiquity. This, according to Smith, is done in order to affirm the 'uniqueness' of Christianity, which cannot therefore have borrowed from religions other than Judaism, which becomes a legitimate progenitor.[340] This criticism should be given due consideration. Mack's proposal should not be dismissed because the Cynics are 'unworthy' progenitors of Christianity. Certainly the Cynics had both noteworthy and admirable proponents. However, surveying the panorama of early Christianity and the Galilean context from which it grew, the popular prophet in the tradition of Elijah and Elisha is surely the more attractive proposal.[341]

Finally, the present author would like to address the issue of the sociological nature of this itinerant group. Malina concludes on the much-vexed question 'Did Jesus intend to found a "church"?', that if Jesus formed a 'faction' (which is what Malina believes) then the definite answer is 'no'.[342] Factions are, according to Malina, ephemeral by nature. They emerge for a certain purpose and dissipate upon success or failure. A sect, however, has an enduring property in that it forms 'fictive kin groups', which Malina sees in Acts and Paul. However, even a superficial reading of Q will show that many sayings in it are intensely critical of the institution of the family, which is 'evidence of the sectarian character of the Q group'.[343] If people in general lived in 'nuclear families living in clusters as production units based, e.g. on crafts, all living in interconnected units',[344] it stands to reason that the disintegration of that unit must have a causal relationship with the formation of a new unit. It is debatable whether the disintegration of the former unit made the latter necessary or the former disintegrated because of the development of the latter.[345] What is not in doubt, however, is that the rules of life described above were the ones that most certainly were judged to have their origin in Jesus and were those that most readily lent themselves to 'fictive family formation'.[346] In other words, if there is one thing that is historically likely about the intention of Jesus regarding His followers, it is that they were part of a family. This, as we shall see, is connected with another fact that remains undisputed, namely, the kingdom of God, about which Jesus certainly taught. This 'fictive family' is in fact the outward manifestation of the kingdom of God.

All the sayings and parables that we will look at, which presumably go back to Jesus, we should expect to speak to the experience of these itinerants.

Sermons

Christ's first major sermon, according to Matthew, is the Sermon on the Mount. In it He presents the core of Christian doctrine and demonstrates the new spirit infused into His revelation. He extols the virtues of the blessed, reinstates the laws of the Pentateuch but commends greater mercy and compassion, condemns the hypocrisy of the divines of that age, reveals the prophetic prayer for His church, admonishes His followers to detach themselves from worldly goods, enjoins them to extinguish every idolatrous thought from their hearts and to focus on their heavenly Father, rebukes those who point to the sins of others but themselves are sinful, warns against teaching those who will not heed, unveils some of the characteristics of the kingdom of heaven on earth, promises unfailing divine assistance to His faithful followers, establishes God's Will as the unerring balance of justice and exalts the station of those who heed His commandments.

Many of these sayings are found in Luke, not in a single sermon, but dispersed throughout his gospel. This material belongs to Q and where Luke probably keeps the order of his source, Matthew has compiled it into a single sermon.

We shall now look at a piece from this sermon, commonly known as the beatitudes, and compare the three versions available:

Matthew 5:3–11	*Luke 6:20–2*	*Thomas*
3. Blessed [are] the poor in spirit: for theirs is the kingdom of heaven	20. Blessed[be ye] poor: for yours is the kingdom of God.	54. Blessed are the poor, for yours is the Kingdom of Heaven
4. Blessed [are] they that mourn: for they shall be comforted.	21b. Blessed [are ye] that weep now: for ye shall laugh.	
5. Blessed [are] the meek: for they shall inherit the earth.		
6. Blessed [are] they which do hunger and thirst after righteousness: for they shall be filled.	21a. Blessed [are ye] that hunger now: for ye shall be filled.	69b. Blessed are the hungry for the belly of him that desires will be filled.
7: Blessed [are] the merciful: for they shall obtain mercy.		
8: Blessed [are] the pure in heart: for they shall see God.		
9: Blessed [are] the peace-makers: for they shall be called the children of God.		
10. Blessed [are] they which are persecuted for righteousness' sake: for theirs is the kingdom of heaven.		69a. Blessed are they who are persecuted within them-selves. It is they who have truly come to know the Fa-ther.
11: Blessed are ye, when [men] shall revile you, and persecute [you], and shall say all manner of evil against you falsely, for my sake.	22: Blessed are ye, when men shall hate you, and when they shall separate you [from their company], and shall reproach [you], and cast out your name as evil, for the Son of man's sake.	68: Jesus said, 'Blessed are you when you are hated and persecuted. Wherever you have been persecuted they will find no Place.

The most striking feature of these logia is the metre[347] that is almost, but not quite, inherent in them. It follows the form:

> Blessed is the [a virtue]:
> for they shall [a reward].

All the verses fall into this metre with the exception of the fourth, where Matthew's insertion of the explanatory note 'and thirst after righteousness' breaks the pattern; the seventh, where 'for righteousness' sake' disrupts the metre; and the last, which one suspects comes from another sermon.

Luke's version throws a great deal of light on the original logia of Jesus as far as it can be reconstructed. First, one should note that Luke's version is directed at a specific group of people, possibly His disciples: 'be ye'/'yours', instead of Matthew's general 'are the'/'theirs'. It is remarkable that Thomas has it both ways in verse 54, so that he has 'are they'/'yours'.[348] If there was this switch in Q, it is likely that Luke and Matthew each decided to stay with one or the other. Therefore it is reasonable to believe that in that particular case, Thomas contains the most original version. Furthermore, Luke has, as his second verse, the same sentence as Matthew has in his fourth verse. It is likely that since Matthew moved so much material into one sermon, the sequence of the internal pieces was changed, so Luke retains the original order.

Luke 6:21a omitted the explanatory note 'and thirst after righteousness' and thus preserved the original metre. Matthew's insertion is made so as to give the saying a more exalted meaning because mere hunger is not relevant to Matthew's audience, whereas social justice is. Thomas is well aware of the original meaning but makes the physical satisfaction optional; for Thomas, asceticism is to be commended. Only Luke retains the logia unchanged, with the possible exception of the word 'now', which he may or may not have added. The same redactional purpose seems to lie behind Matthew's insertion of 'in spirit' (verse 3) so that rather than actual poverty, a more spiritual meaning is derived.[349]

It has already been mentioned that Matthew always changes 'kingdom of God' to 'kingdom of heaven' and in this case receives the support of Thomas. But it appears that Thomas has a similar redactional policy and never once does he have 'kingdom of God' but either 'of heaven', 'of the Father' or just 'kingdom'. In view of these established redactional policies, Luke's version again appears to be the most original.

Surprisingly enough, Luke also ends his discourse with the epilogue-styled sentence that Matthew does, suggesting that the sentence in fact does belong to Q. Luke uses the impersonal and distant 'Son of man's sake', instead of Matthew's 'my sake'. In this case the present author favours Luke's suggestion for 'Son of man's sake', owing to Luke's greater accuracy (so far) and the frequent recurrence of that expression in Q.[350] Although the beatitudes were compiled in Q, their appearance at different places in Thomas seems to suggest that they were originally detached sayings.

Jerome H. Neyrey[351] points out that the 'poor' (πτωχòι) are not people who are barely coping but are those who are so poor that they need to beg to survive. The epilogue describes the effect of living in destitution and the loss of honour that are the immediate consequences of joining Jesus.

Next we will consider some sayings about the kingdom

of God, which is one of the central themes of the gospels. The theme of the first saying is that 'the kingdom of God' or 'the kingdom of heaven' is established within the hearts of men, depending not on whether God will deliver it to an individual but whether that individual is open and will listen to the Word of God. It is not found in Matthew but it is conjectured that it may have been part of Q.

> The kingdom of God cometh not with observation: Neither shall they say, Lo here! or, lo there! for, behold, the kingdom of God is within you' (Luke 17:20–1 KJV).

> If those who lead you say, 'See, the Kingdom is in the sky', then the birds of the sky will precede you. If they say to you, 'It is in the sea', then the fish will precede you. Rather, the Kingdom is inside of you, and it is outside of you (Thomas 3).

> It will not come by watching for it. It will not be a matter of saying 'Here it is' or 'There it is.' Rather, the Kingdom of the Father is spreading out[352] upon the earth, and men do not see it (Thomas 113).

> Take heed lest anyone lead you astray with the words, 'Lo, here!' or 'Lo, there!' for the Son of Man is within you (Mary 4:4–5).

The unity of these sayings is perhaps debatable and therefore redaction criticism can only be used tentatively. All except Luke's version appear to be secondary but the meaning is difficult to discern. In particular, the question of the kingdom of God being within – the meaning of *entos* (ἐντὸς) translated as 'within'[353] in Luke 17:21 – is central for our understanding of this verse. Thomas 3 may not be related to the same saying as Luke or, perhaps, has undergone much redaction. Certainly those who had led people, the Pharisees, never claimed doctrines about the kingdom being in heaven or the sea. If, however, they are related, it is interesting that 'inside' (ⲉⲛⲧⲟⲥ)[354] is contrasted with 'outside', the last part being an addition and the former, which follows Luke, relating to the inner reality.

The Jesus Seminar[355] concluded that Luke's version and Thomas 113 approximate Jesus' actual words, while Thomas 3 has been notably redacted and Mary's version is virtually the words of the author of that book. It should be noted that Luke is translated 'is right there in your presence' (SV). The dismissal of Thomas 3 as a gnostification of the original saying, interpreting it as 'an internal divine spark',[356] is perhaps justified.[357] However, the lexicographical data it supplies[358] suggests that the translation of ἐντὸς as 'midst' is not justified. Thomas 113 has the same preamble as Luke, that the kingdom of God is not perceptible with – as the Coptic renders it – the 'outward looking' (ϭⲱϣⲧ ⲉⲃⲟⲗ) and therefore it is necessary to add at the end of the saying 'and men do not see it'. Invariably, the conclusion must be that whatever the kingdom was, it was not visible to the naked eye. But was it spread out over the whole earth or was it confined to the inside of man? The present author argues that it is both. While the kingdom is the rule of God inside a person, which ultimately is faith that directs the life of those who are faithful, it also spreads, for the spread of the good news goes from heart to heart, directing each to turn towards the kingdom of God.

So while Thomas 113 is theologically congruent with Luke, it is of secondary importance, for the invisible spreading is unintelligible unless there is some theological or other basis for it to be hidden in first place. As with an illness of the body, first one observes that there is a symptom which demonstrates the presence of bacteria. Once one has recognized its invisible yet all too real presence, one can investigate how the disease spreads. The latter requires the former as a prerequisite. While the former is intelligible by itself, the latter is only understandable in a body where the invisible spreading is explained.

Though the Mary text presents only weak evidence because it is late, it does, however, support the theses that the primitive saying redacted by Mary probably carried the significance of Luke.

The reason the present author has discussed this at some length is because there is a considerable consensus against this interpretation. One of the foremost Danish scholars has devoted an entire book to these verses in Luke and has reached the opposite conclusion.[359]

As the last example of source and redaction criticism we shall consider the saying: 'No prophet is accepted in his own country; no physician heals those who know him' (Thomas 31; Mark 6:4 = Matthew 13:57 = Luke 4:23–4 = John 4:44).

> A prophet is not without honour, but in his own country, and among his own kin, and in his own house (Mark 6:4 KJV).

> A prophet is not without honour, save in his own country, and in his own house (Matthew 13:57 KJV).

> And he said unto them, Ye will surely say unto me this proverb, Physician, heal thyself: whatsoever we have heard done in Capernaum, do also here in thy country. And he said, Verily, I say unto you, No prophet is accepted in his own country (Luke 4:23–4 KJV).

> For Jesus himself testified, that a prophet hath no honour in his own country' (John 4:44 KJV).

It is generally believed that there is no Q text behind these sayings and before the publication of Thomas it was difficult to explain the discrepancies between Luke and Mark. Of the two versions, Luke is the simplest, for Mark expands on what the home country really is, namely 'among his own kin, and in his own house'. Matthew takes his text from Mark but decides that 'among his own kin' is redundant, even for him. Whether John has an independent source is not easily determined but at any rate the simplicity of John is only matched by Luke. The two versions of Luke and John are distinguished by the prophet either being acceptable (δεκτός) or honoured (τιμὴν). At the same time, the similarity between Luke and Thomas is striking: there is almost a word for word correspondence.[360] There is an additional connection between Luke and Thomas with the proverb about the physician. The context of Luke suggests that the proverb was common amongst his contemporaries and that it did not originate with Jesus. Accepting that Jesus did indeed cite this proverb in connection with His poor reception at Nazareth, the question becomes, which of the two widely different versions is the more original? In Luke it is used by Jesus' enemies because He had not performed any miracles but in Thomas the proverb is placed in Jesus' defence. Luke's version has the distinct advantage of being short and easily remembered but the disadvantage of being part of, and conforming to, a narrative pattern, by being the words of the opposition. Thomas has the advantage of being catchy and memorable and appearing as words that Jesus could have said in His defence.

Parables

The parable is a short metaphorical narrative which seeks to convey an impression or experience of a general principle. The narrative draws on the common experience of the audience. Conversely, an allegory is the application of a principle to a concrete situation. In its narrative each element corresponds to a concrete and identifiable entity of history. In the gospels we find both parables and allegories but more often than not we find parables that have had introduced into them certain allegorical elements. The elements we find are crafted to point to, for example, the Romans or Israel. A parable is a story that invites an interpretation but is purposely ambivalent so that it creates an insider-outsider environment.[361] The parable can therefore best be understood as an oral entity that was given in different forms, each suited for the situation of the oration. As such, the parable at once asks for interpretation and refuses to formulate one for its audience. Therefore it has been suggested that a certain dichotomy exists between the parabolic and allegorical, the former being hermeneutically open, while the latter seeks to complete the hermeneutic process.

A parable thus has an inside and an outside, a meaning or message and a form or story that conveys it. In an oral recitation the form is conditioned by the audience which receives the message and the message is conditioned by the intention of the reciter. Funk has emphasized that the nature of the parable is not that of an assertion but rather like an event to be experienced.[362] When we therefore speak of a message or the intention of the reciter, we are not speaking of a doctrine or, rather, not a particular formulation of a doctrine. Dan O. Via uses the term 'literary aesthetic object' to define the nature of the parable. Thus, according to Via, interpretation can be had only in a partial sense:

> The meaning distilled from the form-and-content must be given a new form-and-content, a new pattern of connections which relates the original meaning to our time. But since the interpretation of a parable – as distinguished from the parable itself – is not an aesthetic object, the relationship of form to content in the interpretation will not be the same as in the parable.[363]

In terms of Funk's thesis we might say that although we may interpret, interpretation will not evoke the experience, which is at the heart of the parable.

The outside and inside of the parable work together so they can be remembered and understood correctly. This, however, is the ingenious aspect of the parable. The incompleteness requires the audience to decode the hidden message and in the process of decoding the audience makes the message its own.[364] Birger Gerhardsson has proposed that with 'parables one does not primarily wish to inform about something. One wants to *clarify* something in such a way as to draw the audience to him.'[365] This, the present author suggests, is not accurate. The purpose of the parable is not to fine-tune an almost correct opinion of the audience but to change its mind from an entirely fallacious view to something almost completely different. The surprising feature of the narrative part (the outside), the element that strains the hearer's sense of realism, is often also the revolutionary aspect of the message (the inside). At other times the contrast is between the expected simile and the one given. For example, in a parable about the kingdom of God, one would usually expect grandiose imagery rather than simple imagery.

To find the 'original' form of the parable, there are certain features of parables that we should observe. The form is characterized by its ability to lure the listener into a familiar world and then reach an extraordinary and shocking conclusion. This is not only an important mnemonic device but provides the essential challenge to the audience. Funk states:

> It is too little to call the parables as metaphors teaching devices; they are that, but much more. They are language events in which the hearer has to choose between worlds. If he elects the parabolic world, he is invited to dispose himself to concrete reality as it is ordered in the parable, and venture, without benefit of landmark but on the parable's authority, into the future.[366]

It is quite possible that the exact form of a parable is not recoverable. After all, memory only preserves the gist of a story.[367] On the other hand, a story and its interpretation will immediately become connected. The message, such as the audience understands it, becomes a key to remembering the story itself. It is therefore not difficult to understand that certain allegorical elements should emerge, particularly in a textual media. To remove the allegorical application from the parable is not, however, always useful because its original application may be impossible to recover. As an example, Martin Dibelius suggests that the parable of the talents in Luke 19:12–27 allegorically refers to the heavenly return of Christ. Unlike Luke, Matthew has no such interpretation, thus it appears that 'a moral exhortation constitutes the essential content of this narrative', that is to say that the message of the parable is that 'we must use the gifts which God has given to men'.[368] But Dibelius finds it unlikely that Jesus would have used a parable for something that is so morally axiomatic; rather, he finds it more likely that it was applied to the Jews wasting their precious heritage. The present author suggests that the gift in question is not the 'Jewish heritage' but rather the newly given gift, namely the kingdom of God. The (inordinate) multiplication of talents (which refers to the multiplication of members of the kingdom of God) seems to be integral to the shocking effect of the conclusion. The parable therefore refers to an internal admonition rather than an external polemic. The problem that Dibelius notes with the 'axiomatic' nature of the moral of the parable stems from not appreciating the experiential nature of the parable. The parable does not only seek to assert the moral necessity of using one's potential but seeks to make the hearer experience the moral imperative. It is also here that the parable's incompleteness comes into play. The reciter of the parable is aware of the audience's need to experience his message and thus the audience's need provides the parable with closure.

In conclusion, it must be stated that we should make certain that the application of the parable is plausible in the life of the Historical Jesus. We use the term 'application' because the parable does not emerge out of a void. When Jesus first formulated the parable and infused it with experiential content, it was done in the context of a particular situation. We might say that the general principle enunciated in a 'speech event' started with a concrete event. The evolution of the parable may therefore be traced from a single event or context, which then received a general formulation of the principle in a parable. The single principle was applicable to various events and could therefore be allegorized in different ways. The allegory that captures a particular event could, on the other hand, serve to illustrate any number of principles. The parable thus generates experience that leads to action, while the allegory describes experience that leads to reflection and theological formulation.

Again, owing to the vastness of the material, the present author is compelled to address only a selection as an example. Let us first look at the parable of the sower.

Mark places Jesus by the seaside where the multitudes have sought Him. He steps into a ship so that people may hear Him preach. He tells them the story of the sower, who sows wherever he may go: whatever the condition of the soil, it will receive seeds from him:

> And it came to pass, as he sowed, some fell by the way side, and the fowls of the air came and devoured it up. And some fell on stony ground, where it had not much earth; and immediately it sprang up, because it had no depth of earth: But when the sun was up, it was scorched; and because it had no root, it withered away. And some fell among thorns, and the thorns grew up, and choked it, and it yielded no fruit. And other fell on good ground, and did yield fruit that sprang up and increased; and brought forth, some thirty, and some sixty, and some an hundred. And he said unto them, He that hath ears to hear, let him hear (Mark 4:4–9 KJV).

> And when he sowed, some [seeds] fell by the way side, and the fowls came and devoured them up: Some fell upon stony places, where they had not much earth: and forthwith they sprung up, because they had no deepness of earth: And when the sun was up, they were scorched; and because they had no root, they withered away. And some fell among thorns; and the thorns sprung up, and choked them: But other fell into good ground, and brought forth fruit, some an hundredfold, some sixtyfold, some thirtyfold. Who hath ears to hear, let him hear (Matthew 13:4–9 KJV).

> A sower went out to sow his seed: and as he sowed, some fell by the way side; and it was trodden down, and the fowls of the air devoured it. And some fell upon a rock; and as soon as it was sprung up, it withered away, because it lacked moisture. And some fell among thorns; and the thorns sprang up with it, and choked it. And other fell on good ground, and sprang up, and bare fruit an hundred-fold. And when he had said these things, he cried, He that hath ears to hear, let him hear (Luke 8:5–8 KJV).

> Now the sower went out, took a handful (of seeds), and scattered them. Some fell on the road; the birds came and gathered them up. Others fell on the rock, did not take root in the soil, and did not produce ears. And others fell on thorns; they choked the seed(s) and worms ate them. And others fell on the good soil and produced good fruit: it bore sixty per measure and a hundred and twenty per measure (Thomas 9).

The text is reproduced from Mark both in Matthew and in Luke, in the former more faithfully than the latter. Matthew changes the reference to the seeds from it (αὐτό) to them (αὐτά), a change made purely for grammatical reasons. He generalizes so that it becomes a rocky 'place' instead of rocky 'ground' and changes the order of the yield from a decreasing to an increasing order. All of these changes are secondary and of a purely cosmetic nature.

Luke has introduced other and more significant changes. In some of the earliest and most significant manuscripts[369] Luke agrees with Matthew in the grammatical improvement of changing 'it' (αὐτό) to 'them' (αὐτά), which constitutes a 'minor agreement'. Since the improvement is logical, it could easily have been introduced independently. Luke inserts that the seeds could be 'trodden down' and the birds are 'birds of heaven',[370] the seeds did not fall on rocky ground but on an actual rock. For Luke the seed did not immediately grow up but 'as soon as it grew' it withered because it had 'no moisture'. Finally, Luke's seeds only produce a hundredfold.

Neither Matthew nor Luke reveal knowledge of any source other than Mark. The only agreement of interest is that of Luke with Thomas, that the seeds fell onto a rock (ⲉϫⲛ̄ⲧⲡⲉⲧⲣⲁ) but this seems more likely to be a coincidence than anything else. Luke's modifications, which are excellent examples of introductions of allegorical elements, are probably due to the particular relevance he perceived in this parable to his own community. It was probably persecuted and 'trodden under foot', and the tests from the preying birds, were 'heavenly' tests. Luke also indicates that persecution is not the result of receiving the Word but of 'growing', that is to say acting on the Word of God. For Mark, one cannot but react when one receives the Word of God but Luke recognizes, perhaps from his own community, that some may believe but not react out of fear.

Mark provides an interpretation to this parable which is shared by the other synoptics:

> The sower soweth the word. And these are they by the way side, where the word is sown; but when they have heard, Satan cometh immediately, and taketh away the word that was sown in their hearts. And these are they likewise which are sown on stony ground; who, when they have heard the word, immediately receive it with gladness; And have no root in themselves, and so endure but for a time: afterward, when affliction or persecution ariseth for the word's sake, immediately they are offended. And these are they which are sown among thorns; such as hear the word, And the cares of this world, and the deceitfulness of riches, and the

> lusts of other things entering in, choke the word, and it becometh unfruitful. And these are they which are sown on good ground; such as hear the word, and receive [it], and bring forth fruit, some thirtyfold, some sixty, and some an hundred (Mark 4:14–20 KJV = Matthew 13:18–23 = Luke 8:11–15).

Mark interprets the parable as referring to the spreading of the 'word'. The 'birds' are interpreted allegorically as 'Satan' and the seed that sprang up but had no 'deepness of earth' is interpreted as those who receive the 'word' but are unable to thrive owing to 'tribulation and persecution'. The third unsuccessful seed is interpreted as being 'choked' by wealth. The final, successful, seed becomes a fruit-bearing tree, which is understood as the outcome of those who receive the 'word'. Even with this allegorical reading certain things remain open to interpretation, such as what or who 'Satan' is and what the 'fruits' are that those who receive the word 'bring forth'. This Markan interpretation shows signs of being applied to a community that is more like Mark's own than that of the itinerant prophets, the prophets of Jesus.[371] For example, 'persecution' is probably more applicable to a householder than to someone who is wandering and riches are probably more of a test to those who are in places where wealth is accrued. But these are shades of meaning and the Markan interpretation is certainly not far off the mark. The interpretation of the seed as the 'word' (of the kingdom of God) is perhaps slightly more restrictive than if the kingdom of God itself were intended.

The next parable changes the focus from the redemptive nature of the kingdom of God to its eschatological nature.

> Jesus said, 'The Kingdom of the Father is like a man who had [good] seed. His enemy came by night and sowed weeds among the good seed. The man did not allow them to pull up the weeds; he said to them, "I am afraid that you will go intending to pull up the weeds and pull up the wheat along with them." For on the day of the harvest the weeds will be plainly visible, and they will be pulled up and burned' (Thomas 57).

> Another parable put he forth unto them, saying, The kingdom of heaven is likened unto a man which sowed good seed in his field: But while men slept, his enemy came and sowed tares among the wheat, and went his way. But when the blade was sprung up, and brought forth fruit, then appeared the tares also. So the servants of the householder came and said unto him, Sir, didst not thou sow good seed in thy field? from whence then hath it tares? He said unto them, An enemy hath done this. The servants said unto him, Wilt thou then that we go and gather them up? But he said, Nay; lest while ye gather up the tares, ye root up also the wheat with them. Let both grow together until the harvest: and in the time of harvest I will say to the reapers, Gather ye together first the tares, and bind them in bundles to burn them: but gather the wheat into my barn (Matthew 13:24–30 KJV).

There is probably no textual dependence here on the Synoptics. In fact, the amount of variation suggests that the parable most likely circulated in an oral state until it was included in both Matthew and Thomas. This reminds us that parables, although they are longer than other sayings, are easy to remember: even details can be retained because the narrative is memorable and provides a framework for detail.

As a principle, one would assume that Thomas' shorter

version is more primitive. However, in the Thomean version there appear to be omissions because distracting questions are raised. Verses 26 to 28 in Matthew are completely wanting in Thomas. This raises questions such as: To whom does 'them' refer (whom the man did not allow to pull out the weed)? How did he know that the weed had been planted, as there is no mention of it growing up?

The ending of the two parables reveals allegorization. Matthew has amended the ending to suit his particular interpretation (discussed below). Both Matthew and Thomas conclude that there will be a 'time/day of harvest' when the weed will be taken and burned.[372] But Matthew seems closer to the agricultural setting, which he portrays with the bundling of the harvest. Matthew has a more plausible 'time' of harvest, while Thomas has changed it to the 'day' in order to allude allegorically to the Last Day.

Matthew himself interprets the parable:

> He answered and said unto them, He that soweth the good seed is the Son of man; The field is the world; the good seed are the children of the kingdom; but the tares are the children of the wicked [one]; The enemy that sowed them is the devil; the harvest is the end of the world; and the reapers are the angels. As therefore the tares are gathered and burned in the fire; so shall it be in the end of this world. The Son of man shall send forth his angels, and they shall gather out of his kingdom all things that offend, and them which do iniquity; And shall cast them into a furnace of fire: there shall be wailing and gnashing of teeth. Then shall the righteous shine forth as the sun in the kingdom of their Father. Who hath ears to hear, let him hear (Matthew 13:37–43 KJV).

In Matthew's allegorical interpretation the field is the

community of Christians within which there are those who 'do iniquity' and those who are 'righteous'. Such criticism of a community little more than three years old seems unlikely. It is also, therefore, unlikely that the interpretation goes back to the lifetime of Jesus Himself.

The third parable is the parable of the mustard seed:

> And he said, Whereunto shall we liken the kingdom of God? or with what comparison shall we compare it? [It is] like a grain of mustard seed, which, when it is sown in the earth, is less than all the seeds that be in the earth: But when it is sown, it groweth up, and becometh greater than all herbs, and shooteth out great branches; so that the fowls of the air may lodge under the shadow of it (Mark 4: 30–2 KJV).

> Another parable put he forth unto them, saying, The kingdom of heaven is like to a grain of mustard seed, which a man took, and sowed in his field: Which indeed is the least of all seeds: but when it is grown, it is the greatest among herbs, and becometh a tree, so that the birds of the air come and lodge in the branches thereof (Matthew 13:31–2 KJV).

> Then said he, Unto what is the kingdom of God like? and whereunto shall I resemble it? It is like a grain of mustard seed, which a man took, and cast into his garden; and it grew, and waxed a great tree; and the fowls of the air lodged in the branches of it (Luke 13:18–19 KJV).

> It is like a mustard seed, the smallest of all seeds. But when it falls on tilled soil, it produces a great plant and becomes a shelter for birds of the sky (Thomas 20).

There are several agreements between Matthew and Luke

against Mark. It is therefore generally agreed that Q contained this version, which was more developed than both Mark and Thomas. Thomas probably has the most primitive version. Q has the seed sown by a man in a field, whereas Mark merely has it sown in the ground. Q specifically mentions that it becomes a tree, which is not true, for it is an annual shrub, although the Palestinian *sinapis nigra* can grow as tall as three metres.[373] Thomas is simpler than Mark, without any superfluous words or remarks.

The parable is a lesson from nature. Jesus is here teaching that looks are deceptive, that the rule of God starts with the small. The kingdom of God grows slowly but finally gains ascendancy.

Q introduces 'a man' who becomes the actor of the parable and who plants the seed in his own garden. The expansions in Q introduce an element that is at once common to the genre and superfluous to this parable. The introduction of the actor almost certainly belongs to the oral stage, since it does not seem to belong to the redactional pattern of Q. The focus of the parable is on the mustard seed: it is the teacher.

The next parable to consider is that of the leaven.

> Another parable spake he unto them; The kingdom of heaven is like unto leaven, which a woman took, and hid in three measures of meal, till the whole was leavened (Matthew 13:33 KJV).

> It is like leaven, which a woman took and hid in three measures of meal, till the whole was leavened (Luke 13:21 KJV).

> The Kingdom of the Father is like a certain woman. She took a little leaven, [concealed] it in some dough, and

> made it into large loaves. Let him who has ears hear (Thomas 96)[374]

The only difference here is that Q provides the amount of flour, which is not mentioned in Thomas. The three measures may be an allusion to the story in Genesis 18. One of the interesting features of this parable is that it promotes leaven as a good thing while, during Passover, it is not used for bread but is considered non-Kosher.[375] Here again we find the central feature, the illustrative element, in the hands of an unimportant actor. This time, however, the action is attested to by both Q and Thomas and we have no evidence that the parable ever existed without an actor.

The next four parables are the final summary of the properties of the kingdom:

> Again, the kingdom of heaven is like unto treasure hid in a field; the which when a man hath found, he hideth, and for joy thereof goeth and selleth all that he hath, and buyeth that field (Matthew 13:44 KJV).

> The Kingdom is like a man who had a [hidden] treasure in his field without knowing it. And [after] he died, he left it to his son. The son did not know (about the treasure). He inherited the field and sold [it]. And the one who bought it went plowing and found the treasure. He began to lend money at interest to whomever he wished (Thomas 109).

Here Thomas appears far more elaborate than Matthew. Matthew has one person find the treasure in another man's field, whereafter he hides and sells his own property, so as to be able to purchase the field with the hidden treasure. That he does this 'for joy thereof' may be an insertion of

Matthew to cover the doubtful moral nature of such a deception but it could also be regarded as an integral part of the parable. The meaning of the parable seems to be that the people who discover the kingdom of God will gladly sell their earthly treasure in exchange for the treasure hidden within the field, which is the obscure movement of which Jesus is the head.

The version of Thomas is more doubtful. The discovery of the kingdom of God must refer to the followers of Jesus, who draw advantage from their discovery, again with rather dubious morals. The former owners can only conceivably be the Jews, who were formerly the people of God. Thus, after being in the hands of one family (the Jews), the kingdom suddenly falls into the hands of another (Christians or possible the Gentiles). This leads the present author to differ with the conclusion of the Jesus Seminar that Thomas' version is as authentic as Matthew's.[376] The questionable morals,[377] which partly give this version credence, are dubious primarily in a Thomasine connection (see Thomas 95) and as such are suspicious in a variant reading of the same parable. Furthermore, the lending out of the treasure (the kingdom of God) with interest functions poorly in the parable. This, as well as the possible allusion to the Gentile church, leads the present author to conclude that the version of Thomas is secondary.

> Again, the kingdom of heaven is like unto a merchant man, seeking goodly pearls: Who, when he had found one pearl of great price, went and sold all that he had, and bought it (Matthew 13:45–6 KJV).

> The kingdom of the Father is like a merchant who had a consignment of merchandise and who discovered a pearl. That merchant was shrewd. He sold the merchandise and

> bought the pearl alone for himself. You too, seek his unfailing and enduring treasure where no moth comes near to devour and no worm destroys (Thomas 76).

This parable, like the one before it, deals with the renunciation of the disciples who left everything behind them to follow Jesus. The conclusion of Thomas is, of course, secondary as it focuses not on the renunciation as much as the finding. For Thomas, the pearl is *gnosis/sophia* (knowledge/wisdom) which is sought for and through which one finds eternal rest. There seems to be a common oral tradition behind the two versions. Thomas has merely appended a conclusion which has no part in the parable, as it turns to the reader and refers to him in second person.

> Again, the kingdom of heaven is like unto a net, that was cast into the sea, and gathered of every kind: Which, when it was full, they drew to shore, and sat down, and gathered the good into vessels, but cast the bad away. So shall it be at the end of the world: the angels shall come forth, and sever the wicked from among the just, And shall cast them into the furnace of fire: there shall be wailing and gnashing of teeth (Matthew 13:47–50 KJV).

> The Kingdom is like a wise fisherman who cast his net into the sea and drew it up from the sea full of small fish. Among them the wise fisherman found a fine large fish. He threw all the small fish back into the sea and chose the large fish without difficulty. Whoever has ears to hear, let him hear (Thomas 8).

The version of Matthew may have gone through two revisions. The most primitive ended at the first verse: the kingdom of God indiscriminately catches all sorts of people.

This is not possible in the version of Thomas because for him the kingdom is like the wise fisherman who divides his catch. On the other hand, Matthew likens the kingdom to the indiscriminate net. The second revision, which ends at verse 48, has the division which is integral to Thomas but it does not at this stage necessarily refer to the 'end of the world'. The final revision takes Matthew beyond Thomas by referring specifically to the end of the world.

> Therefore every scribe [which is] instructed unto the kingdom of heaven is like unto a man [that is] an householder, which bringeth forth out of his treasure [things] new and old (Matthew 13:52 KJV).

This is probably Matthew's own parable (it is found only in Matthew) about who he considers himself to be, namely a scholar who is trained in the kingdom. The scholar has the ability to bring forth both from the new dispensation and from the old dispensation, which is particularly true of Matthew, who quotes so diligently from the Old Testament.

Summary and Conclusion

We started this chapter by asking the fundamental question of how we received our tradition about what Jesus had said. This line of questioning led us to explore conversion stories, their socio-economic context and the life style of the people. We found that the people who followed Jesus belonged to the lowest social class, the destitute. That Jesus' followers were designated as prophets seems equally significant. The model of discipleship used by Jesus was one already known from past prophetic figures. This meant that when

Jesus' disciples travelled they were acting as prophets, as prophet servants on behalf of the master prophet, namely Jesus. Anyone who accepted any of the disciples accepted Jesus.

We also considered the Cynic hypothesis that has received much support in recent times. Though there was no direct relationship, it served to bring into contrast meaning and modes of expression. The modes of expression were similar both in words and in life styles. Yet the content was different because the context was different, that is, the social situation and the Jewish historical popular background. One of the important differences between the Cynics and the Jesus prophets was the development of a community, a community that became an *ekklesia*, a church.

We then looked at various sayings that are attributed to Jesus. The two first sayings related to the life of the Jesus prophets. The first saying had a form that made it easy to remember, the second did not. The important characteristic of both sayings was the immediate applicability to the life of the Jesus prophets. Memorability and transmission of short sayings often depend on their applicability to real life because the sayings are put into context. As the context changes, the process of recollection changes the saying to fit it.

This became particularly clear in our analysis of parables. The parables, like the last saying, discuss the nature of the kingdom of God. With the exception of two Matthew/Thomas parables, these parables present the kingdom of God in a non-apocalyptic fashion. The kingdom of God, as a concept, undergoes a thorough change in the teachings of Jesus. In Jesus' teachings the kingdom of God is a silent conquest rather than the apocalyptic vision of John the Baptist. Jesus emerges as the fulfilment of John's promise but is quite different from what most probably imagined the Coming One to be. To effect this reversal Jesus used parables as a means of persuading His audience. It is also important to note that though Jesus changed the notion of the kingdom of God, He stayed within the established sign system, although imbuing it with new significance. Rather than rejecting the kingdom of God in an apocalyptic flare, He announced its arrival, albeit in a symbolic sense.

In many significant ways, however, we find points of agreement that would explain why a large number of the followers of the Baptist turned to Jesus. Most of all was Jesus' appeal to the poor, who, as we saw in the last chapter, were also likely to have made up the majority of John the Baptist's followers. In Jesus we see some of John's criticism of the Scribes and, as we shall see, of the temple. Jesus too required just behaviour, the sharing of property and the cessation of oppressive behaviour. In the case of Jesus, however, this is followed by a radical change in life style.

In general we saw a process of developing sensitivity towards moderate communities. Thus we saw a community that retained radical ethics but abandoned radical life styles. This ran parallel to a process of the teachings spreading into higher social spheres.

In addition to the picture of Jesus as an Elijah, in looking at the Gospel of Thomas and Q material we come to see Jesus as a speaker of wisdom. In Q, for example, Jesus becomes the emissary of God's wisdom (Matthew 11:19 = Luke 7:35). Perhaps a more specific image of Jesus is that of Jesus as Solomon (Matthew 12:42 = Luke 11:31).

Theissen in his *A Theory of Primitive Christianity* demonstrates that Jesus taught His poor disciples to act as kings in the sense of adopting royal ethics. Kings and Jesus' disciples rule a kingdom (Q, Matthew 5:3 = Luke 6:20), they judge (Q, Matthew 19:28 = Luke 22:30) and they bring peace (Matthew 5:9).[378] Even the ethics of doing good to enemies had resonances with royal ethics.[379] Being merciful and a benefactor were also royal virtues.[380] The ethics that Jesus taught contribute to the impression that the Solomon figure may have been applied to Him.

We noted in the beginning that Mark worked into his narrative a remark that Jesus taught not like the Scribes but as one having authority. How did the Scribes teach? With the authority of scripture. Jesus' mode of speech and argumentation was based, not on exegesis of scripture but on the authority of His own person, just as we would expect of a popular prophet.

6

The Mighty Works

Next to the words of Jesus stand His deeds. They are equally a part of His revelation, as they are portrayed side by side with His utterances.

While it is popular to believe or disbelieve in the miracles narrated in the gospel, belief is not central to this chapter. Whether or not the miracles took place is outside the purview of science. This is not to say that history cannot discover whether an alleged supernatural event has a natural explanation. On the other hand, history cannot methodologically presume that supernatural events cannot happen, as this is, in itself, a theological presumption.

As for literal and symbolic interpretation, we shall see that each type of interpretation has its value in its respective medium.

An Overview of Transmission and Contextualization

When speaking of miracles in the gospels three words are commonly used in the KJV: 'miracles', 'mighty works' and 'signs'. The word most commonly translated as 'miracle' or 'sign' is the Greek word σημεῖον (*semeion*). This portrays the miracle as a demonstration of God's purpose. Another word used is δύναμις (*dunamis*), which is always translated as 'mighty works' (where miracles are concerned) but is also used, for example, in the Lord's prayer as 'power' or in the Olive Discourse, when speaking of Christ's return 'with power and great glory'. The word portrays God's active involvement and intercession in human affairs. Lastly we should note that the word ἔργον (*ergon*) is also often translated as 'works' but may be better translated as 'deed', as it does not imply anything miraculous. Throughout the Synoptic Gospels, in the KJV, it is a consistent rule that miraculous 'works' are distinguished from deeds by the addition of the word 'mighty'. John, however, employs another language altogether and never once does he use the word δύναμις but instead employs σημεῖον, which is often translated as 'sign' or 'miracle'. This has led to confusion in some translations: 'But if I do, though ye believe not me, believe the works: that ye may know, and believe, that the Father [is] in me, and I in him' (John 10:38 KJV). Here 'works' might be taken to imply miraculous works and the NIV supports this view in its translation: 'But if I do it, even though you do not believe me, believe the miracles, that the Father is in me and I in the Father' (NIV). This is more correctly translated in the Weymouth's New Testament as: 'But if they are, then even if you do not believe me, at least believe the deeds, that you may know and see clearly that the Father is in me, and that I am in the Father' (WEY). The translation of the NIV can be regarded as flawed since the word employed is ἔργοις (i.e. deeds). But could a deed not be a miracle? It certainly could. But as we shall see, it is almost certainly in the plain sense that John intends it.

Be that as it may, most of the narratives about Jesus are a framework around His teachings and discourses and are the construction of the evangelists. Only miracle stories are generally believed to be the reverse, so that the story that circulated was the most memorable part of the story and the words given to Jesus were created to suit the storyline. For example, Jesus said to the man with a crippled hand 'stretch forth your hand' but are those words not merely created for the context of the story? Such statements are – as on those occasions of movement when Jesus says He will go to this or that place – mere narrative devices. It is not, of course, that Jesus did not say mundane things, such as greetings or everyday conversation with those close to Him but these reports do not survive the oral transmission. It is generally agreed that John used a so-called Sign Source, which was a collection of miracle stories which he inserted into his own gospel.[381]

Before we embark on our survey of the miracles of Jesus, we would do well to make some general observations about the literary context of these stories. First it is necessary to establish what type of literature we are dealing with, for this is essential to our understanding of the stories. The stories about miracles are aretological[382] but play other significant roles in the context of the gospel into which they are incorporated. The conclusion of the hypothetical Sign Source is reproduced in John's second to last chapter and again in an exaggerated version in the last chapter. 'Many other signs therefore did Jesus in the presence of the disciples, which are not written in this book: but these are written, that ye may believe that Jesus is the Christ, the Son of God; and that believing ye may have life in his name' (John 20:30–1 ASV).[383]

In other words, for the author of the source material the reason for compiling these miracle stories was to generate faith and ultimately give eternal life.[384] For John this is also an acceptable conclusion for the purpose of his gospel, although for John signs are more than just miracles. To speculate about the purpose of miracle stories before their incorporation of first the Sign Source and then the Gospel of John is both a social analysis and a genre-critical judgement.

Stories which are told about a person who is central in some way to the community in which the story is told reflect the identity of the community. The transition between event and the shaping of the narrative comes through the medium of the individual who sees and recounts the event. That the narrative must be retold to conform to the individual and later to the community in which it was transmitted is a given. The stories are primarily for the use of the community and serve to reinforce its perception of itself. In a comparison of the passion narrative of Mark and John, Crossan writes:

> For Mark, the passion of Jesus starts and ends in agony and desolation. For John, the passion of Jesus starts and ends in control and command. Both speak, equally but divergently, to different times and places, situations and communities. Mark's Jesus speaks to a persecuted community and shows them how to die. John's Jesus speaks to a defeated community and shows them how to live.[385]

An illustration of this may be found in the infancy narrative of Thomas, which contains a miracle that most Christians find repugnant (and rightly so):

> Now the son of Annas the scribe was standing there with Joseph; and he took a branch of willow and with it dispersed the water which Jesus had collected. When Jesus saw what he had done he was angry and said to him, 'insolent, godless ignoramus, what harm did the pools and the waters do to you? Behold, now you also shall wither

> like a tree and shall bear neither leaves nor root nor fruit.' And immediately that child withered up completely (Infancy Thomas 3:1–3).[386]

The miracle in itself is no more extraordinary than some of the miracles found in the canonical writings but it could never be received among orthodox Christians, for this is not the Jesus that Christians follow. If they followed such a person, what would that tell us about Christians? By this the present author does not suggest that Jesus did not shape Christianity, for surely those who followed Jesus believed His teachings and deeds and followed Him and in turn gave the message to those who were willing to accept the image of the Master they had never met, except through those who believed in Him. So the miracles are very relevant, not because they portray history but because they portray the type of person that Jesus was perceived to be. It is important to ask why a particular story was told. This is one of the central questions that will be asked in this survey.

Most scholars today agree that Jesus probably did heal some people, whether psychosomatically or by divine intervention. Numerous independent sources indicate this. But to look for a historical event behind such stories is not only fruitless but goes against the spirit in which the stories are told both orally and, as we shall see, in the gospels.

Now that we have discussed oral tradition, its creation and formation, let us also consider the transition from that state into a textual one. Werner H. Kelber provides the following insight:

> If the process of textualization injects a controversial, metaphorical element into the heroic stories, sharpens the mythoclastical function of the didactic stories, and, as we shall see, introduces a parabolic hermeneutic, one must

> question whether this thrust toward the mythoclastic and parabolic is compatible with the elevation of the most heroic and mythopoetic form to the position of genre determinant.[387]

Three important points raised here are particularly valuable in this discussion. The process of textualization 'introduces a parabolic hermeneutic', which means that the parabolic element of a story may be subconscious when the tradition is in an oral state but when it becomes text the writer is detached from the story. The writer who sees his own text is suddenly able to perceive something in it which may or may not have been in the original, which is difficult when the story is still a part of the narrator. For didactic stories this also means that they become, to a greater degree, expressed through the supernatural. This point will be discussed further below. The last point is that when these stories become part of the gospels they become part of a different genre and do not determine the genre of the work they are included in. It is therefore not logical to call the gospels aretological or even to understand their presence as having the same function as they had before their inclusion. Kelber explains in detail:

> In these [the miracle stories] and other instances, Markan textuality has brought forth significations barely or not at all present in orality . . . This metaphorical proclivity or sign-character of the synoptic miracle stories has frequently been observed, but Madeleine Boucher deserves credit for having boldly linked it with the linguisticality of parables: '. . . the miracles, as they are treated in Mark, are similar to the parables in having more than one level of meaning and are thus subject to the same misunderstanding as the parables.'[388]

Let us first consider the possibility of these parabolic elements that are barely or not at all evident in the oral state. As we will see later, the miracle stories belong to the same social class as the Jesus prophets. If these early Christians thought of Jesus as the 'representative' of God, then they must also have understood His acts to be 'representative' of God. God's miraculous acts through Jesus were 'characteristic' of the way God acted towards His people, in the same way that the parables about the kingdom of God demonstrated the way God acted towards His people. As we may recall from the previous chapter, in the mission commandment the prophets of Jesus also performed healing. In this way they were not emulating Jesus' life and sayings but performed the same message latent in miraculous acts.

But if the gospels are not aretologies, what are they? This is the question which we, with the benefit of the above thoughts, will deal with in our genre-criticism of the gospel. What genre do we understand the gospels to be? Many would say, as did Rudolf Bultmann, that it is a completely new genre which was invented to fill a need in the early Christian community. But most recent studies tend to support the idea that the gospels have enough common ground with Greco-Roman biographies for it to be significant.

The language of the Gospel of Mark has been categorized by some as 'street talk'. This is not quite an accurate description. David E. Aune explains:

> Recently Marius Riesner has demonstrated that many so-called 'Semitisms' in Mark (i.e. Hebrew or Aramaic idioms awkwardly expressed in Greek) are common in Greek popular literature. The style of Mark, therefore, is a popular literary style, even though it does not rise to the literary standards of the highly educated.[389]

Richard A. Burridge set out to test the thesis that the gospels are a type of Greco-Roman biography in his book *What are the Gospels?* In his conclusion he writes:

> In fact, such an approach has now demonstrated from an analysis of many generic features that both the four canonical gospels and the Graeco-Roman βίος exhibit a clear family resemblance. The genre of βίος is flexible and diverse, with variation in the pattern of features from one βίος to another. The gospels also diverge from the pattern in some aspects but not to any greater degree than other βίοι; in other words they have at least as much in common with Graeco-Roman βίοι as the βίοι have with each other. Therefore, the gospels must belong to the genre of βίος.[390]

Well aware of these discrepancies, we now move on with the idea that certain functions within the gospels are similar to that of the Greco-Roman biography. As for the function of the genre as a whole, Aune suggests that 'the unconscious functions of Greco-Roman biography involve the historical legitimation (or discrediting) of a social belief/value system personified in the subject of the biography'.[391]

This description fits well with what we understand to be the function of the aretological material in the gospels. There are two features of this legitimization which are relevant for understanding the purpose of miracle stories within the gospels' literary context: first, the legitimization of the community in terms of what it is and, second, the legitimization of its claims about who Jesus was. The fact that Jesus was the Messiah is, of course, central to the community's legitimization, otherwise it cannot explain its rightful separation from its Jewish roots. This is the reason for the quotations from scripture: proving Jesus to be their fulfilment is an essential aspect of the evangelists' conscious efforts to legitimize Jesus' position and that of His community.

The content of the gospels is not Hellenistic but Israelite/Jewish. Aune in this connection mentions two stories that seem to have served as 'literary paradigms'. First is the story of Moses, who towers above all the Jewish prophets. This story is reflected in the gospels' effort to portray Jesus as 'a new Moses (the pattern reflected in Matthew) and as a means of conceptualizing Jesus as the eschatological Mosaic prophet, a pattern reflected in the fourth gospel'.[392] Thus, says Aune, it is most important in this connection to note that 'the literary framework of the story of Moses in the Pentateuch was influential in shaping the generic features of the Gospels as literature'.[393] The other literary paradigm is 'the Elijah-Elisha cycle', whereby a striking number of miracles have their parallels in the gospels. We shall in the following analysis point out such parallels. As mentioned in previous chapters, there seems to have been a conscious effort to understand Jesus as an Elijah figure. So these parallels may have been formative even at an oral stage.

Charles A. Briggs also presupposes that a Hellenistic influence was partially responsible for the form and structure of the gospels:

> The New Testament writers employed the Greek Language and the Septuagint version. It is probable that the great majority of the earliest Christians were Hellenist. Naturally the influence of Philo and the allegorical method became great. We see that influence already in the epistle to the Hebrews and the Johannine writings.[394]

Practically all miracle narratives are shaped in the form of some Old Testament story that transfers the archetype of the story onto Jesus. So the miracle stories serve in part to describe Jesus as one who has the virtues of the figures of the past. At the same time we can briefly look at some Jewish-Hellenistic biographies that demonstrate how Old Testament biographies are understood as allegorical and thus provide an exegetical key for the stories retold about Jesus.

Before we deal with Philo, who wrote an extensive biography of Moses, we shall first look at Josephus, who was also influenced by this trend. In the introduction to his *Antiquities of the Jews* he sets out to explain his primary source, the Old Testament:

> While our legislator [Moses] speaks some things wisely but enigmatically, and others under a decent of allegory [ἀλληγοροῦντος] but still explains such things as required a direct explication plainly and expressly.[395]

Josephus goes on to say that in the present work he will not explain these allegories but that if God wills it he will do this after its completion. Unfortunately, this later work either was never written or else it has not survived. It is interesting to see that while Josephus is plainly aware of the allegorical nature of scripture,[396] he has no problem using it as history. As we start this survey of the miracles of Jesus, we shall also look at some parallel texts from Philo, by whom Josephus is very obviously influenced.

Miracles may be divided into the categories of effective miracles (i.e. mighty works) and visual miracles (i.e. signs). Some clearly fall into one category and others could be placed in either. The healing miracles may be considered to be effective miracles, whereas the transfiguration of Jesus on Mount Hermon may be considered a visual miracle. If this division of miracles into two categories is acceptable, one may furthermore come to the conclusion that miracles have two purposes. The first is the effective miracle, prompted by the faith of people as exemplified by the statements found in Matthew 9:29–30, 13:58.

The second category, the visual miracles, are performed to increase the faith of the believers. This type of miracle was denied the unbelieving. Mark clearly states that there is 'no sign' for 'this generation' (Mark 8:12) but Matthew (12:38–40) and Luke (11:29–30) include a tradition from Q that elaborates the Markan tradition. The 'sign of the prophet Jonas' is interpreted as the preaching of Jesus, for the Ninevites only heard the preaching of Jonas and repented. It is generally held that Q did not have the elaboration contained in Matthew and that Luke presents Q's true understanding of the 'sign of the Prophet Jonas'.[397] We might say that Q, a sayings document, accepts one sign, which is itself.

Let us now return to the previously discussed chapter in Luke in which some of the unbelieving accuse Jesus of being in league with the Devil. After refuting this notion, Jesus adds: 'But if I with the finger of God cast out devils, no doubt the kingdom of God is come upon you' (Luke 11:20 KJV).

The 'finger of God'[398] is a theophanic symbol[399] from the Pentateuch. It appears in two connections: 1) when God shows Pharaoh His wrath and 2) when God inscribes the Ten Commandments on stone tablets. Thus one may interpret the use of this symbol in two ways: 1) through the power invested by the Father in Jesus He is able to command the evil spirit to leave the tormented. As in its parallel (Exodus 11:20), God stands out as the all-powerful, who shows His mercy by exercising His dominion. 2) One may also interpret this verse using the theophanic symbol as the Holy Spirit, in its parallel through which God reveals His Ten Commandments. In this verse, His revelation frees the sinner from an evil spirit. The exegesis one chooses reflects what one considers to be God's way of dealing with His people. Since this is a part of the Q tradition and the attitude that document shows towards miracles, it seems that the latter option is more plausible. These are followed by allegations of Jesus being in league with the Devil and requests for signs to be shown, which are denied. We should remember that the evangelist is the author of context and the context is what gives the different units their meaning.

Dunn notes that in terms of the attitude towards miracles as creating faith (even with those who have none), Luke is, unlike other New Testament authors, quite positive.[400] Dunn states that the two factors that differentiate Luke from Jesus with regard to miracles are: 1) Jesus 'seems to have rejected outright the idea that miracles were valuable for their propaganda or sign effect' and 2) the 'emphasis he placed on the faith of the one requesting healing'.[401]

An Appraisal of the Different Types of Miracles

Now let us examine several types of miracle portrayed in the gospels. There are many methods available to those wishing to analyse miracles. Particularly well-known, for example, is Gerd Theissen's synchronical and diachronical analysis.[402] The present author will, however, do a fairly simple two-part analysis in which we will 1) look at the purpose of miracle stories in their oral stage and 2) consider the significance given to them by their integration into the written medium.

Healing

In the gospels first and foremost are the miracles of healing illnesses. These include everything from minor sicknesses to actual death. All of these fall into the category of active miracles and, as the above-mentioned definition requires, these miracles are only performed in response to faith.

In Matthew 9:1f we find a story of the man sick of the palsy. Palsy, as does any sickness, causes a loss of honour and social standing. In the specific case of palsy, the illness is particularly debilitating for a craftsman. The illness would not only deprive him of his social standing but also of his ability to carry out his trade and, as a consequence, his ability to survive. It follows that this type of story would have the greatest importance amongst craftsmen, to whom it would give assurance that Jesus could help them should they have such a debilitating illness.

But the evangelist, as has been mentioned, sees a more spiritual side to the story. This is indicated by statements such as: 'And, behold, they brought to him a man sick of the palsy, lying on a bed: and Jesus seeing their faith said unto the sick of the palsy; Son, be of good cheer; thy sins be forgiven thee' (Matthew 9:2 KJV).

Here the faith of the sick is their healing. The addition of the comment 'thy sins be forgiven thee' is thought-provoking, as no mention has been made of the sick man's sins, only his palsy. This clearly demonstrates the allegorical interpretation which Matthew sees in it. For Matthew, sin and disease are the same. Pedersen states that 'Bodily suffering cannot be something isolated. It is the soul that suffers, being dissolved powerless, devoid of vitality, and the power to keep upright.'[403] Here the miracle is probably shaped after Psalm 103:3 about Yahweh. This could have been part of the story in its oral version. Matthew places the story in a larger context, the controversy with the Pharisees. It is in this context that we find an explicit statement regarding the parabolic meaning of the miracle itself. Here Jesus responds to the allegation of the Pharisees about His companionship with publicans and sinners by affirming that: 'They that be whole need not a physician, but they that are sick' (Matthew 9:12 KJV).

Matthew follows with another controversial story which probably circulated in the same environment. Here the illness is a 'withered hand'. In fact the Gospel of the Nazaraean explains that the man was a mason who came to have his health restored by Jesus: 'I was a mason and earned (my) living with (my) hands; I beseech thee, Jesus, to restore to me my health that I may not with ignominy have to beg for my bread.'[404]

The miracle may be best read in the context of Psalm 137:5.[405] Again the controversial story reveals the symbolic interpretation that the evangelist gives to it. Here Jesus' opponents attempt to frame Him by asking if it is lawful to heal on the Sabbath (which it is not). He responds that they themselves would get their sheep out of a hole on a Sabbath (which is lawful) and with almost Mishnaic logic concludes that it must therefore be lawful to do good on a Sabbath (Matthew 12:10–12).[406] The scene is introduced with the seemingly odd query: why should 'they' (the unbelieving Pharisees) ask a question which so directly implied that He, Jesus of Nazareth, had already performed real miracles? The answer may be found in Christ's reply which, if taken at face value, is equally odd since the Pharisees were not shepherds and would probably never be found in such a situation. It would make more sense if it were to be taken as an allusion to Jesus' own title as the shepherd of the lost sheep of Israel (Matthew 15:24). Thus

Matthew, by combining a miracle story and a pronouncement story, presents an allegorical interpretation of the miracle story to his reader. The imagery reappears in Matthew 9:35–6 where Jesus compassionately teaches and heals in villages because 'they fainted, and were scattered abroad, as sheep having no shepherd' (KJV).

Young's literal translation interprets the word σώζω, which is translated 'made whole' in the above verse, as 'saved', as does the KJV on 92 other occasions (out of 110) where the word appears in the New Testament.[407]

Matthew also tells the story of a woman afflicted with a haemorrhage: 'And Jesus having turned about, and having seen her, said, "Be of good courage, daughter, thy faith hath saved thee", and the woman was saved from that hour' (Matthew 9:22 YLT).

This is yet another case of how spiritual and physical health are coupled. This is what Q (Luke 7:22 = Matthew 11:2–6) does with Jesus' response to the enquiry of the followers of John the Baptist. Further, Q couples it with the preaching of the gospel to the poor.

To this one may also add the miracles of casting out devils. This is, of course, not usually accounted as healing but rather as exorcism. The present author's reason for including this in the same category is that many cultures consider evil spirits to be the cause of ill health, both mental and physical. Sinful behaviour was often attributed to the working of evil spirits. Some demons were called after the sickness that they caused such as 'Headache' or 'Fever'.[408]

Josephus reports that a certain Jew called Eleazar freed some men from demons in front of Vespian, his sons and some of his men. This was done with the aid of a ring, the seal of which had been pressed against a root. The ring was then put under the nose of the possessed after which an incantation invoking the name of Solomon was pronounced. Finally he commanded the spirit to overturn a small cup of water to prove to the spectators that it had left the man.[409]

Matthew 8:16 represents Jesus as an exorcist where the act itself is linked to a 'word', which could be his preaching the gospel (most likely the way the evangelist understood it) but could also refer to the form of incantations made by a certain Joshua ben Perahyah in the Jewish environs of Jerusalem in the 2nd and 1st centuries BCE.[410]

Mark 5:1ff presents a curious tradition of Jesus travelling into the domain of Philip where He casts out a demon called Legion into a flock of swine that then precipitates itself into the Sea of Galilee. The Romans had a legion (about 6,000 soldiers) stationed in Syria.[411] The allusion seems almost too clear: these soldiers were like demon-possessed swine, unclean and unwelcome.[412] These elements and allusions seem to be tied together with its original context and probably represent the original intention.

Another tradition found in Matthew 8:5–13, Luke 7:1–10 and John 4:45–54 concerns a Roman official whose servant or slave was sick and who asked Jesus to heal him, which Jesus did from a distance. The Jesus Seminar maintains that there is a Q text behind the story but that John retains a more original version.[413] Reconstruction of all save the centurion's address is difficult, however, since only it has a significant word for word correspondence. In general, the Matthean sense is believed to retain the central thrust of Q, that Jesus was amazed by the great faith shown by the centurion.[414] John's account does not refer to a centurion (ἑκατοντάρχης) but to an official (βασιλικὸς) with no ethnicity attached to him. Kloppenborg therefore seems correct in proposing that Q introduces the theme of Gentile faith into the story.[415] John has its story from the Sign Gospel in which faith was not even an issue and in which verse 48 is believed to be an insertion.[416] According to Kloppenborg, the process of introducing Gentiles into the story had already started in the oral stage prior to it coming into Q.[417] The extent to which this happened, however, remains speculative. The core of the story seems to be that Jesus cured a sick person at a distance at the request of a powerful individual.

In Mark 10:46–52 we hear of Bartimaeus, a beggar from Jericho who is kept back by the crowds but who Jesus called forth and asked what he wanted. The beggar asked for his sight and was granted it through his faith. This follows the repeated pattern of stories of healing: first the disease is noted and its circumstances explained; second, the petition and demonstration of faith; third, the pronouncement of the cure being effected; and last, ascertainment that the cure has in fact taken place. The focus here seems to be on the faith demonstrated by the beggar in his perseverance in wanting to see Jesus regardless of the opposition of the crowd. The social value of such a narrative should not be missed. Not only does it encourage Christians to endure oppression, it speaks to the community and the rights of the socially impaired – those who are commonly on the periphery of the community – to be part of it. Thus Jesus, by His miraculous power, brings those who are outside into the circle of fellowship.

Among healing miracles we find parallels between the healing of lepers in Mark 1:40–5, Matthew 11:4–5 and Luke 7:21–2 with Elisha's healing of Naaman the Syrian (2 Kings 5).

From Philo's *Legum Allegoria* we have an interpretation

of a law, which seems relevant to the above passages:

> 'Cursed again is he who causes a blind man to go astray in the way' (Deut. xxvii. 18) . . . And these also are acts of pleasure, the utterly godless one; for sense by itself is a blind thing, inasmuch as it is irrational, for it is the reasoning faculty that confers sight . . . As it is, pleasure has organized such a shrewd device against the soul, that it has compelled it to employ blind guides, inducing it by delusive wiles to change virtue for evil things, and to surrender its innocence and receive wickedness in lieu of it.[418]

The resurrection stories of John 11:1–45[419] and particularly Luke 7:11–17 have their parallel in Elijah's revival of the son of the widow of Zarephath (1 Kings 17:17–24) and Elisha's raising the son of the Shunammite (2 Kings 4:18–37).

Food and Drink

Next let us look at the miracles that pertain to food and drink. The feeding of the multitudes is one of the most well-known miracles of Jesus. We may place these in the category of effective miracles. Let us now have a look at the context in which these miracles appear.

Mark (7:26–30) tells a story about a woman 'a Greek, a Syrophoenician by race' (Ελληνίς συροφοινίκισσα τῷ γένει), who comes to Jesus to procure a miracle for her daughter who has been possessed by a demon. But instead of granting her wish, Jesus says (verse 27): 'Let the children first be filled: for it is not meet to take the children's bread and cast it to the dogs.' As Theissen notes, 'Then, as now, to call someone a "dog" was an insult.'[420] But the woman shrewdly answers (verse 28): 'Yea, Lord; even the dogs under the table eat of the children's crumbs' (ASV). Whereafter the woman receives her wish. Now why would Jesus insult a woman coming humbly for His help? Theissen suggests that the tension between Tyre and Galilee form the background of this story[421] and it seems reasonable that here the words attributed to Jesus and the Syrophoenician woman are not the constructions of the evangelist but belong to an oral tradition received by Mark. That is, of course, not to say that the oral tradition actually reports Jesus' words; however, the short dialogue has all of the attributes necessary to survive oral transmission. It involves the use of the parabolic and has strong and poignant points. Jesus' statement is in fact a reversal of the actual situation. The Jewish peasants were eating the crumbs off the table of the rich Greek-speaking citizens. Indeed, the nature of the miracle asked for by the woman has no importance for the integrity of the story. What is central here is the imagery, in which salvation (bread on which one can survive) is equated with a miracle.

Mark retains much of the oral wording and purpose while Matthew makes many interpretative comments. Although the favour asked for is an exorcism, which again links the sickness with sin by the term 'lost sheep', the symbol used is that of bread. Jesus' healing power, which has previously been linked to His preaching of the gospel, is for the 'house of Israel'. Being wise and full of faith, however, the appeal of the woman of Canaan (as she is named in Matthew) is accepted and 'crumbs' are given to her.

It is undoubtedly no coincidence that Matthew couples this directly with the miracle of the feeding of the four thousand, while Mark has the story of the healing of the blind and dumb.[422] For Matthew the parabolic language of the miracle with the Canaanite woman points to the interpretation of the miracle of the feeding. In this story Jesus tells His disciples that the multitude that have followed Him are starving and that if nothing is done they will surely die. The disciples object that there is no supply of food but Jesus orders the multitudes to sit, takes the bread, breaks it and, giving thanks, distributes it among them and, blessing the fish, distributes that too. When the multitudes are filled, seven baskets of bread remain.

In its oral stage this miracle may have had two contexts. First and foremost it was a consolation to the poor and destitute, to whom food is always in the forefront of the mind. Second, the miracle may have had a more specific meaning in that the Eucharist is alluded to by the breaking of the bread. The miracle is a fellowship meal in which the poor received a meal from those Christians who had wealth in abundance.

A parallel to this event is found in Elijah's multiplication of 20 loaves for a hundred men (2 Kings 4:42–4).

Mark 8:10–13 follows this event with Jesus' dismissal of the Pharisees (and Sadducees, according to Matthew) and their request for a miracle. Reflecting back on these two events is a short story in which Jesus spoke of the 'leaven of the Pharisees and leaven of Herod' (verse 15). The disciples misunderstood the reference and Jesus reproached them for not seeing or hearing, not perceiving or understanding (verses 17–18). He then referred them to the miracle of the feeding and by that seemingly provided the interpretation of the saying about leaven but in reality Mark is here providing an interpretation for the miracle of feeding. In other words, Mark is letting the reader know that bread is like teaching and that the feeding is to be understood as Jesus teaching His doctrine. This section is an invention of Mark. Here the rebuke to 'this generation', in the previous section, is interpreted as referring to a specific group; the rebuking, directed towards the disciples, itself is characteristic of Mark's polemics against them. Again the pattern of textualization shows a process of spiritualization through the insertion of a metaphorical element.

In the parable of the feast of the kingdom the meal is used as a metaphor for partaking in the kingdom of God: 'For I say unto you, That none of those men which were bidden shall taste of my supper' (Luke 14:24 KJV).

From rabbinical tradition we have the story of the wife of Rabbi Hanina ben Dosa who had no bread but who, out of shame, put the lid on her oven to give the impression that she was baking bread. Her neighbour, however, knowing that she had nothing, became curious when she saw the smoke from Rabbi Hanina ben Dosa's chimney. She went to the house and knocked on the door. The wife retired into a room ashamed. Then a miracle happened and the neighbour saw bread in the oven and dough to spare (Talmud, Ta'anith 24b–35a).

In another tradition Simeon and his son were hiding in a cave and miraculously a water well and a carob tree appeared (Talmud, Shabbath 33b). Elsewhere is a story of a man whose wife was too poor to provide a wet-nurse for his baby and so a miracle occurred and he grew breasts so he could provide for the child himself. This story was a prelude for a discussion about creation between two rabbis (Talmud, Shabbath 53b).

Here we may draw on Philo, who discusses the allegorical meaning of the manna, the miracle of Moses in the desert:

> 'Behold I rain upon you bread out of heaven, and the people shall go out and they shall gather the day's portion for a day, that I may prove them whether they will walk by My law or not' (Exod. xvi. 4). You see that the soul is fed not with the things of earth that decay, but with such words as God shall have poured like rain out of that lofty and pure region of life to which the prophet has given the title of 'heaven'.[423]

Finally, let us evaluate the statements contained in John. The same event of feeding the multitudes is told in John in his sixth chapter. Here the event is followed by a long sermon about Jesus being the bread of life.

The feeding, we recall, involved both bread and fish. Below we will consider how fish play a similar role in the imagery of Christian tradition. Let us consider the miracles concerning catching fish in the lake (Luke 5:1–7). Here Jesus enters a boat with Simon and other disciples and tells them to throw down their nets. Simon objects that they are tired and have been unsuccessful in catching anything all night but accepts Jesus' word. The nets miraculously fill up to breaking point so that an additional ship has to be summoned to bring in the catch.

The story has clearly retained many of its oral features. It shows awareness of such problems as being unable to catch fish, which was undoubtedly a problem with which fishermen were familiar. On the other hand, who but a fisherman could think of a net breaking (i.e. the limitation of tools) or that a boat could become overloaded? These are unlikely to have been conceived of by a retainer. Luke couples the story with the commandment to become fishers of men (Luke 5:10). Thus a metaphor is established: a caught fish is a converted man. The reaction of Peter here is surprising. As Evans comments, 'Conviction of sin is not elsewhere a natural or expected response to miracle' but finds neither the explanation that it is a reaction to the parable nor that it is in reaction to the epiphany to be convincing.[424] But if we suppose that this image is inherited from the community sacrament of conversion, this may lead to an alternative reading. The Didache has the confession of sins on two occasions but in fact may be referring to the same event (4:14,14:1). On the occasion of the day of the Lord, prior to the Eucharist, one makes a confession of sins so that one's 'offering may be pure'. Though the Didache does not associate it with other sacraments, it may be implied that prior to receiving baptism or prior to the two-day fast that precedes it, such a confession took place. Whether this is true or not for the community of the Didache, it remains a fairly plausible explanation for the Lukan text. In addition, John 21:1–8[425] has a similar story with many of the same oral features but without the confession of Peter. Yet in it the same thing happens. Jesus was unknown to the disciples and after the miracle they knew who He was. If the sacrament of baptism is the common 'hidden image' behind these stories, this explains the common thread of going from a state of not knowing Jesus to a state of recognition.

Before we go on to the next group of miracles, we should also consider the miracle mentioned in John where water at a wedding is turned into wine (John 2:1–11).[426] In this story, Mary the mother of Jesus, as well as He and His disciples, were invited to a wedding in Cana. During the feast the wine ran out and Mary informed Jesus. Jesus ordered six stone water jars and when the governor of the feast tasted the water, he found that it had become exquisite wine.

Immediately we detect a difference in the level of

concern from the stories we have looked at so far. Running short of wine during a wedding is hardly life threatening. So in what social milieu would such a miracle be relevant and be able to circulate? Jerome H. Neyrey points out the immense importance of honour in the Mediterranean world and that it was by that system that a human being was measured. Wealth was an important factor in how a family was perceived and weddings were social venues in which a family could display that wealth. Neyrey concludes that 'Insufficiency of wine at a wedding feast would bring incalculable shame on a family'.[427] In other words, we are here looking at a tradition that probably belonged to a middle class or upper lower class.[428]

But in John we find a new meaning for this tradition. One hint about the new meaning is found in the statement of the governor of the feast: 'And saith unto him, Every man at the beginning doth set forth good wine; and when men have well drunk, then that which is worse: [but] thou hast kept the good wine until now' (John 2:10 KJV).

Notice how the comment of the governor of the feast makes little sense unless we understand the account as allegorical. Where earthly wine causes the tastebuds to become numb 'when men have well drunk', the sweet taste of divine wine remains unchanged no matter how inebriated of it a man may be. The dialogue is typical Johannine[429] in that a part of the dialogue seems to be missing. Jesus takes a simple statement of fact (verse 3) to be a request for a miracle that would signal the beginning of His ministry (verse 4).

This particular miracle is sometimes believed to be connected with the Greek god Dionysus, the god of wine.[430] Again we may readily use one of the exegetical keys of Philo.

Here he is interpreting Melchizedek, who instead of water gave Abraham wine:

> But let Melchizedek instead of water offer wine, and give to souls strong drink, that they may be seized by a divine intoxication, more sober than sobriety itself. For he is a priest, even Reason, having as his portion Him that is, and all his thoughts of God are high and vast and sublime: for he is priest of the Most High (Gen. xiv. 18).[431]

In Mark, when Jesus was asked why He and His disciples did not fast (2:18–20), Mark gave a compound of parables in answer. The parable of the bride and groom, which seems integral to the controversy story, is followed by parables about the new and the old (Mark 2:21–2). By compounding the answers about John fasting and Jesus eating with the parable about the new and the old, Mark is allegorizing a problematic attack on Jesus. By doing so, the attack is reversed into a statement about Jesus and spiritual nourishment; traditional piety is contrasted with a new piety. Mark's situation is, however, different from that of Jesus' disciples (who lived with a sort of perpetual fasting) and his community has had to revert to an 'old' type of piety (Mark 2:20). As such, the compilation of the two sets of parables may date back to a pre-Markan source, while verse 2:20 is more likely to have been inserted by Mark himself. The passages discussed above (Mark 2:18–22) have no direct connection with miracles except to show that, as with many other miracle themes, the compounding of any genre in the gospel (apothagemata, pronouncement stories, miracle stories, parables, controversy stories, etc.) is an operation of contextualization and therefore of interpretation. So just as a miracle about food can be given an interpretation, so also can a parable.

Nature

Next we have the category of miracles where nature is involved. Walking on water, controlling the wind and cursing the fig tree: how shall we categorize these? The first two miracles could be regarded as being visual miracles (i.e. these are seen by some people but when they are over, they have no lasting effect on the material world) but in reality they function as effective miracles, as does the last one.

First let us look at the miracle spoken of in the eighth chapter of Luke (verses 22–5). Here Jesus and the disciples cross a lake in a ship, are suddenly surprised by a storm and their lives are endangered. The disciples wake Jesus. Jesus rebukes the winds and waters, which are subdued, and then rebukes the disciples for their lack of faith.

This miracle, like the miracles of catching fish, probably belongs to fishermen or professional sailors. The main concern is the dangers of the sea (or lake, as it were).

Luke has this story from Mark (4:35–41), who included the words of Jesus' rebuke to the winds. The textuality, the symbolic interpretation, is particularly evident in the dialogue, which has none of the properties necessary for surviving oral transmission. Jesus' rebuke signals that the problem of the disciples is not the weather but the disciples' lack of faith. It stands to reason that Jesus did not rebuke them because there was no danger, for Mark makes plain that the danger was very real. But rather than thanking the disciples for waking Him, when all were in such danger that Jesus was required to stand and use His supernatural powers to subdue the storm, He rebukes them for their lack of faith. Thus Mark interprets the sea as a reflection of the disciples' spirits.

A similar oral tradition seems to be behind the story in John 6:16–21.[432] Here Jesus not only commands the winds,

He walks the waves. The metaphor reaches its conclusion when the disciples are about to accept Jesus into the boat and find that they have come to the projected destination. For John, receiving Jesus, metaphorically, into the boat, is to come to the ultimate spiritual destination.

In the Markan version this feature is missing but the Matthean version (Matthew 14:22–33) has a significant addition in which Peter is allowed through his faith in Jesus to walk with Him but is soon discouraged by the wind and starts to sink. This addition serves further to underscore the metaphorical meaning hidden in Mark. Only if one has faith will one not sink in the sea of uncertainty. Nobody is expected to be able to walk on water but people are expected to be faithful.

These miracles are much like Moses crossing the Red Sea with the people of Israel. Here again we may receive insight from Philo, who comments on these passages from Exodus: 'For we also find that when he that sees God is studying flight from the passions; "for the waves became solid in the midst of the sea" (Exod. xv. 8), in order that he that seeth Him that is mighty pass beyond passion.'[433]

Another parallel is Elijah and Elisha's crossing of the river Jordan (2 Kings 2:8, 14). We recall this motif from the discussion in chapter 2 of Theudas the son of Judas the Galilean.

Finally there is the cursing of the fig tree (Mark 11:12–14 and Matthew 21:18–20). In this story Jesus walks along a road and becomes hungry. When He sees a fig tree He approaches it only to find that it has no fruit. Jesus then curses the tree so that it will never bear fruit again. This story is surprising because it portrays Jesus as a destructive person. When we go on to explore its oral origin, we find that there seems to be no reasonable social context.

Certainly one could find people who were dependent on the harvest of such trees but in a miracle originating from such people we would expect Jesus to bless the tree and for it to immediately bring forth fruit. Consensus amongst commentators is that this miracle was originally a parable[434] which was recast as a miracle story. A parable that looks like the miracle can be found in Luke (13:6–9).[435]

If we were able to reconstruct the parable from the miracle, what might it look like? First of all, only the owner of the tree could have been the man pronouncing the curse. Mark, however, makes a curious remark: he states that it was indeed not the right time of year for fruit and thus is in fact defending the tree that Jesus curses. This remark must therefore be an original defence of the tree. Since the defence cannot be uttered by the tree itself, for parables portray natural events not supernatural ones, it follows that a human representative must have uttered this defence. Likewise, neither can the withering be supernatural and must be in the hands of the curser. The parable should start by introducing each of the elements of the narrative: the one who curses (landowner) and its recipient (gardener/fig tree). The final point should be surprising and shock the listener. Thus the present author reconstructs the parable as follows:

> A landowner came to his gardener and commanded: 'Let me now have the fruits of the fig-tree.' The gardener answered: 'But master, it is not yet the season for fruits.'
>
> And the landowner was angry and said: 'Then give it no more water, so it shall dry up.'

There is a peculiar resemblance between this miracle and the one that is found in the infancy narrative of Thomas (cited above), which is probably no coincidence. Whether

Thomas is dependant on Mark or Matthew or whether they have a common source is difficult to ascertain but the interpretation of Thomas is to some degree true in that the tree refers to a person(s) in an allegoric manner. In the above reconstruction the fig tree represents 'this generation', which refused to accept the kingdom of God because it thinks 'it is not the season'.

Appearances

Lastly, let us deal with the miracle of the transfiguration. It, more clearly than any other miracle, falls into the category of visual miracles. The post-resurrection appearances also fall into this category but will be dealt with in detail in chapter 11.

In this story (Matthew 17:1–9), the disciples of the inner circle (Peter, James and John) are brought to a high mountain. There Jesus is transfigured before them and stands in His full glory. Moses and Elijah appear with Him and Peter proposes the immediate construction of a tabernacle but is interrupted by a heavenly voice reiterating the baptismal adoption formula. The disciples, in fear, fall on their faces and look up only at Jesus' encouragement.

It is immediately evident that there is no likely oral precedent. The story has a theological significance. The purpose of telling this miracle is perhaps to counteract a process of association that is taking place within the gospels themselves, namely the identification of Jesus with the two archetypes that are so often reflected on Him, Moses and Elijah. The evangelists make sure to point out that while Jesus has much in common with these revered figures, He remains independent of them and should be given priority.

Crossan in *The Cross that Spoke* argues convincingly that

the tradition itself is a retrojection of the resurrection appearances:

> There [in Mark] it was no longer a Resurrection-ascension appearance or even the proleptic promise of one. Instead, it was a proleptic promise and a vision of the parousia [the return of Jesus] and was to be told to nobody until *after* the Resurrection (9:9) so that it would be clearly understood as a model, not for it but for the parousia.[436]

From the Gospel of Peter (discussed in chapter 1) Crossan draws parallels between Mark's transfiguration and Peter's ascension narratives. Both have a movement to a high place (Peter 10:40, Mark 9:2), in which there are two figures of great brightness (Peter 9:36, Mark 9:3) and finally a voice out of heaven (Peter 10:41, Mark 9:7).

It may also be noted at this point that the fleeing Simeon and his son mentioned in the section on food and drink were called forth by Elijah with the announcement that the emperor was dead and the decree against Simeon was annulled (Talmud, Shabbath 33b).

Miracle and Anthropology

Although we have seen the prophetic figures of Elijah and Elisha in this chapter, there is another, more general category that anthropologists use in looking at religious specialists. Annemarie de Waal Malefijt develops two distinct categories of religious specialist: the priest and the shaman. The shaman receives his or her powers directly from the divine. The priest, however, receives them from being trained in the practice of ritual.[437] It follows that the personal success of the shaman is directly tied to his connection with the divine. The success of the priest, on the other hand, is tied to his performance of the ritual. If the ritual is ineffective it can be attributed to an incorrect performance of the ritual and the ritual can be redone. Significantly de Waal Malefijt notes that

> . . . shamans are more often considered capable of doing both good and evil, while priests are supposedly less capable of using their powers adversely or less inclined to do so. A shaman is believed capable of prompting the spirits by his powers of persuasion, adjuration, and inducement; he can ask the spirits what he wishes to ask. Priests can theoretically bring about undesired results only by wilfully distorting the ritual.[438]

Perhaps with the shaman/priest conflict in mind, Mark or his source explains that Jesus, after curing the leper, commands him to go to the temple, show himself to the priest and make the prescribed offering (Mark 1:40–4).

This essentially seems to be what is at stake in the accusation levelled against Jesus: that He was in league with Beelzebub (Q, Matthew 12:22–30 = Luke 11:14–23). If a priest performs a ritual and exorcizes a demon, it is through the power of the ritual. The predetermined outcome of the ritual is regulated by the priest's training. When a shaman performs an exorcism, he or she adheres to no form but commands the spirit by virtue of his or her own personal power and is therefore free to command it as he or she pleases. For example, when Jesus exorcizes Legion He does so by speaking to it, not in a ritualistic manner but directly in words that are clearly for the occasion. He diagnoses the problem by forcing the spirit to reveal its identity. Once its identity is known, a means of ridding the man of it is found (Mark 5:2–13).[439]

Another example of shamanistic behaviour is found in

Mark's story in 8:22–6 where spit and laying on hands are used as a means of healing. Above we saw Jesus command the winds (Mark 4:35–41). On both occasions we find Jesus acting as an individual using His personal powers to command or remedy the situation. In neither case does He resort to rituals.

Anthropology has also been used, most recently by Crossan, to explain the healing stories.[440] Crossan makes the 'distinction between *curing disease* and *healing illness*'.[441] The first is a biological issue, the second relates to how people feel. While it is not always possible to cure the disease, social conditions can either help or worsen the well-being of the person afflicted. It follows that the social outlook of a community can cause illness and heal illness. As de Waal Malefijt puts it: 'When a person commits an act culturally defined as wrong or evil, and he feels sufficiently guilty about it, his self-condemnation may well make him physically indisposed.'[442] The individual's sense of wrong and right is generally determined by society. As such, it not only regulates how the individual looks at himself but also how other people look at him.

Social pressures did not necessarily stem from sin as such. Paula Fredriksen explains that in 1st century Judaism there were two forms of impurity. The first was Levitical. There were certain things which, if one came into contact with them, caused one to become impure. Amongst these were semen, menstruation blood and corpses. Contact with these could be unintentional and was in no way considered sinful; however, such contact did disqualify people from participation in the temple cult. The other form of impurity, on the other hand, was not morally neutral but was considered sinful. This included illicit sexual activity, ritual infanticide, magic and idolatry. Thus, unlike Levitical impurity, 'moral impurity was not contagious: Contact could not transferred from the agent to a morally innocent third party'.[443] We should not be injudicious in our application of these purity rules since they were probably not as significant in Galilee as they were in Judea, close to the temple. Yet with this in mind it is remarkable to note stories in which Jesus is seen to be in transgression of the purity rules: when He cures a leper Jesus touches the afflicted person (Mark 1:41) and when He heals the woman with ongoing menstrual bleeding (Mark 5:25–34).

As we noted above with the story of Bartimaeus, the early Christian community was taught to be socially inclusive. By developing an ethos that strengthened the status of people who were socially afflicted by their disease the Christian community promoted healing. That is not to say that all healing stories can be explained as social phenomena. As Crossan states: 'Faith heals, and that's a fact. Apart from intentional fakes or tricks, aside from deliberate quacks or charlatans, faith heals or even cures *some* people of *some* illnesses or diseases under *some* circumstances.'[444]

Summary and Conclusion

In this survey we have found a great deal of evidence that the core of the miracle tradition came from the poor and needy. In John we found one exception, the first sign, the wedding in Cana, the exception that proves the rule. Thus miracle stories were told by people affected (directly or indirectly) by loss of status owing to sickness. We saw in the story about Bartimaeus that miracle stories could also provide a basis for social action. Social action was also the basis of miracles about food. Feeding miracles clearly circulated amongst people who were often in need. We saw stories that were of interest to fishermen, both in terms of providing their livelihood and avoiding the hazards of their work.

We also saw that the evangelists were keen on ennobling these stories by giving them symbolic meaning. This was done either by inserting remarks that were not entirely logical in the context of the story or by placing the story in a greater context. We saw that the evangelists made use of allegory, as did Philo, but did not use Philo or his framework.

Some miracle stories seemed to have a different genesis altogether. We saw that the miracle of the fig tree was originally a parable, a parable that explained Jesus' projected act against the temple (discussed in the next chapter). The reason the parable was allegorized to the extent that it became a miracle story must lie in the uniqueness of the event. The event had little value as a general principle. It had little applicability and therefore had to be historicized in order to be transmitted. Another miracle that had a different genesis was the transfiguration. Here the transformation seems to have taken place in the written stage, as Mark recast the resurrection narrative.

From our survey we also found that the theoretical division of miracles into effective and visual, which we proposed at the outset in our general observations about the purpose of miracles, yielded virtually none that could qualify as visual miracles. The sayings tradition (which rejects the visual, faith-generating miracles) became integrated in the gospels with the miracle tradition discussed above and propagated itself as a tradition of faith-based, or faith-generated, miracles. The distinction between the two types of miracles made the integration possible. Yet the discomfort remained to some degree. In part, the solution was to allegorize the miracle stories to bring out meanings other than what seems to have been the intention of the oral version. Allegorization could not, however, remove the issue of faith and its obvious connection with the miracles. This process is seen clearly in Matthew, who solves the dilemma by making faith the source of the miracle. The process is also visible in John's redaction of his Sign Source.

Looking back at the miracles, there are two stories that seem to draw out an issue that we have so far bypassed: What was Jesus' relationship with Gentiles? In chapter 2 we surveyed what appeared to be the problematic relationship between the Jews of the countryside and those in the mostly Greek cities. We saw that a Galilean had given rise to the Fourth Philosophy that objected to the Roman taxes and which later became a terrorist movement that targeted those who collaborated with the Romans. We noted Judas son of Ezekias, a royal pretender who attacked Sepphoris. The obvious negative view that emerges should, however, be moderated. Both Sepphoris and Tiberias had sizeable Jewish populations. Even outside Palestine, we saw, Jews lived amongst Gentiles. Thus at the outset we should recognize that Jews as a whole had no specific position regarding Gentiles.

In chapter 4 we saw various factors that could have implications for John's attitude towards Gentiles. A positive tendency was set in the reduction of the protective efficacy of the Abrahamic covenant, which essentially set equal requirements for Jews and Greeks. We took this as a negative statement towards Jews rather than a positive one towards Gentiles. It also did not mean a slackening of the Law, as we saw John was critical of Antipas' transgression of Jewish Law. On the other hand, we saw that many of his ethical teachings were also directed at people who assisted

Roman overlordship, the soldiers and the tax-collectors. His message to them was not to cease their activity but to perform it equitably.

In chapter 5 we found that the Jesus followers belonged to groups that were predominantly negatively inclined to the activities of Gentiles. This tendency was already seen in the absence of references to major centres of Hellenism in the Christian tradition. Searching the sayings traditions we find several passages that are conceivably relevant to our enquiry. Q (Matthew 22:1–10 = Luke 14:16–24) and Thomas (64) have a parable about a great banquet where guests are invited but all the invited guests turn down the invitation, having given other activities a higher priority. Many elements, particularly in Matthew, suggest an allegorization that applies the parable to the rejection of Israel and subsequently the invitation of other guests as a reference to the Gentile mission.[445] Thomas reads it differently and probably closer to the original context: 'Buyers and merchants [will] not enter the place of my Father' (64:12 SV). It is implausible to think that Jesus perceived His mission to Israel as having 'failed' and therefore turned to the Gentiles. The allegory points to a time when such a failure was somewhat more obvious. Evidence from Paul suggests that the mission to the Gentiles was a project that was started mostly by him. This is corroborated by evidence from Acts. Most likely Jesus was not referring to merchants alone but was referring to the Scribes who, as people who prided themselves on their closeness to God, were too busy with their own doings when God sent Jesus to invite them into the kingdom of God. This is still an allegorization but it refers to a setting that is closer to the Historical Jesus. Q (Matthew 8:11–12 = Luke 13:28–9) has another tradition that predicts the coming of people from the East and West sitting at the table with the patriarchs. This could conceivably follow the Jewish expectation that when God restored Israel and subjugated the Gentile nations, these would in turn come to Jerusalem in reverence.[446] However, Q's rendition presumes that Jews will be thrown out of the kingdom, which again seems entirely unlikely. Mark's small apocalypse (discussed in chapter 8) predicts that the gospel will be preached from the ends of the earth before the arrival of the Son of man (Mark 13:10 = Matthew 24:14). This is countered by two traditions in Matthew that seem to exclude a mission to the Gentiles: Matthew 10:5 as a commandment inculcated in the mission speech and 10:23, which seems to exclude Gentiles because of lack of time before Jesus' return. While Mark in all likelihood created the prediction of the preaching to all nations, Matthew in both cases seems to present received traditions. He is unlikely to have created the limitation of 10:5 since he himself created a resurrection account in which Jesus charged the apostles with the mission to the Gentiles and he is equally unlikely to have invented what clearly must have been a failed prophecy by the time he was writing. Nevertheless, we should not, out of hand, accept Matthew's tradition as historical. Jesus does not appear to have had a negative attitude towards the Samaritans (see chapter 2), as 10:5 suggests. In Q, which is clearly pro-Gentile mission, as well as Didache (1:3) we find the tradition: 'And if ye salute your brethren only, what do ye more than others? do not even the Gentiles the same?' (Matthew 5:47 ASV).[447] This reflects the common Galilean assumption about the behaviour of Gentiles. Since it comes to us through an essentially Gentile-friendly source, we should judge it as probably authentic. Another indication of a negative attitude to Gentiles, or more precisely Hellenic culture, found in Q (Matthew 7:5 = Luke 6:42) is the use of the word 'hypocrite'. The Greek word means 'actor', which was a venerable profession in Greek society but had no parallel in Jewish tradition. The Greek word was likely to have been adopted as a loan word in Aramaic. In the tradition of Jesus, however, it acquires a negative connotation that was probably prevalent in the Jewish society of rural Galilee.

Finally in this chapter we saw some traditions that are relevant to our enquiry. The first tradition considered the exorcism of the demon Legion. Its negative view of Roman military presence is probably closely related to the Galilean (or the Gerasenes area) perception but does not reveal anything significant about Jesus' attitude. The next tradition was from Q and seems to have a very positive attitude towards Gentiles. When we compared it to the tradition in John (or rather the Sign Source), we found that the story originally did not refer to a centurion, or a Gentile for that matter. Again, the tradition says little other than Q's perspective. Finally, we saw the Markan tradition about the Syrophoenician woman. Though the story concludes positively, it reflects the negative attitude that was probably common amongst Jesus' first followers.

In conclusion it must be said that the evidence is on many points contradictory, often reflecting later interests. This in turn suggests that Jesus' attitude in general was not clearly formulated and that His teachings could be extrapolated in ways that were either positive or negative towards Gentiles. On the one hand, there was Jesus' appeal to the socially rejected and His focus on forgiveness. On the other, Jesus' teachings clearly pointed to the problem of Hellenic commercialization. This latter factor is probably very significant. Even though Jesus taught that His disciples should love Gentiles (or any enemy), nonetheless their activities must have seemed unjust and unacceptable. Jesus' mission was to Israel and its 12 tribes (hence the 12 Apostles).[448] The Gentiles would in all likelihood have been accepted by Jesus had they been willing to follow His prescription. Such a thing most probably never happened in Jesus' lifetime, and even assuming that Jesus healed some Gentiles who had heard rumours about Him, this would mean nothing more than that they perceived in Him someone who could provide a service for them of which they were in need.[449]

Our survey of miracles in this chapter also yielded evidence to support the Elijan motifs that we noted in chapters 4 and 5. Overall, the parallels seem not to be part of the scribal process. The story of the miracle, the core of the story, presents the genuine parallels. The parallels are numerous enough to make the Elijah-Elisha figure by far the most dominant one behind the miracle tradition.

A less visible figure is that of Solomon, which we also noted in the previous chapter. We saw that Josephus referred to an incantation that was made in the name of Solomon in order to exorcize a spirit. We noted in chapter 3 that the title 'son of David' used in the healing story in Mark 10:47 in all likelihood referred to Solomon. Thus although the Elijah figure is the most significant in both the sayings tradition and the miracle tradition, there is a small, almost undetectable Solomon figure who may have been significant to some lesser degree.

This chapter and the one that went before have dealt with a huge section of the gospels that fall out of a chronological context. In the following chapter we will resume the chronology at the point at which Jesus appears in Jerusalem for the last time.

7
Jerusalem

In this chapter we shall deal with Jesus' triumphant entry in Jerusalem, the history of the city itself and the circumstances of the events taking place immediately before the Passover.

Matthew 21:1–17
Mark 11:1–19
Luke 19:28 to 20:8
John 12:12–50

The Messianic Entry: Matthew 21:1–11, Mark 11:1–11, Luke 19:28–44, John 12:12–50

In the final stage of Jesus' three-year[450] ministry we find His entry into the city of David, Jerusalem. This event marks the climb towards the apex of His turbulent ministry. Through it the conflict with the authorities was propelled towards its culmination, resulting in the consummation of what is considered by many Christians to be the ultimate goal of Christ's mission.

Jesus was residing in Bethphage and He prepared for His triumphant arrival at Jerusalem by calling on His disciples to procure a colt. The evangelists unanimously interpret this as the fulfilment of the prophecy of Zechariah

(9:9): 'Tell ye the daughter of Sion, Behold, thy King cometh unto thee, meek, and sitting upon an ass, and a colt the foal of an ass' (Matthew 21:5 KJV). 'Fear not, daughter of Sion: behold, thy King cometh, sitting on an ass's colt' (John 12:15 KJV).

Matthew seems to misunderstand the parallel reference to a single animal in Zechariah as a reference to two different animals. As Müller states, the narratives are made to conform with prophecy such as Matthew understands them.[451] Funk and Hoover state that 'the story was conceived to fit the prophecies'.[452] However, every Christian knew that Jesus was Christ, so even if no traditions regarding this period survived, it was logical that He fulfilled scripture.[453] Yet, undoubtedly, Jesus did come 'humbly' rather than as a conquering lord and this is probably the historical core, since it is not part of a Mosaic or Davidic model.[454] In chapters 10 and 11 we will look at large portions of narrative that have exactly the same genesis: the Old Testament.

Returning to John, we see that he interprets the prophecy correctly, as do the two other evangelists, by understanding the double reference to the animal as being one: an 'ass's colt' and not an 'ass' and a 'colt the foal of an ass'. Darby's translation clarifies by rendering it as: 'Rejoice greatly, daughter of Zion; shout, daughter of Jerusalem! Behold, thy King cometh to thee: he is just, and having salvation; lowly and riding upon an ass, even upon a colt the foal of an ass' (Zechariah 9:9 Darby).

This prophecy suits the peaceful nature of Jesus' mission – 'he shall speak peace unto the heathen' – and at the same time links it to His messianic title – 'his dominion [shall be] from sea [even] to sea, and from the river [even] to the ends of the earth' (Zechariah 9:10 KJV).

Amongst those who believe in the historicity of this event, the fetching of the ass is viewed by some modern scholars as an arrangement made prior to the disciples' arrival at Bethphage. Stephen S. Short, however, comes to the opposite conclusion:

> Whilst it is possible that Jesus' knowledge of the location of the colt, and how people would respond to its being untethered, was due to an arrangement He had previously made with its owner, it is more likely that Jesus was exercising here His supernatural knowledge (cf. 1 Sam. 10:2–7).[455]

By what criteria such a thing should be accounted as 'likely', however, remains altogether unexplained.

Doubt has also been cast on the spontaneousness of the awe-striking public response. The duty of every good Jew to make pilgrimage to Jerusalem on Passover may have contributed to a massive Galilean presence, who, it is recorded, wanted Jesus to take the messianic throne.[456] The messianic expectation is also expressed in the use of the call 'Hosanna' (meaning 'save us' from Hebrew *Hosia*; see Mark 11:9–10). This clear reference leaves no doubt what station was attributed to Jesus of Nazareth by the author of this story, as he makes clear reference to the Psalms: 'This [is] the day Jehovah hath made, We rejoice and are glad in it. I beseech Thee, O Jehovah, save, I pray Thee, I beseech Thee, O Jehovah, prosper, I pray Thee. Blessed [is] he who is coming in the name of Jehovah, We blessed you from the house of Jehovah' (Psalms 118:24–6 YLT).

In order to portray Jesus as the Messiah, Mark sets the scene in a manner that resembles that of the proclamation of Jehu as king (2 Kings 9:13). This could come from an oral tradition told by Galilean followers of Jesus.[457]

According to the evangelist, this event is what triggered the intrigues of the enemies of Jesus who plotted to put an end to Him.

The City of David

To get a proper understanding of the boldness of Jesus' declaration, let us put Jerusalem into historical perspective. This city was the place of cultic worship, the centrepiece of the metaphorical Israel.

Jerusalem, the antiquity of which is well-attested,[458] was at the turn of the last millennia BCE made the seat of the kingdom of David. It was here that the king of 'Salem' visited David's illustrious forefather, Abraham. Joshua conquered Jerusalem when its king and some of his allies decided that the peace made between Gibeon and Joshua was a genuine threat against him and decided to make war against Joshua (Joshua 10). David reconquered it from the Jebusites (2 Samuel 5) and brought the Ark of the Covenant[459] into Jerusalem and thereby made it the religious and secular centre of Israel (2 Samuel 6).

Jerusalem was subsequently conquered in 587 BCE by the Babylonians,[460] only to be providentially rescued in 538 BCE by the conquest of the Persians, who allowed it the freedom to rebuild the temple[461] and be placed under the Jewish governor Nehemiah in 445 BCE. Suffering under constant war with Syria and Egypt, Persia's power greatly diminished and it was finally toppled by the conquest of the awe-inspiring king, who at the age of 20 ascended his father's throne: Alexander III the Great of Macedonia.[462] His mighty kingdom was split immediately after his death in 323 BCE between his relatives and generals and conflicts abounded until 276 BCE, when Antigonus II, having established himself in Macedonia, gained sovereignty.

Meanwhile, Israel fell first into Syrian hands and then came under the control of Egypt, which was ruled by the Ptolemaic kings. These were finally defeated in 168 BCE by Antiochus the Great of Syria, who conquered the Holy Land. During his rule Antiochus forbade the temple cult, forced the Jews to eat pork and profaned the temple by erecting an altar to Jupiter. The discontent of the masses boiled over and through a revolution, led by Judas Maccabeus, independence was won in 165 BCE. This is told in the books I and II Maccabees.[463] The Hasmonean dynasty received increasing opposition because of its illegitimate appropriation of the high priest post and Hellenic tendencies. A civil war broke out between Hyracanus and Aristobulus, weakening Palestine further and facilitating the Syro-Palestinian conquest led by Pompey of Rome, who conquered Jerusalem in the year 63 BCE.

He left Hyrcanus, the last of the Hasmoneans, as a nominal sovereign, while Antipater, an Idumean who had supported Hyrcanus throughout, wielded the real power. In 40 BCE, Herod, the son of Antipater, was appointed king of the Jews. After Herod, his son Archelaus ruled from 4 BCE until 6 CE. His reign was a bloody one and his incompetence as a ruler finally became so intolerable that he was removed by Emperor Augustus.[464] Herod Antipas, Archelaus' brother – noted for having John the Baptist executed because John criticized Herod's marriage to Herodias,[465] the wife of his half-brother Philip[466] – became the ruler of Galilee. Philip, the half-brother of Antipas and Archelaus, became the ruler of Northern Transjordan. After Archelaus was deposed, Roman procurators were placed in charge of Judea. When Jesus came to Jerusalem, Pontius Pilatus (Pilate) was in office.

Jesus and the Temple

In the gospel tradition the temple and Jesus interact in two instances. The first has to do with an event in the temple. Mark 11:15–17 tells the story of Jesus' arrival in Jerusalem when He enters the temple and overthrows the table of the money-changers, saying: 'Is it not written, My house shall be called of all nations the house of prayer? but ye have made it a den of thieves.'

The act itself, however, is difficult to make sense of. The event is commonly referred to as the cleansing of the temple. This, as Sanders, Neusner and others have pointed out in recent times, is a highly problematic interpretation of this event. Below we shall consider Sanders's presentation of the issue in *Jesus and Judaism* since he makes it 'the surest starting point' of the 'investigation' of the Historical Jesus.[467] Sanders begins by considering various versions of the 'cleansing' interpretation but states that these suffer under the misapprehension that a 1st century Jew would distinguish between 'practice'/'external' and 'true purpose'/'internal'. This, Sanders states, 'owes more to the nineteenth-century view that what is external is bad than a first century Jewish view'.[468] It is, furthermore, important to note that the practice of having traders of sacrificial animals and money-changers was an absolutely necessary and vital part of temple life. Such traders were not there to serve an elite, corrupt priesthood but rather to serve those who followed the Mosaic law.[469] The historical reality forces us to understand Jesus' action not as an attempt to disrupt temple activity, which would have required quite a few men and certainly would have resulted in Jesus' immediate incarceration, but rather as a symbolic act.[470] So far the line of thought presented is followed as much by Sanders as it is by

Neusner. However, it is in their interpretation of what this symbolic act actually meant that they part ways. Neusner suggests that what in fact was happening was the replacement by Jesus of the Jewish cult (the temple cult) with a new Christian cult (the Eucharist). The table of the temple was replaced with the table of the Eucharist. In the words of Neusner, 'one table overturned, another table set up in place, and both for the same purpose of atonement and expiation of sin'.[471] For reasons that will become apparent in chapter 10, which discusses the Eucharist, this is not an entirely plausible interpretation.

In order to understand Jesus' relationship and thus the event of the 'cleansing', we turn to two synoptic sayings. The first is the beginning of the Little Apocalypse (discussed in the next chapter) in which the disciples remark on the spectacular reconstruction of the temple, to which Jesus replies: 'Seest thou these great buildings? there shall not be left here one stone upon another, which shall not be thrown down' (Mark 13:2 ASV). The application of this saying to the temple could be a Markan construction but there is other synoptic evidence that suggests that the context is indeed correct.

Also from Mark we find the scene from the trial (discussed in chapter 10), in which a witness claims that Jesus had stated: 'I will destroy this temple that is made with hands, and in three days I will build another made without hands' (Mark 14:58 ASV) or in the version found in Matthew: 'I am able to destroy the temple of God, and to build it in three days' (26:61 ASV). Sanders emphasizes that these charges are in both Mark and Matthew watered down.[472] They are depicted as false and are allegorized in order to give a resurrection interpretation to these statements and minimize their potentially political implication.[473] Matthew's reworking of the Markan testimony shows some of his concern: Matthew felt that 'this temple made by hands' would be offensive to Jews, and changed it to 'temple of God'. More significantly, Matthew softens the Markan threat 'I will destroy' by saying 'I am able'.

Sanders finds it 'most striking'[474] that the accusation is found again on the lips of the crowds at the crucifixion: 'Ha! Thou that destroyest the temple, and buildest it in three days' (Mark 15:29 ASV). To the present author this represents minor evidence, since it seems to be no more than a Markan repetition of a theme that he previously used. Luke omits from his gospel narrative both of these instances and yet in Acts, Luke renders the 'false witness' testimony against Stephen thus: 'For we have heard him say, that this Jesus of Nazareth shall destroy this place [the temple]' (Acts 6:14 ASV). John 2:19 provides another independent source on a Jesus saying against the temple: 'Destroy this temple, and in three days I will raise it up' (ASV). John furthermore ties it directly to the 'cleansing' which he, however, places at the beginning of Jesus' ministry.[475] In a sense the embarrassment that the evangelists show in their redaction of the words of Jesus and the synoptist's decontextualizing quotation ('den of thieves') regarding the event is overwhelming proof of the historicity of the 'problematic' relationship Jesus had with the temple.

Crossan is in complete agreement with Sanders on these conclusions: he too sees the event as a 'symbolic destruction of the temple'.[476] He also points to a third independent witness to the logia in Thomas 71: 'I shall destroy this house, and no one will be able to build it . . .' He further feels that Mark betrays knowledge of the true meaning of the 'cleansing' by placing it in the context of the cursing of the fig tree in which the fig tree is symbolically destroyed as a foreshadowing of the destruction of the temple.[477] Finally, Crossan takes the conclusion a step further by stating that the threat of the destruction of the temple was prompted by Jesus' 'indignation' at the temple that had become a symbol of oppression both religiously and politically.[478]

Lastly, as a contribution to our understanding of Jesus' relationship to the temple, we should examine a saying from Lukan material and one from Matthean. In this story told by Jesus (Luke 18:10–14) two men go to the temple. One is a Pharisee, the other a tax-collector. The Pharisee thanks God in his silent prayer that he is more righteous than the sinful tax-collector; the tax-collector confesses to being a sinner and prays for forgiveness. Jesus concludes that the second was forgiven while the first was not.

Matthew 23:16–21 states that one should not swear by the temple, altar, offerings or the gold of the temple. Apparently the latter two were considered valid by the Pharisees, while the first two were considered invalid.[479] This form of legal disputation seems to presume an interest in Pharisaic legalism that is unlikely to have been meaningful to Jesus. Though Jesus may have had radical ideas about vows in general (i.e. that one should not swear at all), nothing historically significant can be extrapolated about the temple.

From the first story we learn two important points: 1) Jesus perceived the temple as the appropriate place in which to receive forgiveness and 2) the problem according to Jesus was the arrogance (not hypocrisy) that motivated the Pharisee's prayer. Though the second point seems to carry the primary thrust of the story, there seems to be an attitude which forms the narrative theme. In consonance with earlier observations, we should perhaps understand the motive behind the pronouncement against the temple as a condemnation of the arrogance that it had come to represent. Continuing this train of thought, we find that in the introduction of the Little Apocalypse (Mark 13:1–2 = Luke 21:5,6) that the prophetic statement against the temple is framed as a response to praise of the temple's magnificence. The temple's reconstruction was financed by exploiting the Palestinian peasantry: the glory was not God's but that of the exploiting rulers.

Crossan states in his book *Who Killed Jesus?* that his 'best historical reconstruction concludes that what led immediately to Jesus' arrest and execution in Jerusalem at Passover was that act of symbolic destruction, in deed and word, against the Temple'.[480] This is indeed where the consensus seems to fall. The exception here is Burton Mack, who considers the whole event to be a Markan fabrication with no historical core.[481] Such a conclusion seems to fly in the face of the strong independent evidence from several sources. The Jesus portrayed by Mack – a Cynic without a programme to effect social change – would not have attacked the temple and thus Mack is forced to presume that Jesus' death in Jerusalem was a mere accident. This conclusion 'led to a flurry of jokes among scholars, such as one about Mack's Jesus being killed in a car crash on the Los Angeles freeway'.[482] Such jokes are entirely misplaced. There should certainly be room in historical analysis for accidents. Even when subsequent generations interpret an event as meaningful, we cannot dismiss the possibility of an accident. However, we must dismiss Mack because the evidence suggests a programmatic Jesus and establishes the attack on the temple as more than Markan fiction.

Summary and Conclusion

We started by looking at Jesus' entry into Jerusalem, an entry that the evangelists saw as Jerusalem receiving its Messiah. We concluded that the details that seemed to be in common between sources were not due to the skill with which oral tradition had recounted the event but rather were due to a tradition of interpretation in which Zechariah 9:9 was understood as a reference to Jesus' entry into the city. We noted that the evangelists took this as the reason for the Jewish plot to have Jesus executed. It is clear that the evangelists had no source that told them that this event had triggered the conspiracy against Jesus – they merely had a tradition of interpretation. Theirs was an educated guess.

However, we saw that another event was in fact also portrayed as a significant factor in motivating intrigues against Jesus, namely His condemnation of the temple. This is problematic because the two themes seem to stem from very different traditions and perspectives of Jesus. The latter tradition, which appears to be historically sound, claims that Jesus was condemned because of prophetic activities. Jesus' condemnation of the temple was typical of an oracle prophet. Two questions emerge from this oracle which, as we saw, is about as historically certain as anything we can say about the life of Jesus. First, what does it tell us about Jesus? And, second, how well does it account for Jesus' execution?

Sanders, as we saw, took this event as the surest thing known to us about Jesus. From this he determined that Jesus was best understood as a restoration prophet, a proclaimer of the imminent arrival of the kingdom of God, just like John the Baptist. Our analysis of the sayings tradition, however, suggests that Jesus' proclamation of the kingdom was radically different from that of John the Baptist. So though the event cannot be ignored, it cannot be made normative for our understanding of Jesus, nor can all the evidence be turned to fit this perception of Jesus. In the next chapter we will look at the eschatological tradition attached to Jesus in order to determine in what sense, if any, He may be understood as an oracle prophet.

As to our second question, the significance of the event with regard to Jesus' execution, we are faced with several problems, some of which cannot yet be satisfactorily addressed. Clearly, the question is: Could Jesus' action against the temple alone be sufficient reason for the Jewish authorities to want to have Him executed? In chapter 2 we learned of an oracle prophet, Jesus son of Hananiah, who came to Jerusalem proclaiming its imminent doom. This brought displeasure to some eminent members of the community, who had him whipped. Being unresponsive, he was brought to the procurator who meted out the same punishment. Clearly, this oracle prophet was not executed, even though he continued his pronouncements for four years. There must therefore be a significant difference between Jesus the son of Hananiah and Jesus the protagonist of the gospels.

One possible explanation suggested by the evangelists was that Jesus' entry into Jerusalem was understood by some as a claim to messiahship. Even if we believe the evangelists to have no specific knowledge of Jesus' entry, they may have known basic facts, such as that Jesus had arrived and had been greeted by crowds. The tradition surveyed so far has revealed that the Solomon figure was applied to Jesus, a thread that appears to intersect both sayings traditions and miracle traditions. If this appears in such primitive traditions, is it conceivable that Jesus' opponents also thought that Jesus was claiming messiahship by using the Solomon figure?

8

The End Foreshadowed

Once Jesus' enemies had been confronted in their stronghold, Jerusalem, they could no longer retreat and so they plotted either to disgrace Him or, if this failed, to put an end to His life. For this reason, according to the gospels, Jesus endeavoured to teach His disciples what was to come and what to look for at His next advent.

These 'passion predictions' or 'passion summaries'[483] (Mark 8:31, 9:31, 10:33; John 12:23) may constitute pre-gospel summaries, kerygma or confessions placed on Jesus' lips. This does not, of course, mean that Jesus did not predict His own end, which indeed would not require any powers of divination; however, in the forms that we find them today, they are the evangelists' own words.

Eschatology and Jesus

Jesus' words about the kingdom of God and its presence has already been discussed at length in chapter 5 but at this juncture we need to make more general observations about the prophecies. It has been argued that since John the Baptist and Paul, Jesus' immediate predecessor and successor, were both apocalyptic advocates then Jesus must also have been apocalyptically minded.[484]

The above statement itself suggests a judgement on the

part of the author which some scholars consider untenable, namely that Jesus did make prophecy. Let us consider Robert J. Miller's critique of Ben Witherington's book *The Jesus Quest*, which itself is a critique of the Jesus Seminar of which Miller is a member. Miller writes: 'Witherington maintains that the historical Jesus was an apocalyptic preacher but an exceptionally odd one: one who wasn't sure whether the End was imminent. According to Witherington, Jesus preached that the End *might* be coming soon. Furthermore, Witherington's Jesus understood himself in terms of the Son of Man in Daniel 7, who, apparently, might or might not be coming soon.'[485]

This strikes at the very heart of what bothers many biblical scholars, namely that it is difficult to produce a coherent picture of exactly what Jesus taught regarding the end of time. Basically, there are three types of chronological eschatologies: realized, near and far eschatology. While the first has already been discussed in chapter 5, the second and third must be considered before we proceed.

By 'near eschatology' is meant the proclamation of the eminent coming of the end of the world. An example of this is found in the message of John the Baptist. The focus of his proclamation is the present generation. The people are warned or promised that they will witness the end and will reap the consequences. Near eschatology is intended to provoke immediate action, the seeking of repentance or renewed efforts to proclaim the new gospel. On the other hand, 'far eschatology' proclaims that the end is somewhere in the distant future. This, of course, has the opposite effect and tends to assist the formation of community and to support those who wish to keep a low profile in the face of present persecution.

Thus both cases can be explained as constructs of the

community in the face of the situation in which it finds itself. But the present author has another proposal for the solution of this inconsistency, one that sides with neither Witherington nor Miller. First, we must accept that some of the sayings that we deal with do not easily fall into any of the three categories. These sayings place the end of the world at some indefinite time. 'Indefinite eschatology'[486] has the great advantage of working well in either type of community. It proclaims that one should be alert and ready to receive the returned Christ. 'But of that day or that hour knoweth no one, not even the angels in heaven, neither the Son but the Father' (Mark 13:32 ASV).

This particular verse is the object of some contention between the two scholars. Miller writes in response to Witherington's claim that it is unthinkable that the early community could have invented such a saying: 'Unbelievable to Witherington, perhaps; but for others it is quite believable that early Christians might well have invented this saying as a way of explaining why Jesus had not been more precise in his predictions, or as a way of taking out insurance on his credibility, just in case the End proved tardy.'[487]

It is notable, however, that the Jesus Seminar did itself admit that 'a later believer would probably not have invented a saying in which Jesus claims that he does not have knowledge of that most important of all dates – the time of his return'.[488]

Bornkamm takes the statement to be Jesus' and suggests that its character is in reality anti-apocalyptic since it refuses to paint detailed pictures of the future world, unlike apocalyptics of His day.[489]

Stratification of Q by Kloppenborg has in recent years been used (amongst others, by members of the Jesus

Seminar, such as Miller) to suggest that the wisdom sayings of Q1 should be given priority and the eschatological sayings of Q2 rejected:

> I don't see any *a priori* reason to think that Jesus did not speak about the judgement (you don't have to be an apocalypticist to do that) or resurrection, or he might have invoked such tropes. I do think that we have a problem on our hands if there is too much of a discontinuity between the strata of Q, for in that case we have to explain how the tradents of Q could tolerate so radical a shift in what it implies about the speaker. Sure, redaction does shift characterization, as a simple comparison of Mark and Matthew indicates. But I'd like to hear from you just how much a change you imagine between Q1 and Q2.[490]

Indeed, failed millennialism could easily explain the need for a wisdom solution, a rationalization of the failure of the ultimate event to manifest itself as expected. Such a transformation could explain the success of Jesus' teachings about the inconspicuously growing kingdom of God in the face of the apparently failed millennialism entailed by John's message. However, just as it is possible to go from failed millennialism to wisdom, it is also possible to go from failed wisdom to millennialism. For some, a wisdom rationalization will not in the long run satisfy their need for a radical improvement of their condition, in other words millennialism. We should therefore be careful not to overestimate the tension between the two positions.

The legitimacy of the historical character of indefinite eschatology does not rest on this saying alone. Q provides a few parables which support the indefinite eschatology. Below we look at some examples of these.

By nature there is a dichotomy between realized

eschatology and indefinite eschatology because one can hardly say that the kingdom of God is present but that it is not known when it will come. This dichotomy is far greater than the one between far and near eschatology, which to some degree can be reconciled. What makes this indefinite-realized dichotomy particularly interesting is that both types occur within independent sources. Mark, Q and Thomas each contain both indefinite and realized eschatology, apparently not noting the problem that must necessarily arise from such a combination.[491] Perhaps the reason is to be found in a saying that is common to Thomas and Luke but appears more original in Thomas: 'Jesus said, "I have cast fire upon the world, and see, I am guarding it until it blazes"' (Thomas 10). 'I have come to set fire to the earth, and how I wish it were already kindled!' (Luke 12:49 NEB).

If this indeed goes back to Jesus, as the Jesus Seminar suggests, then there is reason to believe that Jesus did indeed preach two types of kingdoms, or rather two versions of it. The relationship between the two was apparently quite confusing. The two were interconnected. The first was described as having taken place through the coming of Jesus, was realized through Jesus' gospel and existed without being observed. The second was probably much like Jewish expectations but the extent of the apocalyptic elements must remain in doubt. The above sayings make it clear that the two kingdoms were in reality the same but in different manifestations, one being 'hidden' and the other 'ablaze', or as in the parable of the mustard seed, first it was a small seed and then a magnificent tree.

The near eschatological sayings can be thought of as deriving from the early ministry of Jesus, when Jesus merely appeared to be the follower of John the Baptist. It is possible that what appears to be Mark's implicit claim is in fact true, that is, that Jesus after the arrest of John continued to proclaim the imminent advent of the kingdom of God. Furthermore, it would appear from Mark that it was with this message that Jesus converted His first disciples. According to John 3:22–4 this was happening before the Baptist's arrest, through the baptizing activity of Jesus' disciples (John 4:2).

Jesus' primary audience (i.e. the poor and destitute) were also those who would be most open to the eschatological call of John. So it is conceivable that early converts held onto this message or imagery even after Jesus changed His proclamation to a present kingdom. Such passages could also merely be the constructions of the early communities that found themselves in need of such promises.

The far eschatological sayings may come from the last part of Jesus' ministry, from a few reliable traditions that were later greatly expanded. Such original sayings should be understood in terms of the completion of the initiation of the hidden kingdom of God into the world and a promise of its future impact. The whole set of indefinite eschatological sayings presupposes some sort of far (or near) eschatology, so it seems likely that Jesus did speak of some sort of kingdom which was the manifestation (ablaze) of the one brought by Him.

Jesus the Predicted and the Predictor

What role did Jesus see for Himself in the kingdom that would come with blazes?

This question inevitably collides with the question of what Jesus saw as His role in the kingdom of His present. The sources available on Jesus' claims are very doubtful. There are certain passages in the gospels that may be understood as explaining the apparent lack of known statements or disputes about Jesus' claims to messiahship. These take the form of Jesus' admonitions to those who recognized Him as Messiah to remain silent about it. Peter's confession (Mark 8:27–30) provides an interesting example. Here Jesus questions His disciples first about who people think He is, to which they answer 'John the Baptist; and others, Elijah; but others, One of the prophets' (Mark 8:28 ASV). Then He asks the disciples who they thought He was, to which Peter answers 'Thou art the Christ' (verse 29 ASV), whereafter they are charged to reveal it to no one. This tradition probably includes, through the mouths of the apostles, the opinions that people generally held about Jesus. Jesus then asks the disciples not to tell anyone. Many would say that there is nothing in the gospel to suggest that Jesus ever publicly claimed anything else than prophethood. In chapter 2 we briefly discussed popular prophetic movements and subsequently found that many of the earliest pointers suggested an Elijah motif. In the last chapter we saw how Jesus openly condemned the temple by symbolically destroying it and was later accused for voicing the threat of its actual destruction. It is therefore not strange that a rendition of popular opinion should make Jesus a prophet (and with historical justification), since this fits the profile of a popular oracle prophet.

As far as can be ascertained from the sayings tradition, the message of Jesus was very different from other popular prophets of His time, including that of John the Baptist. Unlike most popular prophetic movements at the time of Jesus, Jesus and His disciples did not propose the introduction of the kingdom of God through the miraculous intervention of God but through the spreading of the divine message. This in itself is so radically different from what a 1st century Jew understood by 'prophet' as to be almost paradoxical.

But Mark is not telling the story to prove that Jesus was a prophet or even that He was the Messiah but rather because of the existence of two communities which advanced disparate claims about who Jesus was. This is dealt with by Mark by constructing a scheme of silence. At first only supernatural creatures knew that Jesus was the Christ and silence was enjoined on them (Mark 1:25, 3:12, 5:43, 7:36, 9:9).[492] Mark is here dealing with the problem of two different bodies of tradition, the first being that Jesus was a prophet (or the prophet) and the other being that Jesus was the Messiah. It is true that in the sayings tradition (Q and Thomas), as Mark must have found, there is not one instance where Jesus is called Christ. That is a rather significant omission. Some have taken this to mean that the tradition that Jesus was the Messiah was a later claim made by followers of Jesus after His death. However, the question could be approached from a different angle. This is done by considering the concept of 'the crucified Messiah'. Paul himself explains: 'but we preach Christ crucified, unto Jews a stumbling block, and unto Gentiles foolishness' (1 Corinthians 1:23 ASV).

The claim that scripture revealed the crucified and resurrected Christ (1 Corinthians 15:3–4) is clearly apologetic in nature, for scripture says no such thing. Therefore Paul must state that it was kept secret in the scriptures (Romans 16:25–6) for it was the actual event that caused it to become manifest. For the Jerusalem community to invent such a difficult position is illogical: it would be inventing 'a stumbling block' and 'foolishness'. To unite two opposites (the paradox of Christ and cross) makes sense only if historical facts necessitated it. From this we may conclude that Jesus probably claimed nothing more than prophethood while in Galilee and that only Jerusalem heard His claims to messiahship. Thomas shows knowledge of the other community's vicw.

> His disciples said to him, 'Twenty-four prophets have spoken in Israel, and they all spoke of you.' He said to them, 'You have disregarded the living one who is in your presence, and have spoken of the dead' (Thomas 52).

> Jesus said to his disciples, 'Compare me to something and tell me what I am like.' Simon Peter said to him, 'You are like a just messenger.' Matthew said to him, 'You are like a wise philosopher.' Thomas said to him, 'Teacher, my mouth is utterly unable to say what you are like' (Thomas 13).

In the first saying Jesus' disciples proclaim Him the promised one of Israel but for Thomas, Jesus is more than the Messiah, He is the 'living one', personified wisdom. The second saying is placed in opposition to the Markan confession of Jesus as Messiah. The Messiah/prophet is less than the wise philosopher and Jesus is even beyond the latter.

We may compare the Jesus movement with popular messianic movements of His time (as we did with prophetic movements). Again the object of such a movement was the establishment of the rule of God but, unlike the prophetic movements, the means of establishing this rule was military power. All evidence available to us, however, suggests that Jesus was not the leader of armed forces. So also in this regard the Jesus movement seems to have claimed something about Jesus which did not fit popular conceptions.

The title 'Son of man' has been suggested to reveal Jesus' proper self-designation but this remains problematic not only with regard to historicity but also about what the term might indicate. We can with some certainty dismiss that the term could have been understood in the context of Daniel. This would require a scribal audience. Below we shall see the term appear in the Olive Discourse in a section that originated in the late thirties. Was this a title used by Jesus to designate Himself? This is certainly the tradition that the gospels reflect. There are no narrative or kerygmatic passages that use the term. The term is found in all independent sources: Q, Mark, John and even Thomas. Otherwise, with the exception of one passage in Acts, the term is nowhere to be found in the New Testament literature. This suggests that it was an early term designating Jesus that fell out of use quite soon. The evidence tentatively suggests that the term was used as a self-designation of humility: the Son of man had no rest (Q: Matthew 8:20 = Luke 9:58 = Thomas 86), he came to minister (Mark 10:45), he dined with outcasts (Q: Matthew 11:19 = Luke 7:34), he came for that which was lost (Luke 19:10). In spite of that humility he was invested with authority to forgive sin and rule over the Sabbath (Mark 2:10, 28). All of these conceivably relate to the Historical Jesus and were used by Jesus' prophets.

In the aftermath of the crucifixion, this humility and servitude were interpreted in terms of the humility of the cross, on the one hand (e.g. Mark 8:31), and His reversal in the exaltation that characterized His return (e.g. Mark 14:62) on the other.[493]

In the coming chapters we shall look at further material to determine whether Jesus claimed to be the Messiah. Provisionally, however, we may assume that Jesus publicly remained ambiguous about the title. Undoubtedly, the military implications were thought inappropriate. If He was ambiguous, we should be cautious about the sayings which clearly are applied to Jesus. Perhaps the scene in Mark 11:27–33, in which Jesus answers the scribe's question about the source of His authority with a counter question about the provenance of John's authority, provides a plausible example of this sort of ambiguity. In the face of opposition from religious authorities, the ambiguity of Jesus' personal claims provided enough uncertainty amongst them to make unified action difficult.

Concluding this section we might speculate that the reason why Jesus may have reasonably changed His claims upon coming to Judea was that prophetic movements had greater appeal in Galilee while messianic movements were more culturally significant in Judea. In Judea, Jerusalem was the place where David placed his seat; it was the place from which current rule emanated. As explained above, neither 'prophet' nor 'Christ' was an appropriate designation for Jesus in the popular sense (and the Jesus movement was, after all, 'popular'). Either designation could have been used by Jesus to convey, in suitable regions, the purpose of His ministry (the establishment of the kingdom of God) but neither designation appropriately explained how this was intended to be done.

The Comforter and the Spirit of Truth: John 14–16

The Gospel of John is unique in its discourse on the Comforter[494] and the Spirit of Truth, also better known as the 'Farewell Discourse'. Unlike the Synoptic Gospels, which contains all four groups of eschatology, John's realized eschatology stands alone and practically unchallenged. In the Farewell Discourse, however, certain elements appear that seem out of place and which indicate what is already held by most Johannine scholars, namely that John has thoroughly edited his source.[495] The Farewell Discourse is, like the Sign Source, from a source that is earlier than the creation of the gospel itself.[496]

Throughout the treatment of this discourse the present author shall, on occasion, refer to the Syriac version of this text. The reason for this is that he believes that although the source may originally have been a Hebrew text,[497] it circulated at some time in a Greek version in Syria prior to its inclusion in John. John probably never saw the Hebrew but only the Greek version. The Greek version may have been translated and circulated in Syria before the translation of the gospels from Greek into Syriac in the 3rd century. This translation, known as the Old Syriac version, is preserved in two extant documents: the Syriac Sinaiticus and the Syriac Cureton. The latter is a later recension of the former but both use Greek manuscripts for their translations. The usefulness of referring to these documents lies in that in a few instances they may have characteristics that go back to the pre-Johannine text.[498] That the translators of the Old Syriac amended their translation in accordance to what sources they had available to them has been argued quite conclusively by Jan Joosten in his 'La Tradition Syriaque des Évangeiles et la Question du "Substrat Araméen" '.[499] Joostan is by no means the first to propose this. Jeffrey P. Lyon notes a list of scholars who have 'shown' that the Old Syriac 'has some connection to western Aramaic, or even Palestinian, [tradition] . . . while the later versions are drawn ever closer to their Greek model'.[500] Although Lyon attributes the 'great majority' of the variant readings in the Old Syriac to the freedom of the translator, he also suggests that some could be caused by 'the presence of an oral kerygma in the early Aramaic-speaking church, cross-contamination from the Diatessaron,[501] and inner-Syriac traditions or errors'.[502]

The first indication of another type of eschatology can already be found in the first verses of chapter 14. Here Jesus promises His disciples a place in the heavenly mansion of His Father where He and His disciples may be reunited (John 14:1–3).[503] This is similar to the Markan promise of the future Eucharistic meal in heaven. Verse 6 is characteristic of John[504] and is probably one of his many contributions to the text. It is intrusive because it changes the theme from what Jesus will do to who Jesus is.

Next is the assertion that Jesus is a messenger, that the words He says are from the Father. If any of this section (14:8–14) goes back to the hypothetical source, it has its core in the doing of deeds (14:12): 'and I will ask the Father, and another Comforter He will give to you, that he may remain with you – to the age; the Spirit of truth, whom the world is not able to receive, because it doth not behold him, nor know him, and ye know him, because he doth remain with you, and shall be in you' (John 14:16–17 YLT).

Here the Paraclete[505] makes its first appearance. The wording of the verse implies that there has been another[506] Paraclete[507] before the one discussed in the discourse ('I will send you "another" Paraclete'). Depending on the audience, this earlier Paraclete was either Jesus Himself, or the prophets of the past. The latter clause in verse 16 does not follow the exegesis proposed so far unless they believed in a Messiah who would stay eternally (which is not entirely foreign to eschatological thought). It is also possible that John is joining two sources here.[508] The core of verse 17 is the inability of the world to receive the Spirit of Truth. The two clauses that follow are probably Johannine explanations. It should also be noted, however, that the conception of being 'in' (Gk. ἐν) has a special significance in John. This we see in the manner it is used only three verses later in 14:20, where Jesus proclaims, 'I am in my Father, and you in me, and I in you.'

'I will not leave you bereaved [or orphans]: {I come unto you.}' (John 14:18 YLT, insertion mine). Here the Cureton perhaps provides a more original reading by omitting the second clause placed in {}. For John these prophecies were fulfilled by Jesus' coming and giving the Holy Spirit to the disciples, so with the insertion of this clause he makes return after the resurrection the delivery of the Paraclete. The clause itself is unclear. Will the disciples not be orphans because Jesus will come and stay or because He will come and deliver the Holy Spirit? 'Jesus answered and said unto him, If a man love me, he will keep my word: and my Father will love him, and we will come unto him, and make our abode with him' (John 14:23 ASV). This is almost paradoxical, because here Jesus and the Father are promised as the ones who will be fulfilling the mandate of the Paraclete. The Cureton changes the 'we' to an 'I'. It remains questionable whether Cureton's version is more original but it seems likely that it has an independent source which developed its own tradition. 'But the Comforter, [which is] the Holy Ghost, whom the Father will send in my name, he shall teach you all things, {and bring all things to your remembrance,} whatsoever I have said unto you' (John 14:26 KJV).

The Holy Ghost[509] is no doubt identified, in this verse, with the Comforter. This verse probably only contains one Johannine interpolation, namely that identification. This is supported by the Old Syriac, which omits the word 'Holy' (ἅγιον). There can be no doubt that this reading was not due to a scribal error nor was it a theological alteration, for it is found also in the patristic writings with the interpretation of it still being Johannine.[510] Just as the words of Jesus are not His own (verse 24), the words of the Paraclete must likewise come from the one who sent Him, namely the Father. John's effort to make the Paraclete a dependant figure probably prompted the insertion of 'in my name', as well as the last clause. The Cureton omits the last clause but inserts 'I say to you', thus striking out one feature that became useless once the apostles had died; for those who had never met Jesus, 'remembrance' was no longer significant.

At the end of chapter 14 Jesus suddenly says: 'Arise, let us go hence' but no actual movement is mentioned (such as 'and they rose and went forth to . . .') and in chapter 15 we find Jesus still giving the Farewell Discourse. This demonstrates poor editing of John's source.

'But when the Comforter is come, whom I will send unto you from the Father, [even] the Spirit of truth, which proceedeth from the Father, he shall testify of me' (John 15:26 KJV). Here the Comforter is one that bears 'witness'[511] concerning Christ. Significantly, He then goes on to enlist His apostles as witnesses as well, 'And ye also shall bear witness', thus making the witnessing of the apostles a separate ordinance and different from that of the witnessing of the Spirit of truth. Also of importance is the use of 'he' instead 'it' (which is used with the Holy Spirit).[512] It is this verse which contains the problematic double procession which split the Orthodox Church from the Catholic. Did the Comforter (or rather Holy Spirit, as it was understood) come from the Father or did it come from both?[513] Probably the clause which gives a procession from Jesus is a Johannine one.

> Nevertheless I tell you the truth; It is expedient for you that I go away: for if I go not away, the Comforter will not come unto you; but if I depart, I will send him unto you. And when he is come, he will reprove the world of sin, and of righteousness, and of judgement: Of sin, because they believe not on me; Of righteousness, because I go to my Father, and ye see me no more; Of judgement, because the prince of this world is judged. I have yet many things to say unto you but ye cannot bear them now. Howbeit when he, the Spirit of truth, is come, he will guide you into all truth: for he shall not speak of himself; but whatsoever he shall hear, [that] shall he speak: and he will shew you things to come (John 16:7–13 KJV).

The archetype described here is a reprover of sins, the manifestation of righteousness and the judge of the world. This portrait suits Christ rather than the Holy Spirit, therefore the subject of the Farewell Discourse could in fact more appropriately apply to the second coming of Christ. Note also that the last clause suggests that the Spirit of truth is prophetic inasmuch as it tells of 'things to come'. Verse 13 in particular brings to mind the Deuteronic prophecy (18:18),[514] which refers to the future prophet like Moses.[515]

In conclusion we find that there appears even in the later Syriac versions to be traces of living inter-Syriac traditions about the Paraclete. As such we saw instances where the Syriac appeared less evolved than the Greek and instances where it appeared to be later and more developed.

Within the New Testament itself we find the Paraclete applied to Jesus Himself (1 John 2:1). Clearly the author here is using the term in a markedly different way than would the author of the gospel, which suggests that a prophetic Paraclete figure may have existed popularly in the Johannine community. At the time 1 John was written, the Jesus prophets were starting to become a problem, as we see in the warnings against false prophets (1 John 4:1). Assuming that 1 John and John both independently portray an archetype, we easily see two important parallel attributes: He deals with sin (John 16:9) and is himself righteous (John 16:10). From chapter 5 we recall that the bearers of Jesus' message were itinerant 'prophets'.

It is to these that we should connect the saying in Mark 3:28–9 that the only unforgivable sin is blasphemy against the Holy Spirit, for in the Didache 11:7 this verse is interpreted as questioning the prophet speaking through the influence of the Holy Spirit. 'Let everyone who comes in the Name of the Lord be received; but when you have tested him you shall know him, for you shall have understanding of true and false' (Didache 12:1, Loeb). The term used for 'true and false' literally means 'right and left', probably alluding to the way of life and the way of death which the Didache supplies in its first chapters. By the time 2 Peter 2:1[516] was written, the Jesus prophets were a thing of the past.

The Johannine Paraclete archetype is probably derived from these itinerant prophets. Though they wandered to many other places than the Johannine community, the term 'Paraclete' was uniquely applied to them there. In time the term developed a life of its own, adding implications as it was applied to Jesus primarily (in retrospection of their life on His) and the Holy Spirit (as it was represented in these prophets).

Looking at later use of 'Paraclete', we see that by and

large it followed the Johannine usage of the text rather than the pre-Johannine.

In mid–2nd century a prophetic apocalyptic movement sprang up in Phrygian Mysia[517] which became known as the Montanists, from their founder Montanus. Aune, following Kurt Aland, identifies 16 'oracles' or prophetic statements that can be reliably attributed to the movement. Amongst these statements we find Montanus' claim to be 'the Father, and the Son and the Paraclete'.[518] These are, according to Aune, not theological statements about the unity of these entities but rather 'self-commendations' that prefaced longer speeches.[519] Elsewhere the Paraclete is said to be in or saying something through the prophet or prophetess. In conclusion, we find that although the term 'Paraclete' was completely identified with the Holy Spirit, it retained its closeness with the prophetic function.

In the Johannine Acts of the 3rd century the invocation 'O Jesus, the Paraclete'[520] appears to echo a popular colloquialism that no longer had any attachment to its origin but was used as a term of exaltation.

In the gospels the Farewell Discourse is chronologically parallel with the great eschatological discourse in the Synoptic Gospels, the Olive Discourse.

The Olive Discourse: Mark 13, Matthew 24–5, Luke 21

We will now look at an example of prophecy from the Synoptic Gospels, namely that of Matthew, which is a compiled discourse like that of the Sermon on the Mount. Its sources are the small apocalypse of Mark 13, Q and a third, uniquely Matthean source. Since the origin of Q has been discussed in chapter 5, we will here start by discussing the origin of the small apocalypse. This chapter was introduced with a discussion of eschatology but the term 'apocalypse' needs to be properly defined before we proceed. D. S. Russell distinguishes the apocalyptic from the prophetic genre by the fact that the former represents the actual revelation and that the content is made to look like a secret book revealed and kept hidden.[521] Though Mark's so-called small apocalypse does not fulfil these criteria completely, there is a sufficient correspondence between it and such books as Daniel or the Revelation of St John that the comparison may yield something of significance. Often the apocalypse is thought of in terms of cataclysmic events, messianic figures and so forth but this is perhaps not helpful. As Esler suggests, this should rather be termed 'millennialism'.[522] Let us therefore call the small apocalypse millennialist. Esler recounts the social conditions under which millennialism can be expected to emerge:

> . . . the local people passionately hope for some imminent, supernatural transformation of the current situation, especially through the destruction of the invading force and the restoration of their traditional lands, lifestyle and beliefs. Often the millennial dream will refer to their reacquisition of political power. It is very common for one particular person, usually with charismatic gifts, to articulate the discontent of his or her people and to shape the vision of the coming restoration of their fortunes.[523]

If the source of the small apocalypse was indeed a book in which Jesus' revelation was thought to have been written down in secret to be unsealed at a time of crisis, this would make Jesus the 'charismatic person' who formulates, through its true author, the hopes of the people. But who were the people and what was the crisis? Gerd Theissen connects, as have many before him, the writing of the small apocalypse with the Caligula crisis in the year 40 CE. In short, the events that led to it are as follows: In Jamnia a newly-erected imperial altar was destroyed by the Jews and Philo's ambassadorial efforts only seemed to worsen the situation. Thus an order was issued by Caligula to the Syrian governor to move two legions and to erect a statue of the emperor in Jerusalem. While the statue was being crafted, a demonstration took place as Jewish leaders were negotiating in Phoenicia. A second negotiation took place in Tiberias and as a result the governor wrote back to Gaius Caligula asking him to withdraw the order. Agrippa intervened in Rome and Gaius accepted. How these events affected the Markan material should, it is hoped, become apparent in the following commentary.

The Olive Discourse found in Matthew 24–5(= Mark 13 = Luke 21) may be divided into five distinct parts: Christ foretells the destruction of the temple, what calamities shall fall, how great they shall be before His coming, the signs of His coming to judgement and the parables.

The sermon starts at the Mount of Olives overlooking the temple. Here it is important to note that Matthew 24:3 alters the meaning of the verse which he has from Mark 13:3–4:

> And as he sat upon the mount of Olives, the disciples came unto him privately, saying, Tell us, when shall these things be? and what [shall be] the sign of thy coming, and of the end of the world? (Matthew 24:3 KJV).

> And as he sat upon the mount of Olives over against the temple, Peter and James and John and Andrew asked him privately, Tell us, when shall these things be? and what [shall be] the sign when all these things shall be fulfilled? (Mark 13: 3–4 KJV).

It is obvious that for Mark the destruction of the temple signals the return of Jesus, for the whole apocalypse is provided to contextualize the question of the disciples regarding the time of the destruction of the temple. For the reader of Mark, 'all these things' can only signify the things Jesus had just prophesied about the temple but for Matthew the temple's destruction is a thing of the past which obviously did not herald the coming of Jesus. Therefore Matthew alters the question so that it specifically refers to the second advent of Jesus.

In Darby's translation the expression 'completion of the age'[524] replaces the more traditional translation from the KJV, 'the end of the world', which is a questionable translation. The Greek text reads 'συντελείας τοῦ αἰῶνος' and is translated in the Vulgate as *consummationis saeculi* (consummation of the age). The world in the sense of the physical world, or rather earth, is usually referred to by the word 'cosmos' (κόσμος).

Then Jesus warns His disciples about following false religious leaders (claiming messiahship) and how they will be troubled by wars, famines, pestilence or earthquakes. These, however, are not the end itself; these are but 'the beginning of sorrows'.

Per Bilde, who thinks that Mark 13 does not represent the forties, counters that there were in fact no prophetic or messianic movements in connection with the Caligula crisis.[525] Theissen's proposal is that the apocalypse is Jewish-Christian and that the prophets are Christian prophets. He points to the possibility of it being a reference to what we have called prophets of Jesus and calls attention to the consonance of the statement in Mark 13:6 and the Montanists mentioned above. Another possibility he suggests is Simon Magus, who was apparently active in Samaria in the late thirties.[526]

To Theissen, however, the mention of 'wars and rumours of wars' is more significant. In chapter 4 we saw that Antipas had been criticized for his marriage with Herodias because it was against Jewish law. However, the marriage was also problematic because Antipas had to divorce his wife, a Nabatean princess. This divorce, a humiliation of the Nabatean king, led to a war in 36–7. Bilde objects that Mark refers to 'wars' in the plural while Josephus refers only to 'a war'.[527] Theissen counters that there was indeed at the same time a war between the Romans and a Persian pretender to the throne.[528] More importantly, Theissen points out that the odd sequence of 'wars' followed by 'rumours of wars' makes sense in this context. Antipas suffered great defeats in his war against Aretas, the Nabatean king, and thus the Syrian legate was commissioned to intervene. He travelled with two legions from Antioch to Ptolemais and continued to Jerusalem alone, and people presumably expected another great war. Having arrived, however, he was informed about the death of Tiberius and the campaign was abandoned.

Rather than going to war with the Nabateans, the Syrian legate could go to Antioch where an earthquake had just hit. Though there is no direct evidence of famine, Theissen suggests that certain requests for tax concessions of agricultural products may indicate a poor harvest.[529] Regarding verse 8, Theissen states:

> In that war [the Nabatean] 'nation [arose] against nation' – Jews against Nabateans. It was a struggle of one 'polis' against another. Both nations had monarchical governments: it is true that Herod Antipas only bore the title of 'tetrarch', but among his Aramaic-speaking people he was called 'king' (cf. Mk 6:14).[530]

Our history is from 'the beginnings of sorrows' (Mark 13:8) to the complete spread of the gospel (Mark 13:10)[531] until 'then shall the end come' (only in Matthew 24:14 but suggested by Mark 13:13). This provides a far eschatological perspective on all of the following prophecies, for certainly spreading the gospel must have seemed an enormous task for the early Christians. Mark 13:9 sets the stage for something that must surely have been a Markan experience.[532] As is well-known from the annals of history, the persecution of the early Christian community was savage and merciless.[533] Theissen sees in Matthew a redaction in which, instead of using Mark's 'apocalyptic topos', he focuses on communal problems which are more pressing.[534]

Then Mark goes on to tie the end of the age to the prophecy of the 'abomination of desolation' (13:14) which refers to Daniel 11:31, generally held to refer to Antiochus Epiphanes, the ruler of Syria who persecuted Jews by taking Jerusalem, stopping worship in the temple and erecting an altar on the altar of burnt-offering.[535] Geza Vermes proposes that this passage should be viewed as a *pesher* on the passage of Daniel,[536] some of the Dead Sea scrolls, like the Nahum Commentary, having striking similarities.[537]

Theissen argues that Mark's text here does not at all refer to the destruction in 70 but rather to the impending threat of Gaius Caligula erecting his statue, the 'desolating sacrilege'.[538]

Bilde grants that this is, indeed, the most direct reference of all to the Caligula crisis but then goes on to raise some objections. Why, he asks, are only those in Judea addressed (clearly the crisis involved all of Israel)? Why should only they flee and why wait until the statue stands in the temple (at which point armed resistance must be presumed to be over)?[539]

Theissen, however, convincingly makes the connection with the following arguments. First of all, he points out that the 'Assumption of Moses', a Jewish work composed between 4 BCE and 30 CE, deals with the theme of Jewish persecution but never uses the term 'desolating sacrilege', revealing that the term was not common and must therefore only have been invoked in the small apocalypse because the term was particularly suited. The word 'sacrilege' or 'abomination' refers to an act against God (such as idolatry) rather than a punishment by God (as the Roman destruction of the temple was invariably perceived in 70). Further, there are grammatical oddities that suggest this: the text reads 'standing where he ought not'[540] and must therefore represent a person; 'standing' also appropriately states what statues do. And, finally, it is not the existence of idols that is the problem; it is that the idol stands 'where he ought not'.

In answer to Bilde, the following is suggested. The original text was a Jewish-Christian leaflet which was circulated only in Jerusalem where people could 'see' (Mark 13:14 uses the word ἴδητε) the statue. From this perspective, everything after verse 14 is regarded as being in the near future.

Mark 13:14–18 encourages a fleeing into the mountains in the hope that this will not occur during the winter. Bilde asks why but Theissen merely shows that there was a general readiness to flee, citing both Philo and Josephus.

Mark 13:19 describes the greatness of these tribulations which are 'such as there hath not been the like from the beginning of the creation which God created until now, and never shall be' (ASV). The parallel passage of Luke interprets these events as follows: 'For these be the days of vengeance, that all things which are written may be fulfilled' (Luke

21:22 KJV). Luke clearly identifies these events with the Roman conquest in 70. 'And they shall fall by the edge of the sword, and shall be led captive into all the nations: and Jerusalem shall be trodden down of the Gentiles, until the times of the Gentiles be fulfilled' (Luke 21:24 ASV).

In the small apocalypse there are a couple of recurrences of warnings against false Christs and prophets (Matthew 24:5, 11, 23–4; Mark 13:6, 21–2; Luke 21:8). While Matthew repeats the theme, Luke has cut the theme away from Mark, his source.

The word 'prophet' does not indicate whether it is a false or true prophet of God. Although the Greek has ψευδοπροφήτης (false-prophet), the New Testament does not seem to be very precise about what a prophet is.[541] Deuteronomy says of the prophet that is to come, that he 'shall speak in my [the Lord's] name' and that he shall be recognized by the fulfilment of His prophecies (Deuteronomy 18:19–20).

The warning of Jesus may well be for His followers to guard themselves against such people as Caphias and Annas, who became religious puppets of political intrigue, or people such as Theudas and Judas of Galilee (Acts 5:36–7). This, however, remains highly doubtful. Later the Christians could draw a new significance from this, as the established communities checked the authority of the local prophets so that the community was not jeopardized by prophetic expectation, driving the community into the desert or to a 'hidden place'.

As we saw, Mark knows that tribulations have been going on for a while and that fleeing is the only response possible and so prays that this is not hindered by practical (the winter, Mark 13:18) or religious-legal (the Sabbath, Matthew 24:20) obstacles.

Mark concludes that his audience will see this outbreak of messianic fervour and will realize that it had been predicted but Matthew inserts a saying about the Son of man coming as lightning so as to contrast the prophetic imperatives of the hidden and distant (Matthew (Q) 24:27–8).[542] 'Lightning' is the most common translation for the word ἀστραπὴ (*astrape)* but it is not always appropriate (e. g. Luke 11:36). Its meaning is somewhat approximated by the word 'shining'. Lightning is not generally known to come from the East and shine in the West, so perhaps it is not lightning but the sun which is intended.[543] If this is the case, then it is not speed but brilliancy which is the point of the passage. It also conveys a sense of regularity and surety. This statement is to be seen as an antipole to the previous warning. Matthew adds, 'For wheresoever the carcase is, there will the eagles be gathered together.' The word ἀετοί translated as 'eagle' is, in fact, a more general expression meaning 'birds that eat meat'. The Hebrew word (נשר,[544] *nesher*) comes from the word to lacerate. Possibly 'eagle' was selected in some translations (Vulgate: *aquila*) because it might refer prophetically to the Roman empire, which used the eagle as its standard. Evans, however, correctly points out that the eagle 'is not a carrion-eating bird'.[545] The proverb is difficult to decipher. Müller suggests that the proverb intends to refer to the certainty with which a vulture finds its carrion.[546] In this case, the context would mean that everyone will spot the Son of man, just as surely as the vulture will find its carrion. However, for a proverb to be retained in use, it has to be both useful in various situations as well as self-explanatory when used in context. We must therefore understand the principle that the proverb illustrates independently of context. The principle is that if you can see the vultures, then you know that there is carrion. So before one has the chance to see the carrion itself one will see its sign, namely the vulture. Applying the proverb in this context therefore means that before one sees the Son of man (the carrion), one will see the signs of the Son of man (the vultures).

This picturesque portrait of the advent of the Son of man may use the Hebrew association of lightning with theophany to display the power of God. The word, rendered in Matthew 24:27 KJV as 'shineth' (φαίνεται, *phainetai*), may also be understood as 'is seen' (ASV), 'appear' (YLT), 'visible' (NIV) or 'flashing' (NJB, NEB, WEY), while James Moffatt's translation 'that shoots' is rather liberal. 'Lightning' is to be used either as a symbol of manifestation or, as hinted at, by using from 'East' to the 'West' to suggest swiftness or at least movement. Although lexically closer to the word 'presence' (*parousia*, literally, 'being alongside'), the context indicates an emphasis on the 'advent' aspect of the word. The parousia is a special feature of the Gospel of Matthew. The Luke parallel text, Luke 17:24, reads: 'so shall also the Son of man be in his day' (RW). Likewise Luke says, 'Even thus shall it be in the day when the Son of man is revealed' (Luke 17:30 RW). It is generally believed that Luke's expression is more original.[547] Another promise of signs is that the moon and sun shall be darkened (Mark 13:24–7 = Matthew 24:29–30 = Luke 21:25–7).[548] Luke inserts the comment: 'Men's hearts failing them for fear, and for looking after those things which are coming on the earth: for the powers of heaven shall be shaken' (Luke 21:26 KJV).

Then Matthew says His sign will appear in the heavens and to identify this sign is no easy task. The 'and' at the beginning of the sentence distinguishes the sign of the Son of man from that of the moon and the sun.[549] The expression used in Matthew 24:29 is a very close description of the events depicted in Joel: 'The earth shall quake before them; the heavens shall tremble: the sun and the moon shall be dark, and the stars shall withdraw their shining' (Joel 2:10 KJV).

These words are quoted by Peter in his Pentecostal sermon (see Acts 2) in which he applied these events to his own days. This is a good example of how a far eschatological tradition is turned into a realized one.[550]

Some suggest that Jesus Himself is, by His coming, the sign of the Son of man.[551] The word 'sign', as mentioned, may also connote a miracle and hence we should explore this as a possibility, 'For as Jonas was a sign unto the Ninevites, so shall also the Son of man be to this generation' (Luke 11:30 KJV). With the warnings against false prophets who display 'great signs', combined with the above statement, we must consider whether Jesus' words were indeed to be His sign or whether the sign of the Son of man may be a reference to Jesus' own person.

Matthew also mentions the sounding of the trumpet. This symbol of the Son of man calling His chosen subjects probably stems from the account of Yahweh's command to Moses that He should make two silver trumpets that should be used for calling to assemblage and to sound alarm. The imagery is further enhanced by the fact that His angels[552] are to go forth and gather the 'elect'.

At this point in Mark, Jesus emphatically introduces a parable: 'Now from the fig tree learn her parable: when her branch is now become tender, and putteth forth its leaves, ye know that the summer is nigh' (Mark 13:28 ASV).

While Matthew follows Mark in associating this parable with the Son of man, Luke is perhaps closer to the original context in which it refers to the coming of the kingdom of

God. It is difficult to ascertain why Luke made this emendation.

The fig tree, one of the major assets of Palestine and a sign of prosperity, grows fruit before it has leaves and so when the 'summer is near' it is time for the fig tree to put forth its fruit. The tree was sometimes thought of as a symbol of the Jewish nation, so one may well ponder whether it is intended that a specific fruit will appear in Israel. In this context it may also be used to remind the disciples to watch out for the signs of the spiritual summer, the return of Christ. In its original setting it is, however, more likely to have referred to Jesus' own time.[553] In other words, we here have a saying of realized eschatology that was made into a far eschatological saying. Mark follows this with a near eschatological statement: 'so ye, also, when these ye may see coming to pass, ye know that it is nigh, at the doors' (Mark 13:29 YLT).

The apparent problem with this statement is that (by implication) this did not come to pass. It may be interesting to look at a similar promise and a possibly more problematic statement: 'Verily I say to you, That there are some of them that stand here, who shall not taste of death, till they shall see the Son of man coming in his kingdom' (Mark 9:1 and Matthew 16:28). Ben Witherington, in his book *Jesus, Paul and the End of the World* argues that this saying originates from Jesus Himself. He points out that the use of 'Amen', as well as the Semitic flavour of the text, such as the expression 'taste death', suggest its authenticity. Indeed, this argument is strengthened by the fact that these were not excluded by the writer of the Gospel of Matthew even after it became apparent that Jesus did not return in the 'kingdom of God come with power'.[554] Witherington suggests that in its original context, as portrayed by Mark, the reference to the 'kingdom of God come with power', probably referred to an event taking place during the time of Jesus, a miracle or even, as the context of Mark suggests, the transfiguration. Elsewhere he notes the difficulty with Matthew 10:23: 'Ye shall not have gone over the cities of Israel, till the Son of man shall have come' (ASV). This, however, he does not find conclusive but rather suggests that the context shows that the remark was an encouragement rather than a prediction.

The word 'generation' (γενεὰ) has been interpreted in various ways so as not to indicate Jesus' contemporaries.[555] One such example would be to think of 'this generation' as a type of people rather than a people of a specific time. 'This generation' was stigmatized by John the Baptist as a 'generation of vipers' which Jesus called 'An evil and adulterous generation seeketh for a sign'. The use of the word 'generation' in this manner may be found in Psalms 12:7 and 112:2.[556]

The next statement seems almost to be in contrast with the previous one: 'But of that day and hour knoweth no man, no, not the angels of heaven but my Father only' (Matthew 24:36 RW). Certain major documents include 'nor the Son'.[557] The originality of this inclusion is attested by its presence in the text of Mark 13:32.

In Q, Jesus further compares the coming in the clouds with the days of Noah (Matthew 24:38–41), when people were also carefree and carried on their lives unaware of their impending judgement. This is also parallelled by a verse in Thomas: 'Two will recline on a couch; one will die, one will live' (Thomas 61:1 SV).

These striking passages, which describe the coming of the Son of man as a cataclysmic event,[558] in fact represent an important part of the apocalypse. The Thomean version is, according to Funk, a 'piece of common wisdom: death strikes when we least expect it and rather arbitrarily'.[559] Schmidt, on the other hand, takes the view that it is a gnostic context, where life and death are spiritual conditions.[560] But the present author finds that it is more likely to be of entirely Christian origin, since it is uninstructive as common lore or in an esoteric setting. Both seem unlikely since the sentence is set in the future tense.

Similarities between the story of Noah and the coming of the Son of man are thus made clear. It is the Day of Judgement which will save the faithful and condemn the unfaithful.[561] The promised deluge is in fact in conflict with the promise of God never to flood the earth again (Genesis 9:15), a theme reiterated by Isaiah (54:9) and also by Sirac:[562] 'Noah was found perfect and righteous; in the time of wrath he was taken in exchange; therefore a remnant was left to the earth when the flood came. Everlasting covenants were made with him that all flesh should not be blotted out by a flood' (Sirac 44:17–18 RAPC).

The concept of eternal covenants[563] is an interesting perspective because it leads to the question of dispensational covenants. One may see this not only as a scene of judgement, though that certainly is central, but also as a promise of a new covenant. The parallel text of Luke adds the story of Lot (Genesis 19:15–28) as another parallel cataclysm. There is in fact quite a bit of debate as to the origin of Luke's verse 17:28. Tuckett proposes that the verse developed in the Lukan version of Q (shown as Q^{lk}).[564] Catchpole, on the other hand, argues convincingly that it is part of Q and that Matthew has redacted it away.[565] 'But the same day that Lot went out of Sodom it rained fire and brimstone from heaven, and destroyed them all. Even thus shall it be in the day when the Son of man is revealed'

(Luke 17:29–30 RW). The last verse implies that the Son of man in fact is hidden from men but that when he is revealed (ἀποκαλύπτεται), mankind will be judged (see above). In this image, the concept of movement (i.e. the *coming* of the Son of man) is completely phased out and one of a transition of states (hidden and revealed) is introduced. This is presumably a transfer of common lore regarding the future appearance of Elijah, who will reveal the Messiah.

Matthew 24:42–4 combines Mark and Q (Thomas also has this parable) to make a prime example of indefinite eschatology:[566]

> Watch therefore: for ye know not what hour your Lord doth come. But know this, that if the goodman of the house had known in what watch the thief would come, he would have watched, and would not have suffered his house to be broken up. Therefore be ye also ready: for in such an hour as ye think not the Son of man cometh (KJV).

The key word here is watch.[567] One may wonder why such a theme was important in the early church. The relevance of either the manifest Christ depicted as descending on a cloud or the hidden Christ coming unseen during the night may have been secondary. The point of the story is that the vigilant are rewarded. Indeed, we find that the entire chapter is dedicated, not so much to the coming itself, as to the signs of the time. Of what importance would the precise hour or day be if when it came it was evident that it had arrived? The answer may lie in the importance not so much of the coming itself but in the consequence of being ready and behaving in a manner appropriate in terms of one's community.

Q presents yet another example through the parable of the 'faithful and wise servant':

> Who then is a faithful and wise servant, whom his lord hath made ruler over his household, to give them meat in due season? Blessed [is] that servant, whom his lord when he cometh shall find so doing. Verily I say unto you, That he shall make him ruler over all his goods. But and if that evil servant shall say in his heart, My lord delayeth his coming; And shall begin to smite [his] fellowservants, and to eat and drink with the drunken; The lord of that servant shall come in a day when he looketh not for [him], and in an hour that he is not aware of, And shall cut him asunder, and appoint [him] his portion with the hypocrites: there shall be weeping and gnashing of teeth (Matthew 24:45–51 KJV).

Here again the conclusion is the unknowability of the hour of the coming of the Son of man. This version of the parable seems to emphasize the importance of being good to the 'fellow-servants'. The parallel text in Luke puts the emphasis differently: 'The lord of that servant will come in a day when he looketh not for him, and at an hour when he is not aware, and will cut him in two, and will appoint him his portion with the unbelievers' (Luke 12:46 RW). Notice here that it is those who 'looketh not for him' that will be judged as 'unbelievers'. This is a very curious conclusion, for it exalts belief in the return to a matter of right faith. Were there any in the Lukan community that doubted that Jesus would return? Had near eschatology, as we see in 1 Thessalonians 4:17, been discredited among some people and made others 'disbelieve'? It is difficult to say.

The Olive Discourse continues into the twenty-fifth chapter with the parable of the ten virgins. We should note that the parable here is prefaced differently than the ones in Matthew 13: it specifically refers to 'that time' (i.e. at the return of Christ), yet deals with 'the kingdom of heaven'.

Here the ten virgins are waiting for the bridegroom. Five of them are foolish and five are prudent (or wise).[568] The prudent virgins have the distinguishing feature of being prepared. When the bridegroom comes, only the wise virgins are ready and are able to follow him to the wedding banquet; the others arrive late and are denied entrance. The bridegroom here plays the role of Christ returning to the world. Those who are alert and are expecting Him will be joined with Him and those who are not alert will be deprived. The conclusion is given at the end of the parable: 'Watch therefore, for ye know neither the day nor the hour wherein the Son of man cometh' (Matthew 25:13 KJV). Catchpole notes that, like the parable of the watchful/obedient servant, this parable also seems to be directed towards being prudent.[569]

Next is the parable of the talents (Matthew 25:14ff).[570] This parable seems to paint a picture of the kingdom of heaven similar to that of the parable of the seed-sower (Matthew 13:3; cf. chapter 5). It too portrays a man who leaves something behind to flourish and grow. The servants of this parable are left with a trust of talents[571] and are expected to employ these to gain more wealth. The first two do this but the last hides away the money and returns it unused at his master's return. He defends himself saying of his own master that he is 'a hard man, reaping where thou didst not sow, and gathering where thou didst not scatter'. One may understand this as the servant having received the ability to spread the 'good news' but failing to do so because it is too hard and claiming that it is not right for the master to ask this of a servant. The gift of God is given freely but if it is not employed then it is given to someone else to fulfil God's purpose.

The Olive Discourse concludes with the vivid picture of

the final judgement. Here the sheep and the goats are divided into two folds, the saved and the lost, drawing on imagery already known to the Jews. The sheep are the chosen people, as can be seen from the twenty-third Psalm, and the goats are the outcasts.[572] The statement in verse 32 that 'before him shall be gathered all the nations' denotes that this judgement will not be confined to one particular group of people but rather the whole earth. 'Then shall the King say unto them on his right hand, Come, ye blessed of my Father, inherit the kingdom prepared for you from the foundation of the world' (Matthew 25:34 KJV).

Here the kingdom is said to have been prepared from the foundation of the world. He praises those on His right side for their charity to Him in His hour of need, when thirsty, hungry, imprisoned, naked and sick. The left side is condemned for ignoring Him in His hour of need. The conclusion of this scenario is that of the final judgement: those who did good were rewarded with 'life eternal' and those who were wicked went away to 'everlasting punishment' (Matthew 25:46). This tradition too seems to go back to a form that is essentially non-eschatological. The theme of the prophets of Jesus lies behind. He who treats those who are (of) the least (ἐλαχίστων) of Jesus' brothers has treated Jesus Himself. The moral teaching predates the eschatological. He that receives the prophet of Jesus has received Jesus Himself.

Summary and Conclusion

In this chapter we have been confronted with some of the most difficult issues relating to the Historical Jesus and the development of prophecy in early Christianity.

We started by exploring a body of Jesus tradition that seemed not only diverse but at times even contradictory. We proposed possible scenarios for near eschatologies in connection with the mission of John the Baptist as well as possible scenarios for far eschatology towards the end of Jesus' own ministry.

There are some near eschatological beliefs reflected in the Pauline literature, most significantly, however, in 1 Thessalonians 4:15–17:

> For this we say unto you by the word of the Lord, that we which are alive [and] remain unto the coming of the Lord shall not prevent them which are asleep. For the Lord himself shall descend from heaven with a shout, with the voice of the archangel, and with the trump of God: and the dead in Christ shall rise first: Then we which are alive [and] remain shall be caught up together with them in the clouds, to meet the Lord in the air: and so shall we ever be with the Lord (KJV).

It is clear from the statement in verse 17 that Paul expected this to happen in his own days, while he was still alive. Many elements of this tradition, which Paul attributes to Jesus, are indeed not his own. The images of the archangel and the trumpet are reflected in a tradition that prompted a redaction in Matthew 24:31. These same images, as well as the resurrection of the dead, appear at the end of Didache's apocalypse (16:6).

The Markan image of Jesus descending from heaven is also reflected in Paul's tradition. We also see that Paul combined the indefinite eschatology of the thief coming in the night with his near eschatological perspective. This perspective was still alive and well at the end of the century when Ignatius wrote to the Ephesians (11:1).

We have one tradition in the sayings tradition in Matthew 10:23 that appears to presume that the disciples could exhaust the villages of Israel before the Son of man arrived. It was proposed that Jesus could have used near eschatology in the context of John the Baptist's message. If this is the case, then 'the Son of man' was Jesus' self-designation that replaced the Baptist's term 'the Coming One' and Jesus was merely alluding to His as yet unrevealed mission. While this is a plausible scenario, it is not the most likely. The tradition is uniquely Matthean and is typical of his source. Clearly Matthew knew Jesus prophets that were against the Gentile mission. We know that some of the sayings of the Jesus prophets were developed by them independently of Jesus. Yet Didache does not clearly suggest that Jesus prophets were engaged in prophesying but were mostly interested in their ethical teachings and their illustration of Jesus' life style. From the Olive Discourse we know that by the mid-thirties some Jesus prophets attached to the Jerusalem community claimed to be Jesus returned (Mark 13:5–6). The apocalypse in the Didache also warns of false prophets in the last days (16:3). The tradition of a grandiose return of Jesus which Mark 13 and 1 Thessalonians 4:15–17 show probably represents a countermove of the scribal community developing its presentation from its knowledge of Jewish scripture. This move effectively disqualified any claims advanced by Jesus prophets. Did the Jesus prophets have traditions in which the Son of man's arrival was expected in the immediate future? An Aramaic expression 'Lord come!' (*maran atha*) is found in both Paul (1 Corinthians 16:22) and Didache (10:6). The tradition of Jesus' immediate return is old and well-attested.

Against this tradition of Jesus' immediate return the following factors should be considered: 1) the need to resolve cognitive dissonance, 2) the tradition is incongruent with the Jesus tradition about the nature of the kingdom of God and 3) the function of prophecy as an ongoing activity.

In the first section of this chapter we discussed the success of Jesus' transformation of millennialism into wisdom, that is to say, a realized eschatology. In an attempt to account for the transition between the first layer of tradition (wisdom) and the second (millennial), we proposed that the opposite process was an equally plausible one.

We looked at tension between realized eschatology and indefinite eschatology as well as the tension between far and near eschatology. These are not only tensions in a theological sense but also a tension in function. We saw in 1 Thessalonians 4:15–5:5 that Paul combined these eschatologies. Both served to urge the Christian community out of its comfort and to be active in its proclamation of the Christian message. The two other eschatologies invoked the opposite process, namely the formation of community. If the end is either in the far future or in some sense already present, there is no reason to warn people of an impending judgement.

So if John the Baptist appealed to millennialism, in a fashion that placed society in a state of tension, making equal requirement of repentance for all, then Jesus brought that tension into relief by transforming it into wisdom. Jesus began a process of social formation, starting a new community which lived according to the radical wisdom of God. That transformation, of course, meant a transition of theology. The image of what the kingdom of God was needed to be reconfigured, a task carried out through the use of parables. We saw that within the sphere of low tension eschatologies, far eschatology could explain the community's far-reaching goal, the spread of the new order. The culmination of social change would make God, once again, the ruler of the world.

How can we then account for the reversion to millennialism? We know that towards the middle of the thirties many Jesus prophets began to proclaim that Jesus was coming, had come and was hidden, or that they themselves were Jesus returned. We have records from the forties of this happening, which suggests that this was something that had already, to some extent, occurred earlier. Mark places these claims by Jesus prophets prior to the outbreak of the Nabatean war in 36–7 and clearly the Markan source was careful about the chronology. This was important for the apocalyptic genre. It is therefore fair to say that these claims arose shortly after Jesus' own execution.

The Jerusalem community dealt with the crucifixion of Jesus by its tradition of the resurrection of Jesus (discussed in chapter 11). This, however, is absolutely absent in the sayings tradition we have explored. Its solution was not to have a resurrected Jesus but to have an imminently returning one.

The reason for this solution can be accounted for in a number of ways. First and foremost, however, was the role Jesus played in relation to His prophets and how they perceived Him. Jesus was, above all, an actor, someone whose activity in the social sphere was significant and valuable. This is clear from both sayings and miracle traditions. As such, a resurrected Jesus had little value. In the resurrection tradition we find apostolic authority (this is discussed in chapter 11) but the authority of the prophets of Jesus was tied to the living Jesus and their emulation of

His life style. It is also most likely that they had greater attachment to Jesus as a person. The hope of being reunited with the person they lost to the cross was probably more attractive than the brief encounter in the resurrection traditions. In the Farewell Discourse we saw the promise that the new Paraclete would stay forever (John 14:16) and it too promised judgement (John 16:11). This is something that seems to permeate every tradition about Jesus' return. It was significant to the prophets of Jesus because they were persecuted in their tradition, something that we have no reason to doubt reflected their actual experience. Again, the resurrected Jesus did not change this injustice the way that the returned Jesus did. In Q (Matthew 11:27 = Luke 10:22), Jesus says, 'All things have been delivered unto me of my Father: and no one knoweth who the Son is, save the Father; and who the Father is, save the Son, and he to whomsoever the Son willeth to reveal him' (ASV). It therefore seems that Jesus as a person must play the role of God's ruler.

Each of these factors probably contributed to the choice of an imminent return of Jesus in the sayings tradition. Yet this does not explain why some of the prophets of Jesus decided that they themselves were the returned Jesus. The answer undoubtedly lies in the relationship of master and disciple. The prophets of Jesus represented Jesus in all respects, they acted with His authority and whatever was done to them was as if it were done to Him. The step from representing to actually being Jesus was probably as hazy for the prophets of Jesus as it was for those who were under their authority.

Christian scribes answered this challenge by composing small apocalypses based on features from Jewish scripture. This did not mean that they did not accept the idea that

Jesus' return was imminent. Both 1 Thessalonians and the composition behind Mark 13 accept that Jesus was about to return. It was not until Mark, Matthew and Luke started to expand and edit it that the synoptic apocalypse placed the return of Jesus in the distant future.

As we noted, however, not all far eschatological statements should be understood as scribal compositions. We saw in many of the reliable traditions about the present kingdom a vision of its evolution into an all-encompassing one. Jesus' personal role in the future kingdom, however, is difficult to determine. Therefore we looked at the role of Jesus and found that there were two traditions about His role in the introduction of the kingdom of God on earth. The first was Galilean and perceived Jesus as a prophet; the second used the terms Christ and Messiah and appears to have perceived Him as a king. Neither of these terms is superior to the other in popular traditions. They appear therefore to have been used more out of convenience than as markers that truly described who Jesus was. Neither designation, be it in the popular version or in the later scribal context, tells us anything significant about Jesus' position in the kingdom. As God's Son, Jesus had, according to Q, been handed all that was with God. In what sense Jesus would remain the ruler is difficult to say. It seems likely, however, that the disciples were promised a reunion with Jesus or support sent by Him in their mission on His behalf. It is important that such remarks of encouragement can be understood entirely apart from millennialism. Indeed, as Kloppenborg remarks, Jesus could easily have referred to both judgement and resurrection without being a millennialist. On the whole, however, these appear to have been unimportant in Jesus' teachings about the kingdom.

In chapter 2 we reviewed a host of popular movements,

both prophetic and messianic. All of them, without fail, were put down and disappeared. Looking particularly at the action prophet who promised an intervention in history by God, just as Q promised on behalf of Jesus, we must ask why these movements failed while Jesus' flourished and continued even after He died. The obvious reason was His form of discipleship, a discipleship that formed a new family, a new life, life that did not wait or provoke the arrival of the kingdom of God but which by its very nature and mode of being was the kingdom of God. The very teachings of Jesus that we looked at in chapter 5 were what ensured that the movement itself carried on even after His death. The survival of the Christian religion proves the mode of discipleship; the mode of discipleship assures us of what the teachings were that formed this particular form of discipleship. Thus, although we cannot be positive that Jesus did not speak of the general resurrection or other apocalyptic topos, these played no integral part in His teachings.

9

The Lord's Last Supper

Matthew 26:1–35
Mark 14:1–25
Luke 22:1–20
John 13:1–38

This chapter deals with the events that led to the arrest of Jesus. We shall discuss the Lord's last supper, the story on which the Eucharist is modelled, the institution of the Christian faith which has been described as 'the heart and the summit of the Church's life'.[573] We shall also deal with the betrayal of Judas Iscariot, one of the most enigmatic characters of the New Testament narrative.

The venue for this event was prepared by Jesus, who sent His disciples with specific instructions on how to find the proper host. The event took place on the outskirts of Jerusalem. The disciples of Jesus were thus sent out to prepare for the celebration (Matthew 26:17–20).

The Betrayal of Judas Iscariot: Matthew 26:21–5, 27:3–10; Mark 14:18–21, 27–31; Luke 22:21–3; John 13:21–38; Acts 1:18, 19

While the disciples were preparing for the celebration of Passover,[574] one of them had secretly, for reasons that are opaque to say the least, plotted to bring down his master. This was Judas Iscariot. Apparently, this disciple of Jesus had been trusted with the finances of the group. Some consider that his name 'Iscariot' may have been a reference to his former allegiance to the Sicarii movement. Horsley, however, as we saw in chapter 2, has determined that the Sicarii were not established until later. Others have more convincingly argued that the name refers to his place of origin, 'Kerioth' ('ish' meaning 'man of').[575]

The motivating force behind the betrayal of Judas has been a mystery that has remained unclear since the early days of Christianity. The fact that Jesus seems to have entrusted him with the treasury of the disciples (John 13:29) has added to the mystery in a way only superseded by his enigmatic suicide. If we are to rely solely on the comments of the evangelists, the motive seems to be that of money. John is the only one who calls him 'the son of perdition' (17:12) and 'a thief' (12:6).[576] The others call him 'traitor' (Luke 6:16) or 'he who betrayed' (Mark 3:19). The charge of 'thief' may be true but can hardly explain the treason, neither does it seem to be a valid reason for Judas to have joined the band of poor wandering disciples. Certainly the meagre resources of this small group was not the incentive for a thief to join up.

It has been speculated that while Judas did not fancy himself a Messiah in his own right, he may have thought that Jesus could be instrumental in creating an uprising against the Romans. This would explain how Judas could both believe Jesus to be the Messiah and then, when He did not fulfil Judas' messianic expectations, betray Him. This, at least, is the hypothesis that Kahlil Gibran suggests in his book *Jesus, The Son of Man* in which he recounts Judas' dialogue with a man who lived outside Jerusalem. Here the distressed Judas explains his actions:

> When first He called us to Him He promised us a kingdom mighty and vast, and in our faith we sought His favour that we might have honourable stations in His court.
>
> We beheld ourselves princes dealing with these Romans as they have dealt with us. And Jesus said much about His kingdom, and I thought He had chosen me a captain of His chariots, and a chief man of His warriors. And I followed His footsteps willingly.
>
> But I found it was not a kingdom that Jesus sought, nor was it from the Romans He would have had us free. His kingdom was the kingdom of the heart. I heard Him talk of love and charity and forgiveness, and the wayside women listened gladly, but my heart grew bitter and I was hardened.[577]

Another suggestion is given by Dorothy Sayers in her radio play *The Man Born to be King*. The play is written with extensive notes in which she comments on the development of the different characters. In a certain sense, she takes the opposite view of Gibran and portrays Judas as initially having a good understanding of Jesus and His spiritual kingdom but then developing a suspicion that Jesus wants a political kingdom so that the treason becomes an attempt to save Jesus from corruption. She describes Judas prior to the betrayal in the following manner:

> He has got the right idea, and holds it with passion and sincerity. But his intellectual pride, his jealousy, and a fundamental lack of generosity make him a ready ground for the sowing of seeds of suspicion. He can trust nobody but himself . . . 'I would kill him with my hands' – if he were to let down my idea of him; that is the key speech.[578]

Both of these are, of course, artists' interpretations. The truth is, unfortunately, that there simply is not enough information to form a psychological profile. We are therefore left with speculation.

According to *The Narrative of Joseph of Arimathaea*, a medieval text, Judas was related to Caiaphas and was, in fact, 'his brother's son to Caiaphas'. This text portrays Judas as having joined Jesus for the sole purpose of betraying Him.[579] There is, however, no indication in the gospels that suggests that this was the case. Whether it is one or the other is difficult to deduce from the biblical text; in fact, the text of the gospels makes it seem like the act of betrayal was impulsive and unpremeditated.

Lastly, according to the Gospel of Judas, which is referred to in the writings of Epiphanius,[580] Judas was an enlightened Gnostic who betrayed Jesus for the purpose of bringing redemption to humankind. The gospel is also mentioned by Irenaeus in his *Against Heresies*:

> They [the Cainites] declare that Judas the traitor was thoroughly acquainted with these things, and that he alone, knowing the truth as no others did, accomplished the mystery of the betrayal; by him all things, both earthly and heavenly, were thus thrown into confusion. They produce a fictitious history of this kind, which they style the Gospel of Judas.[581]

A speculation that has not, to the present author's knowledge, been proposed, is that Judas the disciple who was apparently from Judea, was offended by Jesus' act against the temple. When temple officials solicited for information about the troublemaker, he decided that rather than being caught on the wrong side of the law he would turn in his former master.

Whether Judas was a leading figure amongst the apostles is difficult to say from looking at the biblical text. The fact that he kept the community purse, however, does make it likely. The pejorative perspective given in the gospel, which constantly reminds the reader that it is Judas who will betray Jesus, makes it unlikely that anyone would admit that Judas ever held a high office.

Next we shall consider the death of Judas. Here we have two different accounts of who purchased the land called 'the field of blood' (Akeldama[582]) and how Judas died. In the story given by Matthew (27:3–10), Judas repents and returns the blood money. The money is spent by the priests to purchase the aforesaid land and Judas, in his sorrow, decides to hang himself. Luke (Acts 1:16–20), however, has him purchase the land himself (we must therefore assume that he was unrepentant) and accidentally fall and 'burst asunder in the midst, and all his bowels gushed out'.

The text of Matthew seems to have been derived from an exclusively Matthean tradition. The quotation is from Zechariah 11:12–13 but perhaps with some themes from Jeremiah in mind (a potter, Jeremiah 18 and 19, and the purchase of a field, 32:7).[583] Matthew modifies the text considerably so that it will apply to Judas. On the other hand, some details seem clearly to have been taken from the prophecy. The amount (30 pieces of silver) seems to originate with the prophecy, and although Matthew changes the phraseology so that the money was given for the field, the prophecy's wording about casting it into the House of Yahweh is preserved in the narrative where Judas hurls the money in the temple. Thus there seems to be a narrative tradition that Matthew uses along with a prophetic text. The prophetic text as we read it did not give rise to the narrative but it did come out of what, in all likelihood, was a traditional Christian interpretation of the same prophecy. In other words, the sequence was: the basic facts of the event → the application of the prophecy → the development of narrative → the modification of the text of the prophecy.

The tradition in Acts explicitly cites two Psalms (69:25 and 109:8) in connection with the narrative as its fulfilment. Both seem to have contributed nothing to the tradition. Luke, or his source, had in mind the tradition as it stands when searching for proof that even the end and replacement of Judas were in accordance with scripture.

Another tradition regarding Judas' demise is found in Papias'[584] fourth book of *Expositions of the Oracles of the Lord*:

> Judas was a dreadful, walking example of impiety in this world, with his flesh bloated to such an extent that he could not walk through a space where a wagon could easily pass. Not even the huge bulk of his head could go through! It is related that his eyelids were so swollen that it was absolutely impossible for him to see the light and his eyes could not be seen by a physician, even with the help of a magnifying glass, so far had they sunk from their outward projection . . . He died after many tortures and punishments, in a secluded spot which has remained deserted and uninhabited up to our time. Not even to this day can anybody pass by the place without shielding his nostrils with his hands! Such is that afflux that goes through his flesh [and even pours] out on the ground.[585]

The fact that the account seems to be grossly exaggerated should not deter us from giving this story its proper consideration. It has the advantage over biblical accounts of being much less dramatic and not attempting to tie the land called Akeldama to his death.

Several attempts, some dating as far back as Apollinarius,[586] have been made to reconcile the two biblical accounts. It is suggested that where Acts states that Judas bought the land, it intends to say that he provided the money, whereas Matthew clarifies that it was Caiaphas who made the actual purchase. Judas' death is then explained as follows: When Judas was hanging himself, either the cord or the branch broke or someone intending to stop him from his suicide cut the rope and thus Judas was precipitated into a rocky area where the result is described in Acts.

The attempts to reconcile the two accounts seem to be altogether unsatisfactory. Though the stories constructed are not impossible, each of the two versions was intended to be read independently of the other and hence it is unreasonable to suppose that a reconciliation can be effected.[587]

Lastly, it must be noted that while Luke and Papias have a very negative view of Judas and have him unrepentant, Matthew has him returning the money and taking his own life to seek peace with himself.

The Eucharist

The Lord's Last Supper and the discourse that instituted this practice have already been discussed briefly but before we continue our study of the meaning of this institution we should trace its development through the centuries.

James D. G. Dunn traces two meal traditions that purport to go back to the life of Jesus. The first is the 'fellowship meals' when the followers of Jesus would come together to share a meal. This, as Dunn points out, is not merely a dinner but 'it meant in a very real sense sharing of one's life'.[588] This meal is referred to in the Galilean tradition implicitly in the mission command when the itinerants are commanded to eat whatever is placed in front of them. This form of meal tradition is found in the Didache free of elements from the passion tradition, which we will look at below.[589] In the last chapter we dismissed the idea that Jesus' threat to the temple was connected to the Lord's Supper. At this point, however, we need to qualify this dismissal, since Neusner is right about the connection to sanctification by a meal but is wrong about the meal tradition that he connects it with. The central point is that the meal tradition that can be related to the Historical Jesus belongs to this sort of fellowship meal, which was held repeatedly throughout Jesus' life.

Then there is the other tradition in which Jesus instituted a specific meal practice in view of either a) the impending eschaton or b) the impending sacrificial offering of Jesus Himself as the Passover lamb. It is important to point out that although none of these elements are found in the 'fellowship meal', which was a full and filling meal, it was still a means of sanctification for all those present.

In Corinth we see that Paul had a dual tradition. Before we look at the wording of the sacrament, which belongs to the last meal tradition, there are some circumstances described in Paul's letter which are worthy of note. Paul explains that he had heard that there were some in Corinth who ate before coming to the fellowship meal. Thus in this setting all bring food as they can and then all eat as they need. If, however, the rich eat before they come to the shared meal, they need to eat less and thus bring less and the poor and needy are left no better off (1 Corinthians 11:20–2). Though Paul attributes to the meal another significance, in practice the meal still functioned as a fellowship meal and he both knew and supported this.[590]

Paul, however, is explicit about the origin of the sacrament and its formulation, which he 'received of the Lord' and which was instituted 'in the night in which he was betrayed' (1 Corinthians 11:23 ASV). It is not surprising therefore that Paul's formulation, unlike that of Didache, purports to be in the words of Jesus. Yet we should note the change from the actual sacramental words in 1 Corinthians 11:24–5[591] and the interpretation of Paul in which Jesus is suddenly made to speak of Himself as 'Lord' and 'he' in verse 26.[592] Here the thought of an eschatological meaning of the Eucharist is provoked by the expression 'till he come', which indicates that it was also intended as a reminder to the disciples of the return of Jesus.

In the Gospel of the Ebionite – the Ebionites were a Jewish-Christian community of whom we have reports as far back as Irenaeus[593] – we read that Jesus was asked by His disciples: 'Where wilt thou that we prepare for thee the Passover? and he replied: I do not wish to eat the Passover flesh with you.'[594] This quotation, like the one about John the Baptist from the same gospel, suggests that the Ebionites were vegetarians. There is no evidence to suggest that this was a common practice. Indeed, we should remember that the apostolic mission command, which is outlined in chapter 5, includes the injunction that the disciples should eat whatever was placed in front of them.

There seems to be two different traditions regarding the words of the Eucharist: that presented by Mark (14:22–4) and Matthew (26:26–8) and that presented by Paul and Luke (22:19–20).

> And as they were eating, he took bread, and when he had blessed, he brake it, and gave to them, and said, Take ye: this is my body. And he took a cup, and when he had given thanks, he gave to them: and they all drank of it. And he said unto them, This is my blood of the covenant, which is poured out for many (Mark 14:22–4 ASV).

Mark 14:26 goes on to say that they sang hymns. This in all likelihood refers to Hallel psalms that were commonly sung at Passover (Mishnah: Pesahim 5:7D). We shall look further at these psalms below. In this tradition Jesus identifies the elements of the Eucharist with his own body and blood. His blood is then identified with the 'blood of the covenant which is poured out for many'. Matthew adds what surely is implied in Mark, that the blood poured is 'for the remission of sin'. Paul's tradition is quite similar:

> For I received of the Lord that which also I delivered unto you, that the Lord Jesus in the night in which he was betrayed took bread; and when he had given thanks, he brake it, and said, This is my body, which is for you: this do in remembrance of me. In like manner also the cup, after supper, saying, This cup is the new covenant in my blood: this do, as often as ye drink it, in remembrance of me (1 Corinthians 11:23–5 ASV).

Paul also identifies elements of the Eucharist with Jesus' body and blood but adds that the rite is done in remembrance. He also inserts that the second element is introduced only when the first has been consumed. Luke contains all these elements but also has the Markan element of the blood being poured. The two traditions have much in common and it is likely that they both stem from the same oral tradition, with its origin in the same community but modified in accordance with the local usage.

Mark too knows of an eschatological connection: 'Verily I say to you, I will drink no more of the fruit of the vine, until that day that I drink it new in the kingdom of God' (Mark 14:25 ASV).

In the Didache[595] we find the perspective of those who received the itinerants and how they understood this meal:

> But as touching the eucharistic thanksgiving give ye thanks thus. First, as regards the cup: We give Thee thanks, O our Father, for the holy vine of Thy son David, which Thou madest known unto us through Thy Son Jesus; Thine is the glory for ever and ever. Then as regarding the broken bread: We give Thee thanks, O our Father, for the life and knowledge which Thou didst make known unto us through Thy Son Jesus; Thine is the glory for ever and ever. As this broken bread was scattered upon the mountains and being gathered together became one, so may Thy Church be gathered together from the ends of the earth into Thy kingdom; for Thine is the glory and the power through Jesus Christ for ever and ever (Didache 9:1–4).

This meal is only for people who have been baptized (9:5). This thanksgiving is then followed by the actual meal and is concluded with a prayer:

> And after ye are satisfied thus give ye thanks: We give Thee thanks, Holy Father, for Thy holy name, which Thou hast made to tabernacle in our hearts, and for the knowledge and faith and immortality, which Thou hast made known unto us through Thy Son Jesus; Thine is the glory for ever and ever. Thou, Almighty Master, didst create all things for Thy name's sake, and didst give food and drink unto men for enjoyment, that they might render thanks to Thee; but didst bestow upon us spiritual food and drink and eternal life through Thy Son. Before all things we give Thee thanks that Thou art powerful; Thine is the glory for ever and ever. Remember, Lord, Thy Church to deliver it from all evil and to perfect it in Thy love; and gather it together from the four winds – even the Church which has been sanctified – into Thy kingdom which Thou hast prepared for it; for Thine is the power and the glory for ever and ever. May grace come and may this world pass away. Hosanna to the God of David. If any man is holy,

> let him come; if any man is not, let him repent. Maran Atha. Amen (Didache 10:1–6).

Didache concludes by stating that though this is the form of the community, Jesus prophets can arrange the thanksgiving as they wish (10:7).

This ritual has no myth attached to it. It is not connected to death by a preamble (as given even by Paul) or by content. The elements of the Eucharist are also reversed in Didache 9 so that the vine (the fruit of which is wine) precedes the bread. The vine is identified with the vine of David[596] which was made known (ἐγνώρισας) through Jesus. The vine of one son (or 'child',as παιδός is most appropriately translated) is made known through another son. The bread is in turn identified with life and knowledge. Another analogy is then used: just as the broken bread is scattered on the mountains and is brought back, so also the members of the church are brought together. The concluding prayer repeats the connection between the meal elements and spiritual nourishment (10:3). We should note that there are no allusions to the death of Jesus at all: the meal is 'simply' a thanksgiving for the gifts granted through Jesus' ministry.

Crossan sees in Didache 10:2–4 an earlier version of Didache 9:2–3. In the earlier version the Eucharistic elements have not yet been ritualized; in the later version the two Eucharistic elements have been split and are addressed one at a time.[597]

Possibly it is also this messianic banquet[598] that is intended in the Lord's prayer, which may be translated into English with the words 'give us this day our bread of tomorrow'.[599] But the strong eschatological connotations of the text are not necessarily intended only as referring to some distant future event but also to a near future event, namely the crucifixion.

In the context of the Synoptics, this event takes place on the 15th of Nisan, the first day of the feast, and the meal therefore is the Passover meal, while John places it on the 13th to have the Passover slaughtering the next day.[600] Passover is an annual feast celebrating Israel's deliverance from bondage in Egypt. The actual feast, as it was practised in the 1st century, combined this celebration with the feast of unleavened bread. In John there is no Eucharistic celebration, only Jesus as God's Passover lamb, sacrificed for the sins of the world. However, to understand Paul and the Synoptics we need to understand what happened in a Passover meal, the Seder. Exodus 13:8 explains: 'And thou shalt tell thy son in that day, saying, It is because of that which Jehovah did for me when I came forth out of Egypt' (ASV). That is, this meal celebrated Yahweh as the deliverer of Israel. Not only that: 'this day shall be unto you for a memorial' (Exodus 12:14 KJV). In other words, it was maintained as a day of remembrance. Just as significant was the fact that the meal was a community meal, or at least a family meal (Exodus 12:4, 21). The Didache's ecclesiastical section also refers to the Eucharist in sacrificial terms but makes no connection with Jesus' death. Instead it adopts a more direct parallel with the Jewish temple cult. The cleansing is done not by baths but through confession of sins (14:1–3).

Excursus: The Eucharist Sacrament

From the beginning there were probably different understandings of how the wine and bread were to become the blood and body of Jesus but these were held in different places in the church without it becoming a point of contention until the 9th century. In 1215 the matter was put on record through the Fourth Lateran Council by affirming what is known as the doctrine of transubstantiation, which meant that through the words of the institution the bread and wine were actually physically changed into the body and blood of Christ. Later additions were concomitance,[601] consecration[602] and the doctrine stating that once this change had been effected the elements were holy and should be venerated. All of these doctrines were confirmed by the Council of Trent[603] but the Reformation stirred up this doctrine and the fragmented church began to express different opinions through various denominations powerful enough to escape the influence of the Roman Church. Three major positions were taken by the three leading figures of Protestantism. Martin Luther[604] rejected these doctrines while still accepting that Jesus was really present and that there was a mystery in this sacrament. Ulrich Zwingli[605] had a more Augustinian point of view and propagated a doctrine of spiritual rather than physical presence.[606] John Calvin[607] took what has been called the intermediate point of view, the doctrine known as virtualism.[608]

Development of doctrines relating to the Eucharist has been somewhat free and unfettered within the Roman Catholic Church from about the beginning of the 16th century.

***

Summary and Conclusion

We started this chapter by looking at a conundrum of the Christian tradition. Paul himself mentions in connection with the Eucharist that Jesus was 'handed over' or 'delivered' (παρεδίδετο). Whether Paul was familiar with the figure of Judas is uncertain but it seems reasonable to assume that Paul thought that Jesus had been betrayed and knew a tradition not unlike the one we find in the gospels, where the Eucharist and the betrayal are connected.[609] Betrayal, of course, presupposes that the handing over was an inside job, that someone trusted brought guards to arrest Jesus. All four evangelists, independently of each other, have traditions regarding Judas, a disciple of Jesus who betrayed Him. All other facts regarding Judas remain speculative and doubtful. It appears that very little was in fact known about him and that speculations about his action and later behaviour started in the immediate aftermath of his betrayal. Just like modern authors, the early Christians probed the question of his motives with great imagination and little fact.

Next we turned to the meal tradition, of which there are two. The first tradition we can with certainty attribute to Jesus. This was the meal in which Jesus' prophets would participate, as is reflected in the mission commandments and the Didache. However, there is a step between the mission commandment and the Eucharist described in the Didache. There is likewise a step between the fellowship meal in the mission commandment and the fellowship meal in Paul's letter. The institution has been ritualized. The function is maintained, both with Paul and Didache: it provides for the starving in the community.

Why and how did the tradition go from fellowship meal to ritual? We may look back at Neusner's proposal (chapter 7) that Jesus' destruction of the temple was symbolic of its replacement by the Eucharist. We recall that even after the martyrdom of Jesus, another martyr, Stephen, was accused that he would 'speak words against this holy place, and the law' (Acts 6:13 ASV). Just as before, we find it plausible that there is a core of truth to the charges made by the false witnesses. If the Christians of Jerusalem continued in the tradition of Jesus and had a problematic relationship with the temple and with some aspects of Judean jurisprudence, it seems that the friction was between the Christian community and the Judean Jews. That friction was also felt inside the community. In chapter 4 we saw how this internal friction came to be expressed in Q's temptation narrative. How did Christians handle their exclusion from the temple? They did as Neusner suggests that Jesus did: they replaced it with the Eucharist and as a consequence the fellowship meal that replaced the temple cult came to assimilate some of the temple cult's characteristics.

Crossan states that both 'Paul and Mark agree that it was a Last Supper, but Paul, unlike Mark, commands repetition for remembrance, and Mark, unlike Paul, explicitly describes it as the Passover meal'.[610] What Paul does not state explicitly – that it was a Passover meal – is in fact presupposed by the form and content of the tradition that he cites. Paul's 'remembrance' (which is not Paul's addition) is part of the synthesis of the fellowship meal and the Passover. Just like the people of Israel were commanded to have a Passover meal in remembrance of Yahweh's plagues on Pharaoh which delivered them, Paul commands his Corinthian congregation to hold the Eucharist in remembrance of the Lord being handed over for execution and thus delivering all Christians. This is why, of all traditions that Paul presents as coming from Jesus, this one cannot go without a short narrative introduction.

The elements of the Eucharist most certainly predate the ritual. These were the foods that a struggling community could afford. In the ritual, however, Jesus becomes the Passover lamb, the blood shed at the altar in the temple (2 Chronicles 30:16, 35:11) and its body consumed at the feast. This view is the perception behind the ritualization that informed both Paul and Mark.

John was not content merely to present a ritual with which he was most certainly familiar. Instead he decided to dramatize the event. The correspondence between Jesus' body and bread had already been noted in a dialogue (John 6:35). Now John wanted to take the core of the ritual and dramatize it. Jesus was not only the Passover lamb in a ritual performed on His last Passover, He was the Passover lamb, full stop.

In reality, however, the Synoptics are merely operating from a ritual tradition. They, just like John, do not know that Jesus was betrayed and handed over on a particular day.

From this we may conclude that there was a Christian fellowship meal introduced into the Jerusalem community and that when it could no longer participate in Passover, it started to interpret the events of Jesus' martyrdom in a way that allowed a legitimate reintroduction of elements of the lost Passover. As a result there was an interpretation of the events of Jesus' martyrdom that allowed a legitimate reintroduction of elements of the lost Passover.[611] As we shall see in the following chapter, this understanding was common in Jerusalem but not all that central to Paul's understanding of Jesus' salvific act.

Finally, accepting Crossan's thesis, we see the transformation of a fellowship meal into a meal with ritual elements. The early version merely refers to food and drink, the later version refers to vine (wine) and bread. Between the New Testament tradition and the Didache only the ritualistic elements themselves are held in common and then in reverse order (from bread/wine to wine/bread). Why did the Didache introduce the new ritual? Simply because Didache was a self-regulating document. One need only look at the prescription for baptism (Didache 7) to see the amount of flexibility it needed. The Didache 14 tradition also reflects a later form of Eucharist tradition. Apparently some had become vaguely familiar with the Jerusalem tradition and produced something that in form looked similar to that tradition (the aspect no doubt most easily remembered) but which in content remained true to that community's experience of what the fellowship meal was about.

10

The Crucifixion

Matthew 26:36 – 27:66
Mark 14:26 – 15:47
Luke 22:21 – 23:56
John 12:29 – 19:42

We shall in this chapter sum up the final events leading up to Jesus' crucifixion: the prayer, the capture, Peter's denial and the trial of Jesus. Then we shall deal with the crucifixion itself and its theological implications.

The Last Hours before the Crucifixion

Mark 14:27 (= Matthew 26:31)[612] states that Jesus concludes the Eucharistic scene by stating that now the prophecy of Zechariah 13:7[613] was about to be fulfilled. This connects later with the betrayal of Judas Iscariot, which we discussed in the previous chapter. We saw that the betrayal was interpreted in terms of another prophecy in Zechariah. This prophecy has not been modified, nor was it in need of modification. The sequence was thus: the event (Jesus' death) → application of prophecy → narrative which cites prophecy.

According to the Synoptic Gospels (Mark 14:32–6 = Matthew 26:36–9 = Luke 22:40–2), Jesus and His disciples proceeded to Gethsemane. Here He left His disciples and brought only Peter, John and James. Then, according to Matthew, Jesus 'fell on his face'[614] and prayed: 'Abba, (Father)[615] all things are possible unto thee; remove this cup from me:[616] howbeit not what I will but what thou wilt.'

The implication here is that Jesus does not wish to go through with the crucifixion. This is reflective of Mark's understanding, not of who Jesus was but that this was part of God's purpose and that Jesus willingly submitted to it.

In Luke 22:43–4 an additional two verses are inserted in the narrative in which an angel appears and aids Him as He sweats blood.[617] All three Synoptists record that Jesus returns and finds His chief disciples sleeping. Arousing Peter, He says: 'Simon, sleepest thou? couldest thou not watch one hour? Watch and pray, that ye enter not into temptation: the spirit indeed is willing but the flesh is weak' (Mark 14:36 ASV = Matthew 26:39). This part of the narrative is also a Markan reflection. Here the community and its current persecution is the issue. While they should be out proclaiming the kingdom, they are being weak and relenting under the pressure.

Whereas this marks the end of Luke's narrative, Mark and Matthew both have the same event reoccurring three times, ending with Jesus saying: 'Sleep on now, and take your rest: it is enough; the hour is come; behold, the Son of man is betrayed into the hands of sinners. Arise, let us be going: behold, he that betrayeth me is at hand' (Mark 14:41–2). The last sentence seems to be in conflict with the first. Mark has probably edited away from his original source a sentence between the first and second line which mentioned the passage of time or else the two phrases come from unrelated sources.

Then Judas and the people who have come to apprehend

Jesus appear. Judas gives the customary kiss of greeting as a sign identifying Jesus to the high priest's men. Jesus is seized and brought away to the court. The Synoptic mentions that one of the disciples cut off the ear of the servant of the high priest. In Luke, Jesus is said to have healed the ear of the servant (22:51) and the wielder of the sword[618] is rebuked. Mark seems to be unclear as to the effect of Jesus' words, for he says: 'And they all left him, and fled.' While Matthew immediately clarifies that it was only the disciples who fled, this only becomes apparent from subsequent sections in Mark.[619] John mentions an extraordinary reaction of the guards when Jesus identifies Himself and he records Jesus as saying 'the cup which the Father hath given me, shall I not drink it?' (John 18:11). Mark alone mentions the young man that was present amongst the disciples who wore only linen and was otherwise naked.[620]

Via Dolorosa

According to John, Annas (the father-in-law of Caiaphas, the high priest) was the first to interrogate Jesus. Jesus answered him by saying that He had kept nothing secret and that all of His doctrines and doings were public knowledge. Jesus is thus sent to Caiaphas for interrogation. John[621] states that Jesus was interrogated by Caiaphas whereas the Synoptists state that He was interrogated in the Sanhedrin, the Jewish court of law. Failing to find witnesses that agreed, Jesus Himself was asked, 'Are you the Christ, the Son of the Blessed?' (Mark 14:61 ASV). As His answer (at least in Mark) was the abundantly clear, 'I am', He was condemned to death on the charge of blasphemy. There is some dispute as to the Sanhedrin's ability to pass a death sentence at this time in Jewish history. Haim Cohn points out that according to Talmudic tradition, this right was taken away from the Sanhedrin 'forty years before the destruction of the Temple'.[622] However, the veracity of that tradition has been seriously questioned and the 6 CE date seems more likely.[623] There are several problems connected with the trial in Mark and Matthew in view of Mishnaic Law: 1) a capital trial must be held in daylight, 2) it cannot take place on a day of rest, 3) a death sentence cannot be passed on the first day, 4) the sentence of blasphemy consists of saying the name of Yahweh and 5) the place to gather such a meeting is in the temple rather than the palace of the high priest. Luke, perhaps sensitive to the legal incongruity, amends his version slightly by letting day dawn and omitting the sentencing but still does not resolve points two and three.[624] Catchpole, however, doubts that these rabbinic rules were in place at the time of Jesus.[625] He also concludes that 'Jews could try but they could not execute'.[626] In addition, He finds that the scene introduced by Luke is simpler and 'gives us a block of tradition from a Semitic area, and one more primitive than Mark's tradition, which is also from a Semitic area'.[627]

Meanwhile, Peter follows from a distance (Mark 14:54). When he reaches the courtyard he is questioned thrice and thrice denies his association with Jesus.[628] He then hears the cock crow and is reminded of Jesus' prophecy about his denials (Mark 14:67–72). According to John, a second disciple[629] accompanied Peter and as he knew the high priest,[630] he was able to enter and see the court proceedings (John 18:15–16).

Next Jesus was interrogated by Pontius Pilatus, the prefect[631] of Judea. After a few questions, Pilate turned to the Jews and said that he found no fault in Him.[632] At this point Luke reports that Pilate, discovering that Jesus was from Galilee, decided to send Him to Herod,[633] who was also in Jerusalem, for him to pass judgement. Herod, having interrogated Jesus, mocked Him and sent Him back to Pilate.[634] Pilate then suggested that the customary amnesty[635] could be allowed Him but the crowd called for the release of Jesus Bar Abba (Mark 15:1–11).[636] Crossan proposes that Mark invented this public election of 'Barabbas' as a response to the Zealot movement (of which he was a fictive representative) which was 'chosen' by the Jews and which was ultimately responsible for the destruction of Jerusalem.[637]

Finally, fearing religious upheavals and that reports of sedition left unpunished would reach Rome, Pilate granted the wish of the mob and released Jesus for crucifixion (Mark 15:15). A minimalist proposition would require the involvement of fewer people. Indeed, it is quite plausible to think that Jesus was taken directly by the high priest – who had concluded from reports or observations that Jesus was a threat to the peace – to Pilate, who then relied on the high priest and pronounced judgement without interrogating Jesus. It is even doubtful whether Jesus and Pilate had a common language. This point of view is generally supported by the Jesus Seminar.[638] A majority of the Jesus Seminar also felt that the scenes of the trials were created by the suggestions of Psalm 2.[639] Such a claim seems to stretch the ignorance of the early Christians beyond credibility. The mere statement that the kings and rulers plotted against the Lord and His Messiah does not seem likely to have supplied anything. Blame of some sort must have been assigned by Christians almost immediately after the fact, even before a search of the scripture.

Jesus was then flogged and brought outside the city

(Mark 15:15 = Matthew 27:26 = John 19:1).[640] At some point, presumably because of the flogging, Jesus could carry His cross no longer and a bystander by the name of Simon of Cyrene[641] was compelled to carry it part of the way. On His way out Jesus was offered a mixture of wine and gall to sedate Him and reduce the pain but this He turned down.[642] The place of the crucifixion was Golgotha, which was, according to John 19:41, a garden. In these scenes in particular we find the narrative to be replete with Old Testament allusions.

The narrative of Jesus' passion has been recorded in the Gospel of Peter, which some scholars believe to be an early independent source.[643] A short summary of its peculiarities will therefore be useful before we continue.

In that gospel Jesus is executed by the order of Herod, the Jewish king. It explains that Joseph of Arimathæa was on friendly terms with Pilate and thus was able to solicit for the body of Jesus. Here too there is a friendship between Herod and Pilate, who addresses him as 'brother Pilate' (Ἀδελφὲ Πειλᾶτε) (2:3). Pilate is exonerated even from the maltreatment of Jesus, which is said to have been done by the Jewish people and not by Pilate's soldiers.[644] Some have read docetism[645] into the text because it mentions that 'he kept silence, as one feeling no pain' (αὐτὸς δὲ ἐσιώπα ὡς μηδὲν πόνον ἔχων) (4:1) but on the whole this seems not to be the case.

The words 'Father, forgive them; for they know not what they do' have been interpolated into the text of Luke (23:34) and are not attested by any manuscript older than the 5th century but they are attested by a majority of witnesses and are therefore included in most translations. The words are most likely to have come from those attributed to James the Just by Hegesippus in his 'Memoirs' quoted by Eusebius in *Ecclesiastical History* 2:23: 'I entreat thee, Lord God our Father, forgive them, for they know not what they do.'[646] It is curious that we find once again, as in chapter 4 with the temptation, that a tradition regarding James is transferred to Jesus.

All five gospels (including Peter's) report that Jesus was stripped and his clothes divided for gambling between his malefactors. Here Psalm 22:16–18[647] seems to have been the primary inspiration of the narrative. The details once again appear to be extracted from the psalm, which originally had no messianic connotations. Here it seems clear that the general theme of the psalm attracted the attention of early Christians. There is no citation but a traditional narrative that originated with the psalm. Hence the sequence was: event (humiliating death) → application of psalm → tradition of narrative.

The gospels also record that Jesus was placed between two thieves. Luke reports that while one of the thieves mocked Jesus, the other reproached his companion and asked Jesus if He would remember him in His kingdom.[648] To this Jesus replies: 'Verily I say unto thee, To-day shalt thou be with me in Paradise.'[649] According to Mark and Matthew, both thieves rebuked Jesus while John does not report anything about the thieves. The Gospel of Peter reports a similar story where the thief defends Jesus but does not ask to be remembered by Him; it goes on to say: 'And they were wroth with him, and commanded that his legs should not be broken, that so he might die in torment.'

Jesus, having been placed on the cross,[650] becomes the object of relentless insults from the crowds of onlookers. It is reported that they said, 'He saved others; let him save himself, if this is the Christ of God, his chosen.' The plaque placed on the cross 'THE KING OF THE JEWS' was seen as a mockery of Jesus. John, who records that Jesus' plaque was in Latin, Greek and Hebrew, reports that the Jews resented the inscription and wanted it changed to say that He claimed to be the king rather than was. To this Pilate says, 'What I have written I have written.' This, as well as the fact that Jesus was dressed in royal purple and treated as a king (Mark 15:17–18), may be historical. In the case of Simon bar Giora (discussed in chapter 2), we should recall that the Romans, rather than discrediting him, treated him as king of the Jews. The purpose was to show Rome's ability to execute any royal pretender. It remains, however, doubtful that such a report is based on actual eyewitness accounts and it may be that plausibility was the reason for the introduction of this particular theme.

According to the Toldoth, a hostile Jewish biography of Jesus, He was not crucified but was hanged from a tree:

> In that same hour was he put to death: and it was the sixth hour and the eve of the Passover and the Sabbath. When they had (brought him forth) to hang him on a tree: it brake; for the Ineffable Name[651] was with him. Now when the foolish ones saw that the trees were broken under him, they accounted it for the greatness of his righteousness. Until they brought for him the stock of a carob tree: for while he was yet alive he knew the custom of Israel that they would hang him, and knew his death, and the manner of his being put to death, that at last he would be hanged on a tree. At that time he caused by the Ineffable Name that no tree should bear him; but over the carobstock he uttered not the Ineffable Name: for it is no tree but a plant' (Toldoth 4:19–23).[652]

The last words of Jesus according to Matthew are: 'My God, my God why hast thou forsaken me?' ('*Eli, Eli, lama sabachthani*?' 'אֵלִי אֵלִי לָמָה עֲזַבְתָּנִי'), quoted directly from Psalms 22:1 except for the last word, which is Aramaic and substitutes for the Hebrew word *Azabthani*. Mark is similar but reads: '*Eloi, Eloi, lama sabachthani*?' which is closer to the Aramaic saying (here *lama* works in both Hebrew and Aramaic). The Gospel of Peter has quite a different version: 'My power, my power, thou hast forsaken me' (Ἡ δύναμίς μου, ἡ δύναμις κατέλειψάς με). It clearly does not refer to Psalm 22:1 and has turned a question into a statement.[653] Perhaps Peter is not remodelling the Markan statement but using the sentence from Psalm 22:19. Reading the psalm itself, it becomes evident that the psalm is seen as fulfilled in the events of the passion:

> For dogs have encompassed me; a company of evil-doers have inclosed me; like a lion, they are at my hands and my feet. I may count all my bones; they look and gloat over me. They part my garments among them, and for my vesture do they cast lots (Psalms 22:17–19 JPS).[654]

The purpose of having Jesus say these final words also seems to serve as a reference to the doxology at the end of the psalm, a proclamation of the coming of the kingdom of Yahweh. Rather than being a cry of despair, it is to be perceived as a last proclamation of the coming kingdom of God. The two canonical gospels that report these as Jesus' last words also record that apparently these words were misunderstood by the onlookers as a call to Elijah.

Luke has Jesus' last words as 'Father, into thy hands I commend my spirit', which refers to yet another psalm: 'Into thy hand I commend my spirit: Thou hast redeemed me, O Jehovah, thou God of truth' (Psalms 31:5 ASV).

In John, Jesus calls out that He thirsts and is given some hyssop (19:28–9). Psalm 69:21[655] seems to be behind this scene. Here there is definitely a tradition of interpretation that goes back before John. The motif of hopelessness in the psalm has been changed in order to fit an image of Jesus that is more to John's liking, a Jesus in control of circumstances. The sequence is thus: event (Jesus abandoned to His enemies) → application of psalm → John's receipt of tradition → John's narrative.

John records Jesus' last words as 'It is done' or rather 'It is finished' (τετέλεσται). The same word appears in verse 28, connecting the call for vinegar with fulfilment, making Jesus' statement a triumphant cry of victory. For John, all has come to pass as prophesied and Jesus is in full control of the events transpiring. His call for refreshment is answered with obedience. Prior to this, John records that Jesus gives His mother unto His 'beloved disciple', as both were near by and able to hear Him speak.

Yet for the crucified Jesus to make any of these speeches is implausible since the very nature of crucifixion is death by asphyxiation.[656]

The statement in Mark 15:38 that subsequently the veil of the temple was rent asunder is a curious tradition that cannot easily be attributed to prophecy historicized, the process that we have been observing so far. Alternatively, we might be dealing with a Christian prophecy, namely Jesus' condemnation of the temple. It is conceivable that the followers of Jesus who had come to Jerusalem with Him and had heard His statement against the temple expected its immediate destruction, and in the aftermath of Jesus' crucifixion and the apparent non-fulfilment, understood this to refer to yet another symbolic destruction of the temple.

In the Gospel of the Nazaraeans (10) it is the lintel that breaks rather than the veil. The author may be thinking of the prophecy in Amos 9:1.[657] Here the process seems to be a scribalization of the tradition in Mark 15:38. Its author had a tradition that something happened to the temple but does not have the idea of a failed destruction of the temple. Thus the sequence is: tradition of an event (something destroyed in the temple) → an application of Amos → a narrative.

In Matthew 27:51–3 this theme is extended and earthquakes open the tombs of the saints, who speed out. The theme of these miracles may have been taken from Isaiah 24:19–21.[658] If so, the process started with the conclusion that the kings and rulers had been judged and it followed therefore that the part of the prophecy that preceded must also have happened.

Luke mentions that things happened which made them return 'smiting their breasts' (Luke 23:48 ASV). The Synoptics and Peter report that the onlooking centurion saw the above-mentioned signs and exclaimed, 'Truly this man was the Son of God.' Matthew elaborates and includes as witnesses others who were with the centurion. Luke has the centurion say, 'Certainly this was a righteous man.'[659]

Lastly it is noted by John 19:32–7 that since Jesus died before the sun went down, it was not necessary to expedite His death by breaking His legs, which would have made it impossible to rise and breathe. This is important because it adds to the picture of Jesus as the scapegoat whose bones were not broken. John further states that the soldiers ensured that Jesus was dead by piercing Him with a spear and observing 'blood and water', which proved that He was dead, and thus they left His legs unbroken.

Here again scripture supplies details. Psalm 34:20[660] and Zechariah 12:10[661] each are quoted but it is doubtful that they actually supply the narrative. This is certainly the case with the psalm, which seems to be cited merely to augment Jesus' credentials. In reality, the detail is part of John's scapegoat theme, which starts with John the Baptist and is set into the scene by the positioning of the Passover chronology noted in the previous chapter. The piercing supported by Zechariah is curious to say the least. The possibility of it being read messianicly cannot be altogether dismissed. One modification to the text was, however, necessary to make it appropriate. John had to change 'me' into 'him'.[662] The 'me' refers to Yahweh, or more precisely to His representative, Zechariah.

For the psalm, we can thus see the sequence as follows: theological supposition (Jesus is the scapegoat) → narrative → scriptural support.

It is possible that a reading of Zechariah created the story of the piercing but it seems too much a part of John's theological purpose to make it a plausible interpretational tradition. John 19:35[663] very emphatically calls on a witness, whose testimony can be trusted. So it seems that again the sequence must be: theological supposition (Jesus is the scapegoat) → narrative → scriptural support.

The Theological Implications

Of what import was the crucifixion to Jesus, His apostles and disciples, the Christians of the emerging church and Christians thereafter? Let us first consider what has become termed 'passion predictions'. The Markan passages, having seniority, will be reviewed first.

> And he began to teach them, that the Son of man must suffer many things, and be rejected by the elders, and the chief priests, and the scribes, and be killed, and after three days rise again' (Mark 8:31 ASV).

Mark does not present Jesus as saying these things but as teaching them (διδάσκειν).We are in all likelihood, therefore, dealing with a piece of kerygma or preaching, a sort of central tenet of the community with functions not unlike the ones that emerged in the 2nd century as the Apostolic Creed.[664] Its focus clearly centres around the events of Jerusalem. However, presuming that the sentence has a chronology, the many things that the Son of man must suffer could relate to the things that Jesus suffered prior to coming to Jerusalem. In other words, Jesus' ministry is summed up in that one expression. In chapter 8 we suggested that some of the Son of man sayings emerged in Jerusalem as a reaction to the crucifixion of Jesus, so the focus is not surprising.

The same logia can be found in Matthew 16:21 and Luke 9:22, with notable agreement of detail not found in Mark. Possibly because of their common source, they preferred 'on the third day' instead of 'after three days'.[665] This has been explained by the existence of an Ur-Mark[666], a Q logia or an oral tradition which both Matthew and Luke preferred.

Another significant tradition in Mark reads:

> And he called unto him the multitude with his disciples, and said unto them, If any man would come after me, let him deny himself, and take up his cross, and follow me (Mark 8:34 ASV).

While Matthew and Luke have a parallel text, they are clearly dependent on Mark's version. Q (Matthew 10:37–8 = Luke 14:26–7) has another similar text, which might at first look seem like a development of the former. This logia is perhaps the most significant indication of how the itinerant preachers, perhaps with justification from Jesus' own words, understood His crucifixion. This is the only double tradition regarding the significance of the cross, for it is attested both by Q and Thomas:

> Jesus said, 'Whoever does not hate father and mother cannot be my disciple, and whoever does not hate brothers and sisters, and carry the cross as I do, will not be worthy of me' (Thomas 55 SV).[667]

The expression 'carry the cross' is most certainly not Jesus' and would be totally incomprehensible to any listener of those days as it is not found anywhere in a text prior to the New Testament and is obviously post-crucifixion terminology. The double attestation (Q, Thomas) would place its origin in the first decade after the crucifixion. However, the present author does not believe that its origin lies with Jesus. It is a reaction towards the non-itinerant community who, rather than following the example of Jesus' life style, merely 'believed in the cross'.

Jerome H. Neyrey[668] explains the sociological background of this verse by analysing two of its key themes: family and honour. He concludes that following Jesus meant severing one's family ties and the honour attached to the family and joining a new family in which Jesus offered a restitution of one's lost honour. This has already been discussed at length in chapter 5 but it is important to understand this statement as one of the first reactions to the crucifixion of Jesus that was in some sense critical of the Jerusalem understanding of the event.

Another Markan Son of man saying that we noted in chapter 8 was 'For the Son of man also came not to be ministered unto but to minister, and to give his life a ransom for many' (Mark 10:45 ASV). This is also found in Matthew 20:28 practically verbatim. The first part of the logia states that the reason Jesus came was to minister.[669] The other was to be a 'ransom' for many. The theme of the verses that precede this are on ministering, not on sacrifice. They encourage ministering as a source of greatness, hence the last remark jumps to an entirely different subject and destroys the rhetoric of the verse. It would appear that we are here dealing with a pre-Markan emendation of this saying in the aftermath of the crucifixion, somewhat illustrative of the trend proposed in chapter 8.

There are also the remarks of John the Baptist:

> The next day John seeth Jesus coming unto him, and saith, Behold the Lamb of God, which taketh away the sin of the world. This is he of whom I said, After me cometh a man which is preferred before me: for he was before me. And I knew him not: but that he should be made manifest to Israel, therefore am I come baptizing with water. And John bare record, saying, I saw the Spirit descending from heaven like a dove, and it abode upon him. And I knew him not: but he that sent me to baptize with water, the same said unto me, Upon whom thou shalt see the Spirit descending, and remaining on him, the same is he which baptizeth with the Holy Ghost. And I saw, and bare record that this is the Son of God. Again the next day after John stood, and two of his disciples; And looking upon Jesus as he walked, he saith, Behold the Lamb of God! (John 1:29–36 KJV).

This confession has a rather Johannine bluntness about it.

Only a cursory outline of Paul's theology regarding the significance of the crucifixion is possible here.[670] We shall start by looking at the contents of the Epistle to the Romans.

In the Epistle to the Romans we find that it was Jesus 'who was delivered up for our trespasses, and was raised for our justification' (Romans 4:25 ASV). Here one particular thing becomes apparent, which is that for Paul the Christians are saved because they participate in Christ's crucifixion. Becoming a Christian meant becoming a part of the body of Christ (1 Corinthians 12:27). This was significant because just as one died communally with Christ, one resurrected communally with Him too.

Galatians introduces another theological concept: the cross as a symbol of redemption. For Jews, who do 'works according to the law', this is considered to be their stumbling block and for Gentiles 'foolishness'.[671]

> But far be it from me to glory, save in the cross of our Lord Jesus Christ, through which the world hath been crucified unto me, and I unto the world' (Galatians 6:14 ASV).

Again, it is not scapegoat theology that is implied here but rather a sense of the cross as a transforming power.

> I have been crucified with Christ; and it is no longer I that live but Christ living in me: and that life which I now live in the flesh I live in faith, the faith which is in the Son of God, who loved me, and gave himself up for me' (Galatians 2:20 ASV).

Again, as in Romans, we see that the crucifixion of Christ is transferred to the community so that it partakes in its glory. It is difficult to determine how common Paul's ideas were but Paul at least seems to presume that his audience would understand.[672]

Not withstanding this Pauline conception, Paul has a received tradition:

> . . . that Christ died for our sins according to the scriptures; and that he was buried; and that he hath been raised on the third day according to the scriptures; and that he appeared to Cephas; then to the twelve; then he appeared to above five hundred brethren at once, of whom the greater part remain until now but some are fallen asleep; then he appeared to James; then to all the apostles (1 Corinthians 15:3–7 ASV).

Only the first verse concerns us here, the remainder will be discussed in the next chapter. It is noticeable that the received tradition does not use the Pauline concept of participation but rather uses scapegoat theology. There may also be traces of this theology in Romans 5:10:

> For if, while we were enemies, we were reconciled to God through the death of his Son, much more, being reconciled, shall we be saved by his life (ASV).

The epistle to the Hebrews[673] is written from an altogether different theological perspective. Indeed we may consider it a prime example of scapegoat theology. Here a rich register of Jewish imagery is employed by the author to convey his message about Jesus Christ. Jesus is portrayed as the high priest as well as the scapegoat. While the cross is mentioned (Hebrews 12:2), it is not used as a symbol, for the cross carries no honour in Jewish imagery. 'For we have not a high priest that cannot be touched with the feeling of our infirmities; but one that hath been in all points tempted like as we are, yet without sin' (Hebrews 4:15 ASV). Jesus is proclaimed to be the new high priest who through

His own sacrifice has ended the need for sacrificing. He has taken the ministry from the descendants of Aaron and become high priest in the manner of Melchizedek.[674] Jesus' sacrifice does not, however, bring conditionless remission of sins (Hebrews 10:26).

Being aware of the precise circumstances of the temple cult, and having demonstrated this, the author of Hebrews ostensibly claims that by this final sacrifice a change has come about which renders the cult obsolete (Hebrews 7:27). Jesus is also portrayed as pre-existent, indeed He is from the foundation of the world (Hebrews 9:26).

We may conclude that this epistle seems strongly influenced by the Johannine school of thought, since it shares several features with the Gospel of John. Among these are reverence for the institution of the high priest (John 11:49–51), the perception of Jesus as the sacrificial lamb (John 1:29 *et seq.*, 19:31 *et seq.*) and considering Him to be pre-existent (John 1:1 *et seq.*).[675] The earthly Jesus, however, is almost entirely absent, Hebrews 5:7 and 13:12 being the exceptions.

Another tradition of kerygma comes from speeches in Acts:

> The word which he sent unto the children of Israel, preaching good tidings of peace by Jesus Christ (He is Lord of all.) – that saying ye yourselves know, which was published throughout all Judaea, beginning from Galilee, after the baptism which John preached; even Jesus of Nazareth, how God anointed him with the Holy Spirit and with power: who went about doing good, and healing all that were oppressed of the devil; for God was with him. And we are witnesses of all things which he did both in the country of the Jews, and in Jerusalem; whom also they slew, hanging him on a tree. Him God raised up the third day,

> and gave him to be made manifest, not to all the people but unto witnesses that were chosen before of God, even to us, who ate and drank with him after he rose from the dead. And he charged us to preach unto the people, and to testify that this is he who is ordained of God to be the Judge of the living and the dead. To him bear all the prophets witness, that through his name every one that believeth on him shall receive remission of sins (Acts 10:36–43 ASV).

C. H. Dodd in his book *The Apostolic Preaching* analyses this and other speeches in Acts (2:14–36, 38–9, 3:12–26, 4:8–12). These speeches, he finds good reason to suppose, 'are based upon material which proceed from the Aramaic-speaking Church at Jerusalem, and was substantially earlier than the period at which the book was written'.[676] This he finds particularly true of the above-cited portion. Through correlation he finds the following items to have been the core of Jerusalem's kerygma:

1) The Messianic age has come with Jesus.
2) This took place through His ministry, death and resurrection.
3) He has been exalted to the right hand of God.
4) He has given the Holy Spirit to the church.
5) This age will soon end when He returns to judge the living and dead.
6) An appeal to repent and convert (be baptized).

From this analysis he turns to a comparison with Pauline kerygma. Here Dodd notes that Jesus is not called the Son of God but is spoken of in terms of the Deutero-Isaiah's 'Servant' of God. Jesus did not die for our sins but His ministry, death and resurrection were contributors to salvation. Finally, unlike Paul (Romans 8:34), Jerusalem kerygma does not have Jesus interceding on behalf of Christians.[677] Dodd notes that while there are substantial agreements between Paul and the Jerusalem kerygma, the former lacks references to Jesus' ministry, His miracles and His teachings.[678]

On several counts the position of Hebrews, John and the Jerusalem kerygma may be considered a middle way between the Judeo-Christian right and the Pauline front. We shall now deal with the former, which in many ways can be thought of as the losing party. James should be considered amongst the former and the epistle in his name is certainly an exposition of the position assumed by the moderate Jewish-Christians.[679] The epistle is altogether devoid of opinions regarding the crucifixion and refers to Jesus only twice in passing.

While there is no actual quotation regarding the crucifixion, and none of the Church Fathers record any of the Judeo-Christian beliefs about this event, their attitude to sacrifice may have impacted on their understanding of the event. In the Pseudo-Clementine, Peter states: 'Our Lord neither asserted that there were gods except the Creator of all, nor did He proclaim Himself to be God but He with reason pronounced blessed him who called Him the Son of that God who has arranged the universe.'[680]

This is part of a lengthy dialogue between Simon Magus (a literary disguise of Paul)[681] and Peter (representing the Jewish-Christians). Amongst them we also find:

> Then Simon: 'But the good God [of Simon Magus (or rather Paul)] bestows salvation if he is only acknowledged; but the creator of the world [the God of Peter] demands also that the law be fulfilled.' Then said Peter: 'He saves adulterers and men-slayers, if they know him ; but good,

> and sober, and merciful persons, if they do not know him, in consequence of their having no information concerning him, he does not save! Great and good truly is he whom you proclaim, who is not so much the saviour of the evil, as he is one who shows no mercy to the good.'[682]

Recognitions nonetheless has a rather intriguing crucifixion narrative. It introduces Christ as a prophet like Moses:

> . . . He also of whom he foretold that He should rise up a prophet like unto himself, though He cured every sickness and infirmity among the people, wrought innumerable miracles, and preached eternal life, was hurried by wicked men to the cross; which deed was, however, by His power turned to good. In short, while He was suffering, all the world suffered with Him.[683]

The signs are recounted and, as in Peter, they make the Jews realize their evil deed and divide the people from the priests. But as soon as the signs had passed they returned to their wicked ways, 'some of them, watching the place with all care, when they could not prevent His rising again, said that He was a magician; others pretended that he was stolen away'.[684] However, the gospel stands victorious and the narrative relates 'they often sent to us, and asked us to discourse to them concerning Jesus, whether He were the Prophet whom Moses foretold, who is the eternal Christ. For on this point only does there seem to be any difference between us who believe in Jesus, and the unbelieving Jews.'

Throughout it seems that the crucifixion is not regarded as having any salvatory nature, nor is it the topic of any intra-ecclesiastical debate. It follows that the significance of the event is viewed quite differently from that of the Pauline school and it may even be suggested that the aversion to sacrifices and temple offerings[685] may have arisen as a reaction against the Johannine school.

Excursus: The Crucifixion from the Middle Ages to the Reformation

While the dispute is recorded as late as the 4th century, the Pauline school was by far the most powerful and successful. Augustine may well be considered to be one of the most influential theologians of Western church history. In his *Confessions*, a 13–volume work of largely autobiographical material, he states:

> And lo, there was I received by the scourge of bodily sickness, and I was going down to hell, carrying all the sins which I had committed, both against Thee, and myself, and others, many and grievous, over and above that bond of original sin, whereby we all die in Adam. For Thou hadst not forgiven me any of these things in Christ, nor had He abolished by His Cross the enmity which by my sins I had incurred with Thee.[686]

The influence of Paul is obvious in Augustine and Augustine's influence did not ebb until the 12th century, when Thomas Aquinas entered onto the scene of church history. Before this happened, another significant event occurred outside the church: the emergence of Islam.

The crucifixion was indeed referred to in the Qur'án, and in such manner that left Christians quite appalled:

> That they said (in boast), 'We killed Christ Jesus the son of Mary, the Apostle of Allah'; – but they killed him not, nor crucified him but so it was made to appear to them, and those who differ therein are full of doubts, with no (certain) knowledge but only conjecture to follow, for of

a surety they killed him not (Qur'án: 4:157).[687]

Accordingly, a strong reaction can be found against the Muslims in the writings of the Church Fathers of that time, such as John of Damascus.[688] Also in the Middle Ages we find the sudden appearance of the 'Gospel of Barnabas', which seems to have been composed by a Christian convert to Islam.[689] According to this gospel, it was not Jesus but Judas who was crucified.[690]

The Reformation lent new vigour to the Pauline school through the instrumentality of its chief figure, Martin Luther. In a letter to Melanchthon[691] he wrote (to the great joy of his critics) the following: 'Be a sinner, and let your sins be strong but let your trust in Christ be stronger, and rejoice in Christ who is the victor over sin, death, and the world. We will commit sins while we are here, for this life is not a place where justice resides.'

Also we find in his *The Large Catechism* a commentary of the Apostolic Creed (part II article 10):

> He became man, conceived and born without [any stain of] sin, of the Holy Ghost and of the Virgin Mary, that He might overcome sin; moreover, that He suffered, died and was buried, that He might make satisfaction for me and pay what I owe, not with silver nor gold but with His own precious blood. And all this, in order to become my Lord; for He did none of these for Himself, nor had He any need of it.

* * *

Summary and Conclusion

In the first part of this chapter we reviewed the passion tradition in the five oldest gospels available to us. From this analysis we have two important questions to pose: What can we know about the historical events of the passion and what does the passion tell us about Jesus?

There are two factors in any given passion tradition which should be taken into account when attempting to determine its historicity: 1) how did the tradition come to us and 2) how likely is the scenario in historical context? We may decide that the tradition has a plausible line of transmission from people in the know but at the same time find that the picture is implausible and coloured by, or even invented by, an early source. On the other hand, we may determine that a story appears eminently plausible but find that there is no way that the story is derived from a transmission of tradition and that it is therefore an invention based mostly on plausible inference.

Before we commence, let us sketch two positions represented by the two fronts in the current debate about the Historical Jesus. The first is represented by E. P. Sanders and the second is represented by John Crossan.

Sanders's methodology starts with the facts about which there is least doubt.[692] With regard to Jesus' execution, Sanders finds two facts to be 'firm': 1) that Jesus was executed as a 'would-be' king of the Jews' and 2) that Christians immediately started a non-military messianic movement. These two points are difficult to reconcile. But an 'obvious' solution is at hand: Jesus was not believed to be a military leader but His message could stir up trouble, so the Jews in conjunction with the Romans pre-empted the problem and had Him executed. Sanders goes on to discuss the credibility of various traditions. The trial scenes are not considered to be credible on account of: 1) the question 'are you the son of God' cannot be presupposed from Jesus' public teachings, 2) it appears that the charge of blasphemy was not firmly rooted, 3) there is no connection between witnesses and the charge, and even disregarding the rabbinical definition, the charge seems unwarranted; Sanders can conceive that the speaking and acting against the temple could be construed as blasphemous but, according to the account, the witness did not manage to make that case coherent, 4) it is hard to imagine the chain of transmission that would provide the dialogue, 5) Sanders finds it difficult to imagine the court convening on the first night of Passover (quite apart from the legal issue), 6) the night trial appears to be an expansion of the report to the effect in Mark 15:1 and 7) finally, the evangelist seems to be intent on making the Jews guilty and the Romans innocent. Sanders concludes that it is unlikely that there actually was a trial and that in all likelihood the evangelists are speculating, just as we are.

Sanders goes on to eliminate certain proposed reasons for Jesus' execution. The suggestion of the evangelists that Jewish scholars disapproved of Jesus' teachings or His popularity are dismissed. Sanders holds that Jesus' entry into Jerusalem was regarded as a symbolic act of the kingdom coming humbly but that it did not attract much attention, whereas the act at the temple did. The evidence of kingly pretensions was still missing and Judas provided it. Sanders thinks that the evangelists simply did not know who did what and that the record of various people having been involved is mere guesswork. Sanders presents several cases in which the high priest was the mediator of the Romans. Thus this remains the most likely scenario.

For Crossan the first question is, if the disciples fled and therefore were not witnesses to the events that followed

Jesus' arrest and had only the most meagre details (such as we find in the kerygma of the Jerusalem community), how did one construct a narrative on these bare facts? His answer is that the early Christians searched the scripture in which they believed that Jesus' end had been predicted. Thus for Crossan the beginning of the narrative of the trials lies in Psalm 2.[693] Crossan, unlike Sanders, introduces into his discussion of the Historical Jesus three books with which we are familiar: Thomas, Didache and Peter. While above we consulted Peter and noted some of its distinguishing features, to Crossan, Peter and the trajectory between it and the canonical gospels are crucial to his line of argument.[694] So while Sanders likes to look at broad and solid evidence from the gospels (and then mostly the Synoptics), Crossan looks at minutia in order to consider development in sources. Crossan, engaging the works of Raymond E. Brown, emphasizes that while it is true that the historical development tended to make the passion more and more anti-Jewish, it is untrue that Peter is more anti-Jewish than the canon. Quite to the contrary, Peter makes the distinction that when the authorities discovered they were wrong, they decided to hide it from the people who might turn on them and do them harm (Peter 7:25–8:30). Crossan goes to great lengths to present arguments for the relationship between the various passion narratives. Crossan briefly notes an aspect of the genesis of the trials but does not develop it. The trials and questions posed in them are part of an ongoing experience of Christians put on trial and being questioned. We shall discuss this further below. Thus Crossan concludes that the whole trial scene, whether plausible or implausible, is entirely the creation of the evangelists from the seed sown by Psalm 2.

He concludes that all that was necessary was for Caiaphas and Pilate to agree to rid themselves of a troublemaker. No formal trial or even interrogation was required.[695]

Thus Sanders and Crossan, working from two different directions, the former from historical likelihood and the latter from source and tradition criticism, reach what in substance are very similar conclusions. This gives credence to the central proposition: the evangelists on the whole did not have any substantial information about what happened after Jesus' arrest.

Our own investigation has taken what might be considered a middle way between these approaches. We have worked under the assumption that the process of transmission of oral tradition was ongoing and have not accepted Crossan's thesis of Johannine dependence on the Synoptic passions, all of which, with Peter, were dependent on a Cross Gospel. On the other hand, we have accepted the tradition of Peter into evidence and also accepted that it may have independent traditions. We have not developed everything from prophecy but have certainly noted several instances where it was. We have also engaged issues about the varying degrees of likelihood of different occurrences.

So we return to our two questions: How did the tradition come to us and how plausible is it historically?

To answer the first question we must first review our observations about the historicization of prophecy. A great many instances have been noted in this chapter but others were discussed in chapters 3, 7 and 9.

The two cases in chapter 3 were quite unlike each other. The first started with the assumption that Jesus was the Messiah (and therefore the son of David); the second began with the doctrine of the virgin birth. In these two cases the starting point was a belief about Jesus which led to a particular interpretation of scripture and then to a piece of narrative.

In chapter 7 we saw that the description of Jesus' entry into Jerusalem was built on a text from Zechariah which appeared to be an appropriate messianic text. Three facts made it a suitable text to work on: 1) Jesus was the Messiah, 2) He came to Jerusalem and 3) He was humble. All of these emerge from the text. Details such as that He rode on a particular animal are created from the prophetic text.

In chapter 9 we encountered a dual tradition about the death of Judas. We saw that in some instances where Matthew has details lacking in Luke, such as the amount of money paid to Judas and the manner it was returned to the temple, these had been extracted from the prophecy. However, points of agreement were generally not obtained from prophecy. The tradition as a whole cannot be explained as prophecy historicized. The account of the trial which Crossan saw as emerging from the psalm seems not to have contributed anything as such. Kings, rulers and people all oppose and conspire against Jesus in the passion but surely blame had already been assigned by the Christians of Jerusalem and no other details emerge from the psalm to embellish the trial accounts. That Christians saw the prophecy fulfilled in Jesus' passion is not strange but the psalm's ability to explain the genesis of the passion narrative must remain doubtful.

Moving on to the crucifixion itself, the bare fact of the crucifixion seems to have been known and all else is supposed or prompted by interpretation of scripture. The exceptions seem to be the two thieves on each side of Jesus and the plaque explaining Jesus' crime. Jesus' words are all prompted by scripture. We saw in John an interpretation of a psalm that suited a Synoptic passion well but John less so, indicating that the evangelists had a tradition of prophecy interpretation which John used in his narrative. The evangelists did not need to look through scripture by themselves; it was a community project. We saw how the Gospel of the Nazaraeans had historicized a prophecy in Amos, showing that in Judeo-Christian communities this activity continued to be important. The example of John 19:32–7 cautioned us against assuming that a prophecy always created the event, as on occasion the event is merely supported by a prophecy.

Before we draw conclusions about what can be known about the history behind the passion we need to follow up on Crossan's remark that the passion of Jesus (and specifically he intends the Synoptics) came from an ongoing experience.

Let us look at the question that Jesus is asked. He is asked, 'Are you Christ?' to which Jesus gives two answers: 'I am' and 'ye shall see the Son of man sitting at the right hand of Power, and coming with the clouds of heaven.'

The first part of the answer is strange, in that Mark had made sure that Jesus had kept the secret of His messiahship until then, not even acknowledging it directly. Now, suddenly, the confession of Peter, which is the confession of the community, becomes the confession of Jesus.

As for the other statement, we find Stephen saying, 'Behold, I see the heavens opened, and the Son of Man standing on the right hand of God' (Acts 7:56 ASV). This is surely much more at home with Stephen than with Jesus. The result, according to Acts, was a stoning. As we noted before, however, the charge against Stephen was that they had heard that Jesus was going to destroy the temple (6:13–14).

As with the temptation tradition, the directional pointers are from the writers' immediate present and experience to a past that is interpreted and recounted through the lens of the present. They were the ones who were continually held in suspicion because of their attitude towards the temple and the Law, they were the ones who were asked if Jesus was Christ and they were the ones who, in the face of their martyrdom, looked forward to the Son of man who would establish the kingdom. What appears as a doxology in Acts is probably more correctly formulated in Mark as it was intended, as a threat. That the high priest and the temple authorities continued to be perceived as the main persecutors of the Christian community is reflected in the tradition that Paul received a letter from the high priest to authorize the arrest of Christians in Damascus (Acts 9:1–2).[696]

The question posed by Pilate alters slightly the terminology. Jesus is asked, 'Art thou the King of the Jews?' (Mark 15:2 ASV). This question accurately exemplifies the concerns of the Romans: is Jesus a political pretender to the Jewish throne? What was the central accusation against Christians in the 1st century? Surprisingly, some might find, it was that of 'atheism'. This is attested to in both Christian and Roman sources.

The work known as 'The Martyrdom of Polycarp', generally accepted as a genuine contemporary account, recounts Polycarp's appearance before the pro-consul. Polycarp is encouraged by the pro-consul to swear by Caesar and to say 'Away with the atheists', referring to the Christians, at which point Polycarp looks towards heaven and says, 'Away with the atheists' (Loeb 9:2), referring, of course, to the non-Christians. The pro-consul presses him for the oath and reviling of Christ but Polycarp answers, 'For eighty years have I been his servant, and he has done me no wrong, and how can I blaspheme my King who saved me?' (Loeb 9:3). Of additional interest is the crowd's response in Smyrna when the pro-consul announces Polycarp's confession. Immediately there are cries that he should be burned and that he is the one who has taught 'many neither to offer sacrifice nor worship' (Loeb 12:2).

Similarly, we have the correspondence between Pliny the Younger and Trajan regarding the proper way to interrogate those accused of being Christians. The method was plainly to ask if they were Christians. If they were, they were offered the possibility of escaping capital punishment by worshipping Caesar – Pliny had an image of Trajan with him for that purpose – and then they were to curse Christ.[697]

The problem, of course, was not one of religious intolerance on the part of Romans but one of political loyalty. This is cleverly illustrated by Polycarp's reply that he could not blaspheme his king. A conflict of interest existed, which was precisely the same as the one illustrated in the trial of Jesus in the Synoptics. Polycarp's evasive answer, like that of Matthew and Luke, illustrates the predicament of Christians over this precise question. John makes much of the non-political nature of the kingdom of Jesus. The Romans were in general, however, incapable of understanding Christian behaviour and were puzzled by this odd sect.

Thus, in brief, we come to the conclusion of both Crossan and Sanders that only the historical core of the events that transpired after the arrest of Jesus was known to the early Christians. This core was taken and, through a study of scripture and the experiences of the community, a narrative tradition was begun. We should not think that Christians did not tell stories about the passion of Jesus before the time that Mark or John's Sign Source wrote their narratives. Communities tell stories in order to preserve their identity; storytelling is an integral part of any living community. Christian community traditions were regulated through 'informal control',[698] which is to say that the tradition was not allowed to run wild. Certain facts were immutable because they were important to the community. There were, however, means of holding firm those aspects that were less than essential without committing them to writing. One was scripture because it was already written. Thus if one forgot what happened to Jesus, one needed only to read the appropriate psalm or prophetic text. Another was the authority of present memory. If one could not remember what happened to Jesus precisely and the community was buzzing with recent news of persecutions, details of these would be fused but would ring true with the community as it had the same news. The core of Jesus' passion, however, was preserved in specific forms also, for example by repetition of kerygma, confessions of Jesus the Christ, who was born of the seed of David, did great signs, was tried by Pontius Pilate and condemned to the cross but on the third day rose from the dead and ascended into heaven to the right hand of God.

With these conclusions in place we can go on to the second question of what is likely to have happened. With sources so poor on historical data about the actual events, we can only conjecture what is most probable. Jesus came to Jerusalem with His disciples. He went to the temple and made His pronouncement on it. He was not arrested but caught the attention of the temple authorities, who then reported Him to the high priest. The high priest asked his subordinates to enquire about Him in order to determine whether He was a threat. It was, in all likelihood, at this point that Judas was found. He gave the lead on how to capture Jesus and place a charge that would be acceptable to the Roman prefect. Once captured, Jesus was interrogated by the high priest. The high priest then went to Pilate and told him that a troublemaker had been captured, that He represented a threat to peace and order, that His followers were apparently benign but that He had the ability to gain popular support. Pilate then called on a Roman magistrate to make the death sentence formal. The rest was done by subordinates. Though the gospels say nothing of imprisonment, it is certainly likely that the authorities waited for an opportune time, perhaps when the Galilean presence was less substantial in the period after Passover. So it is, slightly in keeping with Mack, that Vermes concludes that in that period of history in Palestine 'someone could easily lose his life without actually committing any culpable act against the Jewish Law or the Roman state'.[699]

Let us now look at the development of the kerygma of Jerusalem. Though our earliest source is Paul, the kerygma derived from Acts and some of the Son of man sayings appear to represent an earlier and more accurate picture of the earliest Jerusalem kerygma. Paul took the kerygma (which continued to exist in Jerusalem independently), cut out what was for him the non-essential pre-passion ministry and reinterpreted the meaning of the crucifixion so that it became detached from its scapegoat theology. These two variations of the earliest kerygma probably co-existed until the seventies and eighties when the Johannine school emerged out of a Judeo-Hellenistic community. It had strong connections with the Jerusalem community and continued its concept of scapegoat theology.

At the same time something had happened to the overall character of most communities. The Jesus prophets that had been an integral part of the Jerusalem community became naturalized. We see this in the transition of the hierarchy in the church of Corinth. When Paul wrote to them in the fifties, the apostles and the prophets were at the top of the hierarchy (1 Corinthians 12:28–9)[700] but some time in the eighties or thereafter, 1 Clement, which was directed to the community of Corinth, has no mention of prophets. In 1 Clement (42:1–6) apostles are in the past and one no longer tests prophets but converts future bishops and deacons. Ignatius has bishops presiding over the Eucharist (Philadelphians 4:1). Two things had happened in the meantime. First of all, the Christian community of city-dwellers had increased to such a degree that naturalization of prophets became easy. The haves outnumbered the have-nots. This process can clearly be seen in Didache. Until chapter 7 in the Didache it is presumed that the prophet is itinerant but in chapter 8 we see that a prophet can stay in the community and continue to act as a prophet, with the tithe which is due to the temple being given to the prophets, for they are the high priests of the communities (8:3). In chapter 15 we find the reluctant introduction of the office of bishops and deacons, who are set up as people who are also to do the ministry of prophets (15:1). 'Therefore', the Didache admonishes, 'do not despise them, for they are honourable men together with the prophets and teachers' (Loeb 15:2). Clearly this development was not popular but quite necessary.

Another event that probably contributed to this trend was the destruction of most Galilean itinerants in the wake of the Vespian attack on Judea. We know that the poor people of the rural areas were slaughtered and that those who escaped and came to Jerusalem formed the Zealot movements. In light of Jesus' ethics, we cannot imagine that they took up arms or hid with thieves. This, of course, also meant the end of Jerusalem as the centre of Christianity. The Christian community of Jerusalem moved and dispersed.

At any rate, owing to a lack of prophets, the ministry of Jesus started to recede. When the Epistle to the Hebrews was written it contained many of the features that were traditional for the Jerusalem kerygma but the ministry of Jesus was virtually absent.

One part of the community in Jerusalem seems to have held highly Jesus' ethics and portrayed Him as a righteous Jew who followed the Law. These were close to James and stood behind the temptation tradition in Q and the Epistle of James. The Jesus of history was too radical towards the temple to have any significant space in that Epistle and the scapegoat theology was now, in Pauline hands, beginning to take on what seemed like anti-Law conclusions. From Galatians we know that when Paul brought Titus to Jerusalem, some Christians, who Paul refers to as 'false brethren', would not accept Gentile Christians and forced Titus to be circumcised (2:3–4).[701] These were more radical than James, Peter and John who, according to Paul, gave him and Barnabas the right hand of fellowship, and it was decided that Paul and Barnabas would have their mission with the Gentiles while the others would go to the Jews (2:9). These are not, of course, all the same people. While the people behind the temptation in Q are probably identical with or related to the 'false brethren', both were more conservative than James, who was their closest apostle. This party ceased to exist as the Gentile mission became more and more successful. Its authority faded and its project of a strictly circumcised Christianity, which operated within Judaism, became untenable.

Small strands of Judeo-Christians who were opposed to

Paul continued to exist but it is not certain whether they actually opposed what had emerged as Catholic Christianity. Catholic Christianity was by and large Pauline but generally less radical.

11

The Resurrection

Matthew 28:1–20
Mark 16:1–20
Luke 24:1–53
John 20:1 – 21:25
Acts 1:1–26

Perhaps the most central of all events in Christian history, the resurrection towers above even the passion story. It has been regarded as the event that proved definitely the divine identity of Jesus and the truthfulness of the promised general resurrection. In this chapter we will deal with the events that followed the crucifixion and explore some of its theological consequences.

The Burial: Matthew 27:57–66, Mark 15:42–7, Luke 23:50–6, John 19:31–42

The five gospels[702] unanimously name Joseph of Arimathæa the person who was powerful enough to have the body of Jesus given a proper burial. Mark describes him as a member of the council (βουλευτής) who was looking for the coming of the kingdom. Matthew, perhaps feeling that a council member might not be successful in recovering the body, calls him 'a rich man'. Matthew may be suggesting that Joseph of Arimathæa bribed Pilate in order to obtain the body of Jesus. Luke seems less worried about explaining Joseph's ability to procure Jesus' body and more interested in his reasons. Luke states that Joseph was a righteous man who had not consented to the decision of the Sanhedrin. John[703] introduces Joseph as a disciple of Jesus, who out of fear for the 'Jews' kept it a secret. Peter writes of Joseph that he was a friend of Pilate (and of the 'Lord'). Pilate therefore made the request to Herod, who happily obliged.[704] Later Peter mentions him as one who had 'beheld the good thing that he [Jesus] did'.

Crossan[705] provides two possible reasons why Jesus would not have been left to be preyed upon as carrion, the first being the personal piety of an individual[706] and the second communal obligation.[707] His firm conviction, however, remains that Mark invented the story and the other evangelists followed, improved and reconciled it with their own narratives. Mark is ambiguous. Joseph was part of the council (βουλευτής) but was it the same council (the Sanhedrin) that condemned Jesus? He was expecting the kingdom but did he believe that it had come? Matthew and Luke set out to answer these questions, Matthew confirming that he was a disciple and Luke that he was in the Sanhedrin but had not approved of the condemnation of Jesus.

Another interesting point may be drawn from the speech attributed to Paul in Acts 13:26–31[708] which contains elements from a primitive passion narrative (see previous chapter). The narrative given here is short but detailed enough to contain at least a mention of Joseph of Arimathæa but instead it says that the Jews who condemned Jesus were also responsible for His burial.[709] Furthermore, the theme of Jesus being hanged from a tree, which we also saw in the Toldoth, is repeated here. This is an example of how scripture affects the retelling. In Galatians (3:13) Paul states that 'Christ redeemed us from the curse of the law, having become a curse for us; for it is written, Cursed is every one that hangeth on a tree.' This particular reading of scripture (Deuteronomy 21:23 LXX), relating the crucifixion to the curse on the man who is hanged, seems to have affected the oral kerygma attributed to Paul in Acts.

Later legends made Joseph the founder of the church at Lydda and in the Middle Ages he became the bearer of the holy grail to the British Isles.[710]

And so it was, according to the gospels, that Jesus was buried and entered into a proper tomb but problems remained. Some of the evangelists' contemporaries claimed that the conclusion of the story was false, so it was necessary to account for the certainty of the final part of the narrative.

First of all the tomb had to be new, so that Jesus' body alone was placed in it. This in itself was a problem because of the two thieves who were crucified with Jesus, for it is difficult to imagine that Jesus would not be placed in the same tomb as the thieves unless one maintains that Joseph was a disciple. The story of the empty tomb, which we will deal with below, had apparently generated rumours that the disciples of Jesus had stolen His body so that they could claim that He had been resurrected. This is dealt with by Matthew in the following manner:

> Now on the morrow, which is the day after the preparation, the chief priests and the Pharisees were gathered together unto Pilate, saying, Sir, we remember that that deceiver said while he was yet alive, After three days I rise again. Command therefore that the sepulchre be made sure until the third day, lest haply his disciples come and steal him

> away, and say unto the people, He is risen from the dead: and the last error will be worse than the first. Pilate said unto them, Ye have a guard: go, make it as sure as ye can. So they went, and made the sepulchre sure, sealing the stone, the guard being with them (Matthew 27:62–6).

The historicity of this account is difficult to establish. It seems hard to imagine that the 'Jews' should have taken a few allegorical statements (of equally questionable historicity) to imply a promise of resurrection. To furthermore imagine that stealing the body was considered by these 'Jews' a means of establishing this resurrection is straining it unreasonably. Peter seems to have developed this theme further. Here the fear of the stealing of Jesus' body is not explained but the great signs that accompanied His death have made the 'Scribes and Pharisees' realize that they were wrong and they now fear the people's wrath should the body be stolen. The somewhat enigmatic expression in Matthew: 'and the last error (πλάνη) will be worse than the first' may perhaps be better translated as 'And the final deception will be worse than the first' (NEB), meaning that the ministry itself (the first deception) may be less significant than the alleged resurrection (the final deception).

In the Toldoth the gardener removes the body of Jesus in order to prevent the disciples from stealing it and then claiming that He had 'ascended into heaven'. Such Jewish claims are recorded also by Tertullian in his *De Spectaculis* (100.30): 'This is he whom his disciples have stolen secretly, that it may be said, "He has risen", or the gardener abstracted that his lettuces might not be damaged by the crowds of visitors!'

The Empty Tomb: Matthew 28:1–8; Mark 16:1–8; Luke 24:1–8, 12; John 20:1–10

Mark records that 'Mary Magdalene, and Mary the mother of James, and Salome, bought spices, that they might come and anoint him'. Seeing the great rock with which the entrance had been sealed rolled away, they enter and are awestruck when they find an angelic figure there to receive them. The tomb is empty and they are told that Jesus has been raised and gone to Galilee, according to what He had already told them. They were told to share this news with 'the disciples and Peter' and yet they do not do so because they are afraid. Thus ends the Gospel of Mark.[711] The reason for the sudden ending has been the subject of much scholarly debate and we will therefore limit ourselves to mentioning only a few of the suggested solutions.

Werner H. Kelber in his book *The Oral and the Written Gospel* suggests that Mark has the women become 'instrumental in the final and decisive breakdown of oral transmission. Mark, on this reading, has brought the antecedent negativity toward the family to a climax by implicating an important member in the message that failed' (p. 104). This conclusion seems unsatisfactory, for it does not explain the abruptness of the ending, nor does it explain the presence of the other women, amongst whom is Mary Magdalene, who is mentioned before Mary the mother of James. This latter Mary is in all likelihood not to be identified as the mother of Jesus anyway.

Joanna Dewey in her article 'The Gospel of Mark as an Oral-Aural Event'[712] suggests that the lack of conclusion is designed to invoke activity. Mark's audience was part of the continuation of the story. The women were too afraid to tell the good news to their fellow disciples. Were those who made up Marks' audience going to be the subject of that same fear or were they willing to face the persecution and proclaim the gospel?

Crossan believes that the Markan experience of persecution and a belief in Jesus' absence until His return led him to hold that a tradition of resurrection appearances would only induce 'misplaced hopes and disappointed expectations during the terrible days of Jerusalem's Roman siege'.[713] This does not seem likely. As we alluded to in the previous chapter, the resurrection appearances do not seem to propose an active intercession in worldly affairs – there is nothing in the resurrection tradition that suggests that it would give hope under the Roman siege on Jerusalem.

Jesus' promise to appear in Galilee could indicate that some of the first appearance stories came from there. The reason for reporting the women's silence, in this case, may indicate that Mark wished to explain why the story of the empty tomb was relatively new. On the other hand, the reference to Galilee may indicate that this was believed to have been the place of Christ's return (Mark 14:28).[714] It is also possible that there was an ending but that it was removed at some time early in its circulation. That no trace at all should have remained, however, seems unlikely. An answer to the question of Mark's ending will require a fuller discussion of the tradition that remains to us.

As for the women themselves, in Matthew, Salome is omitted from the list and in Luke the group becomes women from Galilee who followed Jesus. At the end of the empty tomb story, Luke finally produces a list: Mary Magdalene, Joanna and Mary the mother of James. Matthew, still confronted with the claims that the body of Jesus has been stolen, asserts that the rock is opened before their eyes by an angel. Indirectly it is asserted that Jesus was able to disappear bodily without the rock being removed. Matthew also makes sure that the guards placed there become witnesses to the event so that it cannot be claimed to be a Christian invention.[715]

While Mark mentions Peter specifically, Matthew addresses the message of Mary to the disciples with no specific reference to any of them in particular. Note how subtly Matthew (28:8)[716] alters the Markan (16:8)[717] text. They departed quickly (ἀπελθοῦσαι ταχὺ) instead of fleeing (ἔφυγον) and not trembling with astonishment (τρόμος καὶ ἔκστασις) but with fear and great joy (φόβου καὶ χαρᾶς μεγάλης).

Luke alters the text even more. Two angelic figures appear who remind them not of Jesus' promise that He would go to Galilee and meet them there but of what He said when He was there (i.e. the passion prediction 9:22, 18:31ff). For Luke, unlike Matthew, the mission to the Gentile starts in Jerusalem and not in Galilee.

For John,[718] Mary Magdalene is alone when visiting the grave and she does not enter[719] but instead runs immediately to Peter and John when she sees that the stone has been moved. Despite not having entered, she reports that someone has removed the body of Jesus to an unknown location. Then these two chief disciples run to the grave. John arrives there first but waits for Peter before he enters. This is typical of John's treatment of these two disciples, who were of equal importance and authority, although John outdoes Peter in his devotion and fervour. Having seen the empty tomb, they leave, believing, like Mary, that the body of Jesus has been removed.[720] Now Mary, standing by the grave and weeping, suddenly sees two angels in the empty tomb[721] but they do not reveal to her the risen Jesus because she turns away.

The Gospel of Peter reports that the guards stationed

outside the tomb witnessed the removal of Jesus by two angelic figures sustaining a third (i.e. Jesus) and a theophanic dialogue between God's voice and a cross which also ascended into heaven.[722] Pilate imposes silence on the guards at the request of the Scribes and Pharisees but once again proclaims himself innocent of the blood of 'the son of God'. The story after this point follows that of Mark, though Peter designates only Mary Magdalene by name amongst the women who went to the grave and omits mention of the Galilee. It otherwise also ends the 'empty tomb scene' with the women fleeing in fear. It goes on to tell a story which appears to be like the apparition story of John 21:1 but the text is wanting from the moment that the disciples step on board Peter's boat.

All stories unanimously make Mary Magdalene amongst the first to discover the empty tomb.

The Appearances

All the gospels have appearance scenes after the empty tomb story, with the exception of the original Mark. Mark's longer ending, which was added later, tells us that Mary Magdalene was the first to see the risen Christ as it is reported in John. In both Matthew and Luke it is the women as a group who see the risen Jesus but only Luke agrees with the long ending of Mark that the disciples first disbelieved. In addition, these two agree that two anonymous disciples met Jesus, though Luke's story is far more extensive and elaborate and it is likely that the tradition had circulated independently. Many of the elaborations found in Luke's version (24:13–35) are clearly the work of the evangelist himself.

The exact relationship between the long ending of

Mark and other evangelists' accounts is not entirely certain. There are some elements that seem to be older in the extra-Markan tradition than their possible canonical counterparts. In particular, the mission command (16:15–18) appears to have an independent tradition. The preaching to the whole creation (πάσῃ τῇ κτίσει) is similar to Colossians 1:23 but is not found in the gospels. The formulation regarding baptism, belief and disbelief in verse 16:16 finds no precise correspondence in the New Testament. The promises to the disciples (believers) that they will be able to expel demons is seen elsewhere (e.g. Luke 10:17), as is the promise of 'new tongues'. In addition to these are promises that they will be able to take serpents and drink deadly poison without harm and heal people by laying on hands (Mark 16:17–18). All of these are connected to the prophets of Jesus, as discussed in chapter 5.

Of particular interest is the reference to speaking in new tongues (γλώσσαις λαλήσουσιν καιναῖς). The practice of speaking in tongues is not directly mentioned elsewhere in the gospels. It is referred to in Acts and in Paul's first epistle to Corinth. Since Paul is our earliest source, it is there that we must start. In Paul's community there were people who, like Paul, could speak in tongues (1 Corinthians 12). Speaking in tongues, known as 'glossolalia' (Greek for 'tongues'), involves, then as today, a person entering into a trance or 'a state of dissociation'[723] which makes him speak involuntarily and uncontrollably. According to studies of present practice, the words spoken have been found not to be actual language, foreign to the speaker or otherwise, but appear to have commonalities across cultural and linguistic boundaries. In this state of mind one becomes detached from reality and enters into a catatonic-like state, often accompanied by feelings of euphoria. Speaking in tongues is therefore believed to be the manifestation of the Holy Spirit. Studies have shown that the practice is learned and that congregations that learn it acquire the speech patterns of their teacher. At the same time, the state can be provoked involuntarily if people are surrounded by others engaged in glossolalia but over a period of time the community glossolalia as a whole tends to fade. Finally, it has been observed that when people who were not baptized started speaking in tongues, it was felt that they were close to God but ritually in danger and therefore in need to be brought into the community.[724] In Paul's case it is clear that glossolalia was perceived as a source of authority.[725]

The story presented in Acts, unlike Paul's, appears not to be based on first-hand experience of what glossolalia is. Paul is well aware that glossolalia is not a foreign tongue, while in Acts that it is precisely why it is considered useful (Acts 2:4–11).[726] The term in Mark 16:17, however, suggests a familiarity with what glossolalia is. This adds to the likelihood that the extra-Markan tradition is an independent one.

Another tradition of interest appears in the Gospel of Mary.[727] In this gospel the resurrected Saviour appears to the disciples and in a classical dialogue teaches them about the nature of existence.[728] After the appearance, the disciples are sad and discouraged by the great challenge of teaching the Gentile population but Mary stands up in their midst and consoles them. At their request she recounts a dialogue with the living Jesus.

> But they were grieved. They wept greatly, saying, 'How shall we go to the gentiles and preach the gospel of the kingdom of the Son of Man? If they did not spare him,

> how will they spare us?' Then Mary stood up, greeted them all, and said to her brethren, 'Do not weep and do not grieve nor be irresolute, for his grace will be entirely with you and will protect you. But rather let us praise his greatness, for he has prepared us and made us into men.' When Mary said this, she turned their hearts to the Good, and they began to discuss the words of the [Saviour].[729]

When she is finished, some of the disciples reject her account, saying that it did not accord with the teachings of the Saviour. Peter in particular states: 'Did he then speak secretly with a woman, in preference to us, and not openly? Are we to turn back and all listen to her? Did he prefer her to us?' But he is rebuked by Levi and the story ends with the disciples leaving to proclaim the gospel.

The conflict between Peter and Mary is a typical motif in gnostic literature and appears in the saying added to the Gospel of Thomas at a later stage:

> Simon Peter said to them, 'Make Mary leave us, for females don't deserve life.' Jesus said, 'Look, I will guide her to make her male, so that she too may become a living spirit resembling you males. For every female who makes herself male will enter the kingdom of Heaven' (Thomas 114 SV).

While these words do not seem to support Mary's superiority, they certainly reflect a perceived conflict between early communities, battled out by the communities' apostolic figures.

How can we best understand this composition? Except for a small cluster of synoptic sayings (Mary 8:10–23), the dialogues are not particularly Christian. It is conceivable that the talks were taken from a non-Christian source and received the narrative from the Christian-Gnostic editor.

This appears to be the case with 'Eugnostos the Blessed' and the Christian revision 'The Sophia of Jesus Christ'.[730] The concluding scene of the first dialogue is rather unique: instead of uplifting the disciples, it makes them weep (Mary 9:6). The Apocryphon of John has John Zebedee falter and doubt until his meeting with the resurrected Jesus (1:11–2:15) but in Mary the mission commandment itself is discouraging. This, along with Mary standing up and encouraging the disciples, seems to be an older Christian narrative.

There are also a few cases where the Christian-Gnostic editors used stories about the apostles that were not of gnostic origin at all. We have, for example, Paul's ascension into the third heaven (2 Corinthians 12:2) used as a motif in the Apocalypse of Paul (19:20–5), the story of Adam and Eve (Genesis 2) and the story of Noah (Genesis 6–9) in the Apocalypse of Adam (69 and 71–3). There need not have been a scriptural basis for the narrative. Reading through the (1 and 2) Apocalypse of James, we find that it contains references both to James the Just's hope for the return of Jesus (the Gospel of the Hebrews) and to his being stoned to death (Josephus and Hegesippus). In all cases the narrative may be slightly compromised by the writer but all dialogues are completely gnostic.

We have already seen that the theme of the conflict between Mary Magdalene and Peter had an oral precursor that found its way into the Gospel of Thomas corpus as a last addition. We likewise know from the Gospel of Philip of the tradition that Mary was the companion of Jesus, His favourite disciple. All of these traditions could be regarded as suspect because they are preserved by texts that are gnostic or appear to have been gnosticized but as narrative traditions they are not particularly gnostic in nature.

There is one passage that needs our special attention before we move on. In Mary 10:10–15 she recounts, 'I saw the Lord in a vision and I said to him, "Lord, I saw you today in a vision." '[731] Pasquir understands the entire dialogue after this to be the vision mentioned at the beginning of the sentence.[732] However, the larger context makes it possible to understand the dialogue as an actual event occasioned by the fact that Mary had had a vision about the Lord. Andrew does not suggest that there was no vision or that the vision was self-conceit; rather he suggests that it is not believable that 'the Saviour said this' (Greek MS εἰρηκέναι). Peter's complaint, 'Did he [the Lord] really speak with a woman without our knowledge (and) not openly' strongly suggests that what is being discussed is not a vision but a conversation that could have been held either without their knowledge or openly, something that is impossible in the case of a vision. What follows is not a vision anyway but a dialogue about the nature of visions. This is also most likely the gnostic editor's work: using the power of a traditional form of authority, namely the living Jesus, in order to assert a new authority, revelation through visions. Thus the author usurps the authority of a traditional source in order to provide for a new, gnostic one. The result is the above-mentioned conflict pointing to the original narrative frame. Unfortunately, the missing pages are necessary to tell us how the dialogue becomes an account of the ascent of the soul. The shift is quite likely due to the gnostic editor's insertion of the dialogue: both themes, vision and ascent, are gnostic and late. The church political issue, on the other hand, is clearly integral to the narrative.[733] As Elaine Pagels points out, Mary lacked the authority of being one of the Twelve and the Gnostics used her as their prototype for an opponent to the priests and bishops that claimed to be Peter's successors.[734] And so when a generation had passed and Peter and Paul came to represent the Catholic majority, more radical groups rallied around figures that in some way seemed peripheral to the earliest community. In the Gospel of Mary, Mary's authority, which stemmed from her closeness to the living Jesus, being His 'companion', was used to empower Gnostics, their theology and their mode of authority (visions).

Matthew has one more problem to deal with before he can return to the disciples, namely the conclusion of the story of the empty tomb. The soldiers returned to report the extraordinary events. They were then paid to be silent (Matthew 28:12). Matthew has the disciples depart immediately. Once they arrive in Galilee, Jesus appears to them but still, Matthew says, 'some doubted', a remark, no doubt, aimed at those contemporary to himself who likewise doubted the resurrection. Here the risen Jesus tells them: 'Go ye therefore, and make disciples of all the nations, baptizing them into the name of the Father and of the Son and of the Holy Spirit: teaching them to observe all things whatsoever I commanded you: and lo, I am with you always, even unto the end of the world' (Matthew 28:19–20 ASV).

Funk and Hoover echo general scholarly agreement when they comment on this speech: 'The commission in Matthew is expressed in Matthew's language and reflects the evangelist's idea of the world mission of the Church.'[735]

Luke notably mentions, within the framework of the story of the two anonymous disciples, that Jesus had also appeared to Peter. This is probably an independent tradition that Luke wanted to include, perhaps because it agrees with the statement of Paul in 1 Corinthians 15:5–8 or the oral tradition it comes from.[736] The story in Luke thus reflects the reconciliation of the extra-Markan tradition of the anonymous resurrection witnesses with a theologically more influential tradition which we know from Paul but which was surely also known to Luke. They are not introduced at the beginning of the narrative, where they are just mentioned as 'two of them [assembled in Jerusalem]' (24:13) but Cleopas is introduced when he speaks in 24:18. The second person may possibly be Simon (Peter), deduced from their statement to the assembled people in Jerusalem in 24:34. Alternatively, Luke may have used the two anonymous disciples to announce the resurrection appearance to Peter but he does not explain how the anonymous disciples came to know about this appearance. Either way, Luke is attempting to reconcile two disparate traditions. In the extra-Markan tradition the first to see the risen Lord is Mary Magdalene (Mark 16:9); in Luke the women are met by a pair of angels (two men), avoiding the problem of Peter's primacy. In order for this to happen, Luke has to separate Peter from the rest of the Eleven – the Eleven designating the remaining apostles after the defection of Judas – so that Peter, and he alone, could be the first to see the risen Lord. A problem, however, arises whether or not Peter is to be identified with one of the anonymous disciples. For when the two disciples arrive they address the Eleven (which, as is clearly implied in Luke 24:9, must include Peter) and proclaim the appearance of the risen Lord.

From there Jesus appears to all of the apostles, 'appearing in their midst' (Luke 24:36). The disciples become afraid because they mistake the risen Jesus for a ghost. Jesus, however, says: 'See my hands and my feet, that it is I myself: handle me, and see; for a spirit hath not flesh and bones, as ye behold me having' (Luke 24:39). As evidence,

Jesus eats a piece of grilled fish in front of them. The story presents some problems in respect to the other stories. First of all, the two anonymous disciples as well as Peter had already met the risen Christ and at least the two anonymous disciples had already seen Him break bread. Yet suddenly it is a question of whether or not this is a ghost (πνεῦμα). The story is designed to answer a specific question about the nature of the resurrection. It should also be noted that verse 24:40 is omitted in some very important manuscripts.[737] In the Gospel of the Nazaraeans the disciples mistake Jesus for a 'bodiless demon'.[738]

John, on the other hand, presents quite a different story. Mary Magdalene, standing at the empty tomb, suddenly encounters Jesus but does not recognize Him.[739] The author of John 21 redacted the Sign Source material to reflect the resurrection scenario, which included the disciples not recognizing Him (John 21:4).[740] Luke has a similar event in his account of the two anonymous disciples wherein Jesus is met but not recognized. This does not, however, suggest a common source or dependency. Rather it suggests a common question. Why did some meet Jesus while others did not? The common answer for the three evangelists is because some could not recognize Him.

Mary, upon recognizing Her master (*rabbouni*, from Aramaic רבוני), is told: 'Touch me not; for I am not yet ascended unto the Father: but go unto my brethren, and say to them, I ascend unto my Father and your Father, and my God and your God' (John 20:17 ASV).

While the language is certainly that of John, the statement is difficult to understand in the context of this narrative. Why should Mary not touch the risen Jesus? The present author suggests that John used a vastly different theology from the other evangelists. It is remarkable that

John has Jesus announce not His resurrection but His ascension. That He has not yet ascended is the reason why He should not be touched. Somehow the situation has changed dramatically by that same evening, when Jesus allows Thomas to touch Him; for when He returns, He has already risen to the Father and then it is suddenly permissible to touch Him. It is likely that John had the scene from Tobit in mind, in which the angel Raphael revealed himself to Tobit and his son Tobias:

> Then they were both troubled, and fell upon their faces: for they feared. But he said unto them, Fear not, for it shall go well with you; praise God therefore. For not of any favour of mine, but by the will of our God I came; wherefore praise him for ever. All these days I did appear unto you; but I did neither eat nor drink, but ye did see a vision. Now therefore give God thanks: for I go up to him that sent me; but write all things which are done in a book.[And he rose in the air].[741] And when they arose, they saw him no more. Then they confessed the great and wonderful works of God, and how the angel of the Lord had appeared unto them (Tobit 12:16–22 APC).

If this indeed is the image that John has in mind, then it adds to the hypothesis that, in John's mind, Jesus did in fact ascend to the Father immediately after His encounter with Mary. This event is to be viewed in context of the event that followed, namely Jesus' appearance to the disciples that very same evening. Here He appears amongst them, although they have locked the door, greets them and says, 'As the Father hath sent me, even so send I you.' This is John's version of the apostolic commission. 'And when he had said this, he breathed on them, and saith unto them, Receive ye the Holy Spirit' (John 20:22 ASV).

To fulfil the apostolic mission it is necessary for them to have the Holy Spirit, and the creation of the church and its continued existence is realized through this event. For this reason Jesus' ascension to the Father becomes the central message of Mary to the disciples.

It must be assumed that John thought of Jesus as being somehow different before and after the ascension. Eight days after the ascension, Jesus appears again to the disciples, amongst whom is Thomas,[742] who was absent the first time and had not believed the other disciples. He puts a condition on his belief: 'Except I shall see in his hands the print of the nails, and put my hand into his side, I will not believe' (John 20:25 ASV). At Jesus' second appearance Thomas is offered the possibility of ascertaining the reality of the resurrection of Jesus. Though Thomas is usually depicted as touching Jesus' side, John never says that he does so and in fact Jesus' response might suggest that he did not: 'Because thou hast seen me, thou hast believed: blessed are they that have not seen, and yet have believed' (John 20:29 ASV).

The appearance to Thomas, which earned him the name 'doubting Thomas', should probably be considered a church political story. Both John and Thomas were patron apostles of the Syrian churches; the author of John, belonging to the former school, launches an indirect censure of the latter.[743]

Another appearance is recorded in John which takes place at Lake Tiberias. It appears to be a regular miracle story which has been slightly modified to fit into the resurrection scenario.[744] The story is probably understood as a metaphor, where the fish which are caught through the assistance of Jesus are seen as men who were miraculously converted in the early church.[745] The redaction consists of the disciples not knowing Him at first and then John recognizing Him (as already mentioned) and Peter's joyous reaction. The dining scene may have been part of the original story but in John's context it is part of the proof of the reality of the resurrection.

And thus appears the last dialogue reported by John between Jesus and Peter. Three times Peter is asked if he loves Jesus. Three times he confirms and three times he is charged to 'feed the flock'. Then Jesus says: 'Verily, verily, I say unto thee, When thou wast young, thou girdedst thyself, and walkedst whither thou wouldest: but when thou shalt be old, thou shalt stretch forth thy hands, and another shall gird thee, and carry thee whither thou wouldest not' (John 21:18 ASV).

It appears as if this tradition circulated prior to the composition of the 21st chapter and that, in view of Peter's martyrdom, a new interpretation was necessary. Earlier, the emphasis was on the old age which Peter would acquire, an age when he would need someone to hold on to.[746] The language, the present author finds, is not particularly Johannine,[747] though the interpretation of the following verse is.

Then in regard to John the disciple there was a report that Jesus had promised that if He wished it to be so, John would live until the time of Jesus' return (John 21:20–2). This tradition or report probably also circulated in the Johannine church, and when John died and Jesus had not yet returned, this also needed explaining. Certainly, the verse demands a new interpretation of an older tradition: 'This saying therefore went forth among the brethren, that that disciple should not die: yet Jesus said not unto him, that he should not die; but, If I will that he tarry till I come, what is that to thee?' (John 21:23 ASV). And with this the

Gospel of John ends and, as with Mark and Matthew, this is sufficient: That Jesus did not just die but was resurrected. Luke, however, wanted to include a story about the ascension of Jesus.

The ascension is described only by Luke both at the end of Luke and at the beginning of Acts. His last words in Luke point to one of the central themes of the second volume, namely the Pentecost: the descending of the Holy Spirit on the apostles and the transfer to them of the authority to conduct the mission: 'Ye are witnesses of these things. And behold, I send forth the promise of my Father upon you: but tarry ye in the city, until ye be clothed with power from on high' (Luke 24:48–9 ASV). Acts also has a resurrection appearance: 'To whom he also showed himself alive after his passion by many proofs, appearing unto them by the space of forty days, and speaking the things concerning the kingdom of God' (Acts 1:3 ASV).

Perhaps here is an indication that gnostic reports circulated that Jesus appeared not only to prove the reality of the resurrection but also had a didactic function, revealing 'things concerning the kingdom'. Such reports are not to be found elsewhere and demonstrate how early distinction may not always have been very clear as to the orthodoxy of certain reports. Alternatively, Luke may have been attempting to supplant such reports and ensure that reports about appearances were limited to the apostles only. Luke himself provides a very orthodox version which, if it existed before Luke wrote it, probably was not originally connected with the resurrection.

> They therefore, when they were come together, asked him, saying, Lord, dost thou at this time restore the kingdom to Israel? And he said unto them, It is not for you to know

> times or seasons, which the Father hath set within His own authority (Acts 1:6–7 ASV).

There is a problem with the account of this event in Acts to do with the limit of 40 days, for Paul still remains unconverted long after Christ's ascension. If Luke is aware of the conflict, he apparently is not troubled by it for he does nothing to rectify it.

Jesus' ascent is described thus:

> And when he had said these things, as they were looking, he was taken up; and a cloud received him out of their sight. And while they were looking steadfastly into heaven as he went, behold, two men stood by them in white apparel; who also said, Ye men of Galilee, why stand ye looking into heaven? this Jesus, who was received up from you into heaven shall so come in like manner as ye beheld him going into heaven (Acts 1:9–11 ASV).

The discrepancies between the prophetic speeches (discussed in chapter 8) and the description of Jesus' ascent, particularly that the cloud was not the medium of transport but was what finally 'received him out of their sight', suggests that Luke has something quite different in mind. There are, for example, certain striking similarities with the story of Elijah's ascension, which we have already discussed. The one taken away is in conversation with another, who shortly after picks up the 'mantle' of responsibility to continue the mission of the first. Or perhaps it is the tradition of Enoch referred to in the Palestinian Targum:

> And Enoch served before the Lord in uprightness after he begat Methuselah three hundred years, and begat sons

> and daughters: and all the days of Enoch with the dwellers on earth were three hundred and sixty and five years: and Enoch served before the Lord in uprightness, and, behold, he was not with the dwellers on earth; for he was withdrawn and went up to the firmament by the Word before the Lord, and his name was called Metatron the great scribe.[748]

Paul had experienced the risen Jesus and claimed for himself apostleship together with those who had lived with the living Jesus or had been related to Him (1 Corinthians 15:5–8).[749] Recalling from the gospel the sudden prominence of 'name-dropping' in the resurrection narrative, it seems that association with the resurrected Christ gave authority. After all, the point of the resurrection was the continued presence of Jesus, whose constant guidance was received through the leaders of the church. In the Gospel of Mary we see that it is in fact not the resurrection that gave Mary authority but that she had recollections of the living Jesus.

Paul's received tradition has two individuals (Peter and James) and two groups (the Twelve and the apostles) and the five hundred who saw the risen Jesus. It has been proposed that two competing traditions have been combined in this tradition. The first tradition has Peter as its head and the second has James.[750]

Though the gospels and Paul unanimously claim that Jesus was raised in accordance with scripture, quotations are suspiciously wanting. This represented a major problem for the early church for nothing in the scripture prepared them for the passion or the resurrection.

Johannes Leipoldt[751] in his article 'The Resurrection Stories' points out that while there are some significant discrepancies between the resurrection stories of Greek and Egyptian gods, they share a common feature: the number three figures prominently as the number of days a deity was dead before being resurrected. The empty tomb story also appears in a novel by Chariton in the beginning of the Christian era but dates are questionable and source dependence is difficult to establish one way or the other. The novel includes a story of the stone being removed and the discovery of an empty tomb, causing great anxiety. Again there are differences. The wife of the protagonist is in fact not dead but only seemingly so. Suetinus reports that a centurion saw Augustus ascending into heaven. Apollinus, the 1st century philosopher, is reported to have predicted his own death and reappeared to his disciples and allowed them to touch him to ascertain that he was not a spirit. He ascended to heaven from a temple at the bidding of angelic voices and reappeared to one man only in a dream to convert him to discipleship. Philostratos, who wrote this account in the 3rd century, is generally maintained to be independent of the gospels but Leipoldt entertains certain doubts in that respect. That these stories have so many parallels with common contemporary literature does not explain (or explain away) the resurrection but it does explain some of the forms that the stories have taken. Another question arises in this connection. If these stories were common, how then does the resurrection explain, as some claim, the emergence of the church? It is difficult to say.

The Theological Significance

There can be no doubt that the concept of resurrection was not a new creation of Christianity. The doctrine of the general resurrection had long been a part of Jewish belief but was, as has been mentioned, disputed by the Sadducees.

It was also believed that when the Messiah was to come, the general resurrection would take place, and so we find that Paul writes (1 Corinthians 15:16–26) that Jesus is the 'first fruit' of the resurrected: His is not a unique resurrection, He is the first of mankind, just like Adam was the first to be overtaken by death. Yet, like Adam, Jesus is more than just the first, He is the archetype. So, according to Paul, this did in fact happen. Jesus was the first to resurrect and by doing so started the general resurrection. All are descendants of Adam and therefore die 'in' Him by inheriting His nature; similarly, all that are 'in' Christ will be raised at His return. This for Paul is a central tenet of his faith. If Jesus was not raised, then all is lost, for there is no general resurrection.

In 2 Corinthians 12:1–6 Paul recounts in the third person a narrative of a man (himself) who had a vision of paradise. Some hold that this story is expressed in the third person out of humility but the present author finds it more likely that it is because of his depersonalized experience that Paul refers to himself as if he were someone else. This unique experience (14 years before Paul writes) could be similar to Paul's earlier experience of the risen Lord. To what extent or in what sense this is true we shall consider further below.[752]

It is difficult to tell exactly what Paul intends with the resurrection, to what degree he spiritualizes the literal Jewish concept and to what degree he adopts it.

An important source of Paul's experience of the risen Lord is given in the three versions in Acts (9:1–22, 22:1–21 and 26:9–23) and it is conceivable that the three are all different oral accounts of the same event.[753] The event is presented as a vision of blinding light and with a voice that addresses him with the words: 'Saul, Saul, why are you persecuting me?' to which he answers, 'Who are you, Lord?' to which He answers, 'I am Jesus whom you are persecuting . . . Now rise up.'

So what was the nature of the resurrection experience? We have already tentatively proposed that it had to do with the disciples' feeling of loss. We will now consider the theory advanced by Gerd Luedemann, Gerd Theissen and Michael Goulder, that these visions of the risen Lord are in fact not only connected with feelings of loss but also of regret. Michael Goulder draws parallels between these experiences and those of Susan Atkins, an accomplice to Charles Manson's series of murders, who experienced a 'conversion vision'. One evening in her cell she was contemplating the terrible things that she had done and considering what her future was. Then, in that hour of doubt and guilt, she saw a blinding light. In it she could distinguish a vague human figure and immediately she knew that it was Jesus. She explains: 'He spoke to me – literally, plainly, matter-of-factly spoke to me in my 9 by 11 prison cell.'[754] After this vision her guilt and bitterness were gone. Here, of course, Paul is the easiest figure to look at for parallels, since we have more reliable information about him than other candidates. We know that he was brought up and became a Pharisee and that he persecuted the church terribly. He did so in his zeal for the law (Philippians 3:5–6). However, according to Theissen, this persecution was born of 'an unconscious conflict with the law'.[755] The description of Atkins's vision bears a remarkable resemblance to the descriptions of Paul's vision in Acts: the blinding light, the conversation with Jesus. Just as Paul fought his doubts about the law by zealously keeping it, he also fought against his attraction to Jesus' community by persecuting it. This dissonance was relieved by the intervention of the vision, after which Paul consciously abandoned his zeal for the law and became a follower of Jesus.

Peter was already a disciple when he had his experience of the risen Lord. Luedemann here perceives something slightly different from a 'conversion vision'. He points to Peter's denial as the event that triggered the vision.[756] When Jesus died, Peter mourned, and Luedemann here draws on various reports of bereaved people to show that they often experience the presence of the lost one. One particular case of note relates to a woman who had lost her father at the age of nine. She was miserable for years. Then one Christmas a stomachache kept her home. The ache subsided and she was lying in her bed when she heard footsteps and then knocking on her door. In came her father, 'shining like gold and transparent like mist. He looked as he had always done.'[757] After this her grief left her and she felt happy again.

Let us now consider James. Wilhelm Pratscher has looked at the tradition in the gospels and concluded that during the lifetime of Jesus His family distanced itself from Him.[758] If this is true, then it can reasonably be assumed that James was torn between his brotherly love/duty towards Jesus and the difficulties he had accepting His teachings and/or His behaviour. The tragic loss of his brother probably combined to trigger a conversion vision, which allowed James to resolve his inner tension and deal with his guilt and, undoubtedly, his grief.

Finally, we may consider Mary Magdalene from whom, according to Luke 8:2 and the extra-Markan tradition (Mark 16:9), Jesus cast out seven demons. Later traditions, as we saw above, seemed to make Mary Magdalene Jesus' closest female companion, to the extent of suggesting some inappropriateness. All traditions presume that she was amongst women or alone in coming to the grave of Jesus. Clearly Mary's experience is closer to that of Peter than that of Paul: hers was a mourner's experience. It would appear from the tradition in the Gospel of Mary that Mary was comforted by her resurrection experience and attempted to comfort the others.

There are two theories to be considered with regard to the five hundred who saw the risen Jesus. The first has been advanced by Michael Goulder, who suggests that this should be explained as 'a collective delusion', comparable to UFO sightings or miracles connected with statues of Mary. In particular, Goulder notes the case of a Bigfoot hunt in South Dakota in 1977 where a few sightings suddenly led to hundreds. Traps were set, footprints were found and the police went after the creature, to no avail.[759] This delusion was strengthened by the community's own need to be confirmed in its belief in Jesus.[760] The wording in 1 Corinthians 15:6 (ἐφάπαξ, all the one time) makes this explanation difficult to accept, since mass delusion implies that the sightings did not occur at the same time.

Luedemann proposes that the origin of the tradition of the five hundred who saw the risen Lord should be understood in terms of a Pentecost event, a mass outbreak of glossolalia.[761] Luedemann notes that Paul himself ultimately reckoned Jesus and the Spirit to be one and the same.[762] The problem with this thesis is that Paul would undoubtedly have had to distinguish between glossolalia and resurrection appearances or accept many of the members of his church in Corinth as his equals. Since Paul received this tradition, there is no reason to assume that he knew anything about the nature of the appearance or that his theological perspective had any impact on his understanding of that tradition. Once this precaution about the Pauline evidence has been noted, however, we would do well to consider it as a plausible hypothesis. If we had heard the resurrection experiences told by these prominent figures, we might have had a similar reaction to that suggested by Goulder. Shortly after Peter had his experience the disciples joined Peter in a glossolalia event and it was interpreted with his experience in mind.

In the gospels the theological issue of the nature of the resurrection needed to be addressed. The Gospel of John (11:23–6) does this in connection with the resurrection of Lazarus:

> Jesus saith unto her, Thy brother shall rise again. Martha saith unto him, I know that he shall rise again in the resurrection at the last day. Jesus said unto her, I am the resurrection, and the life: he that believeth in me, though he were dead, yet shall he live: And whosoever liveth and believeth in me shall never die. Believest thou this? (KJV).

This dialogue illustrates Johannine theology splendidly. For John and Paul, Jesus did inaugurate the resurrection, and he that believes shall never die, he that dies and believes shall live again. If the first is true, then the second statement can only occur if one can believe, or rather receive belief during death. That Jesus is the (general) resurrection is the perspective offered by John. According to him, Jesus' revelation both in deed and in speech has caused people to believe and that belief is the promised resurrection. Unbelief is death and belief is life. The allegory is also shown when Jesus weeps for Lazarus' death (meaningless otherwise, since Jesus knew that he could be resurrected) and 'again groans' at the unbelief of His fellow Jews.

The same understanding is found in this saying from Thomas:

> His disciples said to Him, 'When will the repose of the dead come about, and when will the new world come?' He said to them, 'What you look forward to has already come, but you do not recognize it' (Thomas 51).

The further removed Christian thought became from the problem of the messianic role of the resurrection, the less the tendency was to spiritualize the doctrine and the more it was transferred into a future event. The returned Christ was then expected to initiate the process that failed to occur at His first coming.

The belief was included in the Apostolic Confession[763] from perhaps as early as the 2nd century, which called it 'the resurrection of the body, and the life everlasting'. It has been largely unchallenged since that time. Muslim theology has generally accepted this part of its Judeo-Christian heritage and has developed it further while still maintaining many of the essential concepts.

It is proper, before we conclude this chapter, to address the question of a spiritual afterlife. The matter is difficult to address, for the question gets very little attention in the gospels. Luke introduces us to some unique instances that support the existence of the soul in another (incorporeal?) world. The first is the story of Lazarus (Luke 16:19–31), in which heaven and hell are depicted vividly in a manner presumably current amongst Jesus' contemporaries:

> There was a certain rich man, which was clothed in purple and fine linen, and fared sumptuously every day: And there was a certain beggar named Lazarus, which was laid at his gate, full of sores, And desiring to be fed with the

> crumbs which fell from the rich man's table: moreover the dogs came and licked his sores. And it came to pass, that the beggar died, and was carried by the angels into Abraham's bosom: the rich man also died, and was buried; And in hell he lift up his eyes, being in torments, and seeth Abraham afar off, and Lazarus in his bosom. And he cried and said, Father Abraham, have mercy on me, and send Lazarus, that he may dip the tip of his finger in water, and cool my tongue; for I am tormented in this flame. [25] But Abraham said, Son, remember that thou in thy lifetime receivedst thy good things, and likewise Lazarus evil things: but now he is comforted, and thou art tormented. [26] And beside all this, between us and you there is a great gulf fixed: so that they which would pass from hence to you cannot; neither can they pass to us, that [would come] from thence. [27] Then he said, I pray thee therefore, father, that thou wouldest send him to my father's house: For I have five brethren; that he may testify unto them, lest they also come into this place of torment. Abraham saith unto him, They have Moses and the prophets; let them hear them. And he said, Nay, father Abraham: but if one went unto them from the dead, they will repent. And he said unto him, If they hear not Moses and the prophets, neither will they be persuaded, though one rose from the dead (KJV).

The Jesus Seminar divides the story into two distinct narratives and although they do not justify the division, the present author finds there are good reasons to accept it.[764] The first ends with verse 26 and the other begins with verse 27. The story points out the reversal that happens in the afterlife: the poor man, who was in torment, suddenly finds himself in comfort, while the rich man who was in comfort finds himself in torment. That aspect reaches its climax in verses 25–6 with Abraham's rejection, which serves to illustrate the impossibility of overcoming the division that exists in the afterlife (which in turn serves to illustrate the social divisions in life). The rejection of this minor request is, with Luke's addition, followed by an exceedingly major request for nothing less than a miracle, an incongruence emerging from the fusion of the two stories. Lazarus ceases to be an actor in the second part as the dialogue between Abraham and the rich man goes on. Most significantly, however, is the incongruence between the person portrayed (a rich man) and what Abraham prescribes: Moses and the prophets. We see nothing in the story to suggest that the rich man did not follow the Law and the prophets. Why then is it an issue? The answer is, because Luke has something different in mind than the point illustrated by the first half. Luke is concerned with the fact that Jews (people who read the Law and the prophets) had not converted to the faith of the person who did rise from the dead (namely the faith of Jesus). Abraham's last sentence resounds with the experience of Luke and his community. Luke did something to connect the two stories. There was an oral tradition, a hearsay, about Lazarus who had been resurrected. This was developed further in John's Sign Source, as we saw above. In the original version of the first part, Lazarus was identified merely as 'a poor man', the opposite of 'a rich man'; but Luke, knowing where the narrative was going, chose to give the story a ring of familiarity by using the name Lazarus, although he did not supply a name for the rich man.

The second reference to the afterlife is the more distinctly Lukan story about one of the thieves crucified with Jesus whose words of faith were rewarded with the reply, 'Verily, verily I say unto thee, today thou shalt be with me in Paradise.' These words were discussed in detail in the previous chapter. The lack of direct reference to the matter seems to indicate that in this respect Jesus proposed nothing radical. There was much heated debate on this particular question in 1st century Palestine and yet no logion appears to survive regarding the subject, which would indicate that Jesus probably did not have a very objectionable position. The story contained in Mark 12:18–27 (= Matthew 22:23–33 = Luke 20:27–40) presupposes that Jesus was regarded as holding doctrines that were the opposite of those held by the Sadducees, who posed the question.

Summary and Conclusion

We started this chapter by looking at the story of Jesus' burial. We saw that there was a story about Joseph Arimathæa, who, it was told, ensured that Jesus was properly buried. Historically the story is doubtful. Although both Luke and Matthew present plausible elaborations to explain Joseph's reasons and abilities, yet they fail to convince. As Crossan points out, on the one hand Mark 14:64 states that 'all' the people of the Sanhedrin condemned Jesus, which is not the act of a disciple, secret or otherwise (Matthew's solution in 27:57 and Luke's in 23:50–1). On the other, a pious man would bury not only Jesus but also the two thieves.[765]

Rather than looking for a solution to the Markan problem we should evolve the story backwards. We saw that it was a basic tenet of early Christianity that Jesus was resurrected. This fact was the central starting point and was part of the early church's kerygma but, more significantly, it was part of the early church's experience. So what did one do if opponents claimed that Jesus had not been resurrected, that no proof existed that He had? Christians then returned to their starting point and said: If Jesus had been resurrected, which Christians knew He had, then His body must have disappeared. In a dialogue without the context of the full passion narrative, the first question would be: Can you prove it? Was there an empty grave? Could you be sure that it was His body? And a Christian must naturally assert that it was. Thus emerged the story of the empty tomb.[766] A sequence of questions followed: How is it that He had a tomb for Himself alone? How could the body be taken for burial, for crucified people were usually left to rot? Matthew had an additional set of questions which related to a counterclaim that the disciples had stolen the body of Jesus in order to claim His resurrection. Indeed, Matthew claims that this rumour is still being reported among Jews (28:13–15).

Again we may accept the conclusion about historicity suggested by Crossan. However, there is no need to presuppose that all these questions were not asked before Mark and John's Sign Source started writing their texts. Indeed, we would assume that such questions emerged immediately after the fact.

We should note that, unlike the passion, there seems to be virtually no reference to scripture in the telling of this episode. Why? It would appear that the reason is that the people who were eager to prove that Jesus was the Messiah according to scripture were not the same as those engaged in defending the resurrection of Jesus. To answer that question we will need to evaluate further the question in its various sources.

Let us first consider the function of the resurrection in the writings of Paul. In 1 Corinthians 15:9–10, immediately after Paul's tradition of the resurrection, he explains that he is the least of the apostles yet not withstanding this he works harder than all the others. In Didache an apostle was someone who travelled to a community in order to establish a Christian community and it is undeniably also a sense in which Paul uses the word. However, from the way Paul contextualizes the resurrection tradition in 1 Corinthians, we get the sense that apostles had authority *because* of the resurrection. We get the impression, in fact, that Paul manages to be a full-fledged apostle only because of his resurrection experience. But here we should take care. Is Paul's concern representative of a wider understanding amongst Christians? Undoubtedly, Paul expected that at least some would accept it, yet he equally well knew that some would not accept his authority (2 Corinthians 11).

Our impression, however, is that those most inclined to accept this line of argument were Christians in Corinth. In 2 Corinthians 12 we saw how he recounted his visionary experience. The description of the vision is quite different from Acts' description of Paul's vision of the risen Lord. Yet Paul 'boasts' of this as a vision and revelation of the Lord. There are certain commonalities: dissociation (blinding light and booming voice in Acts and a translation into heaven in 2 Corinthians) and words spoken in revelation (the dialogue in Acts and unknown words in 2 Corinthians).[767]

Finally, we know that in Corinth there were many who spoke in tongues but that Paul could say that he did so more than any of them (1 Corinthians 14:18). Are all these phenomena related? Was Paul particularly prone to dissociative conditions, as he seems to be stating rather frankly to his Corinthian congregation? The evidence seems quite strong.

Where did Paul learn the practice of speaking in

tongues? We can be fairly confident that the practice was not entirely common – there is just too much silence in this regard in our sources. On the other hand, we have evidence from Mark's long ending, from Acts and Paul that suggest that the practice was known outside the Corinthian church. In chapter 5 we briefly noted the episode in 1 Samuel 19:20 where a messenger of Saul encounters a company of prophets and is taken over by God's Spirit. Did some prophets of Jesus practice glossolalia? There is one problem making a direct connection between this scene and the prophets of Jesus. What we see in 1 Samuel 19:20 is, like glossolalia in Corinth and other similar present-day communities, just that: an activity of the community. It could be induced but it could also be taught. The problem is that prophets of Jesus did not stay in communities more than a couple of days. It seems likely that some prophets of Jesus spoke in tongues and that this is what Didache refers to when it speaks of prophets 'enacting a worldly mystery of the Church' (Loeb 11:11). However, since the prophet did not stay to teach glossolalia in a community, transmission of the practice could only happen if someone in the community was highly receptive. This could explain the very meagre but relatively widespread evidence for the occurrence of the practice. Thus we can picture Paul using practices that were taught to him, in all likelihood in Damascus or Antioch, which he brought to his own community. Paul perhaps learned because he was highly susceptible; the Corinthians learned it because they had a teacher who stayed with them.

In the Gospel of Mary we found that there was an attempt to use Mary's authority to establish certain teachings. These teachings, however, were confirmed to Mary, not in a vision, but by the living Jesus to whom she had had particular privilege to speak. Here is something we have to be careful about when we look at the tradition of the canonical gospels: we cannot assume that the apostles were in need of authority conferred by the risen Lord. Unlike Paul, Mary and the apostles had been disciples before Jesus' passion and resurrection and they did not need authority conferred upon them as Paul did. When Paul came into conflict with other apostolic powers, he referred to the risen Lord. As seen in the Gospel of Mary, Mary could refer to her status as the companion of the living Jesus, who taught her secretly. That is, of course, not history but it illustrates the marked difference between Paul and the first people mentioned in his resurrection tradition in 1 Corinthians.

In the canonical gospels we see a string of very different traditions. Matthew, following Mark, knows that Jesus' first appearances were not in Jerusalem but in Galilee (Mark 16:7 = Matthew 28:7). Matthew, however, is not satisfied by having an angel give this message to the women and has Jesus Himself appear to them, essentially to repeat the message of the angel. It is important to note that the women are said to have 'clasped' (ἐκράτησαν) Jesus' feet (Matthew 28:9). This small point correlates with similar remarks in Luke and John.

It should also be noted that three independent traditions – extra-Markan tradition, John and Matthew – each make Mary Magdalene the first witness to the risen Lord. This might be taken to suggest that the tradition is old and may very likely pre-date the tradition that makes Peter the first witness. Luedemann, on the other hand, proposes that Peter was suppressed in the later traditions.[768] However, it may be an entirely futile attempt to identify Peter, Mary or James as first witnesses. No historically certain data is available to ascertain when these three figures had their experiences. Nor were those who were in a position to procure this information interested in such issues; rather, they were interested in who was first in honour. The honour of firstness naturally must have fallen on the person of greatest honour. The modern preoccupation with chronological accuracy had no place in the mind of our sources. The suppression or exaltation of a particular figure was an issue of honour and claims on that figure's behalf were promoted by the communities connected to them.

As a preamble to Jesus' all-important mission statement, He states that He has been given 'authority' (ἐξουσία) over heaven and earth. It is in the context of this authority that Jesus can send His disciples into the world. Jesus concludes His mission statement with the promise: 'I am with you always, to the close of the age' (Matthew 28:20 RSV). This promise places a new perspective on the resurrection: It is about Jesus being present with His disciples.

Luke has a far more extensive tradition. As noted before, for Luke the mission starts not in Galilee but in Jerusalem. Thus when the women return to the disciples they are not believed, for Jesus Himself will appear to them right there in Jerusalem. There is one exception. Peter believes them and runs to the grave himself, only to find it empty (Luke 24:12). Thus the traditional distinction that Peter receives as the first disciple to see the risen Lord, as we saw in Paul's tradition, is maintained. This is done through a clever revision of the tradition received in a more primitive version in the long ending in Mark. In the primitive version, the two people remain anonymous but in Luke one is introduced as Cleopas. If in Mark's long ending it had been known who one was, this would certainly have been important enough to mention. Clearly, many of these additions are developments that came into existence partly because of Luke's tradition that Jesus appeared first to Peter and then to the Twelve (which Mark's long ending has already determined to be Eleven owing to Judas' defection) and the tradition received about two anonymous disciples. The editorial hand is seen in part in the manner in which the names were unnaturally inserted into the narrative and in part by their dependence on the wider framework.

Luke has a discussion between Jesus and Cleopas and the other disciple who had not yet recognized Jesus. Cleopas explains how they were hopeful that Jesus as the Messiah would restore Israel but that He had been crucified yet some women had seen His empty tomb and had been warned by an angel that He was alive. Jesus then rebuked them, saying that they should know from scripture that this was predestined. This is followed by an Eucharistic scene in which Cleopas and the other disciple suddenly recognize who He is, after which He disappears (ἄφαντος). Next He appears to the Eleven. They think that He is a spirit or ghost but He convinces them that He has a body by eating some fish in their presence and then He opens their minds so that they can understand that what had happened was in accordance with scripture. These scenes combine several points. Most important is that the risen Lord is both physical and spiritual. Another point that Luke is emphatic about is that their distress was caused because they did not understand scripture, that it was written that all these things should happen and that the mission to the world should start there in Jerusalem. Thus the mission in Luke is not authorized by the risen Lord but had already been authorized by God in scripture. A possibly older resonance is likely to lie behind the idea of recognizing the risen Lord in the Eucharist. John uses the same theme in His resurrection narrative, which at several points has the risen Lord unrecognized and unbelieved. John too has Jesus appearing suddenly in closed rooms but proving Himself to be both more than spirit and more than man. John's mission statement includes the power to forgive sins (John 20:23). We are reminded of the saying that the Son of man is given the authority to forgive sins (Mark 2:10), which we saw in chapter 8 belonged to the prophets of Jesus, so John's contextualization is well-justified.

A common thread throughout our source is the issue of authority. Luke takes it from the risen Lord and gives it to scripture (Luke 24:45). Otherwise, the empowerment comes through Jesus' authority. The risen Lord uses His authority to send out the disciples. In reality, it is of course the other way around: it is the disciples who use the resurrection of Jesus to empower their mission. When we looked at Paul (early) we asked ourselves if authority really was the central issue behind the resurrection and we answered with Mary (late) that apostles were not in need of authority as they had the authority of the living Jesus. Authority, therefore, though pervasive and integral to the earliest strands of tradition, was a secondary and communally utilitarian reflection of the experience of the risen Lord.

With Mary and Matthew we should also consider that the resurrection was about receiving comfort. In the previous chapters we saw how the passion of Jesus caused the prophets of Jesus to reflect, so that they believed that the absence of Jesus was soon to be relieved by His return. Another response to the passion was grief, which can result in the bereaved experiencing strong and lifelike encounters with the lost person. These experiences were as common in the ancient world as they are today. But unlike today, such experiences were not diagnosed as disorders but were universally understood to be real occurrences.

We saw in the Markan tradition that the first resurrection occurred in Galilee. So the picture that emerges is that in the immediate context of the passion, Jesus' disciples who were with Him in Jerusalem fled from the capital to return to Galilee. There the grief of the disciples meant that some, particularly those who had experienced the arrest and had heard the reports of His end, had visions of Him, primarily comforting them in their grief. Those who received these visions told others. Soon the news spread and made its way back to Jerusalem and the process of enquiry started, which eventually generated narrative.

We are now ready to re-ask the question: Why did Mark omit to narrate the resurrection accounts that he clearly knew? Did he not want to comfort his readers? Mark's ending is probably the byproduct of another intention. All tradition available to Mark had Peter as the first disciple to receive the honour of seeing the risen Jesus. At the time that Mark was writing, this meant that Peter was already amongst the most prominent of Jesus' disciples. Mark had, for reasons that are not entirely clear, a great dislike of Peter and by ending his gospel where he did, Peter does not receive the notice to go to Galilee. People in Galilee still had their visions but not Peter, who remained in Jerusalem. Mark's conclusion showed Peter in a bad light and disempowered him.

The Lukan story of the ascension plays the same role as the Markan omission: it is intended to disempower. There are a few indications that this is indeed the group that he is interested in countering. One is the substitution of their dialogue regarding the resurrection with an orthodox (or, perhaps more accurately, Catholic) dialogue. Another is the transfer of authority to scripture in the resurrection scene. As we noted in chapter 1, it was a conflict about the Old Testament and its sacredness that made the canon of the New Testament necessary. Luke is more concerned than any other evangelist to demonstrate the physicalness of the resurrection. For Luke, this is not just to assert that Jesus is not a spirit but that He is not merely a vision, something that Gnostics believed not only of the resurrection but of Jesus when He was alive.[769]

Concluding Thoughts

Who was Jesus? And who were the disciples that gathered around Him? Who were the people who accepted His message and who were those that rejected it? All these questions can be answered in many different ways. However, none of these questions can be answered without a context. The answer depends on who is asked. We started this book by noting that two categories of people have traditionally made the intensive study of the Bible their business: the theologian and the historian. We also noted that owing to the intersection of the sacred and the historical it was difficult to completely differentiate the two. At the beginning of the last century Albert Schweitzer wrote a book whose criticism of the tendencies that had preceded him in historical studies of Jesus brought virtually all studies of the Historical Jesus to a grinding halt.

> Schweitzer's book had created what might be called a catch–22 in historical Jesus studies: The mark of unbiased scholarship was that it did not try to establish Jesus as relevant for today, but if Jesus is *not* relevant for today, then why study him in the first place? Meanwhile, Christian theology moved decidedly in another direction, that of twentieth-century existentialism for which questions regarding the historical Jesus became increasingly insignificant.[770]

The theological movement, which was headed by Rudulf

Bultmann, shall not concern us here. What is of interest is that the theological position developed in the Historical Jesus field of study may be considered the flip side of Schweitzer's conclusion. History could not be history if it was relevant and Bultmann posited that history was not relevant for the meaning of Jesus. Thus came about what can be perceived as a happy divorce, historians and theologians each agreeing that meaning on the one hand could not (theologically) and on the other hand should not (historically) be attributed to the Jesus of history. As Schweitzer concluded:

> Whatever the ultimate solution may be, the historical Jesus of whom the criticism of the future, taking as its starting-point the problems which have been recognized and admitted, will draw the portrait, can never render modern theology the services which it claimed from its own half-historical, half-modern, Jesus. He will be a Jesus, who was Messiah, and lived as such, either on the ground of a literary fiction of the earliest Evangelist, or on the ground of a purely eschatological Messianic conception.
>
> In either case, He will not be a Jesus Christ to whom religion of the present can ascribe, according to its long-cherished custom, its own thoughts and ideas, as it did with the Jesus of its own making. Nor will He be a figure which can be made by a popular historical treatment so sympathetic and universally intelligible to the multitude. The historical Jesus will be to our time a stranger and an enigma.[771]

So history, unwilling to render service to theology, was thanked and told that its services were not of interest. The inevitable attraction between history and theology was, however, not to hold off for long. Bultmann's 'thanks, but no thanks' was to be overturned a few decades later by his students. The response was to question the assumption about the limitations of historical sources and methodology. The view that the gospels gave Jesus' teachings but not a view of His self-perception had to be revisited. James M. Robinson explained this distinction in his monograph *A New Quest of the Historical Jesus*:

> The German ability to distinguish between *Historie* and *Geschichte* has made it possible, from Bultmann's *Jesus and the Word* on, to look upon oneself as presenting the history (*Geschichte*) of Jesus. Such has not been the case with the terms 'life', 'biography', and 'bios', which continue to be avoided . . . But this should not obscure the crucial fact that Jesus' understanding of his existence, his selfhood, and thus in the higher sense his life, is a possible subject of historical research.[772]

All the same, the new quest is not really characterized by psychological biographies. Instead, we find the Historical Jesus described in terms of categories. Jesus is described as a rabbi,[773] a Cynic,[774] a restoration prophet,[775] a Mediterranean Jewish peasant,[776] a charismatic Hasid,[777] a spirit person[778] and a healer,[779] while some writers combine categories.[780] The purpose of categories, of course, is to ask what Jesus Himself thought He was. If we can understand how Jesus saw Himself, then it becomes possible to understand the key of the biographies, namely the underlying reason for His action. We can then speculate why Jesus taught the people He taught, we can understand the purpose of engaging certain opponents and we can understand His action against the temple, His institution of sacraments and other events of His life. So the exercise is to ask Jesus Himself: 'Who are you?'

We have a host of titles and portraits that show us what others thought of Jesus. We started our third chapter by seeing Jesus through the eyes of a Hellenic Jewish-Christian, the Evangelist John, to whom Jesus appeared as the personification of God's Logos. We went on to see Jesus as a Davidic Messiah, a Son of God, but mostly found that these categories were perspectives that were more at home with the evangelists than with Jesus Himself. The category that the present work has promoted above most others has been the Elijah-Elisha model. The intrinsic value of this model has been its ability to explain Jesus' proclamation through acts and to explain Jesus' mode of discipleship. On the whole, however, it does not seem sufficient to explain the totality of Jesus, His thoughts and His teachings. Categories are important tools but a reduction is inevitable. Even if we concede that Jesus was understood and led people to understand Him as an Elijah figure, as one come with His power and authority to do God's work, can this reasonably answer who Jesus was? Everyone has more than one role to play; the roles we play depend on the people we relate to. This has nothing to do with being hypocritical but has to do with the relationship. A man, for example, is the son of his father and at the same time the father of his child. He is the husband of his wife and the brother of his siblings. The roles are entirely different but are all intrinsic to the person's selfhood. The answer to 'who are you?' becomes an issue of who asks the question. The same must be true about Jesus. To some He was the Master prophet, an Elijah figure, to others He was a compassionate teacher, to some He was a crazy Galilean prophet, to others He was a man of unorthodox views. To some He was a kind stranger who spoke words of comfort, to others He was an irate peasant who spoke words of condemnation. To children He was a kind man who smiled and praised them, to the old a man who offered relief. Not all roles that people saw in Jesus were actually consistent with Jesus' view of Himself. So we come to rely on those whom we deem knew Him best, His followers. In the concluding words of Schweitzer:

> He comes to us as One unknown, without a name, as of old, by the lake-side, He came to those men who knew Him not. He speaks to us the same word: 'Follow thou me!' and sets to the task which He has to fulfil for our time. He commands. And to those who obey Him, whether they be wise or simple, He will reveal Himself in the toils, the conflicts, the sufferings which they shall pass through in His fellowship, and, as an ineffable mystery, they shall learn in their own experience Who He is.[781]

To Schweitzer, to follow Jesus meant that he was to go to Africa as a missionary doctor. In our work with the gospels, however, it has meant that we have sought at all times to ask those that had fellowship with Him the question: 'Who is Jesus of Nazareth?' To our consternation we have found a cacophony of answers and we have been forced to select for reply those we found most likely to be close disciples. This is what history offers us, the view of Jesus as He was seen by those who were closest to Him: Jesus of Nazareth, the prophet who rose to proclaim that the poor and downtrodden, the rejects of society, had been received by God, their Father. Everywhere He went He proclaimed His message, until the day that circumstance took Him away. But the story did not end there.

Appendix 1

Interpretation and Rewriting of the Gospels in the Bahá'í Writings

We shall now undertake a survey of the ways in which the Bahá'í writings use the gospels to relay their own message. In this analysis we shall find that the response in these writings is not only to the gospels but also to the history in which they were written.

Whether using one paradigm or another, much of the gospels can be said to be mythic. That is to say, the story in some sense explains the present reality. Mythography (interpreting myth) is in fact mythopoeia (creation of myth). When the central figures[782] of the Bahá'í Faith and Shoghi Effendi read and interpret the gospels, they are not merely repeating tradition or explaining their 'original' meaning. Rather they are creative, bringing a new significance to old traditions. Therefore we should start by understanding this new creation.

The Bahá'í works on which we will draw will be limited mainly to those written by Bahá'u'lláh, 'Abdu'l-Bahá and Shoghi Effendi. The writings of the Báb have set important hermeneutic precedents but the Báb's use of Christian imagery is primarily Quranic in origin. Bahá'u'lláh, on the other hand, uses and even quotes Christian scripture in a way that provides an important key to Bahá'í hermeneutics. 'Abdu'l-Bahá had contact with and provided interpretations for the first Western Bahá'ís who came from a Christian background. For these Bahá'ís it was important to understand the Bahá'í Faith in terms of their own background and to perceive this new and foreign faith as a fulfilment of the promises of Christianity. Shoghi Effendi was in a similar situation to 'Abdu'l-Bahá but he also had to address the increasing popularity of biblical scholarship.

Bahá'í Theology and Christian Doctrine

In the encounter between the Bahá'í Faith and Christianity, the Bahá'í community had to communicate its own beliefs in the Christian language. In its attempt to do so it was confronted with two factors. The first was the Christian doctrines, the collective understanding of the beliefs of the Christian community, and the second was the gospels, which are held to be holy. These two factors were juxtaposed in the Bahá'í writings in an attempt to make the Bahá'í position accessible to Christian converts.

One of the most immediate issues that had to be tackled was Christian exclusivist views, in particular the Trinitarian eschatology. The Bahá'í writings, therefore, engage mostly the Johannine passages that speak to this issue.

To compare the high Christology of John with that of the Bahá'í writings is indeed not unreasonable. Both belong to a tradition of esoteric and eschatological thought. John came from a developed form of Philonic esoterics with a distinct form of realized eschatology. The Bábí and Bahá'í religions with their origin in Shí'í Islam, and more specifically in the Shaykhí school, are able in their settings to develop a high Christology, or more appropriately for the Bahá'í Faith, theophanology. The near divine reverence with which the Shaykhí school held the Imams, and particularly the Hidden Imam, provides an insightful background for elements of realized eschatology in the Bahá'í Faith.[783] Cole traces the esotericism behind what he calls 'Bahá'í theophanology' to the Mu'tazilí school of theology, which was highly influenced by neo-platonism.[784]

Emerging from these esoteric and eschatological beliefs, the Bahá'í theology develops and expands a concept of unity. The unity of prophethood as formulated in the Bahá'í writings is unique but there are precedents for the concept in both biblical and Quranic literature. Confirmation of the authority of the founders of earlier religions has provided a way for individuals to perceive their conversion to a new community as an extension or updating of their past affiliation.

According to Bahá'u'lláh, the Manifestations of God[785] form the only possible link between God and human beings.[786] As Cole points out, this completely breaks with the Sufi belief that humans can attain direct access to God.[787] Furthermore, Bahá'u'lláh explains that although all of the Manifestations of God are linked together and are equal in the sight of God, they also have 'a distinct individuality, a definitely prescribed mission, a predestined Revelation, and specially designated limitations'.[788]

In the writings of the Báb, the 'Primal Will' appears as the agent through which God reveals His Will to humanity by the Manifestation.[789] Bahá'u'lláh, however, explains that this same Primal Will is the agency through which 'all have stepped out of utter nothingness into the realm of being', which He identifies with God's command.[790] Many parallels can be drawn between the Johannine prologue and some of the imagery found in the Bahá'í writings regarding the Manifestations of God and the Primal Will.

The Johannine prologue, like such writings of Bahá'u'lláh

as the Persian Kalimát-i-Maknúnih (Hidden Words) no. 77[791] and Lawḥ-i-Malláḥu'l-Quds (Tablet of the Holy Mariner), portrays the supernatural entering the mundane world but rather than describing it from a human experience (as in Jesus' parables), the prologue take a divine perspective. Unlike the parable, which attempts to describe the divine with mundane narrative and imagery, theophanic poetry attempts to describe the divine with supramundane narratives and images. Like the parable, however, theophanic poetry maintains polyvalence. 'Abdu'l-Bahá is reported to have remarked that the first verse in the Johannine prologue is 'replete with the greatest meanings' and that its 'applications are illimitable and beyond the power of books or words to contain and express'.[792]

Certainly Bahá'í and present-day Christian theophanology is far more advanced than can be extrapolated directly from the Johannine prologue but the Johannine prologue is also far more advanced than what can reliably be attributed to the Historical Jesus.

In order to translate the Bahá'í idea of Manifestation into Christian Trinitarian language, 'Abdu'l-Bahá in *Some Answered Questions* starts by developing a philosophical framework and superimposes it on the doctrine of the Trinity. This is followed by the citation of the Johannine quotation in order to support the Bahá'í framework.[793] Thus 'Abdu'l-Bahá not only uses the Christian gospels to explain Bahá'í theology but also uses well-established theological ideas to do so.

Often associated with the exclusivity of Christianity was the doctrine of Jesus' virgin birth. In the writings of Bahá'u'lláh we find a significant reference to Mary. In the Kitáb-i-Íqán Bahá'u'lláh uses Mary as an example of how Manifestations are subject to humiliation,[794] a reversal of the Christian usage. Cole is quite right in observing that the story recounted is about social scandal and not a happy Christmas tale.[795] In referring to the conclusion of the story, Bahá'u'lláh brings out the contrast between the reaction of Jesus' (or Mary's) contemporaries and the 'glory of Prophethood'.

'Abdu'l-Bahá was the first Bahá'í to look at Mary as a religious historical figure, comparing her to 'holy' women of other religious traditions. Thus He can use her as an archetypal portrayal of women of the Bábí and Bahá'í dispensations.[796] There is, however, a problem about portraying Mary, the mother of Jesus. While other archetypal figures were renowned for their piety, Mary stood accused of adultery and so the unreserved support of the virgin birth was important for emphasizing this central attribute.

Shoghi Effendi was far more direct about the reasons for accepting the virgin birth:

> It would be sacrilege for a Bahá'í to believe that the parents of Jesus were illegally married and that the latter was consequently of an illegal union. Such a possibility cannot be even conceived by a believer who recognizes the high station of Mary and the Divine Prophethood of Jesus Christ . . . The only alternative therefore is to admit that the birth of Jesus has been miraculous.[797]

Bahá'í theology, in other words, essentially responded positively to the doctrine of the virgin birth. It was a true miracle that led to the birth of Jesus. However, the significance of the event as described in the Bahá'í writings was quite different. The Quranic view was that Mary was placed in disrepute by the miracle. The Bahá'í writings adopt this view but also deal with the problematic exclusivist understanding. In *Some Answered Questions* 'Abdu'l-Bahá points out that the fact that Jesus had no father was not a mark of special excellence, otherwise Adam, who had neither father nor mother, must have been even greater than Jesus.[798]

Christian Narrative as Illustrations

In other instances, the gospels were not marshalled to correct Christian doctrine but used to illustrate a Bahá'í teaching. An example of this is found in Bahá'u'lláh's use of Jesus' opponents.

The Pharisees appear in the Bahá'í writings as the opponents of Jesus, just as they do in the gospels. They appear as archetypal deniers, not only denying Christ but also Muḥammad.[799] The purpose of referring to the Pharisees is to demonstrate that piety and vigilance are no guarantee that one will be able to recognize the Manifestation of God. The Pharisees appear, for example, to reflect the characteristics of priests,[800] which illustrates the oneness not only of the Manifestations and their ongoing mission to humankind but also of those who oppose them.

The practice of comparing and uniting the enemies of God across generations is also found in the gospels. In Q there is the lament of Jerusalem who kills the prophets sent to it: 'O Jerusalem, Jerusalem, that killeth the prophets, and stoneth them that are sent unto her! how often would I have gathered thy children together, even as a hen [gathereth] her own brood under her wings, and ye would not' (Luke 13:34 ASV).

Bahá'u'lláh shows no particular interest in the sectarian nature of 1st century Judaism or the theological differences between various Jewish parties. In referring to Jesus' unique encounter with a Herodian regarding imperial tax (Mark 12:13–17),[801] Bahá'u'lláh makes no mention of the fact that a new group is involved. The Sadducees are not mentioned as a party and the two Sadducees, Annas and Caiaphas, are characterized as 'the most learned among the divines of His day' and 'the high priest'.[802] Annas being the 'most learned' here appears to be contrasted with the most spiritually ignorant act, namely the crucifixion of Jesus. The lack of identification of the sectarian background of Jesus' opponents appears to serve two purposes. First, it is important to Bahá'u'lláh that no appeal to theological difference can justify rejection, let alone opposition to the Manifestation of God. Second, ignoring the theological differentiation helps not to distract from the opponent's illustrative function.

In a similar way, gospel narrative helped to explain the meaning of covenant-breaking.[803] In the gospels we found that there was very little information on Judas and the motive for his betrayal. To explain the nature of covenant-breaking 'Abdu'l-Bahá gives the following explanation for the actions of Judas:

> The case of all of them resembleth the violation of the Covenant by Judas Iscariot and his followers. Consider: hath any result or trace remained after them? Not even a name hath been left by his followers and although a number of Jews sided with him it was as if he had no followers at all. This Judas Iscariot who was the leader of the apostles betrayed Christ for thirty pieces of silver.[804]

'Abdu'l-Bahá here compares the betrayal of Judas to the covenant-breaking of His own days. In order to make the point, He states that Judas had followers who joined him in breaking the covenant. As there is nothing in the gospels that suggests that Judas had a following, and unless one speculates a connection to the Cainites,[805] this is probably best understood as a projection. 'Abdu'l-Bahá's statement that even some 'Jews sided with him' is contrasted with his 'followers', that is to say 'Jews' were those who were not Christians. It seems that 'Abdu'l-Bahá is here reflecting the ability of the covenant-breakers to solicit the help of the Muslim authorities during His own ministry.[806]

> Judas Iscariot was the greatest of the disciples, and he summoned the people to Christ. Then it seemed to him that Jesus was showing increasing regard to the Apostle Peter, and when Jesus said, 'Thou art Peter, and upon this rock I will build My church,' these words addressed to Peter, and this singling out of Peter for special honour, had a marked effect on the Apostle, and kindled envy within the heart of Judas. For this reason he who had once drawn nigh did turn aside, and he who had believed in the Faith denied it, and his love changed to hate, until he became a cause of the crucifixion of that glorious Lord, that manifest Splendour.[807]

In this passage we find another personal experience of 'Abdu'l-Bahá reflected in His account of the Judas narrative. Here it is the appointment of Peter as the 'centre of the Christian covenant' – which Bahá'ís consider to be the equivalent of the centre of the Bahá'í covenant, the position held by 'Abdu'l-Bahá – that causes Judas to betray Jesus. It seems logical to assume that 'Abdu'l-Bahá is not proposing that the motive was the acquisition of the meagre reward money; rather the point is made about leadership.

Just as there are archetypal enemies there are also archetypal protagonists. One example of this is found in Bahá'u'lláh's use of the three wise men. The legend of

Herod's attempt to kill the infant Jesus is mentioned in both the Kitáb-i-Íqán and Epistle to the Son of the Wolf:

> In like manner, when the hour of the Revelation of Jesus drew nigh, a few of the Magi, aware that the star of Jesus had appeared in heaven, sought and followed it, till they came unto the city which was the seat of the Kingdom of Herod. The sway of his sovereignty in those days embraced the whole of that land.
>
> These Magi said: 'Where is He that is born King of the Jews? for we have seen His star in the east and are come to worship Him!' When they had searched, they found out that in Bethlehem, in the land of Judea, the Child had been born. This was the sign that was manifested in the visible heaven. As to the sign in the invisible heaven – the heaven of divine knowledge and understanding – it was Yaḥyá, son of Zachariah, who gave unto the people the tidings of the Manifestation of Jesus. Even as He hath revealed: 'God announceth Yaḥyá to thee, who shall bear witness unto the Word from God, and a great one and chaste.' By the term 'Word' is meant Jesus, Whose coming Yaḥyá foretold. Moreover, in the heavenly Scriptures it is written: 'John the Baptist was preaching in the wilderness of Judea, and saying, Repent ye: for the Kingdom of heaven is at hand.' By John is meant Yaḥyá.[808]

> Consider and call thou to mind the days whereon the Spirit of God (Jesus Christ) appeared, and Herod gave judgement against Him. God, however, aided Him with the hosts of the unseen, and protected Him with truth, and sent Him down unto another land, according to His promise. He, verily, ordaineth what He pleaseth.[809]

Cole sees this as an archetypal portrayal of Jesus and suggests that the explicit mention of the Magi may have been to bring Iranians closer to the infancy narrative.[810] Bahá'u'lláh also supplies some interesting information that is not immediately available from the text in question. Matthew says that the Magi arrived at Jerusalem. Bahá'u-'lláh notes that it was 'the city which was the seat of the Kingdom of Herod', as well as the fact that the 'sway of his [Herod's] sovereignty in those days embraced the whole of that land'. Both of these facts are true but are not obvious from a casual reading of the gospels. Though Jerusalem had and continued to be the seat of Palestinian government, Judea was soon to be wrested from the Herodian dynasty and placed under direct control of Rome. If by 'the whole of that land' is meant Israel, this also is true and changed immediately after the death of Herod the Great when the kingdom was divided among three of his sons. It is noteworthy that neither of these pieces of information has any direct bearing on the story being told. The theme of the passage is the star of Bethlehem, which is the outer star, while John the Baptist is the inner or spiritual star. The information that Jerusalem was the royal seat and that Herod reigned over all of Israel seems to be ornamental in nature. Both features indicate that Bahá'u'lláh, without making it part of the main theme, is using the occasion to cast Herod in the role of the ruler who suppresses the Manifestation of God, which is the role we find him in in Epistle to the Son of the Wolf.

Perhaps even more significantly, Bahá'u'lláh uses John the Baptist as a means of explaining His own relationship with the Báb. Bahá'u'lláh states that the star of Jerusalem was a sign 'in the visible heaven'. This sign was complemented by a sign in 'the heaven of divine knowledge and understanding' in the person of John the Baptist. Bahá'u-'lláh demonstrates that this happens in every dispensation

(Moses, Jesus, Muḥammad and the Báb). It appears as if there is a reversal here. Instead of projecting an archetype back into the past, Bahá'u'lláh seems to be projecting a past archetype into the present. Later, when Bahá'u'lláh reflected back on His life in Epistle to the Son of the Wolf, the Báb Himself became the present-day archetype of John the Baptist.[811]

Cole points to another important passage in Epistle to the Son of the Wolf in which the followers of John the Baptist object to Jesus' proclamation, asking 'wherefore hast thou come' since the 'dispensation' of John had 'not yet ended'.[812] Cole proposes that Bahá'u'lláh may have had contact with the Mandeans, who held the Baptist as a prophet figure and that this may have inspired Him to use this image.[813] As Cole points out and as we have seen in chapter 4, it is possible that there was conflict between Jesus and John's followers. But what about the formulation of the question? The Mandeans would not have levelled such an objection, since they did not consider John the founder of their sect nor did they believe him to have initiated a 'dispensation'.[814] Again the story of the disciples of John is an archetypal device to reflect on the events that transpired in the days of Bahá'u'lláh.

Replacing the Sacred

One use of Christian language in the Bahá'í writings is to replace what is sacred in the Christian religion with new sacredness. One example is the sacred institution of baptism. There is no equivalent act in the Bahá'í Faith. However, it plays such a central role in Christian soteriology that its efficacy had to be addressed. Among the table talks of 'Abdu'l-Bahá recorded in *Some Answered Questions* is one in which He answers two questions relevant to the theme of baptism. The first (chapter 19) relates to the baptism of Jesus and the second (chapter 20) is about the inherent usefulness of the baptismal rite. 'Abdu'l-Bahá explains that 'baptism in the days of John the Baptist was used to awaken and admonish the people to repent from all sin, and to watch for the appearance of the Kingdom of Christ'.[815] 'Abdu'l-Bahá uses this reference to the eschatological nature of the baptism of John to argue against the practice of infant baptism. The practice, states 'Abdu'l-Bahá, is spiritually ineffective, as the child receives no spiritual awakening, no faith and no conversion. This He contrasts with the baptism of John, which, He explains, affected both the external and internal.

In chapter 9 we looked at the practice of the Lord's Supper, which came to be understood as replacing the temple sacrifice. Islam does not have a sanctification ritual parallel to the Jewish and Christian tradition. Islam finds its sanctification through the reading of the Qur'án, which is the highest embodiment of holiness.[816] 'Abdu'l-Bahá connected the Lord's Supper with the Bahá'í Nineteen Day Feast,[817] a feast that has both methods of sanctification, reading the holy writings and communal eating.

Though Christianity replaced the sacredness of the temple with the sacredness of the Eucharist, Islam kept the temple in Jerusalem but later transferred it to Mecca. Bahá'u'lláh too made such a transfer.

Jerusalem generally appears in three contexts in the writings of Bahá'u'lláh. In Epistle to the Son of the Wolf we find an exposition of a passage from Isaiah in which all three come into play.

O Shaykh! Peruse that which Isaiah hath spoken in His

> Book. He saith: 'Get thee up into the high mountain, O Zion, that bringest good tidings; lift up Thy Voice with strength, O Jerusalem, that bringest good tidings. Lift it up, be not afraid; say unto the cities of Judah: "Behold your God! Behold the Lord God will come with strong hand, and His arm shall rule for Him." ' This Day all the signs have appeared. A Great City hath descended from heaven, and Zion trembleth and exulteth with joy at the Revelation of God, for it hath heard the Voice of God on every side. This Day Jerusalem hath attained unto a new Evangel, for in the stead of the sycamore standeth the cedar. Jerusalem is the place of pilgrimage for all the peoples of the world, and hath been named the Holy City. Together with Zion and Palestine, they are all included within these regions. Wherefore, hath it been said: 'Blessed is the man that hath migrated to 'Akká.'
>
> Amos saith: 'The Lord will roar from Zion, and utter His Voice from Jerusalem; and the habitations of the shepherds shall mourn, and the top of Carmel shall wither.'[818]

The first meaning is proposed by the Isaianic passage (40:9) itself. Here Jerusalem becomes a symbol of the people of Judah. Bahá'u'lláh refers next to the Great City, which is the archetypal City of God, the new Jerusalem, which is the Revelation sent from God. In the next sentence Bahá'u-'lláh reverses the symbolic value of Jerusalem back to its Isaianic meaning, as Jerusalem becomes the recipient of the Revelation, the new Evangel. Finally Bahá'u'lláh speaks of the literal Jerusalem, the object of adoration and pilgrimage. Yet even this literal Jerusalem is interesting only as an archetype for the new Holy City, which is 'Akká, the new Qiblih. Bahá'u'lláh then cites Amos 1:2, apparently to connect it with the establishment of a new holy place. The passage is a play on symbols of sacredness.

In the Kitáb-i-Íqán Bahá'u'lláh uses Muḥammad's change of the Qiblih from Jerusalem to Mecca to show the authority of the Manifestation of God to do as He wishes.[819] In Epistle to the Son of the Wolf the Qiblih has been changed to the person of the Manifestation who had taken up residence in 'Akká, the new Jerusalem.[820]

Reforming Eschatology

An important requirement of working in a Christian framework was to transfer eschatological expectancies to a new Bahá'í framework.

'Abdu'l-Bahá describes revelation as a product of divine inspiration and spiritual comprehension.[821] Thus the exposition about the future is likewise regarded to be the fruit of the spiritual perception of Jesus. Jesus' proclamation of the advent of the kingdom of God can, by such a definition, be considered prophetic. The same could be said for millennial or Old Testament prophetic books. By this definition of prophecy, the prophecy of Israel's salvation becomes a legitimate metaphorical description of the peaceful conquest and spectacular coming of Bahá'u'lláh.

A survey of Bahá'u'lláh's use of prophetic New Testament texts will show that not all come from the synoptic texts but some are from the Johannine Farewell Discourse. This Bahá'u'lláh does, in extension of Muslim traditions, with a claim to be the Spirit of Truth.[822]

From our treatment of the Paraclete/Spirit of Truth figure in chapter 8 we found that there were traces of a prophetic source. These traces form the basis of 'Abdu'l-Bahá's argument. 'Abdu'l-Bahá objected to the interpretation of the Paraclete as Holy Spirit, noting that 'The Holy Spirit

(Christ) was already in the world. He came in Jesus when he was born'.[823] Indeed the Holy Spirit was present with the apostles when Jesus sent them to spread His gospel. Thus 'Abdu'l-Bahá states that 'in the Bible the coming of Mohammed [sic] was mentioned in the Gospels as the Advocate'.[824]

Christopher Buck works from Windisch's two-source theory, in which one source deals with the coming of the Paraclete and one with the coming of Jesus. He suggests that Bahá'u'lláh perceives these two distinctive figures and resolves it through the exegesis in which He identifies Himself as the fulfilment of the Paraclete promise.[825] Although Bahá'u'lláh does not refer directly to the Paraclete or the Spirit of Truth in the Kitáb-i-Íqán, Buck identifies a passage in that book that has its origin in an Islamic reading of the Johannine Farewell Discourse.[826] In two works (Súriy al-Mulúk[827] and Lawḥ-i-Aqdas[828]), which were composed after the Kitáb-i-Íqán, Bahá'u'lláh specifically makes the claim to be the Spirit of Truth that will guide 'unto all truth'.

Michael Sours in his *A Study of Bahá'u'lláh's Tablet to the Christians* suggests that 'all truth' is not a reference to all truth (leaving no mysteries at all) but rather to the spiritual eternal truths revealed in every dispensation.[829] Alternatively, the present author would like to suggest that hyperbole is involved. In the Kitáb-i-Íqán Bahá'u'lláh cites a tradition from 'the "Biháru'l-Anvár", the "'Aválim", and the "Yanbú'" of Ṣádiq, son of Muḥammad': 'Knowledge is twenty and seven letters. All that the Prophets have revealed are two letters thereof. No man thus far hath known more than these two letters. But when the Qá'im shall arise, He will cause the remaining twenty and five letters to be made manifest.'[830] He states that this shows how 'great and lofty is His [the Qá'im's] station'.[831]

A more important New Testament text is the Little Apocalypse, several significant prophetic statements of which are referred to in the Bahá'í writings. In the Kitáb-i-Íqán Bahá'u'lláh, following the Matthean (24:3) version of the text, looks at it as an intimation of the return of Jesus. According to Bahá'u'lláh, however, this was not a unique event but something that had happened several times.

'Abdu'l-Bahá connects this event directly to the prophecy of the 'abomination of desolation' in Daniel,[832] which could refer to two different prophecies, one in chapter 9 and one in chapter 12. The prophecy in Daniel 9:27 is commonly held to refer to the crucifixion of Christ[833] but the second one describes a period of time that starts with 'that the continual sacrifice be taken away' (Derby) and ends with 'the abomination that maketh desolate'. 'The end' which Matthew is referring to is at the end of the one thousand two hundred and ninety days (Daniel 12:11).

In a Tablet of encouragement to the Bahá'ís of America, 'Abdu'l-Bahá connects Matthew's version of the 'lightning' logia (Matthew 24:27) to the development of the Bahá'í Faith and particularly its spread to the West.[834]

According to Buck, Bahá'u'lláh's exegesis of Matthew 24:29–31 'is arguably the most detailed exegesis undertaken in the Book of Certitude [Kitáb-i-Íqán]'.[835] Buck rightly suggests that there is more than exegesis involved when the falling stars are interpreted as referring to the priests. Again the archetypal image is invoked by reference to the clerics who always oppose the Manifestations, Jesus and Bahá'u'lláh.[836] Likewise, imagery of the heavenly bodies, the sun and the moon, are religious symbols of an archetypal nature.[837]

This view of Bahá'u'lláh as the return of Christ clashed with another Christian view, namely that of the resurrection.

For if Jesus rose in His body and then ascended in that body, Christians would claim that Jesus had to return in that same body, something that clearly was not true of Bahá'u'lláh.

We saw in chapter 11 that the resurrection was variously understood and perceived in the early Christian community. Below we shall look at various strands of resurrection thought and compare it to the Bahá'í doctrines on the resurrection.

First of all there is an important distinction in Bahá'í exegesis between the resurrection of the Manifestation (Jesus) and the general resurrection. In *Some Answered Questions* (chapter 23) 'Abdu'l-Bahá is asked about the meaning of the resurrection of Christ. He explains that the narrative of the martyrdom, burial and resurrection after three days should be understood allegorically. He explains that it is an allegory for the spirit and morale of the Christian community. At first the Christians were depressed by the tragic death of Jesus but when after three days they 'became assured and steadfast, and began to serve the Cause of Christ, and resolved to spread the divine teachings, putting His counsels into practice, and arising to serve Him, the Reality of Christ became resplendent and His bounty appeared; His religion found life; His teachings and His admonitions became evident and visible'.[838]

In a narrative surprisingly close to that found in the Gospel of Mary 'Abdu'l-Bahá refers to the role of Mary Magdalene after the crucifixion of Jesus:

> It was a woman, Mary Magdalene, who confirmed the wavering disciples in their faith, saying, 'Was it the body of Christ or the reality of Christ that ye have seen crucified? Surely it was His body. His reality is everlasting and eternal; it hath neither beginning nor ending. Therefore,

> why are ye perplexed and discouraged? Christ always spoke of His being crucified.' Mary Magdalene was a mere villager, a peasant woman; yet she became the means of consolation and confirmation to the disciples of Christ.[839]

The general resurrection is when humanity will rise from death into eternal life in paradise. In Bahá'í (and before it, Bábí) theology the Day of Resurrection is understood as the day of the appearance of the Manifestation of God.[840]

As we may recall from chapter 11, Paul had a dual perspective on the resurrection owing to his personal experience on the one hand and received tradition on the other. In the tradition, the resurrection of Jesus was the first and signalled the beginning of the general resurrection but Paul's personal experience, as he recounts it, leaves us with the impression that the physical nature of the resurrection of Jesus was not without problems. As such, Paul was trapped between his vision and an important theological issue of a Jewish-Christian community, which looked forward to the physical resurrection. To what degree his metaphor of the church as the 'body' of Christ figured in Paul's solution to the predicament is difficult to say. If we attribute to it some importance, this would count as a significant parallel to Bahá'í doctrine. 'Abdu'l-Bahá called the discouraged disciples of Jesus 'a lifeless body'.[841] Perhaps the reference to 'spiritual body' (1 Corinthians 15:44) constitutes Paul's solution to his personal quandary.

The narrative of the gospels provides various theological points regarding the nature of the resurrection but relates no personal experience such as Paul's. The gospels, however, are negative theological statements. They are more informative about what the resurrection is not than what it actually is. Regardless of these disparate theological views, the gospels propose one unified point, which is the continued presence of Jesus, and more importantly, perhaps, the legitimacy of the leadership of those apostles who met with the risen Lord and were charged with the affairs of the community. On this issue the Bahá'í doctrine agrees, indeed one might say it is identical, but with a reversal. In the gospels the resurrection accomplishes the establishment of the church; in Bahá'í doctrine the establishment of the church is the resurrection.

Finally, the resurrection belief behind the narrative in the Gospel of Mary has striking similarity to the Bahá'í position. Both make the comforting of the disciples by Mary Magdalene a central point but in the narrative Gospel of Mary there is another central issue, namely the authority invested in Mary by virtue of her ability to recollect the words of the historical or living Jesus. These are dual elements in the Magdalene thought.

'Abdu'l-Bahá's solution is remarkably close to the psychological solution proposed in chapter 11. This solution appears particularly congruent with the general Bahá'í view of miracles that we shall discuss below.

Prophetic Behaviour

The use of Jesus Christ as an archetype in the Bahá'í writings is not limited to protagonists and antagonists but is primarily concerned with the prophet. Some of the religious issues that relate to miracles of early Christianity pertain equally to the Bahá'í Faith.

In chapter 6 we saw that there were two Christian traditions in which requests for miracles as proof of Jesus' claims was condemned categorically (one tradition exempts preaching as an 'allowable miracle'). This parallels

Bahá'u'lláh's own admonition: 'We entreat Our loved ones not to besmirch the hem of Our raiment with the dust of falsehood, neither to allow references to what they have regarded as miracles and prodigies to debase Our rank and station, or to mar the purity and sanctity of Our name.'[842]

Such is the rank of the Manifestations of God that the mention of miracles as proof of their prophethood is to reduce them to sorcerers and conjurers. The Báb in His Dalá'il-i-Sab'ih (The Seven Proofs) condemns the Muslims for requesting miracles. He argues that, according to traditional values of Islam, the Qur'án is believed to be the primary proof of Muḥammad's mission. The Báb, just like Q, argues that this is the same criterion by which His own mission can be judged.[843]

'Abdu'l-Bahá, in His discourse on traditional proofs exemplified by the Book of Daniel, notes the transitory nature of the miraculous proof. He states that He will not 'mention the miracles of Bahá'u'lláh' because it may be maintained that these are false, as the Jews denied the miracles of Jesus. The uncertainty that surrounds the historicity of miracle stories makes them worthless as evidence.[844] 'Abdu'l-Bahá goes on to say that even if one sees a miracle one might think it to be an 'enchantment' rather than a 'miracle', the distinction being that the former is performed by a prophet or holy man by the power of God, while the latter is performed by a conjuror. Thus, 'Abdu'l-Bahá maintains, even those who witness an extraordinary feat cannot be sure that it is a sign of the divine origin of its performer. If we look at the Jewish polemic account of the life of Jesus, the Toldoth, we will see that the contention is not whether or not Jesus performed miracles but whether or not they were divinely sanctioned. The Toldoth maintains that Jesus stole the Ineffable Name from the temple and used its power to perform miracles.

In *Some Answered Questions* 'Abdu'l-Bahá goes back to the issue of historicity by looking at the reports about the momentous events surrounding the crucifixion: the earthquake, the sundering of the veil of the temple and the dead emerging from their graves. 'Abdu'l-Bahá argues that such events, had they really occurred, would surely have been recorded by history and since they are not, surely they should not be taken literally. Furthermore, He argues that had such events occurred, surely the soldiers would have reacted by believing in Jesus and would have either taken down His body or fled in horror. He concludes saying: 'Our purpose is not to deny such miracles; our only meaning is that they do not constitute decisive proofs, and that they have an inner significance.'[845] In a separate chapter (22) the miracles are specifically considered. In this chapter much of what has already been discussed is repeated but there is an additional type of proof of the Manifestation. The behaviour of the Manifestation, His self-sacrifice is a means by which 'people with insight' are able to recognize His station.[846]

At the conclusion of the talk is a summary. First, as a general hermeneutical rule, 'Abdu'l-Bahá states that whenever the 'Holy Books' refer to a physical miracle, it is in reality a spiritual miracle, a metaphor for a spiritual event.

Shoghi Effendi, in *God Passes By*, recounts the events surrounding Bahá'u'lláh's stay in Baghdad. The 'ulamá, having challenged Him to perform a miracle, were shocked when Bahá'u'lláh accepted the challenge to perform any miracle they could agree on, the only condition being that they sign a document stating that, if the miracle were to be performed, they would accept His Cause unreservedly.

Unwilling to meet the conditions, the 'ulamá decided to drop the whole matter:

> 'We have,' Bahá'u'lláh is reported to have commented, when informed of their reaction to this challenge, 'through this all-satisfying, all-embracing message which We sent, revealed and vindicated the miracles of all the Prophets, inasmuch as We left the choice to the 'ulamá themselves, undertaking to reveal whatever they would decide upon.'[847]

If one assembles the ontology that emerges from the Bahá'í writings about the Manifestation which we discussed above, one must conclude that, although the Manifestations of God wield the power to perform any miracle, the veil[848] they carry – their mortal bodies with all their limitations – will not be lifted to demonstrate their glory, which would stifle the free will of the beholder. Rather, when a soul has shown faith, He may confirm that faith by lifting the veil ever so slightly. Thus it was during the days of His manifestation and so it is even in His absence.

With this perspective on miracles, Bahá'u'lláh's teachings not only take on proof value but the content of the teachings are of prime importance.

We may recall from chapter 5 that Matthew 13 has an array of parables all discussing the nature of the kingdom of heaven. The present author understands 'the kingdom of heaven' to mean something equivalent to the Cause of God.[849] If this equivalence is accepted then one may well understand the doctrine of the parables of Matthew 13 to establish the nature of the Cause of God as being the fruit of an open heart receiving the Word of God and the doom of those who neglect it. At the beginning the Word of God seems small and obscure but in the end it establishes its ascendancy in the world. When found, it must be accepted in its entirety and one must renounce the world. Through it judgement is pronounced on each and every person.

We know that among the sayings about the kingdom of God are some of the most authentic words of the Historical Jesus. The Historical Jesus is, in this sense, more interested in social issues than Christians generally perceive the evangelical Jesus to be and therefore His message is more easily comparable to that of Bahá'u'lláh than is usually thought.

New Salvation

The crucifixion became, in early Christianity, the central symbol for Jesus' salvific act. The Bahá'í writings have therefore had to address this tradition as well.

The doctrine of the Bahá'í Faith is somewhat of a new paradigm in resolving the question of the crucifixion of Jesus. Holding both the Qur'án and the Bible as holy, it faces the problem of reconciling the two apparently contradictory accounts which have been such a great source of dispute.[850] In a Tablet to Fatḥ-i-A'ẓam, Bahá'u'lláh unquestionably endorses the gospels' narrative:[851]

> Know thou that when the Son of Man yielded up His breath to God, the whole creation wept with a great weeping. By sacrificing Himself, however, a fresh capacity was infused into all created things. Its evidences, as witnessed in all the peoples of the earth, are now manifest before thee. The deepest wisdom which the sages have uttered, the profoundest learning which any mind hath unfolded, the arts which the ablest hands have produced, the influence exerted by the most potent of rulers, are but manifestations of the quickening power released by His transcendent, His all-pervasive, and resplendent Spirit.[852]

The theological content of this representation of the crucifixion will generally be found to fall short of the uniqueness that Christians generally assign to it. There is, most importantly, no trace of redemption theology, in its traditional sense. A 'fresh capacity', 'learning' and so forth are all very well but what good are these if the crucifixion does not bring the salvation of the individual human soul? The Bahá'í ontology here significantly differs from the Christian evangelical. The evangelical belief in original sin makes an absolute cleansing imperative. The lack of such an absolute act allows for uncertainty about the ultimate destination of one's soul. To accept a Bahá'í ontology is to accept uncertainty about one's own ultimate fate. Is there equivalence? Bahá'u'lláh states that the sacrifice of Jesus promoted progress in the human world. Though such a thing is not absolute in nature, it is, however, universal. Bahá'u'lláh compares His own act of salvation with these words:

> Verily, He (Jesus) said: 'Come ye after Me, and I will make you to become fishers of men.' In this day, however, We say: 'Come ye after Me, that We may make you to become quickeners of mankind.'[853]

In a Bahá'í ontology the physical circumstances are the framework in which spiritual progress is either attained or not. Social laws instituted into the world through revelation are a means by which God creates such a physical framework. One may therefore conclude that in a Bahá'í ontology Bahá'u'lláh is indeed proclaiming Jesus' crucifixion to be a quickening, salvific act.

Regarding the passage in the Tablet to Fatḥ-i-A'ẓam, Buck states:

Given its Islamic milieu, this passage is remarkable for its superlative glorification of Christ. In orthodox Christianity, the 'Work of Christ' is bound up with man's relationship to God, and this aspect of 'functional Christology' is by no means passed over by Bahá'u'lláh. Abandoning the speculative, ontological 'substance Christology' of the classical period, Bahá'u'lláh describes the 'quickening power' (*ta'yíd*) unleashed by Christ's sacrifice and its impact on civilization, bears witness that 'the soul of the sinner' has been 'sanctified' (*tazakkat* – PED 299, s. v. *tazakkí*) and acknowledges that the world has been purified by Christ, the Purifier of the world (*muṭahhir al-'álam* – PED 1259, s. v. *muṭahhir*) . . .

Bahá'u'lláh sees Christ's sacrifice as having an impact not only on the human soul but on the whole panorama of human events. Not only has the individual sinner been saved, but civilization has been quickened as well (on v.n. *isti'dád* – 'fresh capacity' – cf. AED 595 and PED 53). To salvation therefore is added a dimension of the work of Christ which Bahá'u'lláh identifies as 'quickening power' (*ta'yíd*) – often rendered in the Bahá'í writings as 'divine assistance' . . . Thus it is clear that, in Bahá'í doctrine, the work of Christ is extended to civilization itself, spiritually contributing to its social evolution. Identifying Christ with civilization was, historically, a gradual process, in which secular time was merged with sacred time.[854]

Summary and Conclusion

Looking back at the study of both the gospels and the Bahá'í writings one may get the feeling that proving historical or cultural influences on holy scripture somehow diminishes their stature. Such a feeling, however, is, in the present author's opinion, founded on a mistaken criterion of truth. The results arrived at through scientific research have divided people into two major camps: those who feel that science has once and for all proved these scriptures to be worthless pieces of fiction and those who feel that the research has proved that science is hopelessly speculative and ultimately wrong. Both of these conclusions operate under a value system that is inherently foreign to scripture itself.

In his book *The Birth of Christianity* Crossan relates a personal anecdote that may be instructive to reflect upon.[855] Just before the Easter of 1995 Crossan was promoting his book *Who Killed Jesus?* in midtown Manhattan in a Barnes and Noble store. After he had spoken for a while, the floor was opened to people with questions. The first questioner asked why, if Crossan held the Barabbas story to be a Markan invention, he didn't just call it what it was: a lie? The question surprised Crossan because he had never thought of it in that way and he was sure that he was not afraid to call things by their proper name. So why was it inappropriate to call the gospel story about Barabbas 'a lie'? Crossan answered the question in terms of what the gospel is: '*updated* good news' – that is to say, news that spoke to current problems and conditions.

History asks for a static, neutral and non-judgemental retelling of events. It is not that the evangelist is expecting the reader to read it as history and then fraudulently writes a narrative that falls short of its standards. The evangelist is interested in the news, the good news that Jesus of Nazareth had come to bring salvation to all. As far as the evangelist was concerned, that was *the truth*. That truth continued to have an ongoing meaning and to be a truth that manifested itself in many different ways. Updating news also means adapting its form and mode of expression in order to convey the good news to new groups of people.

Salvation itself means widely different things to different people. For some it means an end to injustice and repression; to others it means a new sanctification by an appropriate interpretation of the Law; others mean that they were saved through the coming of the Messiah or the ultimate scapegoat, and finally, others find salvation in the incarnation of the logos/wisdom. All of these things signified salvation to people in different social and cultural settings and thus the question of which was the more truthful rendition becomes highly problematic. The historian may claim that the message closest to the Historical Jesus is more true but not so to the evangelist.

Bahá'u'lláh, in His Lawḥ-i-Ḥikmat (the Tablet of Wisdom), answers a question about creation and its nature.[856] Here Bahá'u'lláh is dealing with two different propositions. One is that creation has always existed; the other is the scriptural concept of creation as a single divine act. Bahá'u'lláh asserts that both of these conceptions are true. He furthermore explains that the difference between them is due to 'the divergences in men's thoughts and opinions'. This is central to religious statements: they attempt to express what is essentially an abstraction and as such can only be understood through the parabolic or illustratory, which in turn appeals to the hearer or reader's practical experience. That practical experience will in turn depend on the social and cultural environment.

Appendix 2

A New Inter-Religious Dialogue

We have now seen how religious tradition renews itself in order to respond to new social and historical conditions. In the introduction and again in the concluding chapter we likened this to a continuous dialogue. Now we shall consider how a new dialogue can also be created between different religious communities. The new dialogue is not different from the old dialogue in either purpose or nature. Dialogue has as its purpose to promote understanding and cooperation. Despite the fact that religions and religious diversity have been around for centuries, inter-religious dialogue is a relatively new phenomenon. The question why there has been a sudden appearance of people of diverse faiths wishing to reach a common understanding must therefore be confronted openly and squarely.

Mary Pat Fisher in her *Religion in the Twenty-first Century* discusses two 'Universalist Religions', Sikhism and the Bahá'í Faith, which 'explicitly attempt to transcend religious boundaries'.[857] She then goes on to discuss 'The Interfaith Movement', which she sees as originating in the Christian ecumenical movement, this movement itself originating in a wish for a unified religion as it was originally.[858] Since we are here specifically interested in dialogue between Bahá'ís and Christians, this distinction is significant. While Bahá'ís have explicit doctrinal interest in a dialogue (which will be discussed in depth below), Christians have no such thing and therefore we must make an enquiry into the origin of Christian interfaith dialogue.

Fisher suggests that interfaith dialogue originated in Christian ecumenism but this still does not explain the transition from interdenominational to inter-religious dialogue. John Hick in his *God and the Universe of Faiths* notes, like Fisher, that increased communication and interdependence, the movement or dislocation of large ethnic and religious communities has made dialogue necessary. For the Judeo-Christian tradition in particular Hick posits a philosophical reason for Christian interest:

> Generally ethnic background is determinative of religious affiliation and thus in some places the chances of becoming Christian are extremely slim. Thus it seems unthinkable that all these other religions are incapable of bringing God's salvation, for that would clearly mean that God had revealed Himself in a 'remarkably limited and ineffective way'.[859]

Another possible influence might be the rise of secularism. As William E. Hordern in his *A Layman's Guide to Protestant Theology* states, summarizing Rufus Jones's position in 1928: 'the great rival of Christianity is no longer Buddhism, Islam, or any of other religions, but secularism.'[860] In a recent television interview the Dalai Lama proposed that Christianity and Buddhism unite in their efforts against the modern rise of the worship of materialism. In a world which is in spiritual decline, moral and ethical values form an important common basis for cooperation.

Thus from a Christian perspective there is a practical reason for dialogue in order to smooth inter-religious social interaction, for example in inter-religious marriage. There are also philosophical reasons, as proposed by Hick, as well as common spiritual goals that may be reached by concerted efforts of the world's religions.

Lastly, there is one point which makes dialogue useful to individuals even if social conditions do not warrant it, philosophical issues do not demand it or spiritual conditions seem not to be so pressing. Meeting people of other religions and entering into dialogue with them gives one a unique possibility to reflect on one's own religion. A Christian reading this book will therefore have the possibility of seeing his or her own religion through the eyes of a follower of another.

Dialogue and accepting that salvation is to be found outside one's own religious affiliation should not lead to apathy. To think that all religious propositions are equally good or equally true in some subjective sense is 'to commit religious suicide'.[861] In Crossan's epilogue to *The Birth of Christianity*, which he calls 'The Character of Your God', he argues that Zeus (of the Greeks), Jupiter (of the Romans) and Yahweh (of the Jews) were not the same God with different names. The distinction was not merely one of name but of values. Yahweh is a God of justice and mercy. This is not merely a theological statement but a statement with profound social implications.

This book should assist the new dialogue, over the old dialogue, in two important ways. First, it should highlight many of the important social and ethical issues that were crucial to the early Christianity that informed the gospels. This will allow the dialogue to develop around issues that affect life and how it is lived instead of metaphysical issues that will change nothing. Second, it treats the gospels not as a divinely dictated text but as an inspired and spiritually living religious text, collected from the Christians who lived in those first decades of Christianity. This will allow the reader to see that even if Christianity started as one, as Fisher suggests, it was a oneness that manifested great diversity. The evangelists accepted these diverse traditions and made them speak together to effectively deliver a coherent message. The new dialogue attempts to do something very similar: to unite diverse religious traditions to form a coherent message for humankind.

First century Christianity produced a surprisingly varied range of literature. As a struggling community it defined itself against the existing society and justified its views, beliefs and ideals to society and itself through already existing standards. Its holy scripture was the Hebrew scripture which we today know as the Old Testament. Some literature was for the administration of the emerging church, some for the edification of its members and some, such as the gospels, explained the existence of the church itself. The gospels explained how the life of Jesus fulfilled Jewish expectations of the Messiah. To this end it told the story of Jesus and linked events to the prophecies in the scripture. This was also done in another type of literature which emerged later: apologetics. This latter brand of literature was largely interested in defending Christian belief against those who stood outside the community.

The early 20th century saw a similar development in the newly-emerged Bahá'í community of the West. It too at first did not have a scripture of its own and was in this respect dependent on the Bible. Correspondence also generally fitted the above pattern, with administration and edification figuring as the purpose of most of it. Literature explaining how Bahá'u'lláh fulfilled Christian expectations also emerged, at first incoherently, but soon with a great deal of consistency. This community too developed the apologetical genre at a later date, when the community had strength enough to turn and face the forces that lay outside it.

The Eastern Bahá'í community offers another set of parallels, being, as it were, brought up in the fire of persecution, living in the society that had rejected its founder and being significant enough to cause the society around it to produce polemics against it. All this served to sharpen the community's perception of itself as a historic event destined to have repercussions that were to be felt outside the society in which it dwelled.

What this tells us about Bahá'í literature is that it is 'natural' to the circumstances of the emerging religious communities. By 'natural' is intended also that it is necessary. The community cannot thrive without guidance, it cannot remain faithful to itself unless it understands itself and cannot spread unless it can justify its own existence.

All of this tells us something about the nature of scripture, namely that it serves the community, it prescribes and describes the social norms of its community, it enacts and reacts to history. Accepting this, we can proceed to study, learn and come to appreciate each other in our respective religious traditions.

As mentioned above, the Bahá'í Faith finds itself religiously obliged to enter into an amicable dialogue with other religions. Thus it is necessary to explore how it can do this.

The end of religious conflict, which the Bahá'í Faith envisages, can only become a reality through the ability of all parties to enter into dialogue, not to seek conversions, but to gain mutual understanding. Dialogue is practical, addresses the mind and is rational in nature. The greatest enemy of a successful dialogue is ignorance, for knowledge of the common basis for dialogue is instrumental to the dialogue itself. The common basis for a Bahá'í-Christian dialogue will therefore necessarily be the Bible and primarily the New Testament.

On the other hand, it is necessary for both parties to turn a critical eye on their own scripture. Various attempts have been made to use critical sciences within a Bahá'í framework of theology. John S. Hatcher's article 'The Validity and Value of an Historical-Critical Approach to the Revealed Works of Bahá'u'lláh'[862] attempts to discuss the nature of revelation and the creative process involved in a social, cultural and historical context. In a paper offered at the same conference, Seena Fazel suggested that exclusivist texts, Christian as well as Bahá'í, should be understood in a historical context. He suggests that the authors of these statements expressed themselves in a particular 'language' or manner because of certain circumstances in which the statements were made.[863]

In 1989 Sen McGlinn wrote an article for his periodical *Soundings* called 'Introduction to the Bible in Modern Research' in which he argued extensively for the relevance of such sciences in Bahá'í studies of the Bible:

> In modern Christianity, then, the greatest functional division is not between Orthodox and Western, or Catholic and Protestant, or even Old World and emergent nations, it is between an undeclared coalition of scholarly understanding of the real nature of the Bible and of Christian doctrine (seeing it as complex, historically conditioned, and all too human) on the one hand; and the popular, conservative, and evangelical understanding of the Bible on the other hand. The latter conceives of the Bible as a single entity, the timeless word of God whose meaning can be read off the page by the light of piety without the benefit of historical method. The extraordinary thing is

> that the Bahá'í Community as I have known it, and much of the popular Bahá'í literature, falls in the latter camp.[864]

McGlinn cites a letter from Shoghi Effendi to support this perception of the historical development: 'The cleavage between the fundamentalists and the liberals among [Christian] adherents is continually widening.'[865] If this perception is true then Bahá'ís have a new front to face in their dialogue with Christianity, a 'coalition' whose commitment lies not with a particular theological point of view but to a particular approach to the biblical sciences. In a dialogue with this group of people, knowledge of these sciences is as essential as knowing the theological particularities of a conservative Christian. From the present author's comparison of the literature of the 1st and 2nd centuries of the Bahá'í Faith and Christianity, it seems all but 'extraordinary' that most popular Bahá'í literature falls into the conservative category. The function of Bahá'í literature has been to relate theologically to the religious community around it and in theology the most outspoken and influential groups have always been the 'conservative' ones.

Robert Stockman in a paper presented at an Irfan Colloquium in December 1993 states:

> We also need to have some confidence that higher biblical criticism, as a technique that fosters independent investigation of truth, will be of use to Bahá'ís in understanding the Bible . . .[866]

McGlinn also says 'that naive assumptions about the Bible will not continue to suffice, both because they are becoming more outmoded and less of a common language', which is in a sense true and in a sense not true at all. It may be said to be true for some Christians but most certainly not all. Thus we must ask ourselves, with whom is this dialogue being held? For McGlinn the answer is clear because he feels that both history and the Bahá'í writings suggest that the future holds 'more intensive' dialogue between the Bahá'í Faith and a group within Christianity, 'Christian clergy and scholars'.[867] Much indicates that this language seems to be becoming more and more popular as well, particularly through the efforts of the Jesus Seminar and the publicity given its findings.

In the Bahá'í Faith, the ability to independently seek out the truth is considered as much a privilege as an obligation and together with the principle of the harmony of science and religion has been the bedrock of the undertaking of this book. 'Abdu'l-Bahá was once asked: 'How shall we determine the truth or error of certain biblical interpretation, as, for instance, the higher criticism and other present-day Christian teachings?' To which He answered: 'Your question is an abstruse and important one. Complete answer to it would require a long time. I will reply to it briefly. The only true Explainer of the Book of God is the Holy Spirit, for no two minds are alike, no two can comprehend alike, no two can speak alike. That is to say, from the mere human standpoint of interpretation there could be neither truth nor agreement.'[868]

Although 'Abdu'l-Bahá does not directly answer the question, which at that time was particularly controversial, He does bring up one important point. Even the application of such critical sciences does not produce truth, for the endeavour itself requires decision-making: which approach to apply, when and what is important and relevant for the general argument. The result is one individual's reconstruction and understanding of a text, one individual's decision of what is relevant and what is irrelevant. Yet the exercise is part of a process in which the end product is not only fact-finding, analysis and conclusion but part of a self-expression. It follows that the present work can in no way claim to be a final product but must remain a temporary result based on the author's personality and the information available to him.

Appendix 3

The Origin of the Didache

Throughout this book we have the used the Didache on the presumption that it tells us something about the period in which the gospels came into being. Below we shall consider the justification for such a presumption, looking at each of the component parts that make up the Didache.

The Two Ways

Two issues relate to the first section of the Didache and are known as the Two Ways. The first concerns the origin of the Two Ways as a whole and its relationship to the Epistle of Barnabas. The second relates to the cluster of sayings of Jesus within the Two Ways.

Adolf von Harnak, the great dogmatic historian, wrote one of the formative studies of the German school, arguing that the Didache was dependent on the Epistle of Barnabas. This perspective long had a hold over the German school with only one significant contending voice. Francis Xavier Funk argued that the reverse was true, that the Epistle of Barnabas was dependent on the Didache. Neither of these positions is held to any significant degree today. A turning point in the debate was the discovery of the Dead Sea scrolls, amongst which was found a document not unlike the one found in the Didache and the Epistle of

Barnabas.[869] Other documents of later Christianity also appear to use a similar document. John S. Kloppenborg charts three families which emerged within Christianity. The first is seen in Barnabas. The second split, with one branch incorporated into Doctrina and the second going into the Didache and from the Didache into the Apostolic Constitutions. The third is seen in the Canons and the Epitome.[870]

Though the Jewish origin of the Two Ways can no longer be questioned, the Christian nature of those versions found in Christian documents is equally undoubted, notwithstanding that no direct reference is made to Christian figures. It is at this point that opinions diverge. Various sayings in the Didache Two Ways resemble those found in the synoptic tradition but are not a precise match with any of the canonical gospels.

The German school, taking its lead from von Harnak, generally chose to explain these sayings as originating from a gospel harmony. Efforts in this regard, however, have failed to convince a majority of scholars in the French and British-American schools, who have adopted different models.

One model from the French school is presented in André Tuilier's 'La Didachè et le Problème Synoptique'.[871] Tuilier proposes that the Didache makes use of Q, which is to be identified with the gospel of the Lord, which the Didache refers to.[872] Tuilier, in contrast with almost all reconstructions of Q, believes that it contained a passion narrative. However, this is far from necessary for an understanding of the Didache, which is remarkable for the paucity of its references to the passion. The one possible exception is found in the apocalypse, which is discussed below.

From the British-American school, Richard Glover came

to a similar conclusion.[873] Where Tuilier charts Q's sayings tradition from an Aramaic text in Tatian's harmony, Glover points to important correlations with Tatian's teacher, Justin Martyr. Indeed, he identifies instances where Didache parts ways with both Matthew and Luke and follows Justin. Among those who support this position is Crossan, who points out to those that would claim dependence that the passages in Q (Matthew 5:39b–42, 44–8 = Luke 6:27–30, 32–6) 'are so different that it is notoriously difficult to decide for sure the sequence and content of that *Q Gospel* section'.[874] Granting the legitimacy of this point, however, we must remember that there are instances in which there is sufficient agreement between Matthew and Luke to establish a disagreement between Q and the Didache. Clearly it is not sufficient to merely propose that the Didache had Q available and used it indiscriminately. If the author of the Didache had Q he must clearly have redacted it, just as both Luke and Matthew did.

Before we consider this possibility, however, two other hypotheses need to be considered. The first was advanced by Bentley Layton in his paper 'The Sources, Date and Transmission of the Didache 1.3b–2.1'.[875] He proposes that the synoptic section in the Two Ways was a later insertion that a redactor collected by using Matthew and Luke. The second hypothesis was advanced by Christopher M. Tuckett in his paper 'Synoptic Tradition in the Didache'.[876] He proposes that the synoptic section is integral to the Two Ways but thinks that the Didache in its entirety used the gospels in their finished state.

Let us first consider Layton's efforts. In his conclusion he himself gives the following description of Didache's redactional pattern: 'The compositor does not hesitate to move back and forth at will from one parallel text to the other or to move backward and forward in the sources in order to extract single words or phrases.'[877] In addition to this he notes that 'theological motives played no important role in determining how the harmony was composed'.[878] It can thus be concluded that the editor made his selection, hopping back and forth, not as a theological redactor but only as a stylistic composer.[879] This is one of the problems with Layton's suggestion: its redactional pattern seems precariously sporadic. It assumes that the composer sat with Luke and Matthew and jumped back and forth, reversing not only the order of parallels but at times switching sources within sentences. The composer's motive for doing this, according to Layton, is to 'plagiarize canonical, hence theologically sound and "primitive Christian" sources for the composition of a pseudonymous "Apostolic" teaching, rather than merely invent such material for himself', to exercise his literary skill and 'disguise the fact of the plagiarization'.[880] On the whole, such motivation does not seem to warrant the radical editorial work that Layton proposes. Certainly Tatian's harmony offers nothing as radical as is proposed here. Another problem with suggesting apostolic pseudonymous editorial intent lies in the use of the Hermea Pastor and Sirac. Though Layton does much to assert that the former was considered canonical enough to be considered apostolic, particularly in the West, there are no actual apostolic claims attached to the work at all. The specific use of Sirac, signalled by 'it is said', represents a similar problem. It too was canonical but hardly conducive to an apostolic image.

Another argument advanced by Layton is that the material all comes from one continuous text in Luke (from 6:20 to 6:33) and Matthew (from 5:39 to 5:48 omitting verses 43 and 45), which he finds cannot be coincidental.

Yet this can be attributed to the fact that both Luke and Matthew used Q and simply did not dislodge the sub-units to any significant degree. Where this happened in Matthew there are holes left by the editor. In other words, there is a noteworthy omission in the Didache's use of Matthew precisely in the seams of Matthew's rearrangement of Q. Another problem surrounds Luke 6:31, which Layton suggests 'doubles' for Didache 1:2.[881] Tuckett is, however, quite right to suggest that Didache 1:2 has a definite Matthean style to it;[882] thus Luke 6:31 becomes another omission.

When Tuckett later analysed the same cluster of synoptic sayings with his own hypothesis in mind, he proposed that the way to determine Didache's dependence on the finished gospels (rather than Q) was to ascertain whether elements within the Didache were attributable to either Matthew's or Luke's redaction of Q. Tuckett, however, was aware that the very nature of this particular Q text made this job especially difficult. When the text diverged in Matthew and Luke it could barely be determined who held the original or indeed if the change was due to the evangelist's redaction or his particular edition of Q, a pre-Matthean or pre-Lukan redaction of Q.[883] Tuckett presents a few occasions which appear to be either Matthean or Lukan redactions.[884]

Before we consider this we must turn to the nature of the problem that was noted by both Crossan and Tuckett. When a tradition shows signs of mutability, that is to say that it is found in many different versions, it indicates that it has oral usage. A tradition that is used in a community (or communities), applied and cited when occasion requires, will naturally have an extensive oral life. Didache 1:2–2:1 and its Q counterpart as a text remain a central exposition of Christian radical ethics. Everyday behaviour was regulated by its sayings and repetition of it in admonition or teaching must therefore also have been daily. Layton, however, emphatically states that postulating 'an "oral source" for the passage cannot magically relieve the critic of the need to explain the conspicuous similarities of the *Didache* to the written source that it parallels'.[885] He thus not only rejects Audet's claim, whom he references, but is at odds with recent German scholars who have come to this conclusion.[886] We need not, however, resort to magic to consider orality a factor. Just as orality influenced the various editions of Q used by Luke and Matthew, we can suppose that a text related to Q had taken shape in Didache's community but had been equally shaped by local oral usage, as were Matthew and Luke's versions.

So the existence of such a text not only seems possible but indeed quite likely. We can thus conclude that the Two Ways in Didache used a Jewish work and inserted into it a 'mini-catechism'[887] which circulated in a written form in the community. Though the fact that it appears independent of the gospels might suggest an early date, this is by no means certain since a document of a similar nature seems to have been available to Justin Martyr as late as the mid–2nd century.[888]

Between Layton and Tuckett there is the issue of whether or not the mini-catechism was integral to the Didache, as the former suggests, or was a later insertion, as suggested by the latter. Layton feels that the hypothesis 'that the compositor of 1.3b–2.1 also compiled the rest of the *Didache*, is no doubt the least attractive (though it is the simplest) – again because of what most critics consider to be the primitive (first century) character of the Christianity reflected in chapters 6.2–16.8'.[889] Thus, because Layton's analysis of the mini-catechism led him to conclude it was dependent on the finished version of the gospels, it seemed plausible to suppose it was a later inclusion into an older catechism, the first edition of Didache. Tuckett observes that the theme of perfection which appears in 1:4 is not only characteristic of Matthew but appears to be important to Didache as a whole.[890] Thus, counter to Layton's argument based on the earliness of the rest of the Didache, Tuckett points to literary evidence suggesting its integral nature. If, however, we retain our original conclusion that the text is independent, these two arguments can be reconciled. The mini-catechism was integral to the Didache in its early 1st century edition.

Sanctity and Piety

The section that follows the Two Ways regulates the individual's behaviour towards God. That is to say that while the first section was about ethical behaviour, this section is about ritual behaviour. Ritual behaviour is an enactment of myth.[891] They are distinct in that one talks about behaviour in the profane, while the other is about behaviour in connection with the sacred. The two, however, are connected. The Didache itself formalizes this connection by requiring the rehearsing of the Two Ways before one can be baptized (7:1). Thus access to the sacred is conditional upon correct behaviour in the profane. Access to the Eucharist is denied to those who are not baptized (9:5) and need to be purified through the confession of sins (14:1).

The first ritual is that of baptism. Here we find the wording to be almost word for word that which we find in Matthew 28:19. Kurt Niederwimmer is correct in assuming that the 'agreement of the formulae is not explained by the Didache's quoting Matthew's gospel but – naturally – by their common dependence on the liturgy,[892] a possibility that Tuckett also concedes.[893]

It should be noted that Didache 9:5 demonstrates knowledge of the earlier baptism, which was only in the name of the Lord.

As noted above, Didache has very strong community confines. Participation in the community required strict compliance with community regulations. Crossan proposes, following Aaron Milavec, that the Didache presupposes an audience that was not familiar with, or for whom it was not natural to follow, Jewish ethics, which are presupposed by the Two Ways. The 'pastoral' intent is to set forth an ethical standard and ensure that it is followed. This is done in order to enable the assimilation of Gentiles into a Jewish-Christian community, particularly with regard to table fellowship.[894] This is quite plausible but does not immediately follow from the nature of the document. The community at Qumran had extensive documents describing the rules of conduct within the community, yet it does not seem there were Gentiles in their midst. Indeed, any community that wishes to access the sacred in purity must ensure that all participants are both aware of the regulations and can be relied on to keep them. Every Jewish sect had some standard in this regard, some strict, some lax.

Nathan Mitchell has another perspective of the author of the Didache. According to him, the Didache is a document whose readers 'think of themselves first and foremost as *Jews*, and who perhaps do not yet believe *in* Jesus'.[895] This latter point will need further consideration but the former will be scrutinized first. The question must therefore be, where were the confines of the community? Who was in and who was out? What did it take to cross the boundaries?

Regardless of earlier affiliation, it is clear that participation in the community required a certain degree of detachment from former associations. Only those who were baptized could participate in the common meal on the Lord's day. If one lived in the Diaspora one had to be cautious about eating with Gentiles because meals could use meat that had been used for idol offering.[896] In Didache 1:3 we saw the Gentiles, as a group, being outsiders. Yet within its own Jewish sphere the Didache knew people who were 'hypocrites'. These were people who fasted Monday and Thursday, while the people of the Didache fasted Wednesday and Friday (8:2). Crossan identifies these hypocrites as conservative elements within the community who wished to maintain Jewish meal restrictions, which the Didache, representing a moderate party, sought to do away with.[897] A more plausible suggestion comes from Niederwimmer, who points out that the description is that of 'pious Jews'.[898] While Crossan recollects the tradition about Paul's confrontation with Peter, Niederwimmer recollects the tradition in Matthew 6:16–18.[899] Fasting is quite different from meal fellowship. In fasting, piety is the issue; in meal fellowship, sanctity is an issue. The problem with the meal was, from the conservative Jewish-Christian perspective, that Gentiles could not be counted on to observe Jewish cleanliness rules. From a Pauline perspective this meant that his community was in danger of being divided and it meant that Gentiles became second-rate citizens in the kingdom of God, cutting them off from access to the sacred. In the case of fasting this was an individual choice from which the community as a whole had little risk or gain. Niederwimmer correctly points out that the Didache does not explain the necessity of fasting but presumes its practice. It brings up fasting only to fix the day on which fasting takes place. The concern here is to differentiate between the Christians and Jews. That Christians fast on days different from those of the Jews is thus made a distinguishing feature. Niederwimmer states that while this witnesses to closeness and interaction with the Jewish community, it also reveals that the Didache community was in 'the process of separating themselves from the religious community of Israel, or else they have already done so'.[900]

The Didache community, however, shows no such separation. These community markers appear to be operating within a Jewish context. Indeed, we can find no definite practice amongst Jews of fasting on Mondays and Thursdays, except in the reference to the Pharisees and later the Rabbinic fathers.[901] The Didache community distinguished itself in a way that probably was only noticeable to those familiar with details of both communities' fasting practices. It appears therefore to be an intersectarian discourse within the confines of Judaism. It is true that the Didache is not specific about the identity of the 'hypocrites', yet this does not warrant the assumption that they are to be identified with 'Jews' in general, since the markers criticized are not generally Jewish but specifically Pharisaic-Rabbinic.

Next the Didache discusses prayer, again mentioning the 'hypocrites' but giving no clue regarding their identity. It appears that it is the content of the prayer that is criticized. The Didache goes on to give the text of the prayer as 'commanded in the gospel'. The text conforms to a greater degree with that of Matthew and to a great extent this includes material which is clearly part of Matthew's redaction. Yet the agreement with Matthew is not, as Glover points out, all that impressive.[902] The Didache adds 'who is in heaven' where Matthew adds 'who is in the heavens'. Thus both added to Q but did so divergently. Glover notes that the Didache agrees with Luke against Matthew in the form of the word 'forgive'.[903] Unfortunately, the text tradition varies here and the best manuscripts have a third reading. The Didache adds a doxology that subsequently became a part of the Matthean text tradition. Notwithstanding differences between the Didache and Matthew, the relationship is unmistakable. Just like the baptismal formula, the prayer is part of a liturgy that was part of an oral usage.[904]

Finally there are two chapters devoted to the Eucharist. These two chapters are, by all accounts, a unique representation of the practice and ritualization of the share meal. Just as with baptism, we find a complete lack of passion myth.[905] Though it has the ritual elements (bread and wine) and then only in the later version of the meal represented by chapter 9, there is no reference to Jesus being handed over as we find in Paul and the gospels.[906] This is particularly striking in the description of the Sunday service, which belongs to the next section (the ecclesiastic), in which Jesus is not the sacrifice but God[907] is the recipient of the sacrifice of the Christians.

Whatever community the Didache came from it seems to have been utterly detached from the prevailing concerns of the Jerusalem community. It is difficult to imagine how these rites could have been used in the face of the pervasive power of the passion tradition. Did the Didache community have no contact with the Pauline or Jerusalem passion tradition? This seems unlikely, so we must explain why it chose its own tradition over the ones prevalent in Jerusalem and in the Pauline community. The explanation is no doubt to be found in the religious imagination behind the Eucharistic passion rite. Theissen explains: 'The identification of bread and wine with the body and blood of Christ touches on one of the deepest taboos in Judaism: the prohibition against consuming blood. Blood was regarded as the seat of life (Gen. 9:4ff)'.[908]

This is significant particularly because it enforced the view that the Didache in its religious imagination does not break with Judaism to the extent that, for example, Paul does. Paul, who for all intents and purposes remained Jewish, was not as restrained by the religious language of Judaism as we see the Didache to be. Jonathan Reed has in his discussion of the '[Hebrew] epic imagination of the Didache' that its 'shift from Israel to the church, from temple to the community, is clearly expressed in these [Eucharistic] prayers. What is less clear is the reason for the shift, and the role which is attributed to Jesus in the shift.'[909] He goes on to conclude that the community of the Didache 'views itself as the true Israel, has grafted itself into the Davidic lineage, and has gathered itself from within the diaspora . . . Furthermore, there is no attempt to justify the new epic, or the community's place within its epic. No reasons are articulated as to why a new temple, new priests, and new sacrifices are necessary.'[910]

This is highly significant. The Didache's confidence that its place within the Hebrew epic need no explanation (i.e. the members of the community need not be supplied with arguments) suggests that the community did not feel that it was, in this regard, challenged by other Jews. The Didache was a community that was confident in its own Jewish nature. Since ritual is the language by which the community shares in their common myth, it must have been an extremely well-established community that could withstand the need to have fellowship with either the Jerusalem or Pauline communities. Furthermore, it does not show the 'tension between Judaism and Hellenistic Christianity that is so evident in the Matthean gospel'.[911]

With regard to Gentiles, Nathan Mitchell is probably right: in the Didache 'the "yoke of the Torah" has *not* been replaced or relaxed by the "yoke of Jesus" '.[912] 'The implication, then, is that the perfect observance of the Torah (as interpreted according to Christian *halakoth*) is the supreme goal of *every* believer's life. In other words, the Didache suggests that one can attain salvation only by becoming a fully observant Jew.'[913]

Ministry

The third section of the Didache concerns the administration of the community. We shall here deal with three different hypotheses. The first is Tuckett's hypothesis that the gospel tradition in this section is dependent on the finished gospels (in particular Matthew). With this we shall consider Kloppenborg's analysis.[914] The second has been advanced by Aaron Milavec[915] and Jonathan A. Draper,[916] who regard the composition of these rules as the act of a single author. Finally, the third hypothesis, advanced by Stephen J. Patterson,[917] suggests that the composition developed in stages.

There are three sayings in this section that are related to the Synoptics. Two of these appear to be related to Matthew. First is the quotation in Didache 11:7. Matthew 12:31–2 here conflates Mark 3:28 and Q (Luke 12:10). Didache, however, only uses the Markan material but in doing so retains Matthew's redaction of the sentence. Koester suggests that the theme of sinning against the Holy Spirit was already in use in Judaism[918] and may therefore be part of the common Judeo-Christian tradition. Tuckett accepts this and therefore concludes that the question of literary dependence cannot definitely be decided 'just on traditionsgeschichtlich grounds'.[919] Kloppenborg, who also accepts Koester's view, points, however, to another important issue, namely interpretation, which 'defies the Marcan and Q (and Matthean) context'.[920] Clearly the meaning of the tradition was not gleaned from the canonical texts available to us. Therefore we must ask if the application of the tradition does not predate the text of the Didache. Since the tradition is marshalled in defence of the prophets being challenged and since the Didache generally attempts to check the authority of the prophets, it seems implausible that the Didache invented this context. This context is indeed, of all those available to us, the most historically plausible. So whether the Didachist knew Matthew or not, he knew its application from community affairs.

The suspect nature of the redactional element also found in the Didache needs to be further considered before it is allowed to weigh against the independence of the Didache. It must readily be acknowledged that Matthew's redaction of Mark is not, as Glover suggests, because of an underlying Q text that Luke has omitted.[921] But what is its origin? It could be construed as a redaction to accommodate the conflation of Mark and Q but this seems unlikely. Matthew so thoroughly redacts and reduces his version of the saying that the verbal correspondence is close to nil. Indeed, the only verbal correspondence is the introductory formula 'I say unto you'. Matthew appears not only to have fixed Mark but appears to have wholly replaced it with his own shorter and less pedantic version. Correspondence between Matthew and Didache therefore seems to be due to common tradition, of which Didache has a shorter and even more primitive version. Didache knows nothing about blasphemy.

It seems more plausible to understand the Matthean redaction as being a conflation of the tradition it has in common with Didache with the text of Mark.

More significant perhaps is the Didache's use of the tradition in Q regarding the worker deserving his wages (in Luke 10:7) or food (Matthew 10:10). Here again it must be admitted that Luke retains Q's wording while Matthew has changed wages to food.[922] Kloppenborg suggests that Matthew has redacted Q out of 'greater sensitivity to the eschatological connotations' of Q's term.[923] Whether this is Matthew's reason is difficult to say. In the Didache, however, we need not speculate. Didache has 'food' because that was indeed what the settled prophets received in pay. Didache 13:3 specifically enumerates that they are to be given the first fruits of 'the produce of the winepress and of the threshing floor and of oxen and sheep'. Verses 5 to 7 seem like a later extension when these basics were not enough. Indeed, the reference to money and clothes but also jars opened for the first time suggests a move from a rural setting where the family unit operated as its own producer for the majority of its needs, to an urban setting where a commercial economy allowed people to trade. This is signalled not only by the reference to money but also by the underlying assumption that when one opens a jar, that is the first time one has access to its contents, as opposed to the situation had one produced it oneself. That verse 3 implies that the reader is a self-sufficient producer is clear from the reference to a winepress and the assumption that the reader had a flock of sheep or oxen to take the first-fruit from.[924] Also the first list has the 'produce of the winepress' which reappears in the second list as 'a jar of wine'. The final verse, which includes money, clothes and possessions, stands in contrast to the version of the saying in verse 1 that specifies 'food' as the sort of payment allowed the 'worker'.

If the saying had taken that form in the community of Didache because of what was in fact practised in the community, there is no reason to assume that this was not also the case in Matthew's community. If Matthew edited his Markan text, as he seems to have done, then he has done so to a version that seems closer to a original setting. Whether Mark retains a more faithful version is in this respect insignificant.

Thus Tuckett's evidence on closer inspection seems rather weak. Somewhat aside from the issue of literary relation, we shall now look at various views regarding the content of this section.

First we shall look at Aaron Milavec's analysis of this section as it relates to distinguishing between 'true' and 'false' prophets. Milavec notes that after one reads about the (optional) role played by the prophets in the Eucharist (see above), 'almost all that one hears about prophets is cautionary. One gains the impression that the community had more to be feared from abusive and wayward prophets than to receive from true ones.'[925] The first issue that Milavec turns to is the function of prophets at the Eucharist.

Here, he points out, the community has its own prayers and the prophet is free to say his own prayer as the spirit moves him. The prophets did not preside over the Eucharist and the community could hold the Eucharist without the presence of a prophet. This seems reasonable enough an assumption. The share meal out of which this Eucharistic practice emerged in a ritualized version did not have anyone presiding. Everyone, rich and poor, came together as equal contributors to a meal. Yet, as Milavec himself suggests, if a prophet convened a Eucharistic meal, 'he would undoubtedly be looked to as the presider over that meal'.[926] He goes on to make the very significant conclusion that this was the problem: 'Prophets had, in the past, tended to take over and even dominate the Eucharist with their charismatic gifts.'[927]

The Didache, or this section, stands at the crossroads between the point at which the prophets were revered as people led by the spirit and the point at which that reverence was abused and taken advantage of. This, unfortunately, only helps to place it in the 1st century. Clearly this was already a problem in the first decade after the crucifixion of Jesus, when prophets attempted to make claims for themselves in Jerusalem. In Corinth, Paul had to lay down ground rules for prophetic behaviour in the community (1 Corinthians 14:29). On the other hand, Matthew's own redactional work shows an ongoing concern for the behaviour of prophets (Matthew 7:15, 24:11).

Draper points to another facet of this issue, namely the ambiguity of leadership. 'The text mentions teachers, apostles, prophets, bishops, and deacons, and it indicates that there is tension among them (15:1–2), affirming them all without resolution to the question of their relative functions and status.'[928] This apparent flux in leadership seems to suggest that the process of establishing a hierarchy, wherein the community's bishops and deacons made it self-sufficient, had not yet occurred.

Draper proposes that Didache 15:1–2 is not a response to the disappearance of charismatic ministry and a step towards the establishment of the non-charismatic leadership. Rather it is the intrusion of charismatic prophets into the prerogatives of bishops and deacons because of unworthy occupants.[929] This fails to convince. Didache is clearly in need of explaining their appearance as people who also have 'the ministry of the prophets and teachers' (15:1).

Their ministry and honour is therefore, in the Didache, modelled (obviously in the loosest terms) on that of the already existing offices. Draper's proposal is also problematic because the Didache unreservedly supports them as 'honourable men' (15:2). Clearly, if they have the qualifications mentioned in verse 1, they are honourable. The problem is that they have to have honour 'together with the prophets and teachers' (15:2). The language of the Didache presupposes a resistance to the introduction of a novel, non-charismatic office. This would seem to place the Didache in a transition period earlier than the firm establishment of that institution in the later part of the 1st century. However, we shall see that the majority of the section can be pushed even further back.

Part of a later development towards the establishment of bishops and deacons, probably intermittent between the itinerant prophet and the bishops and deacons, is the emergence of resident prophets (discussed above in connection with the saying in Didache 13:1). The wording presupposes that resident prophets had in the past been itinerants. The naturalization of itinerant prophets of course promoted the development of bishops and deacons. Itinerants could cover a number of communities, while a resident prophet only covered one. Thus with fewer itinerants, some communities had reluctantly to resort to bishops and deacons.

Evidence for the existence of an earlier edition of the Didache that ended immediately before the section about itinerant prophets settling, emerged in 1923 when L.-Th Lefort discovered a Coptic manuscript in Egypt which appeared to end comfortably with the first clause in Didache 12:2.[930] Though various explanations have been advanced to explain this peculiar ending, considering particularly the expense of producing papyrus manuscripts, it seems unlikely that the scribe would have left such a large area unused for no reason at all.[931] Whether the Coptic manuscript is accepted as evidence of an earlier edition of the Didache, however, is not essential.

In the first section the itinerants are checked, their resources are limited, hospitality to them is restricted to brief periods and their behaviour and teachings are confined to specifics outlined by the Didache itself. This is done under the threat of being declared a false prophet. The rhetoric about a settling prophet is almost the reverse: it is hoped that he or she will take up a craft but if the prophet knows no craft, the community should provide something for him to do. The charge that can be levelled at prophets if they are inactive is 'making traffic of Christ' (12:5). We get the sense that while there is concern about abuse of community resources, there is no concern about abuse of authority. Clearly, when the prophet gives up the 'manners of the Lord' he or she also gives up the charismatic authority that attaches itself to such behaviour. A naturalized prophet represented far less a danger to the stability of the community than an itinerant did.

The next shift appears at the description of the settling prophets in chapter 13. Here the community has become so affluent that it can support a religious professional. At this point the prophet is expected not to work. He receives a fixed income from the community and is thought of as the high priest (13:3). At this stage the resident prophet is a trusted member of the community. There is still a sense of holiness attached to the person of the prophet but he or she is controlled by the community, for the community provides his or her livelihood.

The final stage sees the emergence of a new class, the

bishops and deacons. These had none of the holiness of the former offices and in many eyes were an unworthy replacement of the figures of the past offices.

What we see, therefore, is a very straightforward chronological addition of successive developments in community offices. The community rules were, whenever changes in community life required it, updated to educate the community about how it was to regulate its affairs. If this chronology holds true, then it would appear that the movement to naturalize prophets started in the rural areas and only subsequently emerged in the urban setting where the rest of these rules appear to be at home. This seems the most likely sequence of events since the urban areas were probably visited by more affluent prophets such as Paul, while the rural prophets stayed in the rural areas. The plight of the poor rural prophets needed solving; the urgency of this situation required immediate remedy.

Clearly the Didache available to us today is neither the beginning nor the end of the process of community regulations. Earlier and later editions existed.

The Apocalypse

The final section of Didache (Didache 16) is an apocalypse. The text is unfortunately incomplete but what we have has several significant synoptic parallels.

We shall here consider Tuckett's arguments for dependence and then attempt to place the Didache in its historical context. The material in the apocalypse that shows a relationship with the synoptic tradition is related to the special Matthean source. Thus say those who argue for the Didache's independence, the Didache is dependent not on Matthew but on Matthew's special source. Why else would no use be made of the material that Matthew has from his Markan text? This, Tuckett counters, ignores that 'the Did[ache] 16 contains possible allusions to the synoptic material in four verses common to Matthew and Mark'.[932]

The allusions that Tuckett suggests are not convincing arguments for Didache's dependence on Matthew. There are no verbal agreements with material that stems from Mark and these allusions are all quite understandable as stemming from a largely pre-Matthean framework that in Matthew became conflated with his Markan source.

A careful survey will show that the Didache's apocalypse lacks all significant Markan motifs and has a scheme that diverges considerably. The temple so central to the Markan apocalypse is absent. Instead of merely having deceitful false prophets appear, the Didache singles out one figure, a miracle worker that shall appear as 'a son of God' who will take power over the world (16:4). Then appears judgement day, 'the fiery trial'. Some will be offended and lost, others will be saved by 'the curse itself' (16:5).[933] Then the 'sign of truth' will appear in the sky, then the trumpet will sound and then 'thirdly the resurrection of the dead' (16:6).

This scheme echoes the traditional scheme of 1 Thessalonians 4:16 which Paul cites on the authority of the 'Lord's word' (4:15). Clearly the framework presumed by the Didache is not only not Markan but can definitely be placed away from the Jerusalem context from which it came. Its structure pre-dates Paul's earliest correspondence.[934] On it hinged traditions that the Didache had in common with Matthew, who hinged it on the Markan structure.

Conclusion

Many difficult issues emerge from the challenge of determining the origin of the Didache. Part of the problem of determining the date is due to the evolutionary nature of the document. As we saw in the section on community ministry, there was a clear development starting with controlling itinerants and concluding with the reluctant emergence of bishops and deacons. The document was also mobile. It was flexible enough to adapt to baptism under a great variety of circumstances. Thus we are hard pressed to pin down the precise dates or location of its composition. The fact that the later versions originate in Egypt hardly presents strong evidence for its origin. Though moderately wealthy prophets could afford the transportation that would take them outside Syria-Palestine, the itinerant prophets that the Didache describes could not have afforded such transportation. It is therefore probably in Syria-Palestine that we should place it. The edition that we have at hand appears to date somewhere in the seventies, just a bit earlier than the composition of Matthew, but in the same community. Though the Didache is a composite document, it appears to gather its material from the same community. The distinct lack of Jerusalem tradition suggests that it should be in a place that had authority independent of Jerusalem, that could formulate its own community structure and practice.

Bibliography

Ancient Works

The various ancient texts used in this book with comments from the present author.

Jewish Works

OLD TESTAMENT

Biblia Hebraica [BH]: 3rd edition, edited by Rudolf Kittel (Stuttgart 1937). Hebrew (and Aramaic) text with extensive critical notes divided into significant and less significant variant readings.

Septuaginta [LXX]: 1st edition, editor Ebenhard Nestle died before finishing the work which was completed by Alfred Rahlfs (Stuttgart 1979). This edition contains an extensive critical apparatus.

The Holy Scripture [JPS]: An English Jewish translation produced by the Jewish Publication Society of America (Chicago 1917). Stylistically not unlike the KJV (see below), replacing Yahweh with LORD. Though it removes some of the Christian colouring of other translations, it remains a devotional text rather than a scholarly one.

NEW TESTAMENT

Most of the New Testament translations include an Old Testament text as well. These will be marked OT+.

Apocrypha

LXX: see above.

Biblia Sacra Vulgata [Vul]: Saint Jerome's 4th century translation of the Bible into Latin. Two volumes with text critical notes, Jerome's forewords to each book and a few deuter-canonical books (OT+NT+).

New Jerusalem Bible [NJB]: See below.

New English Bible [NEB]: See below.

King James Version [KJV or AV]: See below.

A few of the New Testament translations include Apocrypha as well. These are marked with Ap+.

RABBINICAL WORKS

The Mishnah: Danby's translation (Oxford 1933) includes excellent critical notes.

The Mishnah, A New Translation: Neusner's translation (Yale 1988) is quite literal.

The Babylonian Talmud: Dr I. Epstein's (Soncino) translation includes excellent comments and critical notes.

(The Hebrew text of these works was available to the author from the MTR Torah Software Package.)

JEWISH HELLENISTIC WORKS

Josephus and Philo: Here the author used 'The Loeb Classical Library' which includes both a Greek text with critical notes as well as a translation. In the case of Josephus, the English translation of Whiston was usually consulted.

Christian Works

NEW TESTAMENT

Novum Testamentum Graece, 27th edition: Nestle-Aland (Stuttgart 1993) is the leading critical text for study of textual criticism. Comes with an extensive critical apparatus, cross-reference and concise manuscript and versional information.

The Greek New Testament, 2nd edition: United Bible Societies (1968) is the leading translation text, fewer critical notes but more detailed. Otherwise as above.

Vul: see above (OT+, Ap+).

Evangelion Da-Mepharreshe (Syric: Separate Gospels): This text prepared by Burkitt (Cambridge 1904) was based mainly on the Curetonian text amended with Sinaic version. Includes a fairly literal translation and critical note keyed mainly to Syrian Church Fathers. Includes a second volume with extensive discussion of grammar, text history and general comments on variant readings.

Old Syriac Gospels: Lewis' text (London 1910) was based mainly on the Sinaic version which is generally considered superior to the Curetonian. Lewis includes two sets of critical notes: the first points out places where the Curetonian varies from the Sinaic, the second points out places where it conforms with other versions. Lewis' comments on variant readings is to be found in her book *Lights on the Four Gospels from the Sinai Palimpsest* (see below).

Biblia Germanica: Luther's own translation was sometimes relevant to an understanding of how this great Protestant reformer understood the Bible.

King James Version [KJV]: By order of James I, this translation was produced without marginal notes for use in church alone. It was published in 1611; several editions with modifications followed. Below are some of the most significant revisions:

American Standard Version [ASV] (1901)

Revised Standard Version [RSV] (1885): Available as an interlinear with the 21st edition of Nestle's Greek text.

Webster [W] (1833)

Revised Webster [RW] (1995)

KJV Independent Translations:

The Holy Bible, A New Translation by James Moffatt (New York 1935)

New International Version [NIV] (1978): Available as a topical study bible; that is to say, with topical references, general and prophetic notes (OT+).

New English Bible [NEB] (1970) (OT+ Ap+)

New Jerusalem Bible [NJB] (1985): A Catholic translation of the Bible into English (OT+ Ap+).

Literal translations provide easy access to text close to the original. One should be cautious about thinking that there is no interpretation involved:

Darby (1889)

Young's Literal Translation [YLT] (1862)

Green's Literal Translation [GLT] (1993)

Emphatic Diaglott [ED] (1942): an interlinear with the Greek texts of B (Vaticanus)

Weymouth [WEY](1912)

Small Audience Translations:

New World Translation of the Holy Scriptures [NWTHS] (1961): Jehovah's Witnesses' own translation. It was crafted to support their theological position and has extensive footnotes and appendices to explain why their translation at places varies from common translations.

Scholars Version [SV] (1993): Published in Funk and Hoover, *The Five Gospels* and Funk, *The Acts of Jesus*, coloured according to the findings of the Jesus Seminar. Includes an explanation for the outcome of the vote. Also Miller, *The Complete Gospels* with notes and introductions.

Synoptic Texts:

The best way to look at the text tradition of the gospels is to get a book that places similar texts next to each other. Huck and Lietzmann, *Synopse der drei ersten Evangelien* has the Greek text. Prado, *Synopsis Evangelica ad usum scholarum, Textum Vulgatae integrum cum praecipuis graeci pericopis compendio praelectionum biblicarum adaptavit* has the Latin text. Thompson, *The Synoptic Gospels, Arranged in Parallel Columns* has the English text.

The Apostolic Fathers:

The Apostolic Fathers: The Loeb Classical Library provides original text versions and translations. See *Josephus* and *Philo*.

The New Testament Apocrypha:

Original language:

The Gospel of Thomas and The Gospel of Philip: see entry at Layton, Bentley below.

The Gospel of Peter: see entry at Mara, M.G. below.

The Gospel of Mary: see entry at Parrott, D.M. as well as the entry at Pasquier, Anne.

The Acts of John: see entry at Junod, Eric, and Jean-Daniel Kaestli below.

English and German:

See entry at Elliott, J.K.

See entry at Hennecke, Edgar, and Wilhelm Schneemelcher.

See entry at Miller, Robert J.

See entry at Robinson, James.

Modern Works

'Abdu'l-Bahá. *Paris Talks*. London: Bahá'í Publishing Trust, 1967.

— *The Promulgation of Universal Peace*. Wilmette, IL: Bahá'í Publishing Trust, 1982.

— *Selections from the Writings of 'Abdu'l-Bahá*. Haifa: Bahá'í World Centre, 1978.

— *Some Answered Questions*. Wilmette, IL: Bahá'í Publishing Trust, 1981.

— *Tablets of Abdul-Baha Abbas*. Chicago: Bahá'í Publishing Society; vol. 1, 1909; vol. 2, 1915; vol. 3, 1916.

Abu'l-Faḍl, Mírzá. *Miracles and Metaphors*. trans. Juan R. Cole. Los Angeles: Kalimát Press, 1981.

Aland, Kurt. *Kurzgefasste Liste der Griechishen Handschriften des Neuen Testaments*. Berlin: Walter de Gruyter, 1994.

Altmann, Alexander. 'In Jewish Philosophy'. *Encyclopedia Judaica*. Jerusalem: Kenter Publishing House, 1972.

Ashton, J. 'Paraclete', in Freedman, *The Anchor Bible Dictionary*. New York: Doubleday, 1992.

Aune, David E. *The New Testament in Its Literary Environment*. Cambridge: James Clarke & Co., 2nd edn. 1988.

— *Prophecy in Early Christianity and the Ancient Mediterranean World*. Michigan: William B. Eerdmans, 1983.

Ayer, Joseph C. *A Source Book for Ancient Church History*. New York: AMS Press, 1970.

The Báb. *Selections from the Writings of the Báb*. trans. Habib Taherzadeh. Haifa: Bahá'í World Centre, 1976.

Bahá'í World Faith. Wilmette, IL: Bahá'í Publishing Trust, 2nd edn. 1976.

Bahá'u'lláh. *Epistle to the Son of the Wolf*. Wilmette, IL: Bahá'í Publishing Trust, 1988.

— *Gleanings from the Writings of Bahá'u'lláh*. Wilmette, IL: Bahá'í Publishing Trust, 1983.

— *The Hidden Words*. Wilmette, IL: Bahá'í Publishing Trust, 1990.

— *Kitáb-i-Íqán*. Wilmette, IL: Bahá'í Publishing Trust, 1989.

— *The Proclamation of Bahá'u'lláh*. Haifa: Bahá'í World Centre, 1967.

— *The Seven Valleys and the Four Valleys*. Wilmette, IL: Bahá'í Publishing Trust, 1991.

— *Tablets of Bahá'u'lláh revealed after the Kitáb-i-Aqdas*. Haifa: Bahá'í World Centre, 1978.

Baigent, Michael, and Richard Leigh. *The Dead Sea Scrolls Deception*. London: Jonathan Cape, 1991.

Balyuzi, H. M. *'Abdu'l-Bahá: The Centre of the Covenant of Bahá'u'lláh*. Oxford: George Ronald, 2nd edn. with minor corr. 1987.

— *The Báb: The Herald of the Day of Days*. Oxford: George Ronald, 1973.

— *Bahá'u'lláh, The King of Glory*. Oxford: George Ronald, 1980.

Bammel, Ernst (ed.). *The Trial of Jesus*. Napperville: Alec R. Allenson Inc., 1970.

Bardy, Gustave. *La conversion au christianisme durant les primiers siècles*. Paris: Aubier, 1949.

Barrett, Charles K. *A Commentary on The First Epistle to the Corinthians*. London: Adam and Charles Black, 2nd edn. 1979.

Ben-Asher, Naomi, and Hayim Leaf (eds.). *The Junior Jewish Encyclopedia*. New York: Shengold Publishers, 5th edn. 1963.

Ben-Zvi, Jizhak. 'The Origin of the Samaritans and their Tribal Divisions', in Dexinger and Pummer, *Die Samaritaner*.

Darmstadt: Wissenschaftliche Buchgesellschaft Darmstadt, 1992.

Betz, Michael. 'Von Gott gezeugt', in Eltester, *Judentum Urchristentum Kirche*. Berlin: Verlag Alfred Töpelmann, 1964.

Betz, Otto. 'Was John the Baptist an Essene?' in Shanks, *Understanding the Dead Sea Scrolls*. London: SPCK, 2nd edn. 1993.

Bilde, Per. 'Afspejler Mark 13 et jødisk apokalyptisk forlæg fra kriseåret 40?' ('Does Mark 13 reflect a Jewish apocalyptic composition from the crisis year 40?'), in Pedersen, *Nytestamentlige Studier*. Århus: Forlaget AROS, 1976.

— *Josefus som historieskriver*. København: GEC Gads, 1983.

Black, Matthew. *An Aramaic Approach to the Gospels and Acts*. Oxford: Clarendon Press, 3rd edn. 1967.

Blackhirst, Rodney. 'Sedition in Judea, Gospel of Barnabas'. *Studies in Western Traditions*, Occasional Paper no. 3, 1996.

Borg, Marcus J. (ed.). *Jesus at 2000*. Colorado: Westview Press, 1997.

— *Jesus: A New Vision. Spirit, Culture, and the Life of Discipleship*. San Francisco: HarperSanFrancisco, 1987.

Borgen, Peder, and Søren Giversen (eds.). *The New Testament and the Hellenistic Judaism*. Århus: Aarhus University Press, 1995.

Bornkamm, Günther. *Jesus of Nazareth*. trans. James M. Robinson. Minneapolis: Fortress Press, 2nd edn. 1995.

Bösen, Willibald. *Galiläa als Lebenraum und Wirkungsfeld Jesu*. Freiburger: Herder, 1990.

Bowden, John. *Who's Who in Theology: From the First Century to the Present*. New York: The Crossroad Publishing Company, 1992.

Bowker, John. *The Targums and Rabbinic Literature, An Introduction to Jewish Interpretation of Scripture*. Cambridge: Cambridge University Press, 1969.

Briggs, Charles A. *General Introduction to the Study of Holy Scripture*. New York: Charles Scribner's Sons, 1899.

Bromiley, G. W. 'Infant Baptism'. Elwell, *Evangelical Dictionary of Theology*, Minnesota: Baker Book House, 1984.

Brown, Raymond E. et al. (eds.). *The Jerome Biblical Commentary*. London: Geoffrey Chapman, 1967.

Brown, Schuyler. *The Origins of Christianity: A Historical Introduction to the New Testament*. Oxford: Oxford University Press, 1993.

Browne, E. G. *A Year Among the Persians*. London, 1893.

Brownlee, W. H. 'John the Baptist in the New Light of Ancient Scrolls', in Stendahl, *The Scrolls and the New Testament*. New York: The Crossroad Publishing Company, 1992.

Bruce, F. F. *The Acts of the Apostles: The Greek Text with Introduction and Commentary*. London: The Tyndale Press, 1953.

— (ed.). *The International Bible Commentary*. Michigan: Zondervan Publishing House, 2nd edn. 1986.

Buck, Christopher. *Paradise and Paradigm: Key Symbols in Persian Christianity and the Bahá'í Faith*. Albany: State University of New York Press, 1999.

— *Symbol and Secret: Qur'an Commentary in Bahá'u'lláh's Kitáb-i Íqán*. Los Angeles: Kalimát Press, 1995.

Bultmann, Rudolf. *Das Evangelium des Johannes*. Göttingen: Dandenhoed & Ruprecht, 18th edn. 1964.

— *Jesus and the Word*. New York: Charles Scribner's Sons, 2nd edn. 1958.

Burney, C. F. *The Poetry of Our Lord: An Examination of the Formal Elements of Hebrew Poetry in the Discourses of Jesus Christ*. Oxford: Clarendon Press, 1925.

Burridge, Richard A. *What are the Gospels? A Comparison with Graeco-Roman Biography*. Cambridge: Cambridge University Press, 1995.

Burrows, Millar. *The Dead Sea Scrolls*. London: Secker & Warburg, 1956.

Catchpole, David R. 'The Problem of the Historicity of the Sanhedrin Trial', in Bammel, *The Trial of Jesus*. Napperville: Alec R. Allenson Inc., 1970.

— *The Quest for Q*. Edinburgh: T & T Clark, 1993.

Chadwick, John. *Lexiographica Graeca*. Oxford: Clarendon Press, 1996.

Charlesworth, James H. 'The Son of David: Solomon and Jesus (Mark 10:47)' in Borgen and Giversen, *The New Testament and the Hellenistic Judaism*. Århus: Aarhus University Press, 1995.

Chilton, Bruce. *Rabbi Jesus, An Intimate Biography*. New York: Doubleday, 2000.

— and Jacob Neusner. *Judaism in the New Testament, Practices and Beliefs*. London: Routledge Inc., 1995.

Cohn, Haim. 'Reflection on the Trial of Jesus', in Neusner and Green, *Judaism and Christianity in the First Century*. New York: Garland Publishing, 1990.

Cohn-Sherbok, Dan, and Lavinia Cohn-Sherbok. *A Short History of Judaism*. Oxford: Oneworld, 1994.

— *A Short Reader in Judaism*. Oxford: Oneworld, 1996.

Cole, Juan R. 'Behold the Man: Bahá'u'lláh on the Life of Jesus', in *Journal of the American Academy of Religion*, vol. LXV, no. 1, Spring 1997.

— 'The Concept of Manifestation in the Bahá'í Writings', in *Bahá'í Studies* 9 (1982).

Comay, Joan, and Ronald Brownrigg. *Who's Who in the Bible, The Old Testament and the Apocrypha, The New Testament*. New York: Wings Books, 1980.

Conzelmann, Hans, and Andreas Lindemann. *Arbeitsbuch zum Neuen Testament*. Tübingen: J. C. B. Mohr, 3rd edn. 1982.

Coupe, Laurence. *Myth*. London: Routledge, 1997.

Creed, John Martin. *The Gospel According to St. Luke: The Greek Text with Introduction, Notes, and Indices*. London: Macmillan 1953.

Cross, F. L. (ed.). *The Oxford Dictionary of the Christian Church*. London: Oxford University Press, 1958.

Cross, Frank Moore. 'Aspects of Samaritan and Jewish History', in Dexinger and Pummer, *Die Samaritaner*. Darmstadt: Wissenschaftliche Buchgesellschaft Darmstadt, 1992.

— 'The Text behind the Text of the Hebrew Bible', in Shanks, *Understanding the Dead Sea Scrolls*. London: SPCK, 2nd edn. 1993.

Crossan, John D. *The Birth of Christianity: Discovering What Happened in the Years Immediately after the Execution of Jesus*. New York: HarperSanFrancisco, 1998.

— *The Cross that Spoke: The Origins of the Passion Narrative*. San Francisco: Harper & Row, 1988.

— Electronic correspondence 2 March 2000 from 'Historical Jesus Methodology' hosted by the electronic discussion group X-Talk and moderated by Mahlon Smith and Jeffrey Gibson.

— *Four Other Gospels: Shadows on the Contours of Canon*. Minneapolis: Winston Press, Seabury Books, 1985.

— *The Historical Jesus: The Life of a Mediterranean Jewish Peasant*. San Francisco: HarperSanFrancisco, 1992.

— *In Parables: The Challenge of the Historical Jesus*. New York: Harper & Row, 1973.

— *Jesus, A Revolutionary Biography*. San Francisco: HarperSanFrancisco, 1994.

— *Who Killed Jesus? Exposing the Roots of Anti-Semitism in the Gospel Story of the Death of Jesus*. San Francisco: Harper, 1995.

Dalman, Rev. Dr. Gustaf H. *Jesus Christ in the Talmud, Midrash, Zohar and the Liturgy of the Synagogue*. trans. A. W. Streane. Cambridge: Deighton, Bell and Co., 1893.

Damm, Rich. *Johannesevangeliet*. København: Gjellerup, 1973.

Daniel, Norman. *Islam and the West: The Making of an Image*. Oxford: Oneworld, 2nd edn. 1993.

Davidson, Ole. *The Narrative Jesus – A Semiotic reading of Mark's Gospel*. Aarhus: Aarhus University Press, 1993.

Davies, Steven. *The Gospel of Thomas and Christian Wisdom*. New York: Seabury Press, 1983.

— *Jesus the Healer: Possession, Trance, and the Origins of Christianity*. New York: Continuum, 1995.

D'Costa, Gavin (ed.). *Resurrection Reconsidered*. Oxford: Oneworld, 1996.

de Jonge, Marinus. 'The So-called Pseudepigrapha of the Old Testament and Early Christianity', in Borgen, *The New Testament and the Hellenistic Judaism*. Århus: Aarhus University Press, 1995.

Detering, Hermann. 'The Dutch Radical Approach to the Pauline Epistles', in *Journal of Higher Criticism*, vol. 3, no.2, Fall 1996, pp. 163–93.

de Waal Malefijt, Annemarie. *Religion and Culture: An Introduction to Anthropology of Religion.* Illinois: Waveland Press, 1968.

Dewey, Joanna. 'The Gospel of Mark as an Oral-Aural Event', in Malbon and McKnight (ed.). *The New Literary Criticism and the New Testament*. Sheffield: Sheffield Academic Press, 1994.

Dexinger, Ferdinand, and Reinhard Pummer (eds.). *Die Samaritaner*. Darmstadt: Wissenschaftliche Buchgesellschaft Darmstadt, 1992.

Dibelius, Martin. *From Tradition to Gospel (orig. title: Die Formgeschichte des Evangeliums)*. trans. Bertram L. Woolf. Cambridge: James Clarke & Co., 1971.

— *Geschichte der urchristlichen Literatur*. München: Kaiser Tascenbücher, 2nd edn. 1990.

Dodd, C. H. *The Apostolic Preaching: And its Developments*. New York: Harper & Row, 1964.

Doughty, Darrell J. 'Pauline Paradigms and Pauline Authenticity', in *Journal of Higher Criticism*, no. 1, Fall 1994.

Douglas, J. D. (ed.). *The New Bible Dictionary*. Michigan: William B. Eerdmans, 1962.

Draper, Jonathan A. 'Social Ambiguity and the Production of Text: Prophets, Teachers, Bishops, and Deacons and the Development of the Jesus Tradition in the Community of the Didache', in Jefford, *The Didache in Context.* Leiden: E.J. Brill, 1995.

Driver, Samuel R. *An Introduction to the Literature of the Old Testament*. New York: Meridian Books, 1956.

Dunn, James D. G. 'Jesus in Oral Memory: The Initial Stages of the Jesus Tradition', presented on an Internet seminar hosted by X-Talk, 25 April – 2 May 2001, moderated by Jeffrey Gibson and Jack Kilmon.

— *Unity and Diversity in the New Testament: An Inquiry into the Character of Earliest Christianity*. London: SCM Press, 1997.

Ehrman, Bart D. *The New Testament: A Historical Introduction to the Early Christian Writings*. Oxford: Oxford University Press, 1997.

Elliott, John H. 'The Jewish Messianic Movement: From Faction to Sect', in Esler, *Modelling Early Christianity*. London: Routledge Inc., 1995.

Elliott, J.K. (ed.). *The Apocryphal New Testament*. Oxford: Clarendon Press, 1993.

Ellison, H. L. 'Matthew', in Bruce, *The International Bible Commentary*. Michigan: Zondervan Publishing House, 2nd edn. 1986.

Eltester, Walther. *Judentum Urchristentum Kirche*. Berlin: Verlag Alfred Töpelmann, 1964.

Elwell, Walter A. (ed.). *Evangelical Dictionary of Theology*. Minnesota: Baker Book House, 1984.

Encyclopedia Judaica. Jerusalem: Kenter Publishing House, 1972.

Epiphanius of Salamis. *The Panarion of Epiphanius of Salamis*. trans. Frank Williams. Leiden: E. J. Brill, 1987.

Esler, Philip F. *The First Christians in their Social Worlds*. London: Routledge Inc., 1994.

— (ed.). *Modelling Early Christianity*. London: Routledge Inc., 1995.

Evans, C. F. *Saint Luke*. London: SCM Press, 1990.

Evans, Craig A. et al. *Nag Hammadi Texts and the Bible: A Synopsis and Index*. Leiden: E.J. Brill, 1993.

Fazel, Seena. 'Understanding Exclusivist Texts', in Momen, *Scripture and Revelation*. Oxford: George Ronald, 1997.

Fine, Steven (ed.). *Jews, Christians, and Polytheists in the Ancient Synagogue: Cultural Interaction during the Greco-Roman Period*. Oxford: Routledge, 1999.

Finegan, Jack. *The Archeology of the New Testament: The Life of Jesus and the Beginning of the Early Church*. New Jersey: Princeton University Press, 1992.

Finley, Moses I. *The Ancient Economy*. London: Penguin Books, 2nd edn. 1992.

Fisher, Mary P. *Religion in the Twenty-first Century*. London: Routledge, 1999.

Fitzmyer, Joseph A. *Essays on the Semitic Background of the New Testament*. London: Geoffrey Chapman, 1971.

Fortna, Robert T. *The Fourth Gospel and its Predecessor*. Edinburgh: Fortress Press, 1988.

— 'Sign Source', in Miller, *The Complete Gospels*. Sonoma: Polebridge Press, 1992.

Franck, Eskil. *Revelation Taught: The Paraclete in the Gospel of John*. Lund: CWK Gleerup, 1985.

Fredriksen, Paula. *Jesus of Nazareth, King of the Jews: A Jewish Life and the Emergence of Christianity*. London: Macmillan, 2nd edn. 2001.

Freedman, David N. (ed.). *The Anchor Bible Dictionary*. New York: Doubleday, 1992.

Freyne, Seán. 'Bandits in Galilee: A Contribution to the Study of Social Conditions in First-Century Palestine', in Neusner, *The Social World of Formative Christianity and Judaism*. Philadelphia: Fortress Press, 1988.

— 'Herodian Economics in Galilee', in Esler, *Modelling Early Christianity*. London: Routledge Inc., 1995.

Friedländer, M. 'The "Pauline" Emancipation from the Law a Product of the Pre-Christian Jewish Diaspora', originally in *Jewish Quarterly Review* – Old Series, 1902, 14:265–302; reprinted in Neusner and Green, *Judaism and Christianity in the First Century*, vol. 3. New York: Garland Publishing, 1990.

Fritz, Volkmar. *Einführung in die biblische Archäologie*. Darmstadt: Wissenschaftliche Buchgesellschaft Darmstadt, 1985.

Funk, Robert W. *The Acts of Jesus: The Search for the Authentic Deeds of Jesus*. San Francisco: HarperSanFrancisco, 1998.

— *Language, Hermeneutic, and Word of God: The Problem of Language in the New Testament and Contemporary Theology*. New York: Harper & Row, 1966.

— and Roy W. Hoover. *The Five Gospels: What Did Jesus Really Say*. New York: HarperSanFrancisco, 1993.

Gerhardsson, Birger. *Jesu liknelser, En genomlysning*. Lund: Novapress, 1999.

Gesenius, Wilhelm. *Hebräisches und Aramäisches Handwörterbuch über das Alte Testament*. Leipzig: Verlag von F. C. W. Vogel, 16th edn. 1915.

Gibran, Kahlil. *Jesus, The Son of Man*. Oxford: Oneworld, 1993.

Gignoux, Philippe. 'L'apocalyptique iranienne est-elle vraiment ancienne?' *Revue de l'histoire des religions*, tome 216, fasc. 2, Avril-Juin 1999.

Gill, John. *An Exposition of the New and Old Testament*. London: Matthew & Leigh, 1809.

Giversen, Søren. *Thomas Evangeliet. ledning, oversættelse og komentarer.* København: GEC Gads, 1959.

Glover, Richard. 'The Didache's Quotations and the Synoptic Gospels', in *New Testament Studies* 5, 1958.

Goldstein, Morris. *Jesus in the Jewish Tradition*. New York: Macmillan, 1950.

Goodenough, Erwin R. *An Introduction to Philo Judaeus*. Oxford: Basil Blackwell, 2nd edn. 1962.

Gordon, Robert P. 'Targums', in 'Translation' in Metzger and Coogan, *The Oxford Companion to the Bible*. Oxford: Oxford Publishing Company, 1993.

Gould, Ezra P. *A Critical and Exegetical Commentary on the Gospel According to St. Mark*. Edinburgh: T. & T. Clark, 1948.

Goulder, Michael. 'The Baseless Fabric of a Vision', in D'Costa, *Resurrection Reconsidered*. Oxford: Oneworld, 1996.

Grant, Michael. *Jesus: An Historian's Review of the Gospels*. New York: Charles Scribner's Sons, 1977.

Grappe, Christian. 'Jean 1,14(–18) dans son contexte et à la lumière de la litérature intertestamentaire', in *Revue d'Histoire et de Philosophie Religieuse*, tome 80, no.1, Janvier-Mars 2000.

Green, Joel B. and Scott McKnight. *Dictionary of Jesus and the Gospels*. Downers Grove, IL: InterVarsity Press, 1992.

Gutmann, Joshua. 'Among the Jewish Sects', in 'Angels and Angelology', in *Encyclopedia Judaica*. Jerusalem: Kenter Publishing House, 1972.

Hadas-Lebel, Mireille. *Flavius Josephus: Eyewitness to Rome's First-Century Conquest of Judea*. New York: Macmillan, 1993.

Hanson, K. C., and Douglas E. Oakman. *Palestine in the Time of Jesus: Social Structures and Social Conflicts*. Minneapolis: Fortress Press, 1998.

Hatcher, John S. 'The Validity and Value of an Historical-Critical Approach to the Revealed Works of Bahá'u'lláh', in Momen, *Scripture and Revelation*. Oxford: George Ronald, 1997.

Hawkin, David J. *The Johannine World: Reflections on the Theology of the Fourth Gospel and Contemporary Society*. New York: State University of New York Press, 1996.

Heaton, E. W. *A Short Introduction to the Old Testament Prophets*. Oxford: Oneworld, 2nd edn. 1996.

Hennecke, Edgar, and Wilhelm Schneemelcher. *Neutestamentliche Apokryphen in deutscher Übersetzung*. Tübingen: J.C.B. Mohr (Paul Siebeck), 1959.

Henry, Matthew. *Matthew Henry's Commentary*. Virginia: McDonald, n.d.

Hewett, James A. *New Testament Greek: A Beginning and Intermediate Grammar*. Peabody: Hendrickson, 1986.

Hick, John. *God and the Universe of Faiths*. Oxford: Oneworld, 2nd edn. 1993.

Hickie, W. J. *Greek-English Lexicon to the New Testament*. Michigan: Baker Book House, 1982.

Hillers, Delbert Roy. 'Demons, Demonology', in *Encyclopedia Judaica*. Jerusalem: Kenter Publishing House, 1972.

Holmes, J. Derek, and Bernard W. Bickers. *A Short History of the Catholic Church*. Kent: Burns & Oates, 1983.

Holy Qur'an, The. trans. Ali Yusuf. n.p.: Islamic Propagation Centre International, 1946.

Hordern, William E. *A Layman's Guide to Protestant Theology*. New York: Macmillan, 1955.

Horsley, Richard A. *Archaeology, History and Society in Galilee: The Social Context and the Rabbis*. Harrisburg: Trinity Press International, 1996.

— and John S. Hanson. *Bandits, Prophets, and Messiahs: Popular Movements at the Time of Jesus*. San Francisco: Harper & Row, 1985.

Huddilston, John H. *Essentials of New Testament Greek*. New York: Macmillan, 1916.

Jacobson, Arland D. 'Divided Families and Christian Origins', in Piper, *The Gospel Behind the Gospels*. New York: E.J. Brill, 1995.

— 'Sayings Gospel Q', in Miller, *The Complete Gospels*. Sonoma: Polebridge Press, 1992.

Japan Will Turn Ablaze. Japan: Bahá'í Publishing Trust, 1974.

Jefford, Clayton N. (ed.). *The Didache in Context: Essays on its Text, History, and Transmission*. Leiden: E.J. Brill, 1995.

— *The Sayings of Jesus in the Teaching of the Twelve Apostles*. Leiden: E. J. Brill, 1989.

Jensen, Hans J. L. *Gammel Testamentlig Religion, En indføring*. Frederiksberg: Anis, 1998.

Jones, F. Stanley and Paul A. Mirecki. 'Considerations on the Coptic Papyrus of the Didache (British Library Oriental Manuscript 9271)', in Jefford, *The Didache in Context*. Leiden: E.J. Brill, 1995.

Joosten, Jan. 'Jésus et l'aveugle-né (*Jn* 9,1–34) dans l'*Évangile de Barnabas* et dans le *Diatessaron*'. *Revue d'Histoire et de Philosophie Religieuses*, 2000, 80e Année, no. 3.

— ' "Le Père envoie le Fils". La provenance occidentale d'une locution Syriaque', in *Revue d'Histoire des Religions*, tome 214, fasc. 3, Juillet-Septembre 1997.

— 'La Tradition Syriaque des Évangeiles et la Question du "Substrat Araméen" ', in *Revue d'Histoire des Religions*, 77 Année, fasc. 3, Juillet-Septembre 1997.

Josephus, Flavius. *The Complete Works of Josephus*. trans. William Whiston. Grand Rapids: Kregel Publications, 3rd edn. 1981.

Junod, Eric, and Jean-Daniel Kaestli (eds.). *Acta Iohannis*. Turnhout: Brepols, 1983.

Kelber, Werner H. *The Oral and the Written Gospel: The Hermeneutics of Speaking and Writing in the Synoptic Tradition, Mark, Paul and Q*. Indianapolis: Indiana University Press, 2nd edn. 1997.

Kjärgaard, Mogens Stiller. *Metaphor and Parable: A Systematic Analysis of the Specific Structure and Cognitive Function of the*

Synoptic Similes and Parables qua Metaphores. Leiden: E. J. Brill, 1986.

Klauck, Hans-Josef. *Die religiöse Umwelt des Urchristentums* (vols. 1 and 2). Stuttgart: Verlag W. Kohlhammer, 1996.

Klijn, A.F.J. *An Introduction to the New Testament*. trans. M. van der Vathorst-Smit. Leiden: E. J. Brill, 1967.

Kloppenborg, John S. *The Formation of Q: Trajectories in Ancient Wisdom Collections*. Philadelphia: Fortress Press, 1987.

— In correspondence 9 November 2000 with Robert J. Miller from electronic seminar on his book *Excavating Q*, hosted by the Synoptic-L list and moderated by Mark Goodacre and Stephen Carlson.

— *The Sayings of Jesus in the Didache*. M.A. thesis, University of St. Michael's College, unpublished, 1976.

— 'The Transformation of Moral Exhortation in Didache 1–5', in Jefford, *The Didache in Context.* Leiden: E.J. Brill, 1995.

Koester, Helmut. *Ancient Christian Gospels, Their History and Development*. London: SCM Press, 1990.

— *History and Literature of Early Christianity*. New York: Walter De Gruyer, 2nd edn. 1987.

— *Synoptische Überlieferung bei den Apostolischen Vätern*. TU 65, Berlin: Akademie, 1957.

Köster, Helmut, and James M. Robinson. *Entwicklungslinien Durch die welt des Frühen Christentums*. Türbingen: J. C. B. Mohr, 1971.

Kutsch, Ernst. 'Passover in the New Testament', in 'Passover', in Roth, *Encyclopedia Judaica*. Jerusalem: Kenter Publishing House, 1972.

Lambden, Stephen. 'Prophecy in the Johannine Farewell Discourse', in Momen, *Scripture and Revelation*. Oxford: George Ronald, 1997.

Lawson, B.T. 'The Crucifixion of Jesus in the Qur'án and Qur'ánic Commentary: A Historical Survey', in *The Bulletin of the Henry Martyn Institute of Islamic Studies*, 1991, vol. 10, no. 2, pp. 34–52 and vol. 10, no. 3, pp. 6–40.

— 'The Dangers of Reading', in Momen, *Scripture and Revelation*. Oxford: George Ronald, 1997.

— 'Seeing Double, The Covenant and the Tablet of Aḥmad or Who is the King, the All-Knowing, the Wise?' Unpublished.

Layton, Bentley (ed.). *Nag Hammadi Codex II, 2–7*. Leiden: E. J. Brill, 1989.

— 'The Sources, Date and Transmission of the Didache 1.3b–2.1', in *Harvard Theological Review* 61, 1968.

Leipoldt, Johannes.'The Resurrection Stories'. trans. Eric Weinberger, in *Journal of Higher Criticism*, vol. 4, no. 2, Fall 1997. *Theologische Literaturzeitung* 12 (1948), pp. 740–2.

Lewis, Agnes S. *Light on the Four Gospels from the Sinai Palimpsest*. London: Williams & Norgate, 1913.

Liddell, H. G., and Scott. *An Intermediate Greek-English Lexicon*. Oxford: Oxford University Press, 1889.

Lights of Guidance: A Bahá'í Reference File. Compiled by Helen Hornby. New Delhi: Bahá'í Publishing Trust, 2nd edn. 1988.

Lovelich, Harry (ed.). *Le Saint Graal: The History of the Holy Grail*, re-ed. Frederick J. Furnivall and Dorothy Kempe. Millwood, NY: Kraus Reprint, 1973.

Luedemann, Gerd. *The Resurrection of Jesus: History, Experience, Theology*. trans. John Bowden. Minneapolis: Fortress Press, 1994.

Luther, Martin. *Dr. Martin Luther's Saemmtliche Schriften*. trans. Erika B. Flores. ed. Johannes G. Walch. St. Louis: Concordia Publishing House, n.d.

— *Triglot Concordia: The Symbolical Books of the Ev. Lutheran Church*. F. Bente and W. H. Dan (eds.). St. Louis: Concordia Publishing House, 1921.

Lyon, Jeffrey P. *Syriac Gospel Translations: A Comparison of the Language and Translations Method used in the Old Syriac, the Diatessaron, and the Peshitto*. Louvain: n.p., 1994.

Maccoby, Hyam. *Paul and Hellenism*. London: SCM Press, 1991.

Mack, Burton L. *The Lost Gospel: The Book of Q and Christian Origins*. New York: HarperSanFrancisco, 1993.

— *A Myth of Innocence: Mark and Christian Origins*. Minneapolis: Fortress Press, 1988.

— *Who Wrote the New Testament? The Making of the Christian Myth*. San Francisco: HarperSanFrancisco, 1995.

Malbon, Elizabeth S., and Edgar V. McKnight (eds.). *The New Literary Criticism and the New Testament*. Sheffield: Sheffield Academic Press, 1994.

Malina, Bruce J. 'Early Christian Groups: Using small group formation theory to explain Christian organizations', in Esler, *Modelling Early Christianity*. London: Routledge, 1995.

— *The Social World of Jesus and the Gospels*. London: Routledge, 1996.

Manen, W.C. Van. 'Romans (Epistle)'. *Encyclopaedia Biblica*. 4 vols. New York: Macmillan, 1899–1903, vol. 4.

Manson, T. W. *The Sayings of Jesus, As Recorded in the Gospels according to St. Matthew and St. Luke Arranged with Introduction and Commentary.* London: SCM Press, 1954.

Mara, M. G. *Évanggile de Pierre*. Paris: Les Éditions du Cerf, 1973.

Marguerat, Daniel. 'La Troisiéme Quête du Jésus de l'histoire', in *Recherches de Science Religieuse*, tome 87, no. 3, Juillet-Septembre 1999.

McGlinn, Sen. 'Introduction to the Bible in Modern Research', in Sen McGlinn (ed.). *Soundings: Essays in Bahá'í Theology*. Dunedin, New Zealand: Open Circle Publishing, 1988.

McGrath, Alistair E. *Historical Theology: An Introduction to the History of Christian Thought*. Malden: Blackwell Publishers Ltd., 1998.

McKenzie, John L. 'The Gospel According to Matthew', in Brown, *The Jerome Biblical Commentary*. London: Geoffrey Chapman, 1967.

McLean, Jack (ed.). *Revisioning the Sacred: New Perspectives on a Bahá'í Theology*. Los Angeles: Kalimát Press, 1997.

Meeks, Wayne. A. *The First Urban Christians: The Social World of the Apostle Paul*. Yale: Yale University Press, 1983.

— *The Origins of Christian Morality: The First Two Centuries*. Yale: Yale University Press, 1993.

Meir, John P. *A Marginal Jew: Rethinking the Historical Jesus*. 2 vols. New York: Doubleday 1991, 1994.

Metzger, Bruce M. *The Early Versions of the New Testament*. Oxford: Clarendon Press, 1977.

— and Michael D. Coogan (eds.). *The Oxford Companion to the Bible*. Oxford: Oxford Publishing Company, 1993.

Milavec, Aaron. 'Distinguishing True and False Prophets: The Protective Wisdom of the Didache', *Journal of Early Christianity*, 2, pp. 117–36, John Hopkins University Press, 1994.

— 'The Saving Efficacy of the Burning Process in Didache 16.5', in Jefford, *The Didache in Context*. Leiden: E.J. Brill, 1995.

Miller, Robert J. 'Can the Historical Jesus be Made Safe for Orthodoxy? A Critique of The Jesus Quest by Ben Witherington III', in *Journal of Higher Criticism* 4/1, Spring 1997.

— *The Complete Gospels: Annotated Scholars Version*. Sonoma: Polebridge Press, 1992.

Mitchell, Nathan. 'Baptism in the Didache', in Jefford, *The Didache in Context*. Leiden: E.J. Brill, 1995.

M'Neile, Alan Hugh. *The Gospel According to St. Matthew: The Greek Text with Introduction, Notes, and Indices*. London: Macmillan, 1952.

Momen, Moojan. *An Introduction to Shi'i Islam*. Oxford: George Ronald, 1985.

— (ed.). *Scripture and Revelation*. Oxford: George Ronald, 1997.

— (ed.). *Selections from the Writings of E. G. Browne on the Bábí and Bahá'í Religions*. Oxford: George Ronald, 1987.

Monneret de Villard, Ugo. *Le Leggende Orientali sui Magi Evangelici*. Vatican: Biblioteca Apostolica Vaticana, 1952.

Müller, Mogens. *Det Gamle Testamente som Kristen bog*. København: Anis, 1997.

— *Kommentar til Mattæusevangeliet*. Aarhus: Aarhus Universitetsforlag, 2000.

— *Mattæusevangeliet fortolket*. København: Det Danske Bibelselskab, 1998.

Murphy-O'Connor, Jerome. 'Jerusalem', in Metzger and Coogan, *The Oxford Companion to the Bible*. Oxford: Oxford Publishing Company, 1993.

Myers, Allen C. (ed.). *The Eerdmans Bible Dictionary*. Michigan: William B. Eerdmans, 1987.

Neirynck, Frans. 'The Apocryphal Gospels and the Gospel of Mark', in Sevrin, *The New Testament in Early Christianity*. Leuven: Leuven University Press, 1989.

— 'The Minor Agreements and Q', in Piper, *The Gospel Behind the Gospels*. New York: E.J. Brill, 1995.

Nepper-Christensen, Paul. *Matthæusevangeliet, En Kommentar*. Århus: Anis, 1988.

Nestle, Eberhard. *Einführung in das greichische Neu Testament*. Göttingen: Vandenhoeck & Ruprecht, 1909.

Nestorius. *The Bazaar of Heracleides*. Driver, G. R. and Leonard Hodgson (eds.). Oxford: Clarendon Press, 1925.

Neusner, Jacob. 'The Absoluteness of Christianity and the Uniqueness of Judaism: Why Salvation is not of the Jews', in Neusner and Green, *Judaism and Christianity in the First Century*. New York: Garland Publishing, 1990.

— *Judaism and Its Social Metaphors: Israel in the History of Jewish Thought*. New York: Cambridge University Press, 1989.

— *The Religious Study of Judaism*. Lanhem: University Press of America, 1986.

— et al. (eds.). *The Social World of Formative Christianity and Judaism*. Philadelphia: Fortress Press, 1988.

— and William S. Green (eds.). *Judaism and Christianity in the First Century*. New York: Garland Publishing, 1990.

Newman, John H. *An Essay on the Development of Christian Doctrine*. New York: Doubleday Image Book, 1960.

Neyrey, Jerome J. 'Loss of wealth, loss of family and loss of honour: The cultural context of the original markarisms in Q', in Esler, *Modelling Early Christianity*. London: Routledge, 1995.

Niederwimmer, Kurt. *The Didache*. Fortress Press, 1998.

Nielsen, Helge K. *Nytestamentlig Græsk, Formlære og Syntaks*. Ringkjøbing: Forlaget Aros, 1974.

Nikiprowetzky, V. 'L'Exégèse de Philon d'Alexandrie dans le De Gigantibus et le Quod Deus sit Immutabilis' in Winston, David, and John M. Dillon (eds.). *Two Treatises of Philo of Alexandria* Chico: Scholars Press, 1983.

Noack, Bent. *Guds rige i os eller iblandt os*. Copenhagen: GCE Gads, 1967.

Nutt, Alfred. *Studies on the Legend of the Holy Grail: With Especial Reference to the Hypothesis of Its Celtic Origin*. New York: Cooper Square, 1965.

Osterhaven, M. E. 'Lord's Supper, Views of', in Elwell, *Evangelical Dictionary of Theology*. Minnesota: Baker Book House, 1984.

Pagels, Elaine. *The Gnostic Gospels*. London: Penguin Books, 3rd edn. 1990.

— *The Origin of Satan*. New York: Random House, 1995.

Paludan, Peter. 'Tempel og synagoge i datidens jødedom', in Pedersen, *Den Nytestamentlige Tids Historie*. Århus: Aarhus Universitetsforlag, 1994.

Pardee, Nancy. 'The Curse that Saves (Didache 16.5)', in Jefford, *The Didache in Context*. Leiden: E.J. Brill, 1995.

Parrott, D. M. (ed.). *Nag Hammadi Codices V, 2–5 and VI with Papyrus Berolinensis 8502*. Leiden: E. J. Brill, 1979.

Pasquier, Anne (ed.). *L'Évangile Selon Marie*. Quebec: Les Presses De L'Université Laval, 1983.

Patterson , Stephen J. 'Askesis and the Early Christian Tradition', in Vaage and Wimbush, *Asceticism and the New Testament*. New York: Routledge, 1999.

— 'Didache 11–13: The Legacy of Radical Itinerancy in Early Christianity', in Jefford, *The Didache in Context*. Leiden: E.J. Brill, 1995.

Pedersen, E. T. *Markusevangeliet fortolket*. København: Det Danske Bibelselskab, 1985.

Pedersen, Sigfried (ed.). *Den Nytestamentlige Tids Historie*. Århus: Aarhus Universitetsforlag, 1994.

— (ed.). *Nytestamentlige Studier*. Århus: Forlaget AROS, 1976.

Piper, Ronald A. (ed.). *The Gospel Behind the Gospels*. New York: E.J. Brill, 1995.

Plummer, Alfred. *A Critical and Exegetical Commentary on the Second Epistle of St. Paul to the Corinthians*. Edinburgh: T. & T. Clark, 1915.

Powell, Mark A. *Jesus as a Figure in History: How Modern Historians View the Man from Galilee*. Louisville: Westminster John Knox Press, 1998.

Pratscher, Wilhelm. *Der Herrenbruder Jakobus und die Jakobustradition*. Göttingen: Vandenhoeck und Ruprecht, 1987.

Quispel, G. *Makarius, Das Thomasevangelium und das Lied von der Perle*. Leiden: E. J. Brill, 1967.

Reed, Jonathan A. 'The Hebrew Epic and the Didache', in Jefford, *The Didache in Context*. Leiden: E.J. Brill, 1995.

Reynolds, Stephen. *The Christian Religious Tradition*. Belmont: Wadsworth Publishing Company, 1977.

Riggs, John. 'The Sacred Food of Didache 9–10 and Second Century Ecclesiologies' in Jefford, *The Didache in Context*. Leiden: E.J. Brill, 1995.

Robinson, James M. (ed.). *The Nag Hammadi Library*. Leiden: E. J. Brill, 2nd edn. 1988.

— *A New Quest of the Historical Jesus*. London: SCM Press, 1959.

Rordorf, W. 'Le problème de la transmision textuelle de Didachè 1.3b–2.1', in *Überlieferungsgeschictliche Untersuchungen*. F. Paschke (ed.). Texte und Untersuchungen zur Geschichte der altchristlichen Literatur, vol. 125, pp. 499–513. Berlin: Akademie-Verlag, 1981.

Rosenthal, Franz. *A Grammar of Biblical Aramaic*. Wiesbaden: Harrassowitz Verlag, 6th edn. 1995.

Roth, Cecil (ed.). *Encyclopedia Judaica*. Jerusalem: Kenter Publishing House, 1972.

Røsæg, Nils A. *Jesus from Galilee and Political Power: A Socio-Historical Investigation*. Oslo: The Free Faculty of Theology (Det Teologiske Menighetsfakultet), 1990.

Rudolph, Kurt. *Gnosis: The Nature and History of Gnosticism*. Robert M. Wilson (ed.). trans. P. W. Coxon, Robert M. Wilson and K. H. Kuhn. San Francisco: HarperSanFrancisco, 1987.

Russell, D. S. 'Apocalyptic Literature', in Metzger and Coogan, *The Oxford Companion to the Bible*. Oxford: Oxford Publishing Company, 1993.

Saldarni, Anthony J. 'Political and Social Roles of the Pharisees and Scribes in Galilee', in *Society of Biblical Literature*, vol. 124, 1988.

Sanders, E. P. 'Common Judaism and the Synagogue in the First Century', in Fine, *Jews, Christians, and Polytheists in the Ancient Synagogue*. Oxford: Routledge, 1999.

— *The Historical Figure of Jesus*. London: Penguin Books, 1993.

— *Jesus and Judaism*. Philadelphia: Fortress Press, 1985.

— *Jewish Law from Jesus to the Mishnah*. London: SCM Press, 1990.

— *Paul and Palestinian Judaism*. London: SCM Press, 1977.

Sandmel, Samuel. 'Palestinian and Hellenistic Judaism and Christianity: The Question of the Comfortable Theory', originally in *Journal of Biblical Literature*, XC (1971); reprinted in Neusner and Green, *Judaism and Christianity in the First Century*, vol. 3. New York: Garland Publishing, 1990.

Sayers, Dorothy L. *The Man Born to be King: A Play-cycle on the Life of our Lord and Saviour Jesus Christ*. San Francisco: Ignatius Press, 1990.

Schiffman, Lawrence H. 'The Sadducean Origins of the Dead Sea Scroll Sect', in Shanks, *Understanding the Dead Sea Scrolls*. London: SPCK, 2nd edn.1993.

Schmidt, Karl O. *Die geheimen Heren-Worte das Thomas-Evangelium*. München: Drei Eichen Verlag, 2nd edn. 1984.

Schneemelcher, Wilhelm. *New Testament Apocrypha*. Cambridge: James Clarke & Co., 1991.

Schnelle, Udo. *The History and Theology of the New Testament Writings*. London: SCM Press, 1998.

Schoeps, Hans J. *Aus Frühchristlicher Zeit*. Tübingen: J.C.B. Mohr, 1950.

Schonfield, Hugh J. *According to the Hebrews*. London: Duckworth, 1937.

Schottroff, Luise. 'Itinerant prophetesses: A feminist analysis of the sayings source Q', in Piper, *The Gospel Behind the Gospels*. New York: E.J. Brill, 1995.

Schwartzman, Sylvan D. 'How well did the Synoptic Evangelists know the Synagogue?', in Neusner and Green, *Judaism and*

Christianity in the First Century (originally *Hebrew Union College Annual*, no. 24, 1953).

Schweitzer, Albert. *Paul and His Interpreters: A Critical History (orig. Geschichte Der Paulinischen Forschung)*. trans. W. Montgomery. London: Adam & Charles Black, 1956.

— *The Quest for the Historical Jesus: A Critical Study of Its Progress from Reimarus to Wrede (orig. Von Reimarus zu Wrede)*. trans. W. Montgomery, London: John Hopkins University Press, 2nd edn.1998.

Sears, William. *Thief in the Night: The Case of the Missing Millennium*. Oxford: George Ronald, 1990.

Selman, Martin, and Martin Manser. *The Macmillan Dictionary of the Bible*. London: Macmillan, 1998.

Sevrin, Jean-Marie (ed.). *The New Testament in Early Christianity: La réception des écrits néotestamentaires dans le christianisme primitif*. Leuven: Leuven University Press, 1989.

Shanks, Hershel (ed.). *Understanding the Dead Sea Scrolls*. London: SPCK, 2nd edn. 1993.

Shoghi Effendi. *God Passes By*. Wilmette, IL: Bahá'í Publishing Trust, 2nd edn. 1979.

— *The Promised Day is Come*. Wilmette, IL: Bahá'í Publishing Trust, rev. edn. 1980.

— *The World Order of Bahá'u'lláh*. Wilmette, IL: Bahá'í Publishing Trust, 2nd edn. 1969.

Smith, Jonathan Z. *Drudgery Divine: On the Comparison of Early Christianities and the Religions of Late Antiquity*. London: University of London, 1990.

Smith, Morton. *Jesus the Magician*. New York: Harper & Row, 1978.

Smith, Peter. *A Concise Encyclopedia of the Bahá'í Faith*. Oxford: Oneworld, 2000.

Smyth, Herbert W. *Greek Grammar*. Harvard: Harvard University Press, 1956.

Sours, Michael W. 'Immanence and Transcendence in Theophanic Symbolism', in *The Journal of Bahá'í Studies*, vol. 5, no. 2, June-September 1992.

— *The Prophecies of Jesus*. Oxford: Oneworld, 1991.

— *A Study of Bahá'u'lláh's Tablet to the Christians*. Oxford: Oneworld, 1990.

Star of the West, vol. 2, no. 13 and vol. 9, no. 1. Oxford: George Ronald, rpt. 1984.

Stark, Rodney. *The Rise of Christianity: A Sociologist Reconsiders History*. Princeton: Princeton University Press, 1996.

Stendahl, Krister (ed.). *The Scrolls and the New Testament*. New York: The Crossroad Publishing Company, 1992.

Stevenson, J. *Creeds, Councils and Controversies*. London: SPCK, 2nd edn. 1989.

Stockman, Robert. 'The Bahá'í Faith and Higher Biblical Criticism'. Unpublished.

Strack, H. L., and Günter Stemberger. *Introduction to the Talmud and Midrash*. trans. Markus Bockmuehl. Minneapolis: Fortress Press, 1992.

Taherzadeh, Adib. *The Revelation of Bahá'u'lláh*, vol. 1. Oxford: George Ronald, 1974.

Tanzer, 'Judaisms of the First Century', in Metzger and Coogan, *The Oxford Companion to the Bible*. Oxford: Oxford Publishing Company, 1993.

Termolen, Rosel. *Apokalypsen, Das Buch der geheimen Offenbarungen*. Augsburg: Pattloch Verlag, 1990.

Theissen, Gerd. *The Gospels in Context*. trans. Linda M. Maloney. Minneapolis: Fortress Press, 1991.

— *Sociology of Early Palestinian Christianity*. trans. John Bowden. Philadelphia: Fortress Press, 1978.

— *A Theory of Primitive Christian Religion*. trans. John Bowden. London: SCM Press, 1999.

— *Urchristliche Wundergeschichten*. Bonn: Güntersloher Verlagshaus, 1974.

— and Annette Merz. *The Historical Jesus: A Comprehensive Guide (German: Der Historische Jesus, Ein Lehrbuch)*. trans. John Bowden. Minneapolis: Fortress Press, 1998.

Tuckett, Christopher M. *Nag Hammadi and The Gospel Tradition*. Edinburgh: T. & T. Clark, 1986.

— *Q and the History of Early Christianity*. Edinburgh: T. & T. Clark, 1996.

— 'Synoptic Tradition in the Didache', in Sevrin, *The New Testament in Early Christianity*. Leuven: Leuven University Press, 1989.

Tuilier, André. 'La Didachè et le Problème Synoptique', in Jefford, *The Didache in Context*. Leiden: E.J. Brill, 1995.

Uro, Risto. 'John the Baptist and the Jesus Movement: What does Q tell us?' in Piper, *The Gospel Behind the Gospels*. New York: E.J. Brill, 1995.

Vaage, Leif E. 'Q and Cynicism: On Comparison and Social Identity', in Piper, *The Gospel Behind the Gospels*. New York: E.J. Brill, 1995.

— and Vincent L. Wimbush (eds.). *Asceticism and the New Testament*. New York: Routledge, 1999.

van der Horst, Pieter W. 'Was the Synagogue a Place of Sabbath Worship before 70 CE?', in Fine, *Jews, Christians, and Polytheists in the Ancient Synagogue*. Oxford: Routledge, 1999.

Vanderkam, James C. *The Dead Sea Scrolls Today*. Michigan: William B Eerdmans, 1994.

Van Der Loos, H. *The Miracles of Jesus*. Leiden: E. J. Brill, 2nd edn. 1968.

Van Groningen, G. *First Century Gnosticism: Its Origin and Motifs*. Leiden: E. J. Brill, 1967.

Varneda, Pere V. *The Historical Method of Flavius Josephus*. Leiden: E. J. Brill, 1986.

Vatican Council II. *Catechism of the Catholic Church*. New York: Doubleday, 1995.

Vermes, Geza. *The Changing Faces of Jesus*. London: Penguin Books, 2000.

— *The Dead Sea Scrolls in English*. London: Penguin Books, 3rd edn. 1987.

— *The Religion of Jesus the Jew*. London: SCM Press, 1993.

Via, Dan O. *The Parables: The Literary and Existential Dimension*. Philadelphia: Fortress Press, 1963.

Vine, W. E. et al. (eds.). *Vine's Complete Expository Dictionary of the Old and New Testament Words*. Nashville: Thomas Nelson, 1985.

Warfield, Benjamin B. *Biblical Doctrines*. Pennsylvania: The Banner of Truth Trust, 2nd edn. 1988.

Watt, William M. *Companion to the Qur'an*. Oxford: Oneworld, 2nd edn. 1994.

— *Religious Truth For Our Time*. Oxford: Oneworld, 1995.

Wedderburn, A. J. M. *Baptism and Resurrection: Studies in Pauline Theology against Its Graeco-Roman Background*. Tübingen: J. C. B. Mohr, 1987.

Williams, Michael A. *Rethinking 'Gnosticism': An Argument for Dismantling a Dubious Category*. Princeton: Princeton University Press, 1996.

Williams, Rowan. 'Between the Cherubim: The Empty Tomb and the Empty Throne', in D'Costa, *Resurrection Reconsidered*. Oxford: Oneworld, 1996.

Williamson, Ronald. *Jews in the Hellenistic World: Philo*. Cambridge: Cambridge University Press, 1989.

Wilson, Ian. *Jesus: The Evidence*. London: Weidenfeld & Nicolson, 1984.

Winston, David, and John M. Dillon (eds.). *Two Treatises of Philo of Alexandria: A Commentary on De Gigantibus and Quod Deus Sit Immutabilis*. Chico: Scholars Press, 1983.

Wise, Michael O. 'Languages of Palestine', in Green and McKnight, *Dictionary of Jesus and the Gospels*. Downers Grove, IL: InterVarsity Press, 1992.

Witherington III, Ben. *Jesus, Paul and the End of the World*. United Kingdom: The Paternoster Press, 1992.

Wright, G. Ernest. 'The Samaritans at Shechem', in Dexinger and Pummer, *Die Samaritaner*. Darmstadt: Wissenschaftliche Buchgesellschaft Darmstadt, 1992.

Zeitlin, Irving M. *Jesus and the Judaism of His Time*. Cambridge: Polity Press, 1988.

Zodhiates, Spiros. *The Complete Word Study Dictionary: New Testament*. Chattanooga: AMG Publishers, 1993.

Notes and References

Introduction

1. Bultmann, *Jesus and the Word*, p. 11.

Chapter 1: ***The Critical Sciences***

2. Fitzmyer in his article '"4QTestimonia" and the New Testament', collected in his *Essays on the Semitic Background of the New Testament*, proposes that the 4QTestimonia belongs to a genre of florilegia, that is to say, an anthology of prophetic proof-texts. It is further proposed that Matthew's various misattributions, introductory formulas, text divergences from the Greek Old Testament (see LXX below) and compound quotations each indicate that his prophetic texts were not collected by the evangelist himself. It is also possible that Paul used such a collection for his epistles.
3. For a reconstruction of Q, see Miller, *Complete Gospels*, pp. 249–300, with introduction and notes by Arland D. Jacobsen.
4. The semeia-Quelle hypothesis, which was proposed by Rudolf Bultmann, supposes that the enumeration of some of the miracles in John is due to a source he used (see Bultmann, *Das Evangelium des Johannes*, p. 78). For a more recent (and more extensive) reconstruction of this source see Miller, *Complete Gospels*, pp. 175–93, with text, introduction and notes by Robert T. Fortna; and Fortna's own book *The Fourth Gospel and its Predecessor*. Fortna argues for a pre-Johannine joining of passion and miracle stories (see ibid. pp. 205–20). Fortna's findings were confirmed

by Edwin D. Freed and Russell B. Hunt's stylistic analysis presented in their article 'Fortna's Signs-source in John', in JBL 1975, vol. 94, pp. 563–79.

5. See Dodd, *Apostolic Preaching*.
6. Dunn, *Unity and Diversity in the New Testament*, p. 328.
7. Conzelmann and Lindemann, *Arbeitsbuch zum Neuen Testament*, p. 7.
8. Koester, *History and Literature of Early Christianity*, pp. 8–11.
9. Dunn, *Unity and Diversity in the New Testament*, p. 376.
10. Koester, *Ancient Christian Gospels*, p. 80.
11. Davis, *Gospel of Thomas and Christian Wisdom*, p. 3.
12. Koester, *Ancient Christian Gospels*, p. 85.
13. Davis, *Gospel of Thomas and Christian Wisdom*, devotes all of chapter 2 to the question 'Is the Gospel of Thomas Gnostic?' (pp. 18–35), to which his resounding answer is 'no'.
14. See Koester, *Ancient Christian Gospels*, and Davis, *Gospel of Thomas and Christian Wisdom*. Crossan states that the Gospel of Thomas lies on the 'ambiguous borderline between Gnostic and Catholic Christianity' (*Four Other Gospels*, p. 34). K. O. Schmidt calls the author of Thomas 'a mystic' (*Das Thomas-Evangelium*, p. 12). Quispel states that Thomas is no more Gnostic than is John (*Makarius, Das Thomas-evangelium und das Lied von der Perle*, p. 71).
15. Koester, *Ancient Christian Gospels*, pp. 81–2.
16. Crossan, *Four Other Gospels*, p. 28.
17. For a comprehensive look at authorities that pronounced it as dependent, see Mara, *Évangile de Pierre*, pp. 17–18.
18. The latest conceivable date.
19. The work is quoted by Eusebius (H.E. 5.22.1), who dates the book from 180 to 192.
20. The most thorough treatment of Crossan's hypothesis is to be found in his book *The Cross that Spoke*.
21. Koester, *Ancient Christian Gospels*, pp. 219–20.
22. Miller, *Complete Gospels*, pp. 189–93.
23. Crossan, *Four Other Gospels*, pp. 91–121, and Koester, *Ancient Christian Gospels*, pp. 293–303. For a criticism of

the independence of both Peter and Secret Mark see Frans Neirynck's paper 'The Apocryphal Gospels and the Gospel of Mark', in Sevrin, *The New Testament in Early Christianity*, pp. 123–70.

24. See King's introduction in Robinson, *Nag Hammadi Library*, pp. 523–4.
25. Tuckett writes, '. . . it is impossible to say whether G[ospel of]Mary is dependent on Matthew or Luke or a prior source' (*Nag Hammadi and the Gospel Tradition,* p. 37).
26. Jefford, *The Sayings of Jesus in the Teaching of the Twelve Apostles*, pp. 3–17.
27. Paul Sebastian, Jean-Paul Audet, Andre Taulier and Willy Rordorf were proponents of this school, while Edouard Massaux suggested that the Didache was dependent on the Gospel of Matthew (Jefford, ibid. pp. 4–7).
28. Proponents include Adolf von Harnack, Adam Krawutzcky, Adolf Hilgenfeld, Theodore Zahn, G. Wolhenberg, Paul Drews, J. Leipoldt, Rudolf Knopf, Klaus Wengst and Wolf Dietrich but with the highly significant dissenting voices of F. X. Funk and Helmut Köster. The latter contend that at least some of the traditions appear to have been derived from an oral source (Jefford, ibid. pp. 7–11).
29. Proponents include F. W. Farrar, Philip Schaff, Canon Spence, R. D. Hitcock, Francis Brown, Charles Taylor, B. B. Warfield, J. Rendel Harris, Kirsopp Lake, J. B. Lightfoot, Jan Greyvenstein, J. Armitage Robinson, James Muilenburg, F. C. Burkitt, R. H. Connolly, J. M. Creed, B. H. Streeter, Richard Glover, F. E. Vokes, John S. Kloppenborg, Edgar J. Goodspeed, Robert A. Kraft, George Eldon Ladd, Bentley Layton and Arthur Vööbus (Jefford, ibid. pp. 11–17.) More recently, as we shall see, Crossan has taken a position that seems closer to the French than most British-Americans are willing to consider.

Chapter 2: ***The Jewish Context***

30. Tanzer, 'Judaisms of the first century', in Metzger and Coogan, *Oxford Companion to the Bible*, p. 391.
31. Chilton, *Judaism in the New Testament*, p. 19.
32. Malina, 'Early Christian Groups, Using small group theory to explain Christian organizations', in Esler, *Modelling Early Christianity*, p. 99.
33. For a description of the Mishnah, see below.
34. Zeitlin, *Jesus and the Judaism of His Time*, p. 15.
35. ibid. p. 14.
36. See Elliott, 'The Jewish Messianic Movement: From Faction to Sect', in Esler, *Modelling Early Christianity*.
37. Malina, 'Early Christian Groups, Using small group theory to explain Christian organizations', in ibid. p. 107.
38. Chilton, *Judaism in the New Testament*, p. 29. Neusner, on the other hand, in his article 'The Absoluteness of Christianity and the Uniqueness of Judaism' (see Neusner and Green, *Judaism and Christianity in the First Century*, p. 658) proposes that the Pharisees did not have a fictive family nor were their 'social affiliations . . . homologous'.
39. Zeitlin, *Jesus and the Judaism of His Time*, p. 16.
40. Horsley and Hanson, *Bandits, Prophets, and Messiahs*, p. 27.
41. Jewish historian. Born Flavius Josephus in 37 CE in Jerusalem, died in Rome at the beginning of the 2nd century.
42. Jewish philosopher. Born Philo Judaeus in Alexandria, Egypt, sometime in the first decade BCE, died 45 CE.
43. The concept of man being both a spiritual and material entity was alien to the ancient Judaic religion. The concept of the soul, as we understand it today, was likewise very rare in the Old Testament. The formulation of Genesis clearly shows this: 'and man became a living soul' (2:7 KJV). He was not given a soul, he became it, just like the animals: 'Let the earth bring forth living souls after their kind, cattle, and creeping thing, and beast of the earth, after their kind' (1:24 Darby). Likewise the concept of the God

of Israel being the only real God was also a later development: 'Thou shalt have no other gods before me' (Exodus 20:3 KJV). The first commandment does not imply that there are no other gods, just that they should not be followed, for He is 'a jealous God' (20:5).

44. See also the parable in Matthew 13:52 discussed in chapter 5.
45. This is discussed in detail in chapters 5 and 6.
46. Josephus, *Antiquities of the Jews*, 17:2:4.
47. ibid. 18:1:3.
48. ibid. 13:10:6.
49. The Mishnah (Baba Qamma 8:1) prescribes precisely how the value of an injury is calculated.
50. A Jew not living in Israel but being an expatriate because of war. This is discussed further in chapter 7.
51. Mishnah, Aboth 1:12–15, cited in *A Short Reader in Judaism*, p. 57. The translation given here varies greatly from Danby's but is fairly close to Neusner's.
52. Mishnah Aboth 3:11. Horsley, *Archaeology, History and Society in Galilee*, pp. 186–7.
53. Only Acts (23:8) lists unbelief in spirits and angels. Though most accept this statement, Joshua Gutmann, in his section 'Among the Jewish Sects' in 'Angels and Angelology' in *Encyclopedia Judaica,* states that this is 'undoubtedly a false assumption, derived from the Sadducees' rejection of apocalyptic teachings' (p. 962). Gutmann, however, presents no evidence to support the supposition. One point could be raised in support of this position, namely the silence in Josephus regarding this rejection (*Antiquities* 18:1:4, *Wars* 2:8:14). This may be accounted for by recognizing that there is no precise Greek equivalent to the Jewish conception of angels; angels are hardly mentioned by Josephus at all. Philo overcame this by identifying angels with the demons of Greek philosophers (see Alexander Altmann's section 'In Jewish Philosophy' of the same article, p. 972). There were certain conservative trends in the prophetic tradition which seem to have

removed angels from the scene (see Bernars J. Bamberger's section 'Silence of the Prophets' in the above-mentioned article, p. 959). Fletcher-Louis (*Luke-Acts: Angels Christology and Soteriology*, pp. 57–61) proposes that Luke actually conglomerates angel and spirit into one concept and contextualizes it specifically to the afterlife. In conclusion, the present author finds no reason to doubt Acts' assertion that the Sadducees rejected the notion of angels which was indeed prominent in the apocalyptic tradition that they so disliked. Whether they allowed for angels outside a resurrection context, as Fletcher-Louis proposes, is difficult to ascertain.

54. The covenant of God, as used in this context, means that God sends His Law through His Prophets and by obedience to that Law we receive God's protection.
55. Josephus, *Antiquities of the Jews*, 13:10:6.
56. By this we should not understand a personal survival. In early Old Testament thought one came from dust and returned to dust (Genesis 3:19), that was it. It is Yahweh whose breath animates the living (man and animal alike) and unto Him His breath returns upon death. All must die. The righteous lives long and well and becomes the father of many children; the unrighteous lives a short and miserable life and his family will, if it survives, bear the misfortune of the head of the family (see Jensen, *Gammel Testamentlig Religion*, pp. 82–91).
57. De Jonge in his article 'The so-called Pseudepigrapha of the Old Testament and Early Christianity' states that 'in the Testaments of the Twelve Patriarchs we find severe criticism of the leaders of Israel . . . at the same time, the desire to stress the continuity and connection in the persons of the patriarchs, the fathers of Israel' (in Borgen, *New Testament and Hellenistic Judaism*, p. 64).
58. See Tanzer, 'Judaisms of the First Century', in Metzger and Coogan, *Oxford Companion to the Bible*, p. 393.
59. The Law (literally the five-volumed work), the first five books of the Bible, attributed to Moses.

60. Mishnah, Niddah 4:2.
61. There are other problems involved in identifying the Essenes with the community in Qumran. In Baigent and Leigh's *The Dead Sea Scrolls Deception* some of these are pointed out: 1) Philo states that the Essenes did not have a cult of animal sacrifice and yet the Temple Scroll has precise instructions in this regard and 2) Herod the Great was, according to Josephus, on good terms with the Essenes but Qumran literature seems very hostile towards the Herodian dynasty (pp.170–1). It seems likely that the fact that the Qumran sect kept a different calendar meant that the day of sacrifice would be different from that of Jerusalem and would therefore be understood as not being a real sacrifice. The discussion of the identity of the Qumran sect has at present reached a fairly strong consensus on the Essene. Connections with early Christianity have been summarily dismissed, particularly through the carbon dating of significant texts. Baigent and Leigh, following Robert Eisenman, for example, have hypothesized extensively that the Teacher of Righteousness is James the brother of Jesus while Paul is the Liar found in the Habakkuk Commentary (see chapter 13, *The Dead Sea Scrolls Deception*), a text that is radio carbon dated to prior to the birth of Jesus (see Vermes, *The Complete Dead Sea Scrolls in English*, p. 478). For a discussion for and against the Essene hypothesis read Lawrence H. Schiffman, 'The Sadducean Origins of the Dead Sea Scroll Sect', in Shanks, *Understanding the Dead Sea Scrolls*, pp. 35–49 and James C. Vanerkam's response in 'The People of the Dead Sea Scrolls: Essenes or Sadducees?' in ibid. pp. 50–62. Vanderkam's more comprehensive argument is to be found in his book *The Dead Sea Scrolls Today*, pp. 71–95.
62. Pliny the Elder, *Natural History*, 5:15:73.
63. Josephus, *Jewish Wars*, 2:8:2–13.
64. Here the Community Rule would be expected to have such a reference. This has been challenged by the finding of female skeletons along with those of children in the

periphery of the Qumran cemetery. Generally, however, these can be accounted for in other ways; for example, perhaps their burial was allowed out of some attachment other than marital (see Vermes, *Dead Sea Scrolls*, pp. 8–9).

65. Three years was also the time it took for someone to gain full membership of the sect.
66. The Old Testament is divided into three canonical layers. The Law (the Pentateuch), the Prophets (Joshua, Judges, Samuel, Kings, Isaiah, Jeremiah, Ezekiel and the twelve minor prophets) and Other Writings (Psalms, Proverbs, Job, Song of Solomon, Ruth, Lamentations, Ecclesiastes, Esther, Daniel, Chronicles, Ezra and Nehemiah).
67. Josephus, *Life of Flavius Josephus*, 2.
68. ibid. pp. 27–9. See Hadas-Lebel, *Flavius Josephus, Eyewitness to Rome's First-Century Conquest of Judea*.
69. The lack of reference to angels in Josephus' summary of doctrines is typical and they are absent also in his description of the Pharisees and Sadducees, perhaps because the concept was difficult for his Gentile readers.
70. Many manuscripts add 'the Christ' but the most significant (P66, 75, a, B, C, W) omit it.
71. Adv. Hear. I 23,3.
72. Van Groningen, *First Century Gnosticism*, p. 137.
73. ibid. p. 138.
74. ibid. p. 139.
75. The Samaritan Pentateuch, cited in Cohn-Sherbok and Cohn-Sherbok, *Short Reader in Judaism*, pp. 52–3.
76. G. Ernest Wright concludes this from an archeological survey of the Samaritan ruins at Shechem in which the period in question shows a time of abandonment and reconstruction (see 'The Samaritans at Shechem' in Dexinger and Pummer, *Die Samaritaner*) while Frank Moore Cross observed a division between the Samaritan Palaeo-Hebrew script and the Judean script starting in that period (see 'Aspects of Samaritan and Jewish History' in Dexinger and Pummer, *Die Samaritaner*). Cross also places the Samaritan text in the 1st century but makes it part of

an older line of the Palestinian text family that separated itself from a Babylonian family in the 4th century BCE (see Cross, 'The Text behind the Text of the Hebrew Bible' in Shanks, *Understanding the Dead Sea Scrolls*, pp. 147–8).

77. Jizhak Ben-Zvi in 'The Origin of the Samaritans and their Tribal Divisions', in Dexinger and Pummer, *Die Samaritaner*, extrapolates the following figures: 27,000 (p. 187) were led into captivity out of a population of 60,000 (p. 188).
78. See Ezra 4:1–4 where they are the unnamed 'adversaries of Judah and Benjamin'.
79. Epiphanius of Salamis, *The Panarion of Epiphanius of Salamis*, 1.1.20.
80. Josephus, *Antiquities* 18:1:6; see also *Wars* 2:8:1.
81. Josephus, *Wars* 2:17:8.
82. ibid. 2:13:3.
83. Horsley and Hanson, *Bandits, Prophets, and Messiahs*, pp. 202–11.
84. ibid. pp. 211–16.
85. Josephus, *Wars* 4:3:3–4; see Horsley and Hanson, *Bandits, Prophets, and Messiahs*, pp. 220–3.
86. Josephus, *Wars* 4:3:6.
87. Horsley and Hanson, *Bandits, Prophets, and Messiahs*, p. 70.
88. Freyne, 'Bandits in Galilee: A Contribution to the Study of Social Conditions in First-Century Palestine' in Neusner, *The Social World of Formative Christianity and Judaism*, p. 64.
89. Josephus, *Wars* 2:12:2.
90. ibid. 1:16:2.
91. ibid. 1:10:5.
92. Josephus, *Antiquities* 20:1:1.
93. Josephus, *Wars* 2:12:2.
94. ibid. 2:12:5.
95. ibid. 2:13:2.
96. ibid. 4:9:7.
97. ibid. 7:2:1.
98. ibid. 2:4:1 and Josephus, *Antiquities* 17:10:5.
99. Josephus, *Wars* 6:5:3.

100. ibid. 6:6:2.
101. ibid. 2:8:12.
102. Josephus, *Antiquities* 17:2:4.
103. Josephus, *Wars* 3:8:9.
104. Josephus, *Antiquities* 18:4:1.
105. ibid. 20:5:1.
106. ibid. 20:8:6.
107. ibid. 20:8:10.
108. Aune, *New Testament and Its Literary Environment*, p. 12.
109. Friedländer, 'The "Pauline" Emancipation from the Law a Product of the Pre-Christian Jewish Diaspora', originally in *Jewish Quarterly Review* – Old Series', 1902, 14:265–302; reprinted in Neusner, *Judaism and Christianity in the First Century*, book 3, part 1, pp.179–216. See also Sandmel, 'Palestinian and Hellenistic Judaism and Christianity: The Question of the Comfortable Theory', originally in *Journal of Biblical Literature*, XC (1971), III, pp. 333–6, reprinted in Neusner, *Judaism and Christianity in the First Century*, book 3, part 2, pp. 223–34.
110. The term, which is borrowed from Greek, means against the Law and refers to the idea that Christians are released from observance of the Law.
111. Stark, *Rise of Christianity*, chapter 3. Alternatively, Maccoby explains it as different Gentile groupings that had been close to Jews, such as disenchanted God-fearers or those offended by Jewish claims to superiority (*Paul and Hellenism*, pp. 31–2).
112. ibid.
113. Sanders, 'Common Judaism and the Synagogue in the First Century', in Fine, *Jews, Christians, and Polytheists*, p. 2.
114. Whether there was worship has been an issue of some dispute. Pieter W. van der Horst weighs the arguments for and against in his article 'Was the Synagogue a Place of Sabbath Worship before 70 CE?' and concludes that even if one supposes that there was no prayer, the reading of the Torah would still in the Jewish mind mean worship (Fine, *Jews, Christians, and Polytheists*, p. 36).

115. Sanders, 'Common Judaism and the Synagogue in the First Century', in Fine, *Jews, Christians, and Polytheists*, p. 7.
116. Mack, *The Lost Gospel*, p. 53.
117. Horsley, *Archaeology, History and Society in Galilee*, p. 173.
118. Mack, *The Lost Gospel*, p. 54.
119. That Galilee was called thus out of spite in Judean lore is unlikely. The expression is found nowhere in the Mishnah, the Jerusalem Talmud (though Galilee is mentioned) and occurs only twice in the Babylonian Talmud (Sanhedrin 94b and 104b), on both occasions while citing Isaiah. In neither case is there any comment on the meaning of the expression nor does it seem to have held any negative connotations.
120. MT stands for Masoritic Text, which is a text of the Old Testament and will be discussed below.
121. The word ἔθνος, which reflects well the meaning of the Hebrew text, is often understood as meaning 'gentile'.
122. Though omitted from B and C, it is most likely a part of the original translation.
123. Freyne, 'Bandits in Galilee: A Contribution to the Study of Social Conditions in First-Century Palestine', in Neusner, *Social World of Formative Christianity and Judaism*, p. 52.
124. Horsley, *Archaeology, History and Society in Galilee*, pp. 25–6.
125. The present author is here summarizing conclusions from some 80 pages. Chapters 11–13 deal with this subject.
126. Freyne in his article 'Herodian Economics in Galilee', in Esler, *Modelling Early Christianity*, challenges the theory of urban exploitation of the rural areas and instead suggests that Antipas' economic reforms brought increased wealth for all strata of Galilean society (p. 40).
127. Theissen, *Sociology of Early Palestinian Christianity*, pp. 68–9; Meeks, *First Urban Christians*, pp. 14–16; Horsley, *Archaeology, History and Society in Galilee*, pp. 118–30.
128. Though Mack states this quite categorically, this is not entirely true. The synagogue found in Gamla is dated towards the beginning of the 1st century (Paludan, 'Tempel

og synagoge i datidens jødedom' in Pedersen, *Den Nytestamentlige Tids Historie*, p. 258, but see Fritz, *Einführung in die biblische Archäologie*, p. 218). Hanson and Oakman point out Josephus' mention of a synagogue in Caesarea which they state is 'documentary evidence of first-century synagogue buildings used within Palestine' (Hanson and Oakman, *Palestine in the Time of Jesus*, p. 77). The evidence from the gospels is questionable. Sylvan D. Schwartzman in his article 'How well did the Synoptic Evangelists know the Synagogue', in Neusner and Green, *Judaism and Christianity in the First Century* (originally *Hebrew Union College Annual*, 24:115–32, 1953) argues that even counting on diversity between Palestinian and Diaspora synagogues, the evangelists' knowledge of this institution seems wanting. Paludan traces the development of the synagogue buildings from the Galilean model to a model resembling that of the Diaspora (Paludan, ibid. p. 259). Horsley surveys archaeological evidence and does not find evidence for any Galilean synagogues in the 1st century (see chapter 6, 'Before Synagogues were Buildings' in *Archaeology, History and Society in Galilee*). Significantly he notes that the building and maintenance of a public building required resources that villages very seldom had available to them. Therefore, Galilean villages generally did not have synagogues as communal religious institutions (ibid. p. 134). Religious celebration thus had forms that did not require such public buildings (ibid. p. 132).

129. Mack, *The Lost Gospel*, p. 59.
130. ibid.
131. ibid.
132. Mack, *Myth of Innocence, Mark and Christian Origins*, pp.12–13.
133. Horsley and Hanson, *Bandits, Prophets, and Messiahs*, pp. 5–6. See also Horsley, *Archaeology, History and Society in Galilee*, pp. 173.
134. See Theissen and Merz, *The Historical Jesus*, pp. 176–7; Josephus, *Life of Flavius Josephus*, 12.

135. Horsley, *Archaeology, History and Society in Galilee*, p. 174.
136. Mack, *The Lost Gospel*, p. 60.
137. Neusner, *Judaism and Its Social Metaphors*, p. 24.
138. ibid. p. 27.
139. For further discussion on the origin of Q itself, see chapter 5; for the dating of Q, see chapter 4.
140. The present author's own conclusions match those arrived at by the sociological analysis of John H. Elliott in his 'The Jewish Messianic Movement', in Esler, *Modelling Early Christianity*, in which he surveys the transition of the 'Jesus faction' to the 'Jesus sect'.
141. Saldarni, 'Political and Social Roles of the Pharisees and Scribes in Galilee', in *Society of Biblical Literature*, vol. 124 (1988), p. 205. Horsley similarly proposes that Pharisees periodically visited villages as retainers of the temple state (Horsley, *Archaeology, History and Society in Galilee*, p. 152). However, it appears unlikely that they received any assistance from either Herod or his son Antipas to promote the Judean laws for which neither cared (ibid. p. 34).
142. Mack, *Myth of Innocence, Mark and Christian Origins*, p.61.
143. ibid. p. 10, n. 4.
144. Horsley and Hanson, *Bandits, Prophets, and Messiahs*, p. xv.
145. Josephus, *Antiquities* 18:1:1. Loeb's translation differs here considerably. It is, however, Whiston's translation that is closer to the Greek text. ' . . . κακόν τε οὐκ ἔστιν, οὗ μὴ φυέντος ἐκ τῶνδε τῶν ἀνδρῶν καὶ περαιτέρω τοῦ εἰπεῖν ἀνεπλήσθη τὸ ἔθνος. The translation in Loeb (Louis H. Feldman) is: 'and so these men sowed the seed of every kind of misery, which so afflicted the nation that words are inadequate.' Feldman, wrongly, in the present author's opinion, attaches τοῦ εἰπεῖν (of say) to Josephus (i.e. his inability to express the evil (κακόν) that sprang from these men), while Whiston connects it to the men themselves (τῶν ἀνδρῶν). To translate τοῦ εἰπεῖν as 'doctrine' is perhaps to suggest more cogency than Josephus intends. It seems to suggest invective speech rather than doctrinal discourse. Horsley quite correctly points out that the name

'Judas the Galilean' suggests that he was from Galilee but that he was active in Judea (Horsley, *Archaeology, History and Society in Galilee*, p. 33). Notwithstanding this, he undoubtedly represented a Galilean attitude, appealing to people to peacefully resist taxation in a bid for independence.

146. See Zeitlin, *Jesus and the Judaism of His Time*, p. 35.
147. Theissen and Merz, *Historical Jesus*, p. 178.
148. ibid. pp. 177–8.
149. Vermes, *Changing Faces of Jesus*, p. 228.
150. The Mishnah, besides often referring to the authority of a second person with phrases such as 'Rabbi Johanan ben Zakki said to his students' or 'Rabbi Joshua says', always gives the source at the beginning of the quotation, except for anonymous sources.
151. Mishnah, Aboth 1:1–2:8.
152. By 'mythical' the present author means a piece of lore that is used by a group as constituting common ground for self-perception. Myths follow different paradigms. Creation myths, fertility myths, hero myths and deliverance myths are necessary patterns for explaining community existence, behaviour and hope. Laurence Coupe in his book *Myth* explains that creation myths presume that the creative event took place outside a historical framework in 'sacred time'. The community, however, finds itself in 'profane time' but through various sacred acts or re-enactments finds its way to cross over into'sacred time' (p. 58). In the case of the myth about the creation of the Mishnah tradition, the tradition originates in the sacred time on Sinai along with the written Torah and the re-enactment occurs through the ongoing interpretation of the Law by Hillel, Shammai and successive generations.
153. The Mishnah is the authoritative record of the Tannaim, an academy where Pharisees gathered.
154. This is another point worth noting. One did not follow teachers of two contending schools. The Mishnah does not

hide that these two disagreed but somehow they are still believed to be the Oral Torah.

155. The oldest Mishnah MS belongs to the 7th century CE (Strack and Stemberger, *Introduction to the Talmud and Midrash*, p. 140), whilst the oldest mention of a Babylonian Talmud MS is from the 10th century (p. 209).
156. At times the Targums are more interpretative than normal translation would allow.
157. See below.
158. The Masoretes were the Jewish scholars responsible for the insertion of vowel signs in the Old Testament. The former texts were written in traditional Hebrew without vowels, just as is the case with traditional Arabic and Persian. In both the Old Testament and the Qur'án the adaptation of a vowel system was necessary for clarity. These scholars are reputed to have started their work in the 6th century.
159. Briggs, *Study of Holy Scripture*, p. 210.
160. See Robert P. Gordon's section on 'Targums' in the entry 'Translation', in Metzger and Coogan, *The Oxford Companion to the Bible*, pp. 754–5.
161. The Mishnah (Megillah 2:1) states that '[if] he read it in Aramaic translation or any [other] language, he has not fulfilled his obligation . . . Still, one who speaks a foreign language who heard it in Assyrian [Hebrew], has fulfilled his obligation' (trans. Neusner).
162. Manuscripts in book format were preferred because it was easier to locate texts in codices and because both sides of the paper could be used.
163. Although Hebrew was generally known only by Scribes, some believe that it was more common as vernacular in Galilee (where this event took place). The evidence of Jesus' literacy is undermined by the fact that no text survives that can plausibly be attributed to Him. Jesus' means of communication seems only to have been oral. As to the language Jesus spoke in, Theissen and Merz write: 'The vernacular in Palestine was Aramaic, and in

Galilee a dialect of Aramaic was spoken . . . Whereas only a minority believes that he presented his teachings wholly or partly in Hebrew, there is a lively discussion as to whether we should suppose that Jesus spoke Greek. In view of the clearly recognizable way in which Jesus turned to the simple population of the villages and small towns of Galilee, that seems more improbable' (*Historical Jesus*, p. 169). An entirely optimistic suggestion is advanced by Michael O. Wise in his article 'Languages of Palestine': 'We simply do not know precisely how to characterize the Aramaic dialect which Jesus spoke, either regarding morphology or lexicon. One may also conclude that Jesus probably knew both the H[igh form] and one or more L[ow] forms of Hebrew, and that he had at least a minimal competence in Greek' (in Green and McKnight, *Dictionary of Jesus and the Gospels*, p. 443). Fredriksen points out that even educated Jews of Judea had problems speaking Greek (*Jesus of Nazareth, King of the Jews*, p. 164). It is therefore hard to believe that Jesus could speak more than the most rudimentary Greek and it certainly seems improbable that He could teach in that language. Horsley comes to a similarly moderate conclusion from his survey of Galilean evidence (*Archaeology, History and Society in Galilee,* chapter 7, 'Languages and Cultural Traditions').

164. As we recall from above, the synagogue model is not likely to have been in place in Galilee at this point. Indeed, there is no archeological evidence of synagogues in Nazareth before the 3rd century. (Cf. Finegan, *Archeology of the New Testament,* pp. 49,51. Finegan, however, presupposes its presence based on Luke's tradition and other later literary witnesses. ibid. pp. 61–2.)

165. Müller notes that the LXX version of the book of Jeremiah is about one-sixth shorter than the Hebrew text. Amongst the Qumran texts, however, both the short and the longer versions were found (*Det Gamle Testamente som Kristen bog*, p. 16).

Chapter 3: ***The Birth of a New Dispensation***

166. Something pertaining to the nature of Christ.
167. Greek civilization was exported to different parts of the world mainly by Alexander the Great during his conquests (336–23 BCE). It introduced new centres of learning such as the great library in Alexandria and a large variety of sciences. It was also introduced into the Judaic culture with some success. Its major achievements are the writing of the Septuagint and the emergence of such philosophers as Philo Judaeus, who introduced works on allegorical interpretation and on Logos.
168. Admittedly, there are very few Hellenistic elements in Christ's self-portrayal or even in the Synoptic Gospels (i.e. Matthew, Mark and Luke); and John, which has some Hellenistic elements, met with opposition and was the last gospel to receive canonical status (for a discussion of the canon see chapter 1).
169. For a thorough discussion of Hellenistic Judaism see Grappe, 'Jean 1,14(–18) dans son contexte et à la lumière de la litérature intertestamentaire', in *Revue d'Histoire et de Philosophie Religieuse*, tome 80, #1, Janvier-Mars, 2000, pp. 153–69.
170. Present author's translation; Nikiprowetzky 'L'Exégèse de Philon d'Alexandrie dans le De Gigantibus et le Quod Deus sit Immutabilis', in Winston and Dillon, *Two Treatises of Philo of Alexandria*, p. 14.
171. ibid. p. 19.
172. Zeitlin, *Jesus and the Judaism of His Time*, p. 40.
173. It seems that the Messiah was in fact expected to be pre-existent, as mentioned in the apocryphal prophecy of 2 Esdras 13:26: 'this is he [the Messiah] whom the Most High has been keeping for many ages, who will himself deliver his creation; and he will direct those who are left' (RAPC, insertion mine).
174. The literary style called 'Wisdom literature' includes Psalms, Proverbs, Ecclesiastes and Job. These are solemn

testimony to the high regard given by the Jews to wisdom, even to the degree of using it as a theophanic symbol (see Psalms 136:1–5 and 104:24–5, Job 28:19 and Proverbs 2:6 and 3:19). This is seen particularly in the Deutero-canonical books. The Book of Wisdom (9:9): 'With you [the Lord] is Wisdom, she who knows your works, she who was present when you made the world . . .' (NJB); and Ecclesiasticus (1:4): 'Wisdom was created before everything, prudent understanding subsists from remotest ages'(NJB). Jesus also employs a personified Wisdom in His saying: 'wisdom is justified of all her children' (Matthew 11:19, Luke 7:35 and therefore belongs to Q). The Midrash (2nd century Jewish book of interpretation) states a similar thing of the Torah (the Law revealed by Moses): 'Through the Torah God created the world, the Torah was his helper and his tool. With its aid he set boundaries to the deep, ordered the orbits of the sun and the moon and formed all of nature. Without the Torah the world would disappear' (Midrash, Tanh B. cited in Cohn-Sherbok and Cohn-Sherbok, *A Short Reader in Judaism*, p. 91).

175. Köster, *Entwicklunslinien durch die welt des Frühen Christentums*, p. 97.

176. Arius (256–366 CE), a prominent presbyter (i.e. an elder who has been given a certain amount of authority in a community) of Alexandria.

177. ἀνόμοιος, Greek for 'unlike'; opposite of *homoi-ousios*, 'same substance'.

178. The Nicene Creed was succeeded by 11 Arian creeds (see Stevenson, *Creeds, Councils and Controversies*, p. 8ff) until finally power reverted to the opposite party and the Nicene Creed was reinstituted in Constantinople in 381 CE. The power of the Arian party in the interim is often ignored yet for a period Christianity was Arian and those in opposition, such as Athenasius, were exiled and anathemized (see Ayer, *Source Book for Ancient Church History*, p. 297).

179. The double bracketed clause, called the 'filioque' (Latin for 'and the Son') clause, was included in the Western church and was first accepted and believed authentic in the Frankish Empire in the 6th century. Although the addition was resisted for some time in Rome, it was accepted in the 10th century and ultimately sparked a controversy between the Catholic and Orthodox Churches (see Cross, *The Oxford Dictionary of the Christian Church*, p. 504).
180. The Nicene Creed, cited in Reynolds, *The Christian Religious Tradition*, pp. 62–3.
181. Marcellus of Ancyra (?–374 CE): Bishop who held to the Nicene Creed and the doctrine of Modalism – the idea that God is One but appears to humanity in three ways: as the Father, the Son and the Holy Ghost.
182. Definition of Chalcedon (451 AD) cited in Reynolds, *The Christian Religious Tradition*, pp. 69–70.
183. Nestorius (c. 380–450 CE) was the Bishop of Constantinople.
184. Nestorius, *The Bazaar of Heracleides*, p. 15.
185. The Westminster Confession of Faith is one of the early Presbyterian creeds, written in the middle of the 17th century.
186. Westminster Confession of Faith, para. 6.044.
187. Philo wrote at the beginning of the 1st century and published many of his works as he completed them. The present author finds the similarities between Philo's statements about the Logos and Moses and the Johannine statements about the Logos and Jesus so striking that it seems the latter are best understood by proposing that they were informed directly by the former.
188. In Bruce, *International Bible Commentary*, p. 1232.
189. This phraseology is also used in the new Italian translation *La Bibbia – nuovissima versione dai testi originali* and the *Biblia Germanica – 1545* translated by Martin Luther, the father of Protestantism, in his later years.
190. The effect of saying that 'God is the Word' is the same as saying 'God is spirit' (John 4:24 RSV) (spirit the God,

πνεῦμα ὁ θεός) or 'God is a Spirit' (KJV). God is not equated with a Spirit, rather Spirit is descriptive of God.

191. Williamson, *Jews in the Hellenistic World: Philo*, p. 110.
192. ibid. p. 107.
193. ibid. p. 113.
194 Goodenough, *Introduction to Philo Judaeus*, p. 100.
195. Williamson, *Jews in the Hellenistic World: Philo*, p. 116.
196. Although the word *katelaban* (κατέλαβεν) translated as 'comprehendeth' can be thought of as the action of surrounding or seizing something, it is also translated as 'overpowered' (Weymouth), 'admit, or, receive' (AV Note) and even 'overcome' (RSV).
197. Williamson, *Jews in the Hellenistic World: Philo*, pp. 106–7.
198. The theme of the man sent by God to make the announcement (rather than 'testify', which is Johannine) that all may believe, is from the Sign Source. (Miller, *Complete Gospels*, p. 180, see commentary in footnote.)
199. Though John is not gnostic, it often employs imagery that would be understood by people familiar with Gnosticism. In Gnosticism the name was not merely the appellation of an object or entity but was a key to its very being. Once one knew the names of the Aeons (gods) that prevented the soul's voyage to God ('the Good'), such as Terror, Error and Oblivion, one had power over them and could pass them unhindered.
200. The verb translated as 'made' (or more appropriately 'became', since the voice is middle deponent), γινομαι, here rendered in 2. Aorist denotes transition. Because of the popular word 'incarnation', this is how we have come to think of it. However, there is no preposition to indicate the nature of the change in state. The natural translation therefore is 'became'. In other words, there is a transition from being something to being something else. From a larger context this, however, seems untenable, for surely John could not have meant that the Logos ceased to be Logos in order to become flesh. Hence the preposition 'in' has been deemed appropriate (as an implied

preposition) and so the Logos is therefore thought to have been enfleshed (rather than transformed).

201. Goodenough, *Introduction to Philo Judaeus*, p. 34.
202. Williamson, *Jews in the Hellenistic World: Philo*, pp. 117–18.
203. ibid. See illustration on p. 105.
204. Vine, *Vine's Complete Expository Dictionary*, p. 447.
205. This is also regarded as part of the Sign Source (Miller, *Complete Gospels*, p. 181; see commentary in footnote). This may be the Sign Source's way of starting with the beginning (John predicting the sacrifice of Jesus, the final sign), or may be John's wording (or John using the Sign Source's wording) to connect John's witness with the Logos.
206. Wisdom 7:22 uses the designation for Wisdom itself. As a prophetic designation it is found in the Testament of Benjamin 9:2 and an equivalent term is found in the Dead Sea scrolls and in reference to Bar Kochba, the 2nd century insurrectionist.
207. Grappe, 'Jean 1,14(–18) dans son contexte et à la lumière de la litérature intertestamentaire', in *Revue d'Histoire et de Philosophie Religieuse*, tome 80, #1 Janvier-Mars, 2000, p. 165.
208. Aaron, the brother of Moses who shared His prophetic office. The office was inherited and hence the title became a sign of office. It is by virtue of this tradition that the high priest, in the opinion of John (11:49–52) may make truthful and God-inspired predictions.
209. Kings, Chronicles and Samuel.
210. As mentioned, Matthew's redactional arrangement allows him to show how history has come, by regular intervals of 14 generations, to three major events: the advents of Abraham and David and the Babylonian exile. Now, after the passing of another 14 generations since the exile, another major historical event may be expected, such as the coming of the Messiah.
211. The NJB says: 'son of Matthat, son of Levi', whereas the KJV says: 'Which was [the son] of Matthat, which was [the son] of Levi'. One is left wondering why the connecting

word 'son' is used in the NJB but appears only as an insertion in the KJV. The Greek text in reality only provides the name list with the word *tou*, which means 'of' (since it is the genitive masculine definite article), connecting each name (with the exception of Joseph, of course) as it is translated in Darby's translation. This rendering of the text could suggest that immediate sonship is not implied and that a physical relationship is implied rather than a legal one.

212. As Creed points out, the genealogy relies on the LXX and not the Hebrew text (*Gospel According to St. Luke*, p. 59), therefore it is not likely to have an origin outside Luke's own community.

213. David himself was declared to be the 'firstborn' (Psalms 89:27). It was therefore logical that the Messiah when He came would also be the Son of God. The high priest when interrogating Jesus asked Him, 'Art thou the Christ, the Son of the Blessed?' (Mark 14:61). The blasphemy was not that there could be a Son of God – otherwise the high priest would be the blasphemer – but that Jesus the son of a carpenter made such a claim for Himself. For an extensive review of the concept of divine adoption see Michael Betz's article 'Von Gott gezeugt', in Eltester, *Judentum Urchristentum Kirche*, outlining its development from the ancient orient through the Old Testament, Targums and Midrash to the Qumran sectarians and the New Testament authors.

214. Dalman, *Jesus Christ in the Talmud, Midrash, Zohar and the Liturgy of the Synagogue*, p. 86.

215. ibid. p. 87.

216. Funk and Hoover, *Five Gospels*, p. 105.

217. Mark has another instance of the title of 'son of David' in the story of Bartimaeus. Here, however, it appears to be a reference to Jesus' Salomonic ability to heal (see Charlesworth, 'The Son of David: Solomon and Jesus (Mark 10:47)' in Borgen and Giversen, *The New Testament and Hellenistic Judaism*, pp. 72–87).

218. Horsley and Hanson have analysed two different strands of messianic movements, one popular and the other official or scribal. In the former, election rather than kinship was the criterion, whereas in the latter the promise to David was central. The earliest Jesus movements were popular in nature, so we find in this passage a witness of a popular ideology being promoted in a 'hostile' scribal environment (see Horsley and Hanson, *Bandits, Prophets, and Messiahs*, pp. 88–134).
219. Malina, *Social World of Jesus and the Gospels*, p. 102.
220. One must distinguish between immaculate, which implies sinlessness (not necessarily virgin), and virgin birth, which is the act of a virgin (not necessarily sinless) giving birth.
221. M'Neile, *The Gospel According to St. Matthew*, p. 10; Ellison, 'Matthew', in Bruce, *International Bible Commentary*, p. 1122; but Müller, *Kommentar til Mathæusevangeliet*, p. 92 and McKenzie in Brown, *Jerome Biblical Commentary*, p. 67. The dispute is difficult to resolve and depends to some extent on how one views the language of Matthew as compared, for example, with the LXX or whether one sees a Semitic background for the passage. On review, however, the present author is more inclined to see discontinuity between the language of the LXX and Matthew and not to see a Semitic background to it (since it is Matthew's narrative product) and is therefore inclined to understand it as the English text is usually understood.
222. Crossan, *Jesus, A Revolutionary Biography*, pp. 16–21.
223. Goldstein, Toldoth 1:3.
224. Tertullian, *De Spectaculis* 100.30.
225. Origen, *Contra Celsum* 1.28.
226. The word *mágoi* stems from *megas*, meaning 'great'. It was a title which could be used both to offer respect, as on this occasion, but also to mean a sorcerer, as seen in Acts 13:6.
227. This apocryphal work, along with a host of other similar works such as the Gospel of Pseudo-Matthew, the Infancy Gospel of Thomas and the Gospel of the Nativity of Mary, contains accounts of the alleged deeds of Jesus as a child

which many Christians would find offensive. The Arabic Gospel of Infancy, however, is perhaps the source of some of the traditions related in Qur'án 5:113:'I strengthened thee with the holy spirit, so that thou didst speak to the people in childhood and in maturity . . . Thou makest out of clay, as it were, the figure of a bird, by My leave, and thou breathest into it, and it becometh a bird by My leave . . . and the unbelievers among them said: "This is nothing but evident magic"' (Ali). The Arabic Gospel of the Infancy 38: 'And He had made figures of birds and sparrows, which flew when He told them to fly, and stood still when He told them to stand, and ate and drank when He handed them food and drink. After the boys had gone away and told this to their parents, their fathers said to them: My sons, take care not to keep company with him again, for he is a wizard . . .'

228. Monneret de Villard here suggests that it is possible a correction was made in the original Syriac text where Nud (ܢܘܕ) was substituted for the original Nur (ܢܘܪ), meaning fire, light or brightness.

229. Monneret de Villard, *Leggende orientali sui Magi Evangelici*, p. 125, translation mine. Schoeps suggests in *Aus Frühchristlicher Zeit,* p. 32, that the identification of Zoroaster with Nimrod has its origin in a hostile rabbinic tradition.

230. Recent efforts to date the Zoroastrian apocalypse to an earlier period have received severe criticism from Philippe Gignoux,'L'apocalyptique iranienne est-elle vraiment ancienne?', in *Revue de l'Histoire des Religions*, tome 216, fasc. 2, Avril-Juin 1999.

231. Monneret de Villard, *Leggende sui Magi Evangelici*, p. 129 and parallel at p. 131.

232. Nepper-Christensen, *Matthæusevangeliet*, pp. 37–9.

233. To be distinguished from Herod Antipas, the tetrarch who was a descendant of Herod the Great.

234. There is a difficulty in fixing the year of Jesus' birth. In Luke 3:1 Tiberius is mentioned as being in the fifteenth year of his reign when John the Baptist started his ministry,

which would mean the year was 29 CE (since he was made emperor in 14 CE). Luke goes on to say that 'Jesus himself began to be about thirty years of age' (3:23). Taking into consideration the imprecision of the statement 'about thirty', some have speculated that Jesus could have been closer to 31 in the year 29 CE, which would place his birth in the year 2 BCE. Sanders discusses the standard reckoning developed by Dionysius Exiguus (Sanders, *The Historical Figure of Jesus*, pp. 11–12).

235. Leviticus 12:2–6 requires that a child be circumcised eight days after his birth and on the fortieth day the mother must sacrifice a 'lamb of the first year' and 'a young pigeon, or a turtledove', 'unto the door of the tabernacle of the congregation, unto the priest'.

236. For a complete discussion see Theissen and Merz, *Historical Jesus*, pp. 153–60.

237. Herod had ten wives, of which the most notable were Doris, Mariamne, Mariamne II, Malathace the Samaritan and Cleopatra of Jerusalem.

238. The sign of Caesar, who held divine status for the Romans, was considered a great breach of the Law against having images of gods.

239. Josephus, *Jewish Wars*, 1:33:6.

240. The genesis of Mark's literary scheme, first proposed by Wrede, will be discussed in chapter 8.

Chapter 4: **Baptism**

241. Tuckett states: '. . . in Q God says "I will send my messenger before *you* to prepare *your* way." Thus John is the expected Elijah who will prepare the way for *Jesus*' (*Q and the History of Early Christianity*, p. 133; italics original).

242. Davies reads Thomas 4 ('The man old in days will not hesitate to ask a small child of seven days old about the place of life, and he will live') as referring to this: 'The idea of a baby of *seven* days may have reference to the fact that Jewish proselyte baptism took place seven days after

circumcision. The event of circumcision was of greater significance than baptism and was considered the time of rebirth. One reborn after circumcision would be a child of seven days at the time of baptism' (*The Gospel of Thomas and Christian Wisdom*, p. 121).

243. Bardy, *La conversion au christianisme durant les primiers siècles*, p. 107.
244. It is important to note, however, that it was only John the Baptist who performed the baptism of his movement. When John was executed, his movement had no way of bringing in new disciples.
245. A few early manuscripts such as A and W change 'the prophet Isaiah' into 'the prophets'.
246. Catchpole, *The Quest for Q*, p. 71.
247. Meeks finds the purification ritual used prior to contact with the temple to be the most significant antecedent to the baptismal rite (*The First Urban Christians*, p. 151). Others, such as W. H. Brownlee, have suggested a connection with the Qumran (see 'John the Baptist in the New Light of Ancient Scrolls' in Stendahl, *The Scrolls and the New Testament*, pp. 33–53 and Betz, 'Was John the Baptist an Essene?', in Shanks, *Understanding the Dead Sea Scrolls*, pp. 205–14). In general, these must be considered related, in the sense that they enabled a ritual purity. John the Baptist, however, required a single baptism that would provide safety during the coming apocalypse.
248. Repent is rather a weak translation of μετανοεῖτε, which implies more than feeling bad or acknowledging wrongdoing; it implies a change of heart. Perhaps a better translation would be 'Mend your ways'. In Christianity baptism continued to have a strong relation to the individual's moral behaviour (see Meeks, *The Origins of Christian Morality*, pp. 92–6).
249. Science of the end of time, including expectations of miracles, the appearance of the Messiah and the establishment of His theocratic regime of conquest and rule.
250. Josephus, trans. Whiston, *Antiquities of the Jews*, 18:5:2.

251. Crossan, too, thinks Josephus' account is apologetic (*Jesus, A Revolutionary Biography*, p. 34).
252. Uro, 'John the Baptist and the Jesus Movement: What does Q tell us?' in Piper, *The Gospel Behind the Gospels*.
253. ibid. pp. 254–5.
254. Uro points out that John's baptism to 'the remission of sin' is unlikely to be a Christian invention (ibid. p. 249).
255. Theissen, *A Theory of Primitive Christian Religion*, p. 127.
256. Kloppenborg notes that there are inconsistencies between the Baptist's description of the Coming One and the criteria cited by Jesus (*The Formation of Q*, p. 94). The inconsistency indicates that the title and the apocalyptic function are not the invention of Christian collectors but are in all likelihood historical (ibid. p. 104).
257. 'Behold, I will send my messenger, and he shall prepare the way before me: and the Lord, whom ye seek, shall suddenly come to his temple, even the messenger of the covenant, whom ye delight in: behold, he shall come, saith the LORD of hosts.'
258. Theissen, *A Theory of Primitive Christian Religion*, pp. 39–41.
259. Neirynck, 'The Minor Agreements and Q', in Piper, *The Gospel Behind the Gospels*, pp. 68–9. Uro includes it in his reconstruction (ibid. p. 256).
260. Josephus, however, mentions that it was held by some that Antipas' end was a divine punishment because of the execution of John the Baptist. Bilde comments that Josephus seems to follow a didactic pattern in which he demonstrates how unrighteousness is punished by God. This pattern is applied to Antipater, Arkelaus, Pilate and finally Herod Antipas (*Josefus som Historieskriver*, p. 150).
261. Theissen, *The Gospels in Context,* p. 83.
262. Aune analyses this speech and concludes that it 'bears little resemblance to prophetic speeches in the OT; neither John himself nor early Christian traditionists attempt to pattern this speech to fit OT prophetic models' (*Prophecy in Early Christianity and the Ancient Mediterranean World,* p. 130). This, along with its vivid and easily remembered imagery,

suggests that it represents an accurate recounting of an oral tradition.

263. The words attributed to John the Baptist belong to Q (see Luke 3:7 and Matthew 3:7) but the source does not seem to state who the words are directed against. Tuckett embarks on a lengthy analysis (*Q and the History of Early Christianity*, pp.110–16) after which he concludes that it was most likely directed towards the Pharisees. We discussed the role of Pharisees in chapter 2 and came to the conclusion that they were not as prominent as one might assume from the gospels. However, it is possible that Matthew is right that they came from Jerusalem in order to evaluate the message of John.

264. Tuckett mentions that the contrast made here between Jesus and John seems to be an allegorical interpretation of the parable that precedes this saying. He is, however, critical of those who would make it secondary on a whim (*Q and the History of Early Christianity*, p.176). On the issue of allegory and its rejection in recent studies, see the next chapter's section on parables.

265. On the other hand, Theissen builds a plausible case for a popular tradition that would attribute such powers and ill-will to the Herodian women (*The Gospels in Context*, pp. 88–91).

266. Theissen here in particular looks at coins minted by Herod which carry the reed on one side (*The Gospels in Context*, p. 30).

267. ibid. p. 37.

268. See Creed, *The Gospel According to St. Luke*, pp. 52–3.

269. In the Ebionite Gospel this pedigree is also recorded.

270. The Gospel of the Nazaraeans solves this problem in another manner: 'Behold the mother of the Lord and his brothers said to him, "John the Baptist baptizes for the forgiveness of sins; let us go and be baptized by him." But he said to them, "In what have I sinned that I should go and be baptized by him? Unless perhaps what I have said is ignorance."' In the Ebionite John falls to his knees and

says, 'I pray you, Lord, baptize me,' to which Jesus, refusing, answers, 'Suffer it, for thus it is fitting that all should be accomplished.'

271. Evans, *Saint Luke*, p. 246. Funk and Hoover agree: *The Five Gospels*, p. 133.

272. The words employed (σωματικῷ εἴδει) are typical of the language of Luke. Those who favour apostolic authorship of the third gospel will often appeal to such wording, as here exemplified, to show that the writer was used to using medical language.

273. As mentioned above, this is regarded as part of the Sign Source.

274. Manson understands the question as implying that the Baptist had hoped that Jesus was the one but that something that Jesus had done had brought this into doubt (*The Sayings of Jesus,* pp. 66–7; also Müller, *Kommentar til Mathæusevangeliet*, p. 276). If Q, however, had intended what Manson suggests, we should expect some sort of explanation to this effect. Therefore it seems most likely that Q thought that John had heard about Jesus and had become hopeful (see M'Neile, *The Gospel According to St. Matthew*, p. 152). If John had become disillusioned with Jesus, why would he have sent disciples with such a simple question? The implication is that John had come to believe that Jesus was the one he had proclaimed and now only wanted to hear that Jesus Himself confirmed his belief in Him.

275. D is a 6th century manuscript presently located in Cambridge. This special deviation of the D manuscript may be attributed to one of two things. First, it may be a conscious insertion by an Ebionite scribe who adjusted it to the 'Gospel of the Ebionite' which contains the same use of Psalm 2:7. Another possibility is that the quote had been included in parental manuscripts as a footnote and then was accidentally included by a scribe as a part of the text.

276. Müller, *Mattæusevangeliet fortolket*, p. 359.

277. Wedderburn, *Baptism and Resurrection*, p. 57. See also M'Neile, *The Gospel According to St. Matthew*, p. 436.
278. Bruce, *International Bible Commentary*, p. 1123.
279. Müller, *Mattæusevangeliet fortolket*, p. 51.
280. Wedderburn, *Baptism and Resurrection*, pp. 62–3.
281. The Didache (7:4) does not identify a particular institution that performed the baptism but merely calls the individual who performs the rite ὁ βαπτίζων (the baptizer). Since the role of the baptizer is explained in detail, it must be presumed that even the neophyte was required to know how to perform baptism. Paul notes that certain people in Corinth prided themselves in being baptized by this or that apostle. He does not, however, make clear that there are any restrictions on the people who perform this rite (1 Corinthians 1:10ff).
282. The Baptist Confession of Faith (1689).
283. For a discussion of the development of infant baptism see Newman, *An Essay on the Development of Christian Doctrine*, pp.139–41, as well as G. W. Bromiley's article 'Infant Baptism' in Elwell, *Evangelical Dictionary of Theology*, pp.116–17. It is quite clear that the confession of faith was an integral aspect of baptism from the earliest times (see Bardy, *La conversion au christianisme durant les primiers siècles*, pp. 171–2). Dunn is also supportive of the view that baptism was mostly understood as a proclamation of faith and therefore not likely to have been administered to infants (*Unity and Diversity in the New Testament*, pp. 160–1).
284. Pedersen, *Markusevangeliet fortolket*, p. 29.
285. The present author will argue below that the temptation story has a Judeo-Christian origin. It would appear from the two widely different traditions, Mark and Q, that there was an ancient myth which they had in common.
286. Pedersen, *Markusevangeliet fortolket*, p. 30.
287. This is suggested, for example, by Evans, *Saint Luke*, pp. 257–8.
288. Evans, ibid. p. 256; Manson, *The Sayings of Jesus*, pp. 42–3. Creed also finds Matthew's third temptation to be a more

climatic end but uses it to argue the view that Matthew retains the original order (*The Gospel According to St. Luke*, p. 63). This order has also been chosen in more recent times by Mack, *The Lost Gospel*, p. 82, and Jacobson in Miller, *The Complete Gospels*, p. 255.

289. Evans (ibid.) suggests that the change was made by Matthew because he felt that the climax of the temptation should be the worship of the Devil. This may very well be but it remains somewhat speculative.
290. Theissen, *The Gospels in Context*, pp. 206–21.
291. It should, however, be noted that Tuckett questions the stratification (*Q and the History of Early Christianity*, pp. 419–20). For the argument for this stratification see Kloppenborg, *The Formation of Q*, particularly pp. 247–8.
292. Both Evans (*Saint Luke*, p. 259) and Müller (*Mattæusevangeliet fortolket*, p. 55) note the similarity but fail to use it as an interpretational key. Evans states that there is no basis in rabbinic tradition 'that the messiah would reveal himself on the roof of the temple' (Evans, *Saint Luke*, p. 260).
293. Chronicler of the 2nd century who, as here, is preserved by citation of Eusebius in his *Ecclesiastical History* (II 23).
294. Here Eusebius quotes Clement, *Outlines*, book 8 that James 'was thrown down from the pinnacle of the temple and beaten to death with a fuller's club' (*Ecclesiastical History* II 1).
295. This text is slightly damaged at the end of the page so we cannot be certain of all the details. However, we can be certain that it contained all the details of Hegesippus as well as additional embellishments. See Robinson, *The Nag Hammadi Library*, pp. 269–70 for an introduction and p. 275 for relevant text.
296. Josephus, *Antiquities of the Jews*, 20:9:1.
297. It has been suggested (granting its uncertainty) that references to stoning were inserted by Eusebius in order to harmonize with Josephus, whom he cites afterwards (see Pratscher, *Der Herrenbruder Jakobus und die Jakobustradition*,

p. 105). This, however, is unlikely since the stoning seems to be presumed by the Rechabite who stops it. Either way the apocalypse from the period is a witness that stoning was integral to the martyrdom narrative.

298. See Crossan, *Birth of Christianity*, pp. 469–76.
299. Book 1, chapter 70: 'Much blood is shed; there is a confused flight, in the midst of which that enemy attacked James, and threw him headlong from the top of the steps; and supposing him to be dead, he cared not to inflict further violence upon him.'
300. We see this in Thomas 14 and Mark 2:18–20.
301. This title, we noted in the last chapter, was typical of the beliefs of the evangelists' community. In chapter 8 we shall see that such titles, which were attached to messiahship, are at home in a Judean setting.
302. Manson, *The Sayings of Jesus*, p. 44.
303. de Waal Malefijt, *Religion and Culture*, p. 269.
304. Elliott, *The Apocryphal New Testament*, pp. 9–10.
305. Taanith 1:6.
306. H. E. 2:23.
307. Hegesippus' description, it should be noted, matches that of someone who has taken a Nazirite vow (Numbers 6:1–21 and Mishnah: Nazir). What the Mishnah describes is a form of communal Nazirite vow.
308. Josephus, *Antiquities of the Jews* 20:9:1.
309. Hegesippus states that James used to go into the holy place all the time to pray for the people.
310. Pagels, *The Origin of Satan*, p. 39.
311. See Numbers 22, the story of Balaam.
312. Pagels, *The Origin of Satan*, p. 42.
313. Where most translations read 'tested' or 'tried' the ASV uses the possibly more satisfying 'proved'.
314. Bornkamm, *Jesus of Nazareth*, p. 56.
315. The Pharisees did this by the popularization of priestly duties and the Essene by performing cultic acts using a different calendar and by their open animosity towards the current high priests.

Chapter 5: ***The Proclamation of Christ***

316. Schuyler Brown in *The Origin of Christianity: A Historical Introduction to the New Testament* discusses this as the primary method behind the 'new quest' (pp. 49–50).
317. John D. Crossan devotes a great deal of research to these classes and their situation in his 'Cross-Cultural Anthropology' chapter in *The Birth of Christianity*. To understand the economic situation in the Roman Empire read Finley, *The Ancient Economy*, in particular chapters 2, 3 and 4 which discuss 'Orders and Status', 'Masters and Slaves' and 'Landlords and Peasants'. It should furthermore be noted that generally farmers were also artisans. Farmers were not participants in a commercial economy but independently provided their own nourishment and produced their own tools (Horsley, *Archaeology, History and Society in Galilee*, pp. 74–5).
318. Luise Schottroff in her article 'Itinerant prophetesses: A feminist analysis of the sayings source Q', in Piper, *The Gospel Behind the Gospels*, demonstrates that though Q is written from a male perspective it provides evidence of the presence of women amongst these disciples operating as equals with men. Crossan reaches the same conclusion. He does so by an analysis of the saying about the break-up of families and the Markan injunction regarding travelling in pairs (*The Birth of Christianity*, p. 378ff). Crossan's proposition that husband-wife couples travelled together as itinerant preachers is strengthened by Jesus' strong injunction against divorce (see Sanders, *The Historical Figure of Jesus*, pp. 198–200), which suggests that the break-up of the family did not include husbands and wives. Paul tells us that both Peter and James the brother of Jesus were married (1 Corinthians 9:5).
319. Freyne, 'Herodian Economics in Galilee', in Esler, *Modelling Early Christianity*.
320. Crossan, *The Birth of Christianity*, p. 179.

321. For an exploration of the relationship between Sepphoris and Tiberias with its Galilean surroundings see Horsley, 'Sepphoris and Tiberias, Monuments of Urbanization', chapter 2, *Archaeology, History and Society in Galilee*.
322. Theissen, *A Theory of Primitive Christian Religion*, pp. 100–7.
323. Patterson, 'Askesis and the Early Christian Tradition', in Vaage and Wimbush, *Ascetism and the New Testament*, p. 51.
324. Patterson calls this form of performance *askesis* (see 'Askesis and the Early Christian Tradition', in Vaage and Wimbush, *Ascetism and the New Testament*, p. 65) while Theissen refers to it as 'self-stigmatization' *(A Theory of Primitive Christian Religion*, p. 143).
325. Theissen gives a thorough treatment of the nature of early Christian movements in his *Sociology of Early Palestinian Christianity*. Particular attention should be given to 'The Role of Wandering Charismatics' (pp. 8–16) and 'The Role of Sympathizers in the Local Communities' (pp. 17–23).
326. Kelber, *The Oral and the Written Gospel*, p. 101.
327. Considering Kelber's thesis, Jonathan A. Draper has pointed out it 'seems that the beginning of this process of textualization may be observed in the Didache also ('Social Ambiguity and the Production of Text: Prophets, Teachers, Bishops, and Deacons and the Development of the Jesus Tradition in the Community of the Didache', in Jefford, *The Didache in Context*, p. 305). Following Niederwimmer, Patterson has looked at the stratification of the Didache 11–13, identifying the less hostile set of rules as belonging to the earliest strata ('Didache 11–13: The Legacy of Radical Itinerancy in Early Christianity', in Jefford, *The Didache in Context*, pp. 317–18).
328. The Hebrew characterizes the husband as a בני־הנביאים, often translated as 'sons of the prophets', which denotes belonging to a group of prophets. The word בני, deriving from בנה (meaning 'build'), has nuances ranging from 'son' to 'building'. The NJB translates the term as 'member of the prophetic brotherhood', the Moffat as 'member of the prophets' guild' and NIV as 'company of prophets'.

329. In *A Short Introduction to the Old Testament Prophets*, E. W. Heaton explains the distinguishing features of institutional prophets who live at courts and assist the king (p. 32) and the independent prophets who live isolated and peripheral to society (p. 42).
330. It goes without saying that the community expected a prophet of Jesus to admonish the people to live as he himself did but that they would not generally embrace his life style. They would embrace the prophet's radical ethics (Didache 1–6) but not his radical life style.
331. Theissen was perhaps one of the first scholars to note this similarity *(Sociology of Early Palestinian Christianity*, pp. 14–15) but in recent times more support has been found, amongst others including Burton Mack (*The Lost Gospel*) and Leif Vaage ('Q and Cynicism: On Comparison and Social Identity', in Piper, *The Gospel Behind the Gospels*).
332. For a discussion of Cynicism and some of the problems isolating its doctrines from Stoicism, see Klauck, *Die religiöse Umwelt des Urchristentums*, vol. 2, pp. 107–31.
333. Kloppenborg, *The Formation of Q*, p. 324.
334. In Meeks's discussion of the concept of conversion in Greek philosophy he notes three characteristics of moral conversion: 'First, popular philosophy stresses how hard it is to be good. The life of virtue is an *agon*, a struggle, a contest, a race to be run. Second, the choice between the easy life of vice and the difficult life of virtue is an exceedingly lonely one. Third, indispensable to the proper choice is the right kind of education (*paideia*). It follows that philosophical conversion and the virtuous life to which it leads are attainable only by an elite' (*The Origins of Christian Morality*, p. 24). He goes on to discuss a conversion story told under the name of Diogenes, the founder of Cynicism, in which a son of 'extremely prosperous parents' invites him to his 'banquet hall adorned all about with inscriptions and gold'. Needing to spit, Diogenes finds no place appropriate to do so except on his host, who, of course, rebukes him. He answers that only he was unadorned,

which his host immediately interprets as a challenge to his education. In response to the challenge, the host decides to become a Cynic himself. It is noteworthy that rather than distributing the wealth to the poor, as we have in Christian narratives, the wealth reverts to the convert's family (ibid. pp. 24–5).

335. Klauck, *Die religiöse Umwelt des Urchristentums*, vol. 2, p. 112. This is, of course, the logical consequence of the attitude discussed in the previous note.

336. Crossan, *The Birth of Christianity*, p. 280.

337. ibid. p. 334. This is quite a change of tone from Crossan's earlier publication, *Jesus, A Revolutionary Biography*, in which he states: 'The Historical Jesus was a *peasant Jewish Cynic*' (p. 129). It is not surprising that Crossan's position is misunderstood by some (see, for example Daniel Marguerat in 'La Troisiéme Quête' du Jésus de l'histoire', in *Recherches de Science Religieuse*, Juillet-Septembre 1999, tome 87, numéro 3, p. 405, in which he equates the views of Crossan with those of Mack). Crossan (in electronic correspondence 2 March 2000 from 'Historical Jesus Methodology' hosted by the electronic discussion list X-Talk and moderated by Mahlon Smith and Jeffrey Gibson) explained: 'My first engagement with any connection between Cynicism and/or Q and/or the Historical Jesus was in 1990 and it was by invitation of others. My initial response, with my own work on the Historical Jesus well on its way to completion, was this. If anyone wants to talk about a "Cynic Jesus", then they better imagine what a Jewish peasant Cynic would look like. I did not want, then or now, to get entangled on questions beyond proof or disproof: Was there Cynicism in urbanized Galilee (for example Sepphoris) and, if so, might Jesus have known about it? I could explain Jesus, to my own satisfaction, without even a mention of any Cynic hypothesis. The subtitle of my book was, therefore, *A Mediterranean Jewish Peasant* and not *A Mediterranean Jewish Cynic* . . . anyone who thinks that Burton Mack and I are saying the same

thing in general or even when we mention Cynicism has not read us very carefully.' Besides the entirely unlikely transmission of Cynicism from Sepphoris or Tiberias, Horsley notes that there 'appears to have been only a thin veneer of cosmopolitan culture in the cities of Galilee shortly after they were (re)built by Antipas. That is hardly the sort of cultural atmosphere in which Cynic philosophers would have flourished and somehow influenced or provided models for Galilean villagers' (*Archaeology, History and Society in Galilee*, p. 69).

338. Mack, *Who Wrote the New Testament*, p. 51.
339. Leif E. Vaage's article 'Q and Cynicism: On Comparison and Social Identity', in Piper, *The Gospel Behind the Gospels*, pp. 199–229, convincingly refutes some of the charges of Tuckett. Yet it is precisely on 'social identity' that the present author finds the comparison least useful. Rather, it is the means by which the social reform is promoted through *askesis* which is most instructive.
340. Smith, *Drudgery Divine*, pp. 36–53.
341. Mack attributes the theme of Elijah-Elisha to a group known as 'the Congregation of Israel', which was responsible for the miracle stories (*A Myth of Innocence*, pp. 91–3). As we have seen above and will see further below, the Elijah-Elisha figure is not easily placed in a single strand of tradition but seems appropriate to several strands. Mack's dismissal of this image as historical, made on the basis of evidence that 'Jesus was unconcerned about specifically Jewish traditions' (ibid. p. 92), is also unconvincing.
342. Malina, 'Early Christian Groups, Using small group formation theory to explain Christian organizations', in Esler, *Modelling Early Christianity*, p. 110.
343. Jacobson, 'Divided Families and Christian Origins', in Piper, *The Gospel Behind the Gospels*, p. 375.
344. ibid. p. 379.
345. Crossan considers the issue as it is debated between Theissen and Horsley. He concludes that the itinerants

determined what were the necessities of life; that is to say, their life of destitution (and we should presume the break-up of families) was made virtuous and thus to be commended and pursued (*Birth of Christianity*, pp. 280–1).

346. Jacobson, 'Divided Families and Christian Origins', in Piper, *The Gospel Behind the Gospels*, p. 375.
347. The metre is the beat or rhythm of poetry or music.
348. This verse in Thomas is only available in Coptic. Here it reads ⲚⲈ Ⲛ ϨⲎⲔⲈ (are the poor) and ⲦⲰ ⲦⲚ̄ (yours).
349. It also ruins the end rhyme that we find in a reconstruction of the original Aramaic saying. However, keeping 'and thirst' in verse 6 in Matthew would make a better rhyme than if it were omitted. See Burney, *The Poetry of our Lord*, p. 166.
350. According to Manson, Matthew changed 'Son of Man' into the personal pronoun elsewhere (*The Sayings of Jesus*, p. 48).
351. Neyrey, 'Loss of Wealth, Loss of Family and Loss of Honour', in Esler, *Modelling Early Christianity*. See also Finley, *The Ancient Economy*, p. 41.
352. Most translations read 'is spread' as if it were a completed action. The ⲈⲤ in ⲈⲤⲠⲞⲢϢ indicates an ongoing action and should therefore be translated as 'is spreading'. The present author is grateful to Mike Grodin, whose interlinear of Coptic Thomas and personal correspondence pointed this out.
353. Only the NIV, YLT, WEY and ASV agree with the KJV about 'within'. The NWT along with some respected translations such as the RSV, DBY and the JMTB translate it as 'in your midst', while the NJB and NEB say 'amongst you'. The interpretation thus reached is that Jesus is in fact pointing to Himself. He would then be stating that He was the representative of the kingdom of God on earth, which the present author finds theologically consistent. But this is not contextually or philologically acceptable. The word occurs in only one other place in the New Testament and that is in Matthew 23:26, where *entos* ('inside') occurs as

an antonym to *ektos* (εκτος, outside) calling on the Pharisees to clean their souls before their bodies. Similarly *entos* appears in the LXX: 'My heart was hot *within* me' (Psalms 39:3); 'Bless the LORD, O my soul: and all that is *within* me, bless his holy name' (Psalms 103:1); 'and my heart is wounded *within* me' (Psalms 109:22); 'They also rebuilt the sanctuary and the *interior* of the temple' (1 Maccabees 4:48); 'the *centre* is inlaid with ebony' (Songs 3:10); 'but *inwardly* he is full of deceit' (Ecclesiasticus 19:26); 'Therefore my heart shall sound like an harp for Moab, and my *inward* parts for Kirharesh' (Isaiah 16:11); 'my *inward* parts are turned in me: and I have retained no strength' (Daniel 10:16; only in θ). The Vulgate agrees with KJV saying *intra vos est* (literally 'inside you (pl.) is'). Finally, the context of the previous verse of Luke 17:21 makes it clear that it comes 'not with observation', or rather is not to be seen by outward signs but 'within'. See also Liddell and Scott, *An Intermediate Greek-English Lexicon*, p. 266.

354. Thomas 3 is available in Greek. This is the Greek word as it is rendered in the manuscript with Coptic lettering.
355. The Jesus Seminar is a group of scholars who met in the mid–80s to build a scholarly consensus on the Historical Jesus and publish it to as wide an audience as possible. The result was published in Funk and Hoover, *The Five Gospels, What Did Jesus Really Say*. They went on to deliberate about which of the acts attributed to Jesus were actually performed by Him. This was published in Funk, *The Acts of Jesus, The Search for the Authentic Deeds of Jesus*. For a survey see Powell, *Jesus as a Figure in History, How Modern Historians View the Man from Galilee*, pp. 65–81.
356. Funk and Hoover, *The Five Gospels*, p. 365.
357. For objections to reading Thomas as Gnostic, see the discussion in chapter 1 about the Gospel of Thomas.
358. In both Thomas and Mary ⲘⲠⲈⲦⲚ̄ϨⲞⲨⲚ is translated as 'within'.
359. Bent Noack, *Guds rige i os eller i blandt os.*

360. The only difference is in the word order and in the word *no* (οὐκ) instead of *no one* (οὐδεὶς).
361. This insider-outsider relationship is spelled out by Mark (4:33–4). It is not likely that Jesus explained the parables, for it is implicit in the nature of parables that they are understandable by their target audience. If they are not understood, then they fail in their purpose, which is to convey meaning.
362. See Kjärgaard, *Metaphor and Parable*, p. 160.
363. Via, *The Parables*, p. 44.
364. This, of course, presumes a generally positive disposition to the message. It is clear that some members of the audience could hear the message and reject it (as presupposed, for example, by Luke 11:45, 20:19).
365. Translated from the Swedish with original italics. Gerhardsson, *Jesu liknelser* (*The Parables of Jesus*), p. 16.
366. Funk, *Language, Hermeneutics, and the Word of God*, p. 162.
367. See Crossan, *Birth of Christianity*, part II: 'Memory and Orality', pp. 47–89.
368. Dibelius, *From Tradition to Gospel*, p. 255.
369. Papyrus 75 of the 3rd century and B of the 4th.
370. D and W of the 5th century and the Old Syriac as well as Italic manuscripts (a, b, d, e, ff2, l, q).
371. Crossan comments that 'the parable exhibits rather heavily the characteristics of translation Greek from an Aramaic original' (*In Parables*, pp. 41–2).
372. Matthew has 'the time of harvest' καιρῷ τοῦ θερισμοῦ while Thomas has the 'day of harvest' ϩⲙ̄ ⲫⲟⲟⲩ ⲅⲁⲣ ⲙ̄ⲡⲱϩ̄ⲥ̄.
373. See 'Mustard' in Myers, *The Eerdmans Bible Dictionary*, p. 738. Harrison notes that some report sizes up to 15 feet ('Plants' in Douglas, *The New Bible Dictionary*, p. 1006). See also 'Mustard Seed' in Selman and Manser, *The Macmillan Dictionary of the Bible*, p. 136.
374. The word 'concealed' is not complete in the manuscript ([ⲁⲥϩⲟ]ⲡϥ) and so the reconstruction is not completely certain, although it is extremely likely. When these gaps appear in a manuscript they are called 'lacuna'.

375. Funk and Hoover, *The Five Gospels*, p. 195.
376. ibid. p. 530.
377. Money lending is the theme of another parable contained only in Luke (16:1–13). It presents several interpretational problems because it requires understanding the economic situation of 1st century Palestine. Because money lending with interest was not legal (see Leviticus 25:36–7), it was common for the creditor to write the sum owed including the commission of the lender, so the money would be not be recoverable in a court of law. The parable of the dishonest manager is thus that when the master of the manager returns and finds his manager has used his property in this dishonest way, he fires him. The dishonest manager then hurries to his creditors and has them rewrite the note for the amount that was actually lent, whereupon the master receives him back and calls him prudent. The present author interprets the parable as referring to the kingdom of God, which was the absent master returned. The former sinner (the dishonest manager) repents and is received back into the good will of his master.
378. Theissen, *A Theory of Primitive Christian Religion*, p. 85.
379. ibid. pp. 86–7.
380. ibid. pp. 90–2.

Chapter 6: ***The Mighty Works***

381. See chapter 1.
382. From *arete*, which is 'powerful acts'. In this category are those stories that enumerate the great, often miraculous deeds of gods or holy people.
383. Miller, *The Complete Gospels*, p. 193; see commentary in footnote.
384. So say many ancient manuscripts such as a, C, D, L and Y as well as the Vulgate and the Old Syriac.
385. Crossan, *The Birth of Christianity*, p. 143.
386. Elliott, *The Apocryphal New Testament*, p. 76.

387. Kelber, *The Oral and the Written Gospel*, pp. 119–20. Kelber describes 'mythoclastic' as being that which 'challenges the hearers' sense of reality', while 'mythopoetic' is that which 'fosters continuity with culture' (ibid. pp.76–7).
388. ibid. pp. 110–11.
389. Aune, *The New Testament in Its Literary Environment*, p. 47.
390. Burridge, *What are the Gospels?* p. 258.
391. Aune, *The New Testament in Its Literary Environment*, p. 35.
392. ibid. p. 39.
393. ibid.
394. Briggs, *General Introduction to the Study of Holy Scripture*, p. 448.
395. Josephus, trans. Whiston, *Antiquity of the Jews*, int.4, insertion mine.
396. In his recounting of the creation he again is caught up in the allegory: 'but Moses said it was one day, – the cause of which I am able to give even now; but because I have promised to give such reasons for all things in a treatise by itself, I shall put off its exposition till that time.'
397. 'Almost all agree that Matthew's interpretation of the "sign of Jonah" in Matt 12:40, interpreting the reference in terms of the time of Jonah's sojourn in the belly of the fish, is secondary in relation to Luke's shorter and more enigmatic version' (Tuckett, *Q and the History of Early Christianity*, p. 257).
398. Matthew 12:27–8 has the 'spirit of God' but Luke's version is generally considered more primitive.
399. Theophany is the Greek word for 'appearance of God'; a theophanic symbol is that which appears instead of God, for example, the fire which Moses saw on Sinai or the man who wrestled with Jacob, after which he received the name 'Israel'.
400. Dunn, *Unity and Diversity in the New Testament*, p. 182.
401. ibid. p. 185.
402. See Theissen, *Urchristliche Wundergeschichten*. The journal *Semeia 11: Early Christian Miracle Stories* devoted most of the issue to discussing Theissen's methodology.

403. Pedersen, 'Israel, its Life and Culture', in Van der Loos, *The Miracles of Jesus*, p. 261.
404. Cited by Jerome in his Commentary on Matthew 12:13, in Schneemelcher, *New Testament Apocrypha*, vol. 1, p. 160.
405. Psalms 137:5: 'If I forget you, O Jerusalem, let my right hand wither!' (RSV).
406. The legal presumption of Matthew, which the present author has placed in parentheses, is in fact not a given. The question would be answered differently depending on the sect asked and the manner in which the healing was carried out. For a comprehensive treatment of the issue, see Sanders, *Jewish Law from Jesus to the Mishnah*, pp. 20–2. Theissen points out that the issue really is not the Sabbath law but has to do with Jesus' appropriation of priestly authority (*A Theory of Primitive Christian Religion*, p. 112).
407. By σώζω is meant 'to preserve'. In this connection one may be saved from death and, by implication, be healed. Often the narrative does not allow the understanding of σώζω as making whole or the act of healing.
408. Cf. Hillers, 'Demons, Demonology', in *Encyclopedia Judaica*, p. 1522. For an extensive list of demon names and the illnesses they caused, see Charlesworth, 'The Son of David: Solomon and Jesus', in Borgen, *The New Testament and Hellenistic Judaism*, pp. 81–2.
409. Josephus, *Antiquities of the Jews*, 8:2:5.
410. Charlesworth, 'The Son of David: Solomon and Jesus', in Borgen, *The New Testament and Hellenistic Judaism*, p. 78.
411. Hanson and Oakman, *Palestine in the Time of Jesus*, p. 67.
412. See in particularly Theissen, *The Gospels in Context*, pp. 109–12.
413. Funk, *The Acts of Jesus*, pp. 44–6.
414. Catchpole, *The Quest for Q*, pp. 280–308. He argues extensively that Luke's additions are a Lukan redaction and fit his particular vision of the mission of Jesus. He also proposes that the centurion's subservitude is Christological rather than a Jewish/Gentile issue and that indeed the term

used for centurion need not refer to a Roman soldier at all. Tuckett, however, counters that while Christology is central, it is impossible to evade the sense that the centurion is indeed very much a Gentile (*Q and the History of Early Christianity*, p. 396).

415. Kloppenborg, *The Formation of Q*, pp. 117–21.
416. Miller, *The Complete Gospels*, p. 183.
417. Kloppenborg, *The Formation of Q*, p. 120.
418. Philo, *Legum Allegoria*, XXXV.
419. Miller, *The Complete Gospels*, p. 185.
420. Theissen, *The Gospels in Context*, p. 62. See also footnote 1 on the page that discusses the use of the word 'dog' in insults. Van der Loos asserts the opposite opinion (*The Miracles of Jesus*, p. 413).
421. ibid. pp. 66–80.
422. The Matthean omission may also be understood by the behaviour that Jesus showed in connection with these healing activities. Matthew also omits the healing of the blind man of Bethsaida found in Mark 8:21–6 (Nepper-Christensen, *Matthæusevangeliet*, p. 192). Pedersen associates this behaviour with Hellenistic miracle narratives (*Markusevangeliet*, p. 110).
423. Philo, *Legum Allegoria*, LVI.
424. Evans, *St. Luke*, p. 290.
425. Included in Fortna, 'Sign Source', in Miller, *The Complete Gospels*, p. 183. Fortna places this as the third sign in the source (*The Fourth Gospel and its Predecessor*, p. 65ff).
426. Included in Fortna, 'Sign Source', in Miller, *The Complete Gospels*, p. 182. Fortna places this as the first sign in the source (*The Fourth Gospel and its Predecessor*, p. 49ff).
427. Neyrey, 'Loss of wealth, loss of family and loss of honour, The cultural context of the original markarisms in Q', in Esler, *Modelling Early Christianity*, p. 142.
428. Two cities are candidates for the location of this story: Khirbet Qana, whose ruins reveal considerable urbanization, and Kefar Kenna, a village which is still inhabited today (Finegan, *The Archeology of the New Testament*,

pp. 62–3). Bösen seems to presume that it is the former (see map in *Galiläa*, p. 59), while Finegan seems to favour the latter. The present author favours the former because 1) the unqualified name Cana would by default refer to the town rather than a small village and 2) it suits better the social profile of the miracle.

429. The style is perhaps more appropriately attributed to the Sign Source that John used but this is by no means certain. Similar constructs are found in the Johannine discourses which have an altogether different origin.
430. Van der Loos, *The Miracles of Jesus*, p. 602. See also Damm, *Johannesevangeliet*, p. 58.
431. Philo, *Legum Allegoria*, XXVI.
432. Miller, *The Complete Gospels*, p. 185.
433. Philo, *Legum Allegoria*, LX.
434. See Funk, *The Acts of Jesus*, p. 229; Pedersen, *Markusevangeliet fortolket*, p. 159 and Müller, *Mattæusevangeliet fortolket*, p. 250.
435. The difference between the version in Luke and the one reconstructed below is its reference to the three years after which the man had come to check on the fig tree. This could be taken to support the Johannine chronology that says that Jesus went to Jerusalem three times.
436. Crossan, *The Cross that Spoke*, p. 350, italics original, insertion mine.
437. de Waal Malefijt, *Religion and Culture*, p. 229. Pharisees would not technically fall into this category but their 'popular priesthood' would make this distinction insignificant.
438. ibid. p. 237.
439. On exorcism see ibid. pp. 249–62. It is of special interest to this story that one means of exorcism is to 'bribe' the spirit (ibid. p. 260), as Jesus seems to be doing when he allows Legion to flee into a herd of swine. Also, the revelation of its name is in line with an exorcist's attempt to curb the power of the spirit over the possessed body (ibid.).

440. Crossan, *The Birth of Christianity*, pp. 293–304. His earlier discussion of miracles in *The Historical Jesus* (pp. 303–54) is less marked by anthropological interests.
441. ibid. p. 294.
442. de Waal Malefijt, *Religion and Culture*, p. 248.
443. Fredriksen, *Jesus of Nazareth, King of the Jews*, p. 68.
444. Crossan, *The Birth of Christianity*, p. 297. Italics original.
445. Kloppenborg believes this intention to be already present in Q (*The Formation of Q*, pp. 229–30).
446. Sanders, *Jesus and Judaism*, p. 214.
447. Luke 6:33 replaces 'Gentiles' with 'sinners' but the Matthean version is almost universally regarded as the original (see Tuckett, *Q and the History of Early Christianity*, p. 22, n. 20, and Catchpole, *The Quest for Q*, p. 102).
448. Sanders, *The Historical Figure of Jesus*, pp. 120–2.
449. The relationship between an individual who sought a magician was discontinued after the services were rendered. In the Greek world the individual would feel no particular commitment to the magician (see Stark, *The Rise of Christianity*, p. 205).

Chapter 7: ***Jerusalem***

450. The length of the ministry of Jesus is based on the number of Passovers accounted for in the Gospel of John. Since it recorded that Jesus was 'about thirty years of age' (Luke 3:23) when He started His ministry, it is commonly held that it ended when He was 33. The actual length is difficult to establish. Irenaeus claims that Jesus, in order to sanctify all ages, lived to the age of 50, so that even the old could receive the blessing. To this end he claims the support of John the apostle as well as other unnamed apostles (Adv. Hear. II, 22:4–5).
451. Müller, *Mattæusevangeliet fortolket*, p. 245.
452. Funk and Hoover, *The Five Gospels*, p. 228.
453. Crossan, *Jesus, A Revolutionary Biography*, p. 145.

454. ibid. p. 129. Sanders sees it as 'likely' that Jesus acted out the prophecy of Zechariah (*The Historical Figure of Jesus*, p. 84) but following Horsley's distinction of popular models, the present author is inclined towards Crossan's judgement. A popular movement would not be able to interpret the act as an enactment of an obscure prophecy with which it was highly unlikely to be familiar.

455. Short, in Bruce, *International Bible Commentary*, p. 1172.

456. John 6:14–15 mentions that a multitude wanted to take Jesus by force to make Him king. It seems reasonable to assume that Jesus had a larger following in Galilee and the northern regions, where He spent most of His ministry, than He had in Judea.

457. If the Galilean peasantry wanted to proclaim Jesus their king this would indeed have been a proper enactment of a popular tradition of the Northern Kingdom. Elisha sent one of his prophet servants (2 Kings 9:1) to Jehu so that he could be anointed and make war on the ungodly of King Ahab's family (2 Kings 9:6–10).

458. 'The earliest attestation of Jerusalem's name is in the Egyptian Execration Text of the nineteenth and eighteenth centuries BCE in a form that must be a transcription of the Semitic *Urusalim*, which appears in the Amarna letters of the fourteenth century BCE' (Murphy-O'Connor, 'Jerusalem' in Metzger and Coogan, *The Oxford Companion to the Bible*, p. 349).

459. The Ark of the Covenant was a box containing the original tablets of the Ten Commandments: '[There was] nothing in the ark save the two tables of stone, which Moses put there at Horeb, when the LORD made [a covenant] with the children of Israel, when they came out of the land of Egypt' (1 Kings 8:9 KJV).

460. This is usually referred to as the 'exile' and the following period as the 'post-exile' or 'second temple'. During the Babylonian conquest, the temple (built by King Solomon) was destroyed. Hence, the period between its construction

in 960 BCE and its first destruction is referred to as the first temple.

461. The second temple endured from its construction in 520 BCE until its fateful and final destruction by Roman troops under the command of Titus in the year 70 CE.
462. Alexander, undoubtedly one of history's greatest military leaders, managed to conquer all of the Persian empire, the Syrians and the Egyptians; all paid tribute to him. His unexpected death was caused by a fever caught on his way home from his last battles in 323 BCE.
463. These two books belong to the Catholic canon.
464. This change from Herod to Archelaus is noted in the Gospel of Matthew (2:22): 'But when he heard that Archelaus did reign in Judaea in the room of his father Herod, he was afraid to go thither: notwithstanding, being warned of God in a dream, he turned aside into the parts of Galilee . . .'
465. She was the daughter of Aristobulus, the son Herod put to death, and was therefore niece to both her husbands.
466. Not to be confused with the tetrarch of Trachonitis. He was the son of Herod the Great by Mariamne.
467. Sanders, *Jesus and Judaism*, p. 61.
468. ibid. p. 63.
469. ibid. p. 65.
470. ibid. p. 69.
471. Neusner, 'The Absoluteness of Christianity and the Uniqueness of Judaism, Why Salvation is not of the Jews', in Neusner and Green, *Judaism and Christianity in the First Century*, vol. 3, part 1, p. 656.
472. Sanders, *Jesus and Judaism*, p. 72.
473. Though Sanders quotes Josephus' remark that the holder of the temple held the whole Jewish people in his power (*Antiquity of the Jews*, 15:248), he makes nothing much of it in terms of political ramifications.
474. Sanders, *Jesus and Judaism*, p. 72.
475. This relocation is, according to Fortna, a relocation by John, who found it at the end of the Sign Source (Fortna,

'Sign Source' in Miller, *The Complete Gospels*, p. 187). For Fortna's arguments see *The Fourth Gospel and its Predecessor*, pp. 119, 120, 124 and 126ff.

476. Crossan, *Jesus, A Revolutionary Biography*, p. 130.
477. For a discussion of this miracle story see chapter 6.
478. Crossan, *Jesus, A Revolutionary Biography*, p. 133.
479. Regarding the historical likelihood that this accurately portrays Pharisaic legal thought, see Sanders, *Jewish Law from Jesus to the Mishnah*, p. 55.
480. Crossan, *Who Killed Jesus?*, p. 65.
481. Mack, *A Myth of Innocence*, pp. 291–2.
482. Powell, *Jesus as a Figure in History*, p. 28.

Chapter 8: **The End Foreshadowed**

483. Theissen and Merz, *The Historical Jesus*, p. 483; Dibelius, *From Tradition to Gospel*, p. 225. For an exposition on the integration of these formulas into Mark's narrative frame see Mack, *A Myth of Innocence*, pp. 278–81.
484. An example of this is Paula Fredriksen. Chapter 3 of her book *Jesus of Nazareth, King of the Jews*, 'Trajectories: Paul, the Gospels, and Jesus' (pp. 74–154) is devoted to this thesis.
485. Miller, 'Can the Historical Jesus be Made Safe for Orthodoxy? A Critique of The Jesus Quest by Ben Witherington III', in JHC 4/1 (Spring 1997), p. 127. Emphasis original.
486. By this term the present author intends statements that place the eschaton or the end at an unknown time.
487. Miller, 'Can the Historical Jesus be Made Safe for Orthodoxy?' in JHC 4/1 (Spring 1997), p. 129.
488. Funk and Hoover, *The Five Gospels*, p. 114.
489. Bornkamm, *Jesus of Nazareth*, p. 67. John Kloppenborg uses the same terminology in reference to Q 17:23–37 (correspondence 9 November 2000 with Robert J. Miller from electronic seminar on his book *Excavating Q* hosted by the Synoptic-L list and moderated by Mark Goodacre and Stephen Carlson).

490. Kloppenborg, in correspondence 9 November 2000 with Robert J. Miller from electronic seminar on his book *Excavating Q* hosted by the Synoptic-L list and moderated by Mark Goodacre and Stephen Carlson.

491. John is, in fact, the only source that does not have these two eschatologies. John has purposely made all of his text realized eschatology.

492. According to Udo Schnelle, the framework of Jesus' 'messianic secret' in Mark has been at the centre of Markan research since 'the groundbreaking study of William Wrede' *(The History and Theology of the New Testament Writings*, p. 214). For a thorough discussion of the messianic secret see Schnelle's treatment (ibid. pp. 210–17).

493. For a summary of other suggested solutions to the Son of man terminology see Dunn, *Unity and Diversity in the New Testament*, pp. 35–40.

494. The Greek word *Parakleton* (παράκλητον) is translated mainly as 'Comforter' but is only translated thus when the word is used in its broadest terms. The word may, in a stricter sense, be translated as 'Counsellor' (as the RSV) or 'Advocate' (as the Weymouth and the NEB). The NJB, on the other hand, does not translate it but merely writes 'Paraclete' and then explains in a footnote that 'the Gk word means "advocate", "counsellor", "protector"'. James Moffatt's translation uses an even broader term, 'Helper', leaving the historical judicial use of the word and applying its literal meaning 'Called to one's side'.

495. B. H. Streeter made an analogy in which he found the recovery of the sources used by John to be as likely as the reconstruction of a pig from a string of sausages (see *The Four Gospels*, p. 337, cited in Hawkin, *The Johannine World*, p. 48). More recent work amongst Johannine scholars seems to be more optimistic about the possibility of reconstructing the sources behind John.

496. The hypothesis of a prophetic or angelic archetypal origin has been voiced by previous commentators (see J. Ashton's

article 'Paraclete' in Freedman, *The Anchor Bible Dictionary*, vol. 5, pp. 152–3).

497. Hypothesis of a primitive Hebrew text is quite conjectural and is as such not crucial for this analysis.

498. To connect the original Hebrew text with an eyewitness to Jesus is completely futile. The Hebrew text, if it existed, may have filled no more than a dozen lines, from which the Greek came into being and was expanded.

499. Joostan in his article in *Revue d'Histoire des Religions*, 77 Année, f. 3, jul.- sept., 1997 as well as ' "Le Père envoie le Fils". La provenance occidentale d'une locution Syriaque', in ibid. Tome 214, f. 3, jul.- sept., 1997 demonstrates that the translators of the Old Syriac employed distinct Western Aramaic dialects, as opposed to the local Syriac (Western Aramaic), showing that they used oral lore to supplement their translation. The latter article works with the word 'sent' which is rendered either 'ܫܕܪܗ', which is Syriac, or 'ܫܠܚܗ' which is the Palestinian word. The present author has found no occurrences of the latter and six of the former in the test we will be dealing with, showing that the text had no Palestinian oral tradition which fits with the hypothesis so far.

500. Lyon, *Syriac Gospel Translations*, p. 5.

501. The Diatessaron is a harmony of the four gospels (though some conjecture a fifth, Jewish-Christian, gospel was also used) written by Tatian about 170 CE in Syriac (though this too has been questioned). Lyon is not convinced that the consensus that the Old Syriac is secondary is in fact true (ibid. pp. 203–7).

502. ibid. p. 192.

503. Addai, reputably the founder of Christianity in Eddesa (Syria) in the 1st century, also refers to this passage saying, 'to the same Places that the Son hath gone to prepare for every one worthy of them' (Burkitt, *Evangelion Da-Mepharreshe*, vol. 1, p. 507).

504. There are few places where Jesus speaks of Himself emphatically with the words 'I am the . . .' (ἐγώ εἰμι).

505. The word is thoroughly Greek and does not have a good Semitic counterpart. In the Syriac text the word appears as a loan word from the Greek.

506. The Greek ἄλλον is to be understood as 'another of same type' as opposed to ἕτερος, which is understood as 'another of a different type'.

507. Here the Sinaiticus reads ܦܪܩܠܝܛܐ while the Cureton reads ܦܪܩܠܛܐ. This latter reading is most certainly the true reading and the former is most likely to be a shaky scribal hand (only Lewis notes this variant reading while Burkitt passes over it, giving only the Cureton reading). The former reading has been used to suggest that *periklutos* is intended in the Syriac text. This cannot be abduced from the reading, nor is it even likely to be an original reading since even in the Sinaiticus it is used only once out of the four times the word appears.

508. Matthew Black in his *An Aramaic Approach to the Gospels and Acts* comments on the translation of ἵνα (that) with the Syriac d^e^ (ܕ), which in this verse is supported by Old Latin manuscripts. He calls this 'a piece of valuable evidence for an Aramaic tradition behind a Johannine saying of Jesus' (p. 77).

509. The KJV uses the archaic word 'Ghost' (from the Germanic *geist*) which, in modern translations, has been superseded by the more common 'Spirit' (from the Latin *spiritus*), the same word found in the title 'The Spirit of Truth' (to *pneuma tes aletheias*, τὸ πνεῦμα τῆς ἀληθείας).

510. Cyrilliona is hardly quoting this text when he writes: 'The Spirit shall come with His tongues, and the Paraclete with His revelations.' Here 'Spirit' is masculine (though it is usually feminine in Syriac; see Burkitt, *Evangelion Da-Mepharreshe*, vol. 2, p. 151). In *Doctrina Apostolorum* we read: 'What time I have ascended unto my Father, I will send (ܡܫܕܪ) you the spirit, the Paraclete, who will teach you everything that it is right for you to know and to make known.' The gender here, again, is masculine but otherwise we have the recurring phrase 'that spirit, the Paraclete',

which must have been common phraseology until the Peshitta (see ibid. p. 108). The significance of gender will be discussed below.

511. In his masterful doctoral thesis *Revelation Taught: The Paraclete in the Gospel of John*, pp. 56–7, Eskil Franck suggests that the word 'witness' (*μαρτυρεῖν)* should be used as Philo does in the sense of being didactic, teaching.

512. While Spirit is neuter, the only physical appearance of the Holy Spirit in the gospel is the dove, which is feminine; the Paraclete is masculine. But in John 16:13 as well as 15:26, the masculine demonstrative pronoun ἐκεῖνος (translated 'he') appears in reference to the Spirit of truth. In the latter case this can be explained as a carrying through of the thought of the Paraclete from the beginning of the sentence, bypassing the Spirit of truth and making the Paraclete the object of the demonstrative pronoun. This is much more difficult to imagine in the former case, for here the Paraclete and the demonstrative pronoun are separated by three verses, whereas the Spirit of truth appears there just before it. This can be explained by the existence of a Hebrew archetype, for unlike Syriac, in which 'spirit' is feminine, the Hebrew word רוח can be masculine.

513. This is discussed in endnote 179 in chapter 3.

514. 'I will raise them up a Prophet from among their brethren, like unto thee, and will put my words in his mouth; and he shall speak unto them all that I shall command him' (KJV).

515. Black notes that in this verse the use of the present participle to 'express a future tense' is an Aramaicism (*An Aramaic Approach to the Gospels and Acts*, pp. 131–2).

516. 'But there were false prophets also among the people, even as there shall be false teachers among you, who privily shall bring in damnable heresies, even denying the Lord that bought them, and bring upon themselves swift destruction' (KJV).

517. Present-day Turkey.

518. Aune, *Prophecy in Early Christianity*, p. 314.
519. ibid. p. 315.
520. The POxy 850, which is the only surviving fragment of this speech, reads 'Ιηυ ὁ παράκλητος'. Unfortunately, a lacuna in the document makes it impossible to determine how the sentence continues. Assuming that it follows the style of the rest of the discourse, it seems likely that it went on to specify to whom Jesus was Paraclete. Junod and Kaestli, at any rate, add τῶν (the genitive plural definite article) in brackets (*Acta Iohannis*, p. 119).
521. Russell, 'Apocalyptic Literature', in Metzger and Coogan, *The Oxford Companion to the Bible*, pp. 34–6.
522. Esler, *The First Christians in their Social Worlds*, p. 97.
523. ibid. p. 99.
524. Both the NIV and the NEB read also 'the end of the age'. Jehovah Witnesses have for doctrinal reasons (they believe that Jesus returned in 1914 and is now controlling their governing body) insisted that the word *parousias* should be translated as 'presence' ('the sign of your presence and the conclusion of the system of things?'). The distinction, however, is of minor significance: He shall leave (to return to the Father). When He is yet again present, he shall have 'come' or 'returned'.
525. Bilde, 'Afspejler Mark 13 et jødisk apokalyptisk forlæg fra kriseåret 40?' ('Does Mark 13 reflect a Jewish apocalyptic composition from the crisis year 40?'), in Pedersen, *Nytestamentlige Studier*, pp. 105–34. It is in part Bilde whom Theissen answers in his exposition. While it is true that no prophets arose in direct connection with the Caligula crisis, the Samaritan prophet discussed in chapter 2 arose in 36 CE.
526. Theissen, *The Gospels in Context*, p. 153.
527. ibid. p. 114.
528. ibid. p. 154.
529. ibid. p. 155.
530. ibid.

531. The problem of defining 'the world' (*oikoumene*, οἰκουμένη) lies in that the word was sometimes used as a reference to the civilized (Greek) world as opposed to the one settled by 'barbarians'. It was sometimes used to refer to the Roman empire and sometimes to the whole inhabited earth. Neither does the clarification 'for a witness unto all nations' afford much help since the word *ethnos* (ἔθνεσιν) can mean anything from the smallest group of people, like a family, to the largest, the entire Gentile population. No doubt 'the whole earth' has grown throughout history as more and more of the earth has become accessible through the development of transport. At the time of Christ, 'the whole earth' probably included little more than some of Europe, the Middle East and northern Africa.
532. We know that prior to his conversion, in either 33 or 35, Paul had been active in persecuting the church. For issues of chronology, see Koester, *History and Literature of Early Christianity*, pp. 101–4.
533. Stark, *The Rise of Christianity*, chapter 6, 'The Martyrs: Sacrifice as Rational Choice'.
534. Theissen, *The Gospels in Context*, pp. 273–4.
535. See Driver, *Introduction to the Literature of the Old Testament*, pp. 491–2.
536. Vermes, *The Religion of Jesus the Jew*, p. 62.
537. Vermes, *The Dead Sea Scrolls in English*, pp. 279–82.
538. Theissen, *The Gospels in Context*, pp. 128–9.
539. Bilde, 'Afspejler Mark 13 et jødisk apokalyptisk forlæg fra kriseåret 40?' ('Does Mark 13 reflect a Jewish apocalyptic composition from the crisis year 40?'), in Pedersen, *Nytestamentlige Studier*, pp. 117–18.
540. ASV is supported by WEY, Moffatt and NEB.
541. As mentioned earlier, John views the prophecy of Caiaphas as being 'not of himself: but being high priest that year', he rightly foresaw the sacrifice of Jesus. The character and acts of Caiaphas, however, deny that he was rightly guided by God. His appointment to the office of high priest was based on politics rather than religion.

542. Although this has already been discussed, it should be noted that some scholars suggest that the title 'Son of man', which probably comes from Daniel 7:13, was only used by Christ to refer to His future appearance (Witherington, *Jesus, Paul and the End of the World*, pp. 39, 172 but p. 170), while others suggest that it originally referred to people in general (Funk and Hoover, *The Five Gospels*, p. 77). If the latter be the case, 'but the Son of man hath not where to lay [his] head' (Matthew 8:20; Luke 9:58) would be a general bemoaning of mankind's state but few passages allow for this understanding. The above text is also found in the Gospel of Thomas (logia 86). Theissen connects it directly with the itinerants (*Sociology of Early Palestinian Christianity*, p. 10).

543. Tuckett, like most, understands *astraph* in the conventional sense and interprets the lightning as a sign of the suddenness with which the Son of man will appear (*Q and the History of Early Christianity*, p. 159) Catchpole, however, concurs: 'To say that the lightning ἐξέρχεται from the east and shines as far as to the west (Matt 24:27) is to use language more appropriate to the sun than lightning' (*The Quest for Q*, p. 253).

544. The word appears in the Hebrew text in Psalms 103:5 and in the LXX has the above-mentioned Greek word.

545. Evans, *Saint Luke*, p. 633.

546. Müller, *Kommentar til Matthæusevangeliet*, p. 499.

547. Catchpole, *The Quest for Q*, p. 253: 'a powerful consensus'.

548. Theissen holds this section to have been part of Mark's original source (*The Gospels in Context*, p. 130). It is obvious that this draws from Old Testament imagery.

549. The sun and the moon are commonly-used terms with regard to time. The day when the sun no longer gives its light is, in a sense, the end of time. Psalms 72:5 'They shall fear thee as long as the sun and moon endure, throughout all generations' (KJV). So this could be just another way of saying 'at the end of time', which extends beyond 'all generations'.

550. Generally the process is believed to work the other way so that realized eschatology is reworked into far eschatology. This example should alert us that the opposite could also happen.
551. Matthew is unique in mentioning the 'sign of the Son of man'.
552. (ἀγγέλους) in the strictest sense means 'messengers', 'bringers of tidings'.
553. Matthew 16:3 uses the allegory of seasons to convey that of spiritual springtime: 'And in the morning, [It will be] foul weather to day: for the heaven is red and lowering. Ye know how to discern the face of the heaven; but ye cannot [discern] the signs of the times.'
554. Witherington also notes that Matthew substitutes this expression with 'the Son of man coming in his kingdom', demonstrating that he understood this to be a future event (*Jesus, Paul and the End of the World*, p. 38). This, however, remains questionable. When Matthew wrote in c. 80, was near eschatology not becoming increasingly untenable? Most of those who personally heard Jesus were dead or dying.
555. Witherington rejects this and writes 'such attempts usually assume that "all these things" include the coming of the Son of Man, which is unlikely' (ibid. p. 44).
556. The LXX reflects this usage in Greek as well and uses the words 'τῆς γενεᾶς ταύτης' (this generation, LXX: Psalm 11:8) and γενεὰ (generation LXX: Psalm 111:2). Note the first example implies that 'this generation' will endure 'for ever', while the other identifies the seed of the man that fears God with the generation of the upright.
557. The inclusion is held by most scholars to be authentic and is included in most modern translations such as ASV, RSV, ED, NEB, NJB and NIV. A majority of manuscripts exclude it such as $\aleph^1$, L and W as well as the Vulgate, Syriac and Coptic versions but it is included in $\aleph^{*,2}$, B, D, Θ, f^{13} and some Italian and Latin manuscripts.
558. Cataclysm (κατακλυσμοῦ); literally, 'flood'.

559. Funk and Hoover, *The Five Gospels*, p. 507.
560. Schmidt, *Das Thomas-Evangelium*, p. 149.
561. Luise Schottroff in her article 'Itinerant prophetesses: A feminist analysis of the sayings source Q', in Piper, *The Gospel Behind the Gospels* notes that the reference to the women grinding at the mill indicates that women were considered equals and were themselves responsible for their spiritual survival (p. 360).
562. Sirac was written by Jesus Ben Sira, the son of Eleazar who, according to his own statement, lived in Jerusalem but travelled extensively. It was written not for personal gain but for 'all who seek instruction' (Sirac 24:34 RAPC).
563. 'διαθήκην αἰώνιον' (*diathekai aionos*, or Latin *testamenti saeculi*); the word 'eternal' or 'age' has been dealt with earlier in this chapter.
564. Tuckett, *Q and the History of Early Christianity*, p. 159.
565. Catchpole, *The Quest for Q*, p. 248ff.
566. This image is extremely well-documented in several independent sources. Its appearance in 1 Thessalonians 5:2, the Gospel of Thomas (21:3, 103) and Q 12:39–40 makes it likely that it is an early oral tradition. Funk and Hoover comment that 'sayings about Jesus' return "like a thief in the night" were common in early Christian tradition' and that the language therefore was 'Christianized language and was not formulated by Jesus'. They further add, 'The use of the phrase "son of Adam" also makes it likely that this verse is a Christian expression' (*The Five Gospels*, p. 252). Such a conclusion is, in the present author's opinion, completely unsatisfactory in view of the material available and seems to presume a unified Christian language at a very early stage.
567. The Greek word for watch, *gregorete*, and Latin, *vigilante*, were popular names in the early church. From the Greek, the name 'Gregory' has survived.
568. The numbers here seem of no consequence but, as in the previous chapter, judgement falls equally both ways: half are lost, the others are saved.

569. Catchpole, *The Quest for Q*, p. 57.
570. This seems to have a fair amount of material in common with the parable in Luke 19:11. The great number of discrepancies, however, have cast doubt as to whether these are the same parables or two different ones. The present author has elected to assume the latter.
571. A talent is a weight measure (one talent is approximately 34 kg). It is difficult to say what metal is referred to: the Syric and Arabic manuscripts say silver, the Ethiopian says gold. Whether one or the other, a true fortune was given to all his servants.
572. The goat was often associated with sin because it was used for sacrifice for the remission of the sins of the people of Israel. Leviticus 16:10 relates how lots were cast between two goats, one to be killed for the sacrifice and the other, the scapegoat, to be let free in the dessert. The positioning of the sheep at the right hand is used to denote favour. The king would seat one at his right side as a special place of honour.

Chapter 9: ***The Lord's Last Supper***

573. Council II. *Catechism of the Catholic Church*, p. 394, para. 1407.
574. There seems to be a discrepancy between the Synoptic Gospels (Matthew, Mark and Luke) and John as to whether this event took place during Passover. This discrepancy, as we shall see below, appears to be because of divergent interpretations of the Lord's Supper tradition.
575. Kerioth is in the southern part of Judea. All the other disciples were from Galilee and it is difficult to imagine that a 'foreigner' of Galilee would know of Jesus' claims or even have heard of Him in such an early part of His ministry so as to become a companion. On the other hand, one document (D, dating from the 5th century) adds the words 'from Kariot' (ἀπὸ Καρυώτου) in John 12:4.

576. The word *kleptes* (κλέπτης) implies one who steals through treason or subtlety.
577. Gibran, *Jesus, The Son of Man*, pp. 174–5.
578. Sayers, *The Man Born to be King*, p. 136.
579. Elliott, *The Apocryphal New Testament*, p. 219.
580. Epiphanius, Haer. 30:1:5.
581. Irenaeus, *Against Heresies*, 1:31:1.
582. Akeldama (Aramaic for 'field of blood') is, according to Eusebius, located south of the valley of Hinnom.
583. Dunn, *Unity and Diversity in the New Testament*, p. 93.
584. Papias was the Bishop of Hierapolis in Asia Minor. He was the disciple of John (which John is uncertain) and companion of St Polycarp (one letter of whom survives as well as an account of his death). He lived in the period 60 to 130 CE and therefore the tradition given is of considerable importance. None of his works have survived, apart from quotations in the Church Fathers' writings.
585. *The Apostolic Fathers*, pp. 380–1.
586. Apollinarius was Bishop of Leodicea, born c. 310, died 390.
587. Very few scholars today believe that either Luke or Matthew was dependent on the other.
588. Dunn, *Unity and Diversity in the New Testament*, p. 162.
589. Crossan, *Jesus, A Revolutionary Biography*, p. 130.
590. Meeks, *The First Urban Christians*, pp. 67–70.
591. 'And when he had given thanks, he brake [it], and said, Take, eat: this is my body, which is broken for you: this do in remembrance of me. After the same manner also [he took] the cup, when he had supped, saying, This cup is the new testament in my blood: this do ye, as oft as ye drink [it], in remembrance of me' (1 Corinthians 11:24–5 KJV).
592. 'For as often as ye eat this bread, and drink this cup, ye do shew the Lord's death till he come' (1 Corinthians 11:26 KJV).
593. Irenaeus, *Against Heresies*, 4:33:4. Irenaeus wrote at the end of the 2nd century but most certainly the sect existed

before that in some form or another, perhaps taking its origin in Jerusalem.

594. Epiphanius, Haer. 30:22:4.
595. Didache was discussed in chapter 1. St Ignatius also mentions the practice (Letter to the Philadelphians, 4).
596. Reed comments that this may allude either to Israel as a whole (Ezekiel 15) or to the Davidic lineage in particular (Ezekiel 17). Reed, 'The Hebrew Epic and the Didache', in Jefford, *The Didache in Context*, p. 220.
597. Crossan, *The Birth of Christianity*, pp. 436–8. Cf. Crossan, *The Historical Jesus*, pp. 360–7. John Riggs concurs ('The Sacred Food of Didache 9–10 and Second-century Ecclesiologies', in Jefford, *The Didache in Context*, p. 265).
598. A similar thought was current amongst the Qumran sect which refers to this event in its writings.
599. The word often rendered 'daily' (ἐπιούσιον) is a very uncommon Greek word. The word has been translated differently in all the oldest translations available. The Latin reads 'supersubstantial', the Syriac reads 'eternal' in one and 'necessary' in another, the Sahidic reads 'to come' and the Middle Egyptian and Boheric reads 'tomorrow's'. This last reading is also supported by the ancient Syriac gospel called the Gospel of the Nazaraeans.
600. Ernst Kutsch reflects the consensus in this regard ('Passover in the New Testament' in his article 'Passover' in Roth, *Encyclopedia Judaica*, pp. 171–2).
601. This doctrine – that the body and blood are both present in each of the wine and bread – meant that when wine was no longer given to the laity, they would still receive full communion through the bread alone.
602. This refers to the doctrine that the high moment of the Eucharist was no longer the communion itself but rather the transubstantiation or the change of the elements.
603. Held in the period 1545 to 1563.
604. Born in 1483 and often referred to as the father of Protestantism, he became an Augustinian monk in 1505 and from then onwards started to develop doctrines

increasingly divergent from those of the Roman Catholic Church. This led to the composition of his 95 theses, which triggered a summons to Rome and the ever-widening rift between himself and the church. Though Luther was against removing wine from the laity in the sacrament, he believed the church doctrine of consubstantiation.

605. Swiss reformer, 1484–1531.
606. Osterhaven in 'Lord's Supper, Views of', in Elwell, *Evangelical Dictionary of Theology*, pp. 653–6.
607. French reformer, 1509–64.
608. The doctrine held that there was a spiritual presence of Jesus in the elements.
609. Crossan is emphatic that παρεδίδετο should not be translated as 'betrayed' but as 'handed over', meaning that God handed over the Lord (*The Birth of Christianity*, p. 439). However, Liddell-Scott refers to Thucydides' use of it thus, besides which the reference to it happening on the night of the Lord's supper seems to suggest some narrative like the gospels, even if we take it to mean that Jesus was handed over by God.
610. Crossan, *The Birth of Christianity*, p. 434.
611. Theissen, *A Theory of Primitive Christian Religion*, pp. 129–31.

Chapter 10: ***The Crucifixion***

612. 'And Jesus saith unto them, All ye shall be offended because of me this night: for it is written, I will smite the shepherd, and the sheep shall be scattered' (Mark 14:27).
613. 'Awake, O sword, against my shepherd, and against the man [that is] my fellow, saith the LORD of hosts: smite the shepherd, and the sheep shall be scattered: and I will turn mine hand upon the little ones' (Zechariah 13:7).
614. The expression 'fall on one's face' used by Matthew expresses a particular devotion. It is found also in Luke 5:12. According to Maimon (Hilch. Tephilla, ch. 5. sect. 14, 15, cited by Gill, *An Exposition of the New and Old Testament*, in his commentary on this verse), this is only

to be done by 'he that knows in himself that he is righteous, as Joshua'. Mark does not use this expression and Luke says that He 'kneeled'.

615. Abba has been understood in various ways. The Greek addition ὁ πατήρ (Father, or the Father) is obviously only an insertion of the evangelist as an explanation to an audience that was unfamiliar with Hebrew. It could be the Hebrew word אב (ab) but may also have been a corruption of the Syriac ܐܒܝ (abi) 'my father'; this is the wording of Matthew.

616. 'This cup' is an expression denoting an evil fate. It is to be found in Psalms 75:8 and Isaiah 51:17.

617. These two verses are omitted by all the oldest witnesses (P75, א[1], A, B, N, T, W and Syriac Sinaiticus and Boheric versions) and are generally not regarded as part of the original Luke (Nestle-Aland and Westcott and Hort mark it as an early insertion).

618. According to John, Peter was the wielder of the sword. Also, John gives the name of the servant of the high priest: Malchus.

619. It appears as though Mark is using a narrative that does not belong in this context: that Jesus is about to be apprehended but wards off the attackers with a remark of some sort (perhaps the tabooed name of God, Yahweh).

620. The Secret Gospel of Mark, which, as we discussed in chapter 1, Helmut Koester suggests may be a source of the Gospel of Mark, contains a story in which Jesus raises a young man: 'And after six days Jesus told him what to do, and in the evening the youth comes to him, wearing a linen cloth over his naked body. And he remained with him that night, for Jesus taught him the mystery of the Kingdom of God.' With the above as a working theory, the book is probably to be dated sometime near the turn of the 1st century.

621. According to Fortna, this comes from the Sign Source which, however, was much shorter, excluding verses 18:30–3, 34–7, 40 – 19:6, 19:7–13 (Miller, *The Complete*

Gospels, pp. 190–1). For an analysis of the pre-Johannine material see Fortna, *The Fourth Gospel and its Predecessor*, pp. 173–6.

622. Cohn, 'Reflection on the Trial of Jesus', in Neusner and Green, *Judaism and Christianity in the First Century*, p. 282.
623. Catchpole, 'The Problem of the Historicity of the Sanhedrin Trial', in Bammel, *The Trial of Jesus*, p. 59.
624. Theissen and Merz, *The Historical Jesus*, p. 461.
625. Catchpole, 'The Problem of the Historicity of the Sanhedrin Trial' in Bammel, *The Trial of Jesus*, pp. 58–9.
626. ibid. p. 63.
627. ibid. p. 65.
628. Werner Kelber maintains that this story serves Mark's anti-disciple plot to discredit his oral predecessors (*The Oral and the Written Gospel*, p. 128). It is, however, also possible to see it as a consolation for those Christians who were persecuted and dissimulated their faith. The issue of historicity will be discussed in the next chapter.
629. Some ancient manuscripts read 'the other disciple' ($\aleph^2$ and C are the most notable) instead of 'another disciple' (supported by the most ancient witnesses). The first presumably implies that this disciple refers to 'the beloved disciple' or John. This is regarded as part of the Sign Source (see Miller, *The Complete Gospels*, p. 180).
630. The oldest witness to this text, Papyri 66 (dated about 200 CE), does not mention that the other disciple was acquainted with the high priest.
631. The gospels (Matthew 27:2, Luke 3:1) refer to Pilate only as governor (ήγεμονι), though the formal title, according to both Josephus and Tacitus, was held to be 'procurator'. In 1961, however, an inscription was found in which Pilate dedicated a temple to the people of Caesarea under the title of 'prefect'. Finegan comments that 'the two terms are therefore broadly interchangeable, "prefect" seems to have been more of a military title and "procurator" to have carried more of the connotation of financial administration; also "prefect" seems to have been preferred in the time

of Augustus, "procurator" to have become the prevailing title from Claudius (41–54) onward' (*The Archeology of the New Testament*, p. 139; see also Theissen and Merz, *The Historical Jesus*, p. 455).

632. This has been deemed rather unlikely by a few critics, owing to the historical descriptions that have reached us. They find it unlikely that Pilate would let anyone go who had been accused of sedition, much less one who had not denied this when questioned. Generally, the Synoptists put the entire blame on the Jews and hold them responsible.

633. This seems altogether unlikely, since Herod had no jurisdiction in Jerusalem.

634. The final remark, which comes from a Lukan source, 'And Herod and Pilate became friends with each other that very day: for before they were at enmity between themselves' does not seem to align completely with the Synoptist attitude to Pilate. Here Pilate becomes friendly with Herod and is probably considered equally guilty. Works later appeared that tended to reinforce the synoptic point of view and the 5th–6th century work called *Acts of Pilate* exonerates him with the following words: 'And now, lo, one that was uncircumcised but circumcised in heart, took water and washed his hands before the sun, saying: I am Innocent of the blood of this just person: see ye to it.'

635. Theissen and Merz state that there is no evidence and indeed a curious silence as to the existence of a custom of granting amnesty but notes two instances, one in Egypt (mentioned in Papyrus Florentinus no. 61) and another in Palestine (mentioned by Josephus in *Antiquities* 20:9:5), where amnesty was indeed given (*The Historical Jesus*, pp. 465–6). In the first instance the culprit was to be flogged but the governor was under pressure from the crowd, so he was released. In the other case the procurator, Albinus, was leaving his office and decided, in order to leave Jerusalem on a good note, to execute all prisoners worthy of death and to set free petty thieves with a fine.

Not only does it seem implausible that the pro-Roman Josephus would not mention such a tradition but the two exceptions seem to the present author to underscore the implausibility that a procurator (let alone a prefect) would grant amnesty to one condemned to death.

636. This name, found only in the text of the Syriac Sinaiticus (and certain minor documents), has received much support, especially from F. C. Burkitt (see *Evangelion da-Mepharreshe*, vol. 2, p. 277–8), and is with some reluctance used in the main text of Nestle-Aland while Westcott and Hort's text uses the Greek majority text.
637. *Jesus, A Revolutionary Biography*, p. 143.
638. Funk, *The Acts of Jesus*, pp. 146–52. See also Crossan, *Who Killed Jesus?*, p. 82–117.
639. ibid. p. 152.
640. See Hebrews 13:12: 'Wherefore Jesus also, that he might sanctify the people with his own blood, suffered without the gate.' The author of the Hebrews seems to be using an analogy based on a fact known from a traditional narrative.
641. Cyrene (Κυρηναῖον) was a city (now Tripoli) in Upper Libya, North Africa. Mark mentions that Simon Cyrene was the father of Alexander and Rufus, who must somehow have been known to the audience of this gospel. Some who believe that Mark composed his gospel in Rome feel that it is not unlikely that it is the same Rufus who is mentioned by Paul in Romans 16:13.
642. Matthew alone mentions this (27:34). Those who take the Nazarite vow are not allowed to drink this brew (Numbers 6:3). This differs from the drink Jesus was offered on the cross, which was a refreshing drink. The Talmud (Sanhedrin 43a) allows a drink of wine mixed with incense to be given to one who is to be put to death.
643. See chapter 1.
644. The historical Pilate was undoubtedly neither a monster, as Josephus portrays him, nor a man of innocence, as the

gospels portray him (see Crossan, *Jesus, A Revolutionary Biography*, pp.136–40).

645. The belief that Jesus only 'appeared' to be real and that He was in reality a spiritual creature who could therefore feel no pain. This belief is found in some strands of Gnosticism. Arthur J. Dewey notes that this is based on Isaiah 53:7 and does not imply docetism (Miller, *The Complete Gospels*, p. 403 n. 4:1).

646. There is a word for word correspondence between the two texts.

647. 'For dogs have compassed me: the assembly of the wicked have enclosed me: they pierced my hands and my feet. I may tell all my bones: they look [and] stare upon me. They part my garments among them, and cast lots upon my vesture' (KJV).

648. In an infancy narrative from the 5th or 6th century named 'The Arabic Gospel of the Infancy of Our Saviour', the two thieves are met by the holy family in a desert area. The goodly thief (named Titus) pleads with his companion (Dumachus) to leave the family alone and is recompensed with the infant Jesus' prophecy: 'O mother, the Jews will crucify me at Jerusalem; And these two thieves will be raised upon the cross along with me, Titus on my right hand and Dumachus on my left; and after that day Titus shall go before me into paradise' (Elliott, *The Apocryphal New Testament*, p. 105).

649. This verse represents a real problem for those who believe in 'soul sleep', such as some Baptist theologians (see the Forty-two Articles of Edward VI) as well as the Jehovah Witnesses. In their translation, the Jehovah Witnesses place the comma after 'today' so that the verse reads: 'Truly I tell you today, you will be with me in Paradise.' While in a footnote they appeal to the fact that there is no comma in the Greek uncials and the Syriac Cureton which supports their translation, the idiomatic expression 'Verily, I say unto you' (ἀμήν σοι λέγω or similar phraseology) appears

over 70 times, none placed in a time frame. Placing the comma after 'today' therefore seems unnatural.

650. The immense pain already endured by Jesus – the flogging, the crown of thorns and general beating by the soldiers – now culminates in the piercing of His wrists and placing His feet on top of each other and hammering them to the cross. The pain resulting from relieving the pressure on either feet or wrists would have produced cramps that inhibited breathing. It is thus difficult to believe that Jesus could have cried out loud (see Crossan, *Jesus, A Revolutionary Biography*, p. 125).

651. That is, the name of Yahweh. According to the Toldoth, Jesus was able to do miracles because He had stolen the 'Ineffable Name' from the foundation-stone in the temple of Jerusalem (2:2, 3).

652. Schonfield, *According to the Hebrews.* See also Goldstein's shorter text in *Jesus in the Jewish Tradition*.

653. The word 'God' was sometimes substituted with 'Power', as is seen in Eusebius' *Ecclesiastical History*, 2:23. The words of James the Just are reported as being 'He himself sitteth in heaven at the right hand of the great Power, and is about to come upon the clouds of heaven.'

654. JPS (Jewish Publishing Society of America, 1917). Two things are notable: 1) the numbering is off by one verse because they follow the traditional Masoritic Text and 2) the interpretation of כארי which is rendered 'pierced' in the Christian translations and 'are at' in the Jewish. Another possible translation is 'bound', which was suggested in the Danish pre-publication version 92. The LXX uses the word ὤρυξαν which means 'dig'.

655. 'They gave me also gall for my meat; and in my thirst they gave me vinegar to drink.'

656. Crossan, *The Cross that Spoke*, pp. 163–4.

657. 'I saw the Lord standing upon the altar: and he said, Smite the lintel of the door, that the posts may shake: and cut them in the head, all of them; and I will slay the last of them with the sword: he that fleeth of them shall not flee

away, and he that escapeth of them shall not be delivered' (KJV).

658. 'The earth is utterly broken down, the earth is clean dissolved, the earth is moved exceedingly. The earth shall reel to and fro like a drunkard, and shall be removed like a cottage; and the transgression thereof shall be heavy upon it; and it shall fall, and not rise again. And it shall come to pass in that day, [that] the LORD shall punish the host of the high ones [that are] on high, and the kings of the earth upon the earth' (KJV).

659. Crossan points out that to Mark it is not the resurrection but the manner of Jesus' death that convinces the centurion that Jesus was the Son of God *(The Cross that Spoke*, pp. 348–9).

660. 'He keepeth all his bones: not one of them is broken' (KJV).

661. 'And I will pour upon the house of David, and upon the inhabitants of Jerusalem, the spirit of grace and of supplications: and they shall look upon me whom they have pierced, and they shall mourn for him, as one mourneth for [his] only [son], and shall be in bitterness for him, as one that is in bitterness for [his] firstborn' (KJV).

662. This modification is, in all likelihood, the reason why some Christian scribes changed most Greek and some (less significant) Hebrew texts to conform to John.

663. 'And he that saw [it] bare record, and his record is true: and he knoweth that he saith true, that ye might believe' (KJV).

664. McGrath, *Historical Theology*, pp. 30–1.

665. This is what has been termed a 'minor agreement' and the Greek texts show other agreements between Matthew and Luke but also divergences from Mark.

666. Koester's theory was discussed in chapter 1.

667. The Greek text is not extant in this case and only the Coptic is available. 'Deserving' has been suggested as a better translation for ⲛ̄ⲁⲝⲓⲟⲥ (translated 'worthy' above), yet the word stems from the Greek ἄξιος usually translated as 'worthy'. The Thomas text seems to present the most

primitive version of this logia, and variations in Matthew and Luke (who never agree against the Thomas text) represent changes made by them.

668. Neyrey, 'Loss of Wealth, Loss of Family and Loss of Honour', in Esler, *Modelling Early Christianity*.
669. διακονῆσαι 'to minister', to help or assist
670. The theology of Paul is usually deduced from the 'indisputable' authentic Pauline epistles (Romans, 1 and 2 Corinthians, Galatians, Philippians, Philemon, 1 Thessalonians). These epistles (sometimes termed 'Principal Epistles' or 'Hauptbriefe') have been disputed by the so-called 'Dutch Radical' (see Hermann Detering, 'The Dutch Radical Approach to the Pauline Epistles', JHC 3/2 (Fall 1996), pp. 163–93), as well as F. C. Baur, who retained only Romans, 1 and 2 Corinthians and Galatians (the four letters). Darrell J. Doughty suggests that the authenticity of the Pauline literature is only maintained through reliance on works that likewise dated early on the basis of a faulty paradigm (see Darrell J. Doughty, 'Pauline Paradigms and Pauline Authenticity', JHC 1, Fall 1994, pp. 95–128). This is neither the appropriate forum nor does space allow for the proper consideration of the points raised by Doughty but with these reservations in mind we shall continue the survey on the assumption that the 'Principal Epistles' are authentic. This, of course, need not be the case for the contents to have value. The material is unquestionably an exposition of the theology of early Christianity, whether from Paul's own hand or from a Pauline school (on the latter view see W.C. Van Manen, 'Romans (Epistle)', in *Encyclopaedia Biblica*, vol. 4).
671. Galatians 5:11 as well as 1 Corinthians 1:18, 23.
672. Sanders, *Paul and Palestinian Judaism*, p. 453.
673. This epistle is anonymous and was attributed to Paul only at the end of the 2nd century by Clement of Alexandria. This we have from Eusebius, who mentions it in *Ecclesiastical History*, VI. 14. However, the work was already quoted in 96 CE by Clement of Rome in his (first) epistle to the

Corinthians. While some of the objections raised about the authorship of the Pauline literature could be equally well raised about the Clementine, the present author is willing to propose that a date near thc end of the 1st or beginning of the 2nd century is plausible. This is mainly because the end of the temple cult (70 CE) could not be in the too distant past.

674. This was the king of Salem who greeted Abraham (Genesis 14:18–20). He is subsequently mentioned only once in the Old Testament, in Psalms 110:4. Hebrews 5 deals extensively with him as a Christ-like figure. Melchizedek was already a significant messianic figure in 1st century Judaism, as witnessed both by the Dead Sea scrolls (see 11QMelc in Vermes, *The Dead Sea Scrolls in English*, pp. 300–1) and the Talmud (see Sukkah 52b, where he is referred to as 'the Righteous Priest' but also in a negative sense in Nedarim 32b). Later the figure was used by some Gnostics (see the document and introduction in Robinson, *The Nag Hammadi Library*, pp. 438–44).
675. The expression 'from the foundation of the world' ἀπὸ καταβολῆς κόσμου appears in Hebrews 9:26 and Revelation of John 13:8, 17:8 in talking of Jesus.
676. Dodd, *The Apostolic Preaching*, p. 20.
677. ibid. p. 25–6.
678. ibid. p. 27.
679. Dunn, *Unity and Diversity in the New Testament*, pp. 251–2, 263–5. Schnelle, *The History and Theology of the New Testament Writings*, pp. 383–98. Koester, *History and Literature of Early Christianity*, pp.156–7.
680. Homily 16.
681. See Fitzmyer, *Essays on the Semitic Background of the New Testament*, p. 449 n26.
682. Recognitions 55.
683. Recognitions 41.
684. Recognitions 42.
685. The Gospel of the Ebionites quotes Jesus as stating, 'I have come to abolish the sacrifices: if you do not cease from

sacrificing, the wrath [of God] will not cease from weighing upon you' (Epiphanius, adv. Haer. 30:16).

686. Augustine, *Confessions* 5.9.16.
687. Translation of Ali Yusuf.
688. See Daniel, *Islam and the West*, p. 13.
689. Apparently not fully aware of the teachings of the Qur'án, the author wrote several things that were contradictory with the Qur'án itself. It is extant today only in Spanish and Italian manuscripts, which may confidently be dated to the 15th century. Alternatively to the thesis that the gospel was a fully Muslim composition, Rodney Blackhirst's paper 'Sedition in Judea, Gospel of Barnabas' (in *Studies in Western Traditions*, Occasional Paper', no. 3, 1996, p. 84) proposes that the gospel was in fact originally a Judeo-Christian work which a later Muslim editor changed to suit his own theological views. The present author would like to thank Dr Blackhirst for allowing him to read his paper 'Barnabas and Gospels: Was There an Early Gospel of Barnabas?' prior to its publication. Blackhirst is amongst a small but increasing consensus that there is an older Christian substratum to the Gospel of Barnabas. The *Revue d'Histoire et de Philosophie Religieuses*, 2000, 80e Année, no. 3, 9:1–34 carried an article by Jan Joosten ('Jésus et l'aveugle-né (*Jn* 9,1–34) dans l'*Évangile de Barnabas* et dans le *Diatessaron*', pp. 359–69) which demonstrated a relationship with the Diatessaron, the early Syriac gospel harmony from 200 CE.
690. This belief was current among many Muslims, even at the time of William of Tripoli (Daniel, *Islam and the West*, p. 194).
691. Letter no. 99, 1 August 1521.
692. On Sanders's methodology see Powell, *Jesus as a Figure of History*, p.116. The reverse of this methodological view is tinkering with minutia, trying to dissect tradition, which Sanders finds will not 'greatly advance' our knowledge (see e.g. Sanders, *Jesus and Judaism*, p. 299).
693. Crossan, *Who Killed Jesus?*, pp. 82–5.

694. Crossan's two books on the passion are *The Cross that Spoke*, which is an extensive academic work, and *Who Killed Jesus?*, a shorter and more popular version, with a slightly greater emphasis on the historicity issue and less discussion of various sources.
695. Crossan, *Who Killed Jesus?*, p. 117.
696. That the high priest or the Sanhedrin could do this is generally disbelieved. See Brown, *The Origins of Christianity*, p. 110; Koester, *History and Literature of Early Christianity*, vol. 2, p. 99 but Bruce, *The Acts of the Apostles*, pp. 196–7.
697. Correspondence between Trajan and Pliny the Younger about Christians is cited with commentary in Crossan, *The Birth of Christianity*, pp. 4–8.
698. This thesis has recently been advanced in the paper 'Jesus in Oral Memory: The Initial Stages of the Jesus Tradition' by James D. G. Dunn on an Internet seminar hosted by X-Talk, 25 April–2 May 2001 and moderated by Jeffrey Gibson and Jack Kilmon.
699. Vermes, *The Changing Faces of Jesus*, p. 260.
700. Meeks, *The First Urban Christians*, pp. 134–5.
701. ibid. pp. 112–13.

Chapter 11: ***The Resurrection***

702. I here include the Gospel of Peter, mentioned in the preceding chapter.
703. The Sign Source, according to Fortna, mentions Joseph but not the reason for him not being openly a disciple (or, indeed, that he was not open about it; Miller, *The Complete Gospels*, p. 192). 'In v. 38 qualification of Joseph of Arimathæa's discipleship (**but secretly for fear of the Jews**) is anachronistic and surely Johannine' (Fortna, *The Fourth Gospel and its Predecessor*, p. 186, emphasis original).
704. Perhaps the friendly tone between Pilate and Herod is a sign of a common tradition shared by Luke and Peter (see previous chapter).
705. Crossan, *The Birth of Christianity,* p. 555.

706. Tobit 2:4 tells how the pious Tobit recovered the body of a fellow Jew for burial.
707. The Mishnah (Sanhedrin 6:5–6) states that two tombs should be kept for criminals (one for those beheaded or strangled and one for those who were stoned or burnt). After a year they were honourably re-buried but without public mourning.
708. 'Men [and] brethren, children of the stock of Abraham, and whosoever among you feareth God, to you is the word of this salvation sent. For they that dwell at Jerusalem, and their rulers, because they knew him not, nor yet the voices of the prophets which are read every sabbath day, they have fulfilled [them] in condemning [him]. And though they found no cause of death [in him], yet desired they Pilate that he should be slain. And when they had fulfilled all that was written of him, they took [him] down from the tree, and laid [him] in a sepulchre. But God raised him from the dead: And he was seen many days of them which came up with him from Galilee to Jerusalem, who are his witnesses unto the people' (Acts 13:26–31 KJV).
709. There appears to be a similar tradition in John 19:31–7 in which the Jews' request appears to presume a Jewish burial (see Luedemann, *The Resurrection of Jesus*, pp. 43–4).
710. Extensive legends about him and Nicodemus are found in the Gospel of Nicodemus dating from the 4th century. More extensive literature developed in the British Isles, where it was combined with Celtic folktales (see for example Nutt, *Studies on the Legend of the Holy Grail;* for the text and introduction see Lovelich, et al., *Le Saint Graal: The History of the Holy Grail*).
711. The abrupt ending of the Gospel of Mark has prompted early scribes to produce endings that were more satisfactory, one long and one short. The long one is attested by very ancient manuscripts: A, C, D, W and Q as well as most versions (i.e. translations) with the exception of the Syriac Sinaiticus, the Sahidic and the Armenian. The long ending is included in the Vulgate and is considered canonical by

Catholics in accordance with the Tridentine decree on the canon.

712. Dewey, 'The Gospel of Mark as an Oral-Aural Event', in Malbon and McKnight, *The New Literary Criticism and the New Testament*, pp. 145ff.
713. Crossan, *The Cross that Spoke*, p. 348.
714. Koester, *History and Literature of Early Christianity*, p. 170.
715. According to 2nd century Justin Martyr, the following was the accusation of the Jews (*Dialogues with Trypho*, chapter 107): 'a godless and lawless heresy had sprung from one Jesus, a Galilaean deceiver, whom we crucified, but his disciples stole him by night from the tomb, where he was laid when unfastened from the cross, and now deceive men by asserting that he has risen from the dead and ascended to heaven.'
716. 'And they departed quickly from the sepulchre with fear and great joy; and did run to bring his disciples word' (Matthew 28:8 KJV).
717. 'And they went out quickly, and fled from the sepulchre; for they trembled and were amazed: neither said they any thing to any [man]; for they were afraid' (Mark 16:8 KJV).
718. This is regarded as part of the Sign Source (Miller, *The Complete Gospels*, p. 180).
719. Matthew also omits mentioning the women entering but it is difficult to determine whether or not this is an intentional omission.
720. John here is slightly ambiguous, for it says only that they believed, which could mean that they believed Jesus was resurrected. The following verse, however, seems to exclude this, for it claims that they had still not understood scripture. Hence, it must mean that they believed Mary.
721. Rowan Williams in his article 'Between the Cherubim: The Empty Tomb and the Empty Throne' (in D'Costa, *Resurrection Reconsidered*) suggests that John alludes to an Old Testament motif here. The two cherubs sit at the feet and the head where Jesus lay, just as the cherubs of the mercy seat of the ark stand on each side of the place where the

God of Israel Himself would be if He was personified. So, Williams argues, for John there is a presence in the absence of Jesus.

722. Crossan sees the transfiguration (discussed in chapter 6) as a retrojection of this tradition and that the two angelic figures were identified by Mark as Elijah and Moses *(The Cross that Spoke*, p. 350).

723. A term used by Felicitas Goodman, who has studied the practice in its present usage. See Meeks, *The First Urban Christians*, p. 119.

724. Esler, *The First Christians in their Social Worlds*, pp. 41–3.

725. Meeks, *The First Urban Christians,* pp. 119–21.

726. Esler, *The First Christians in their Social Worlds*, p. 49.

727. The Gospel of Mary is a gnostic writing from the beginning of the 2nd century and, arguably, may be independent of the canonical gospels (see chapter 1). It should be noted that the Gnostics often perceived Mary Magdalene as the most prominent disciple of Jesus. The Gospel of Philip says that Jesus loved her more than the other disciples and that He used to kiss her (ⲁⲥⲡⲁⲍⲉ ⲙ̄ⲙⲟⲥ), which created jealousy amongst them. The present author is of the opinion that the tradition of Mary consoling the disciples stems from a feminine oral tradition.

728. This is the typical gnostic scene. The dialogue functions as a teaching/revelatory text, where gnostic doctrines are expounded.

729. Robinson, *The Nag Hammadi Library*, p. 525.

730. Douglas M. Parrott has placed them side by side in Robinson, *The Nag Hammadi Library,* pp. 220–43.

731. MacRae and Wilson's (Robinson, *The Nag Hammadi Library*) translation seems consistent in its meaning with King's (Miller, *The Complete Gospels*) and Pasquier's *(L'Évangile selon Marie*).

732. Pasquier, *L'Évangile selon Marie,* p. 71. See also Pagels, *The Gnostic Gospels,* p. 42.

733. Pasquier does much to show the redactional nature of the second speech *(L'Évangeile selon Marie*, pp. 7–13).

734. Pagels, *The Gnostic Gospels*, p. 44.
735. Funk and Hoover, *The Five Gospels*, p. 270.
736. Paul preambles the passion-resurrection account with the words: 'For I delivered unto you first of all that which also I received' (ASV). The term παρέλαβον (received) is used previously by Paul in reference to having received the Eucharist tradition (1 Corinthians 11:23) and in his letter to the Galatians (1:12) he states that he did not receive his gospel from men but from God. There can be little doubt that here, as with the Eucharistic tradition, the meaning of 'received' implied that it was received from the church (Barrett, *A Commentary on The First Epistle to the Corinthians*, p. 337). Luedemann suggests that this formula has its origin no later than two years after the crucifixion of Jesus (*The Resurrection of Jesus*, p. 38).
737. It is omitted by codex Beaza (D) some Italic copies (a, b, d, e, ff2, l, r1) as well as the Old Syriac. Marcion also omits it from his copy of Luke. It is included in Papyrus 75, A, B, C, W and many other significant sources. It is a difficult call. Tischendorf's 8th edition and Nestle/Aland's 25th exclude it (though the 27th includes it). Westcott/Hort and Vogels include it but mark it as very doubtful, while von Soden merely marks it as questionable.
738. Jerome, On Isaiah. See Elliott, *The Apocryphal New Testament*, p. 13.
739. Mary here believes Him to be a gardener. This is perhaps the source of later Jewish stories, such as in the Toldoth and Tertullian, that the gardener removed Jesus' body.
740. Fortna, *The Fourth Gospel and its Predecessor*, p. 71.
741. The sentence in brackets (καὶ ἀνέβη) is found in the Sinaiticus (א) but not in the Vaticanus (B) or in the Alexandrinus (A). The translation is from the NJB whose editors decided that this was the more accurate reading.
742. Thomas Didymus is in fact a double name, Thomas being 'twin' in Aramaic and Didymus being the same in Greek. Therefore the Syriac version omits the clause, giving the explanation in John 20:24. Thomas' original name was,

according to Eusebius (H.E. i.13), Judas and is, by the Old Syriac versions, identified as the enquirer called in John 14:22 'Judas (not Iscariot)'. The Syriac Acts of Thomas, composed towards the end of the 2nd century, also calls him 'Judas Thomas' ܝܗܘܕܐ ܬܐܘܡܐ.

743. This was the school that authored the Gospel of Thomas.
744. Fortna believes this to be a relocation by John from his Sign Source (Miller, *The Complete Gospels*, p. 184)
745. The metaphor of fish as converts, as in Mark 1:17, was discussed in chapter 6.
746. See Bultmann, *Das Evangelium des Johannes*, pp. 552–3.
747. The present author is here at odds with Robert W. Funk who believes both this and the prophecy that follows to be the composition of John.
748. The Targum of Jonathan Ben Uzziel on the Book of Genesis, Chapter 5, cited in Bowker, *The Targums and Rabbinic Literature*, p.142. This rabbi was one of the contemporaries of Gamaliel I (active around 30–50 CE) and a prominent student of the famed Hillel.
749. It should particularly be noted that Paul, in 1 Corinthians 15:11, directly places his own testimony equal with those other apostles who experienced the resurrection.
750. Luedemann, *The Resurrection of Jesus,* pp. 36–7. See also Pratscher, '2.1.3 1 Kor 15,7 als Rivalitätsformel', *Der Herrenbruder Jakobus und die Jakobustradition*, p. 35f.
751. Leipoldt, 'The Resurrection Stories', JHC 4/2 (Fall 1997), pp. 138–49. *Theologische Literaturzeitung* 12 (1948), pp. 740–2. Translated by Eric Weinberger.
752. See discussion in Plummer, *A Critical and Exegetical Commentary on the Second Epistle of St. Paul to the Corinthians,* pp. 336–47.
753. This thesis was advanced by Dunn in his unpublished paper 'Jesus in Oral Memory: The Initial Stages of the Jesus Tradition'. Dunn explains that since each tradition originates from the same author, we can disregard problems of distinct editorial practices and we can be certain that the same event is being referred to in all three cases.

Despite the fact that same author is behind all three accounts and as striking as are the commonalities, even more striking are the differences. Did Saul 's companion fall to the ground or only Saul? Did they hear the voice? Saul's blindness and Ananias are prominent in two accounts but go unnoticed in the third. In one account Saul receives his mission to the Gentiles on the road, in the second through Ananias and the third later, in Jerusalem. Luedemann, however, sees them as 'genetically' related, the two other accounts being redacted to the narrative context (*The Resurrection of Jesus*, p. 63).

754. Cited in Goulder, 'The Baseless Fabric of a Vision' in D'Costa, *Resurrection Reconsidered*, p. 49.
755. Theissen, *A Theory of Primitive Christian Religion*, p. 218. See also Luedemann, *The Resurrection of Jesus*, pp. 79–84.
756. Luedemann considers the denial a historical fact and finds the saying of Mark 8:33 'too sharp not to be authentic' (*The Resurrection of Jesus*, p. 95). As we find the account in Mark, there appear to be many literary developments. It also appears likely (as mentioned in the previous chapter) that Peter fled, possibly to Galilee, with the other disciples after Jesus was arrested. Yet for the purposes of a psychological profile it is sufficient to assume that the historical core of the narrative was that Peter felt guilt over this abandonment and perhaps had even been forced to recant his discipleship when asked.
757. Cited in Luedemann, *The Resurrection of Jesus*, p. 98.
758. Pratscher, *Der Herrenbruder Jakobus und die Jakobustradition*, pp. 13–27.
759. Goulder, 'The Baseless Fabric of a Vision' in D'Costa, *Resurrection Reconsidered*, p. 53.
760. ibid. p. 54.
761. Luedemann, *The Resurrection of Jesus*, pp. 102–8.
762. ibid. pp. 104–5.
763. McGrath, *Historical Theology*, pp. 30–1.
764. Funk and Hoover, *The Five Gospels*, pp. 360–2.
765. Crossan, *Who Killed Jesus*? pp. 172–3.

766. The opinion that there never was an empty tomb has been supported in recent times by such scholars as Crossan, *Who Killed Jesus?* ch. 6; Mack, *A Myth of Innocence*, pp. 308–9; Luedemann, *The Resurrection of Jesus*, p. 117; Goulder, 'The Baseless Fabric of a Vision', in D'Costa, *Resurrection Reconsidered*, p. 57. For a comprehensive survey see Thiessen and Merz, *The Historical Jesus*, pp. 475–508
767. Luedemann too argues, against a 'modern Protestant . . . "anti–visionary complex" ', that the two experiences are related (*The Resurrection of Jesus*, p. 69).
768. ibid. p. 85.
769. See Rudolph, *Gnosis: The Nature and History of Gnosticism*, pp. 157–8, and Williams, *Rethinking 'Gnosticism'*, p. 126ff.

Concluding Thoughts

770. Powell, *Jesus as a Figure in History*, p. 18.
771. Schweitzer, *The Quest of the Historical Jesus*, pp. 398–9.
772. Robinson, *A New Quest of the Historical Jesus*, pp. 71–2.
773. This category has been the most common amongst scholars of Jewish background. More recently, however, it has been used by Bruce Chilton in his *Rabbi Jesus, An Intimate Biography*.
774. See Mack, *The Lost Gospel*.
775. See Sanders, *Jesus and Judaism* and *The Historical Figure of Jesus*.
776. Crossan, *The Historical Jesus: The Life of a Mediterranean Jewish Peasant* and *Jesus, A Revolutionary Biography*.
777. Vermes, *The Changing Faces of Jesus*.
778. Borg, *Jesus, A New Vision*.
779. As a general category this has been used by Steven Davies, *Jesus the Healer: Possession, Trance, and the Origins of Christianity* and Morton Smith, *Jesus the Magician*.
780. One example of this is John Meir, *A Marginal Jew*.
781. Schweitzer, *The Quest of the Historical Jesus*, p. 403.

Appendix 1: ***Interpretation and Rewriting of the Gospels in the Bahá'í Writings***

782. This expression refers specifically to the Báb, Bahá'u'lláh and 'Abdu'l-Bahá (see Shoghi Effendi, *World Order*, pp. 131–2).
783. In particular, the belief that one creates heaven and hell, depending on one's deeds, is a significant eschatological feature (Momen, *An Introduction to Shi'i Islam*, p. 227).
784. For a thorough treatment of the origins of Bahá'í theophanology read Cole, 'The Concept of Manifestation in the Bahá'í Writings', in *Bahá'í Studies*, vol. 9 (1982), pp.1–38.
785. 'Manifestation of God' is the term applied to the major prophets of God, in particular those who come with 'a new Book'.
786. Bahá'u'lláh, *Gleanings*, p. 66.
787. Cole, 'The Concept of Manifestation in the Bahá'í Writings', in *Bahá'í Studies*, vol. 9 (1982), pp.1–38.
788. Bahá'u'lláh, *Kitáb-i-Íqán*, p. 176.
789. The Báb, *Selections*, p. 126.
790. Bahá'u'lláh, *Kitáb-i-Íqán*, p. 98.
791. 'O Son of Justice! In the night-season the beauty of the immortal Being hath repaired from the emerald height of fidelity unto the Sadratu'l-Muntahá, and wept with such a weeping that the concourse on high and the dwellers of the realms above wailed at His lamenting. Whereupon there was asked, Why the wailing and weeping? He made reply: As bidden I waited expectant upon the hill of faithfulness, yet inhaled not from them that dwell on earth the fragrance of fidelity. Then summoned to return I beheld, and lo! certain doves of holiness were sore tried within the claws of the dogs of earth. Thereupon the Maid of heaven hastened forth unveiled and resplendent from Her mystic mansion, and asked of their names, and all were told but one. And when urged, the first letter thereof was uttered, whereupon the dwellers of the celestial

chambers rushed forth out of their habitation of glory. And whilst the second letter was pronounced they fell down, one and all, upon the dust. At that moment a voice was heard from the inmost shrine: "Thus far and no farther." Verily We bear witness to that which they have done and now are doing' (Bahá'u'lláh, *Hidden Words*, Persian no. 77).

792. Reported in 'Abdu'l-Bahá, *Promulgation*, p. 154.
793. 'Abdu'l-Bahá, *Some Answered Questions*, pp. 113–15.
794. Bahá'u'lláh, *Kitáb-i-Íqán*, pp. 56–7.
795. Cole, 'Behold the Man: Bahá'u'lláh on the Life of Jesus', in *Journal of the American Academy of Religion*, vol. 65, no.1, Spring 1997, p. 51.
796. 'Abdu'l-Bahá, *Japan Will Turn Ablaze*, p. 46 and 'Abdu'l-Bahá, *Paris Talks*, p. 47.
797. From a letter of Shoghi Effendi to an individual, 1 October 1935, *Lights of Guidance*, no. 1641, p. 491.
798. 'Abdu'l-Bahá, *Some Answered Questions*, pp. 89–90.
799. Lawḥ-i-Burhán in Bahá'u'lláh, *Tablets*, p. 206.
800. Compare with Bahá'u'lláh's admonition to the monks in *Epistle to the Son of the Wolf*, p. 49.
801. Bahá'u'lláh, *Epistle to the Son of the Wolf*, pp. 89–90.
802. Bahá'u'lláh, *Gleanings*, p. 83.
803. In the Bahá'í Faith, publicly denying the line of succession or rebelling against the 'Centre of the Covenant', the head of the religion and working to undermine the covenant. The term 'covenant-breaker' has a significant antecedent in S͟hí'í Islam in which covenant-breakers were those who sided against the Imam 'Alí, Prophet Muḥammad's rightful successor. I would like to thank Todd Lawson for a copy of his unpublished paper 'Seeing Double, The Covenant and the Tablet of Aḥmad or Who is the King, the All-Knowing, the Wise?'
804. 'Abdu'l-Bahá, *Selections*, p. 212.
805. The gnostic group that authored the Gospel of Judas.
806. See Balyuzi, *'Abdu'l-Bahá*, pp. 90–125.
807. 'Abdu'l-Bahá, *Selections*, p. 163.
808. Bahá'u'lláh, *Kitáb-i-Íqán*, pp. 64–5.

809. Bahá'u'lláh, *Epistle to the Son of the Wolf*, p. 58.
810. Cole, 'The Concept of Manifestation in the Bahá'í Writings', in *Bahá'í Studies* 9 (1982), pp. 1–38. Christopher Buck suggests that 'Bahá'u'lláh's acceptance of the star of the Magi as literal perhaps reflects the interpretive perpetuation of a biblical metaphor taken literally' *(Symbol and Secret*, p. 121).
811. Bahá'u'lláh, *Epistle to the Son of the Wolf*, p. 158.
812. ibid. p. 157.
813. Cole, 'Behold the Man: Bahá'u'lláh on the Life of Jesus', in *Journal of the American Academy of Religion*, vol. 65, no. 1, Spring 1997, p. 53.
814. Rudolph, *Gnosis*, p. 363.
815. 'Abdu'l-Bahá, *Some Answered Questions*, pp. 94–5.
816. Lawson, 'The Dangers of Reading', in Momen, *Scripture and Revelation*, pp. 198–201.
817. See *Bahá'í World Faith*, pp. 390–1, 407–8; 'Abdu'l-Bahá, *Selections*, p. 78.
818. Bahá'u'lláh, *Epistle to the Son of the Wolf*, pp. 144–5.
819. Bahá'u'lláh, *Kitáb-i-Íqán*, pp. 49–51.
820. 'In the Arabic Bayán the Báb changed it to He whom God shall make Manifest, stating that it would move as he moved. Bahá'u'lláh confirmed this change in the *Kitáb-i-Aqdas*, identifying his own "Most Holy Presence" with "the Centre round which circle the Concourse on High". After his death the *qiblah* became his tomb at Bahjí' ('Qiblah', in Smith, *A Concise Encyclopedia of the Bahá'í Faith*, p. 284).
821. 'Abdu'l-Bahá, *Some Answered Questions*, p. 252.
822. See Lambden, 'Prophecy in the Johannine Farewell Discourse', in Momen, *Scripture and Revelation*, pp. 69ff.
823. *Star of the West*, vol. 9, no. 1, p. 7. From notes of Mrs Herron, 1900.
824. ibid. The Guardian confirms that ' "Mt. Paran" and "Paraclete" refer to Muḥammad's Revelation' (*Lights of Guidance*, p. 495, no. 1662). Browne in his book *A Year Among the Persians* records his discourse on the topic with the Bahá'ís of Isfahan: 'I know that the Muhammadans assert that the

prophecies which we apply to this descent of the Holy Spirit were intended to refer to Muhammad; that the word παράκλητος they would substitute περικλυτός, which is nearly equivalent to Ahmad or Muhammad, signifying one "praised", or "illustrious".'

825. Buck, *Symbol and Secret*, p. 114.
826. ibid. pp. 114–15; Bahá'u'lláh, *Kitáb-i-Íqán*, p. 20.
827. See Bahá'u'lláh, *Gleanings*, p. 246.
828. See Bahá'u'lláh, *Tablets*, p. 12.
829. Sours, *Study of Bahá'u'lláh's Tablet to the Christians*, p. 100.
830. Bahá'u'lláh, *Kitáb-i-Íqán*, p. 243.
831. ibid. p. 244.
832. 'Abdu'l-Bahá, *Some Answered Questions*, pp. 42–3.
833. 'Abdu'l-Bahá confirms this interpretation and expounds it in *Some Answered Questions*, pp. 36– 44. See also Sears, *Thief in the Night* and Sours, *The Prophecies of Jesus*. The selfsame interpretation is noted in Driver in his *Introduction to the Literature of the Old Testament*, p. 494.
834. *Star of the West*, vol. 2, no. 13, p. 3.
835. Buck, *Symbols and Secrets*, p. 121.
836. ibid. pp. 121–2.
837. Buck provides an extensive analysis of the contents and the devices used in the exposition of Matthew 24:29–31 in the Íqán. See in particular ibid. pp. 121–6.
838. 'Abdu'l-Bahá, *Some Answered Questions*, p. 104.
839. 'Abdu'l-Bahá, *Promulgation of Universal Peace*, p. 282.
840. The Báb, *Selections*, p. 78, and Bahá'u'lláh, *Kitáb-i-Íqán*, p. 170.
841. 'Abdu'l-Bahá, *Some Answered Questions*, p. 104.
842. Bahá'u'lláh, *Epistle to the Son of the Wolf*, p. 33.
843. The Báb, *Selections*, p. 120. The entire work is found in a French translation by Nicolas.
844. 'Abdu'l-Bahá, *Some Answered Questions*, p. 37.
845. ibid. p. 38.
846. ibid. p. 101.
847. Shoghi Effendi, *God Passes By*, p. 144.

848. The imagery of the veil, which is often used in the writings of Bahá'u'lláh, possibly has its origin in the story of Moses putting on a veil because His face shone after communing with Yahweh (Exodus 34:28–35).
849. The term 'Cause of God' in Bahá'í terminology refers to the Will of God manifest in this world. It comes into the world through the Prophets and their revelation. It then becomes embodied in the religious institution that follows the ascension of the Prophet. When people are confronted with the truth of the new revelation, God judges them according to their reaction: some will be receptive, others will be unmoved.
850. For an in-depth treatment of the Quranic text and the history of its interpretation see Lawson, 'The Crucifixion of Jesus in the Qur'án and Qur'ánic Commentary: A Historical Survey' in *The Bulletin of the Henry Martyn Institute of Islamic Studies*, 1991, vol. 10, no. 2, pp. 34–52 and vol. 10, no. 3, pp. 6–40.
851. Shoghi Effendi explains in a letter of 14 July 1943 written on his behalf to an individual believer: 'The Crucifixion as recounted in the New Testament is correct. The meaning of the Quranic version is that the spirit of Christ was not crucified. There is no conflict between the two' (*Lights of Guidance*, p. 492, para. 1646).
852. Bahá'u'lláh, *Gleanings*, pp. 85–6.
853. Bahá'u'lláh, Tablet to Pope Pius IX, cited by Shoghi Effendi in *The Promised Day is Come*, p. 106.
854. Buck, *Paradise and Paradigm*, pp. 230–1.
855. Crossan, *The Birth of Christianity*, pp. 523–5.
856. Bahá'u'lláh, *Tablets*, pp. 140–1.

Appendix 2: ***A New Inter-Religious Dialogue***

857. Fisher, *Religion in the Twenty-first Century*, p. 106.
858. ibid. p. 111.
859. Hick, *God and the Universe of Faiths*, p. 17.
860. Hordern, *A Layman's Guide to Protestant Theology*, p. 234.

861. Hick, *God and the Universe of Faiths*, p. 16.
862. Hatcher, 'The Validity and Value of an Historical-Critical Approach to the Revealed Works of Bahá'u'lláh', in Momen, *Scripture and Revelation*, pp. 27–52.
863. Fazel, 'Understanding Exclusivist Texts', in ibid. pp. 239–82.
864. McGlinn, 'Introduction to the Bible in Modern Research', in *Soundings*, pp. 24–5.
865. Shoghi Effendi, *World Order*, p. 183.
866. The author would like to thank Mr Stockman for making this unpublished paper available. The title of the paper 'The Bahá'í Faith and Higher Biblical Criticism' is called 'Modern Biblical Interpretation and the Bahá'í Faith' in Momen, *Scripture and Revelation,* p. vii.
867. McGlinn, 'Introduction to the Bible in Modern Research', in *Soundings*, pp. 24–5.
868. 'Abdu'l-Bahá, *Promulgation*, p. 212.

Appendix 3: ***The Origin of the Didache***

869. See Vermes, *The Complete Dead Sea Scrolls in English*, pp. 101–2 for a translation of the Manual of Discipline.
870. Kloppenborg, 'The Transformation of Moral Exhortation in Didache 1–5', in Jefford, *The Didache in Context*, pp. 88–97.
871. 'La Didachè et le Problème Synoptique', in Jefford, *The Didache in Context*, pp. 110–30.
872. ibid. p. 118.
873. Glover, 'The Didache's Quotations and the Synoptic Gospels', in *New Testament Studies* 5, 1958, pp. 12–29.
874. Crossan, *The Birth of Christianity*, p. 385.
875. Layton, 'The Sources, Date and Transmission of the Didache 1.3b–2.1, in *Harvard Theological Review* 61 (1968), pp. 343–83.
876. Tuckett, 'Synoptic Tradition in the Didache', in Sevrin, *The New Testament in Early Christianity*, pp. 197–230.
877. ibid. p. 370.

878. ibid. p. 372.
879. Layton notes some occasions where the editor has improved the overall style of Q, in terms of structure, through his editorial activity. Cf. Didache 1:3b (p. 353), 1:5 (p. 361).
880. ibid. p. 372.
881. ibid. p. 370.
882. Tuckett, 'Synoptic Tradition in the Didache', in Sevrin, *The New Testament in Early Christianity*, pp. 210–11.
883. ibid. p. 216.
884. ibid. pp. 217–30.
885. Layton, 'The Sources, Date and Transmission of the Didache 1.3b–2.1, in *Harvard Theological Review* 61 (1968), p. 372.
886. See Kurt Niederwimmer, *The Didache* and Helmut Koester, *Synoptische Überlieferung bei den Apostolischen Vätern*.
887. Crossan, *The Birth of Christianity*, p. 387.
888. See Glover above.
889. Layton, 'The Sources, Date and Transmission of the Didache 1.3b–2.1, in *Harvard Theological Review* 61 (1968), p. 380.
890. Tuckett, 'Synoptic Tradition in the Didache', in Sevrin, *The New Testament in Early Christianity*, p. 226. See also Rordorf, *Le problème de la transmision textuelle de Didachè 1.3b–2.1* for additional connections between the mini-catechism and the rest of Didache.
891. Theissen, *A Theory of Primitive Christian Religion*, p. 121.
892. Niederwimmer, *The Didache*, p. 127.
893. Tuckett, 'Synoptic Tradition in the Didache', in Sevrin, *The New Testament in Early Christianity*, p. 212.
894. Crossan, *The Birth of Christianity*, p. 367.
895. Mitchell, 'Baptism in the Didache', in Jefford, *The Didache in Context*, p. 232.
896. See in particular Sanders, *Jewish Law from Jesus to the Mishnah*, pp. 272–308.
897. Crossan, *The Birth of Christianity*, pp. 367–8.
898. Niederwimmer, *The Didache*, p. 131.

899. Crossan, *The Birth of Christianity*, p. 368. Niederwimmer, *The Didache*, p. 131 n. 2. Niederwimmer counters the suggestion that this is directly dependent on Matthew by pointing out that the rules of fasting in Didache are quite different from those of Matthew.
900. Niederwimmer, *The Didache*, p. 132. See also Jefford, *The Sayings of Jesus in the Teachings of the Twelve Apostles*, p. 137.
901. See Sanders, *Jewish Law from Jesus to the Mishnah*, pp. 81–4.
902. Glover, 'The Didache's Quotations and the Synoptic Gospels', in *New Testament Studies* 5, 1958, p. 19.
903. ibid.
904. See also Tuckett, 'Synoptic Tradition in the Didache', in Sevrin, *The New Testament in Early Christianity*, p. 212.
905. Thus Mitchell notes that the 'favourite baptismal motifs and images of Pauline Christianity are absent from the Didache' (Mitchell, 'Baptism in the Didache', in Jefford, *The Didache in Context*, p. 237).
906. For a discussion of the relationship between the two Eucharistic traditions in chapters 9 and 10, see Crossan, *The Birth of Christianity*, pp. 436–4; and Riggs, 'The Sacred Food of Didache 9–10 and Second Century Ecclesiologies', in Jefford, *The Didache in Context*, pp. 265–6.
907. The Didache uses the word Lord (κύριος) of both Jesus and God. In this case the quotation is from Malachi and must therefore be thought of as God's speech to man.
908. Theissen, *A Theory of Primitive Christian Religion*, p. 132.
909. Reed, 'The Hebrew Epic and the Didache', in Jefford, *The Didache in Context*, p. 221.
910. ibid. p. 224–5.
911. Jefford, *The Sayings of Jesus in the Teachings of the Twelve Apostles*, p. 102. Jefford is here commenting on chapters 1 to 5. However, as has been pointed out, the Didache seems even in its criticism of the 'hypocrites' not to presume a criticism of Judaism in general but rather a criticism of a particular prominent opposition party within Judaism.

912. Mitchell, 'Baptism in the Didache', in Jefford, *The Didache in Context*, p. 232. As Jefford states: 'The Didachist was anxious to weld the two yokes into a single system' (*The Sayings of Jesus in the Teaching of the Twelve Apostles*, p. 102).
913. Mitchell, ibid.
914. Kloppenborg, *The Sayings of Jesus in the Didache*.
915. Milavec, 'Distinguishing True and False Prophets: The Protective Wisdom of the Didache', in *Journal of Early Christianity*, 2, pp. 117–36.
916. Draper, 'Social Ambiguity and the Production of Text: Prophets, Teachers, Bishops, and Deacons and the Development of the Jesus Tradition in the Community of the Didache', in Jefford, *The Didache in Context*, pp. 284–312.
917. Patterson, 'Didache 11–13: The Legacy of Radical Itinerancy in Early Christianity', in Jefford, *The Didache in Context*, pp. 313–29.
918. Koester, *Synoptische Überlieferung bei den Apostolischen Vätern*, p. 216.
919. Tuckett, 'Synoptic Tradition in the Didache', in Sevrin, *The New Testament in Early Christianity*, p. 208.
920. Kloppenborg, *The Sayings of Jesus in the Didache*.
921. See Glover, 'The Didache's Quotations and the Synoptic Gospels', in *New Testament Studies* 5, 1958, p. 20.
922. Tuckett, 'Synoptic Tradition in the Didache', in Sevrin, *The New Testament in Early Christianity*, p. 210; Kloppenborg, *The Sayings of Jesus in the Didache*, pp. 128–9.
923. Kloppenborg, *The Sayings of Jesus in the Didache*, p. 130.
924. There is also a structural reason to presume that Didache 13:1–4 is part of first edition to which verses 5–7 are a later addition. Verses 1–3 present a closed list of items to be tithed, why they are to be tithed (because the prophet is the high priest) and what is to be done if there is no resident prophet. The verses that follow add items to the list of things to be tithed. Here we see a sort of formula 'according to commandments' that assumes something that is not evident from the artificial context that is created by the combination of these two sections.

925. Milavec, 'Distinguishing True and False Prophets: The Protective Wisdom of the Didache', in *Journal of Early Christianity*, 2, p. 117.
926. ibid. p. 131.
927. ibid.
928. Draper, 'Social Ambiguity and the Production of Text: Prophets, Teachers, Bishops, and Deacons and the Development of the Jesus Tradition in the Community of the Didache', in Jefford, *The Didache in Context*, p. 290.
929. ibid. p. 291.
930. For text, translation, comments on emendations of previous readings and a discussion of the history and nature of the Coptic manuscript, see Jones and Mirecki, 'Considerations on the Coptic Papyrus of the Didache (British Library Oriental Manuscript 9271)' in Jefford, *The Didache in Context*, p. 47.
931. For discussion of these issues see Patterson, 'Didache 11–13: The Legacy of Radical Itinerancy in Early Christianity' in Jefford, *The Didache in Context*, p. 313–29. Jones and Mirecki also consider Patterson's hypothesis but are sceptical (ibid. pp. 72–83).
932. Tuckett, 'Synoptic Tradition in the Didache', in Sevrin, *The New Testament in Early Christianity*, p. 201.
933. The term 'the curse' has been the subject of much debate. Many have resolved to understand it as a reference to Jesus being a curse in the sense of Paul's language in Galatians 3:13. Aaron Milavec and Nancy Pardee have both objected to this as it fails the larger context of the Didache (see Milavec, 'The Saving Efficacy of the Burning Process in Didache 16.5', in Jefford, *The Didache in Context*, pp. 131–55 and Pardee, 'The Curse that Saves (Didache 16.5)', in Jefford, *The Didache in Context*, pp. 156–76.
934. It is believed to have been written by Paul while he was in Corinth in 50 CE. See Schnelle, *The History and Theology of the New Testament Writings*, p. 44, and Koester, *History and Literature of Early Christianity*, p. 112.

Index

This index is alphabetized word by word. Hyphens are treated as spaces; articles and prepositions in sub-headings are ignored. Thus *'King James Version'* precedes 'Kingdom' and 'Ha-Nasi' precedes 'halakhah', and 'in the Bahá'í Faith' precedes 'baptismal formula'.

Index to Scripture

Old Testament

New Testament